LiVE TV

Also by Chris Horrie

Disaster!
The rise and fall of *News on Sunday*
Anatomy of a business failure

Stick It Up Your Punter!
The rise and fall of the *Sun*

Sick as a Parrot
Football and Television

Fuzzy Monsters
Fear and Loathing at the BBC

LiVE TV

Tellybrats and Topless Darts The Uncut Story of Tabloid Television

Chris Horrie and Adam Nathan

POCKET
BOOKS

LONDON · SYDNEY · NEW YORK · TOKYO · SINGAPORE · TORONTO

First published in Great Britain by Simon & Schuster
UK Ltd, 1999
This edition first published by Pocket Books, 1999
An imprint of Simon & Schuster UK Ltd
A Viacom company

1 3 5 7 9 10 8 6 4 2

Simon & Schuster UK Ltd
Africa House
64-78 Kingsway
London WC2B 6AH

Simon & Schuster Australia
Sydney

A CIP catalogue record for this book is available
from the British Library

ISBN 0-671-01574-5

Printed and bound in Great Britain by
Caledonian International Book Manufacturing Ltd, Glasgow

For Tom, Lotte, Clare and Gita

CONTENTS

large number of underemployed drunks on the payroll, is denounced as a creep and a rotter for his pains, resulting in a move to London and a failed plan to take over the Sun, which leads him to unleash a tidal wave of steamy Kiss-and-Tell Bonk Journalism at the News of the World amid more conflict, denunciations and back-stabbing before he relaunches a newspaper aimed at television-obsessed female yuppies and hires Janet Street-Porter as a television critic ting up a Network of City TV stations with Janet's help but is frustrated by a great many Short-Sighted and Smooth-Talkin' Americans, takes over the Daily Mirror instead, thus picking up the nickname 'Rommel' ('because Monty was on our side'), tries again to get City TV off the ground but is pipped at the post by the Daily Mail, but at the same time manages to make friends with some Very Important People in the cable industry who, at last, want to Do Business

Chapter Eight 122

In which Janet makes Der Vampyr and wins yet more honours and awards but does not become controller of BBC 1 or BBC 2 or anything else for that matter and so meets her old friends in the Independent Sector and considers joining them but thinks again and takes a new job at the BBC for a few months before moving to Mirror Television to be united with Kelvin MacKenzie – of all people – in the launch of L!ve TV, and a Mirror-owned version of Channel 5

Chapter Nine 130

In which Kelvin MacKenzie grows weary of editing his beloved Currant Bun and makes an Unexpected Move to become Managing Director of Sky TV where, at first, he Makes All the Right Noises

Chapter Ten 149

In which Kelvin is courted by the cable bosses and comes to fear a Bidding War and so decides to take a firm line when the Sports Agents turn up asking for more money, but then makes a rather serious mistake over boxing, falls out with Sam Chisholm and leaves Sky TV

Chapter Eleven 158

In which Monty worries about his Share Price but finally realises his Dream by launching a version of his City TV idea which is to be called L!ve TV and at the same time puts the Mirror at the disposal of the cable companies to promote cable subscriptions as part of a Somewhat Convoluted plan to capture the Premier League football rights from Sky with a series of arrangements which are Very Crafty and bear the hallmark of His Sneakiness, and is then joined at the Mirror by Kelvin

Chapter Twelve 165

PART II: THE LAUNCH OF L!VE TV

Chapter Thirteen 179

Chapter Fourteen 193

Chapter Fifteen 212

Row and a split right down the middle of the management of Mirror
Television

Chapter Sixteen

*In which the Tellybrats start to find life difficult at L!ve TV but reckon that
the Poor Sods on the technical side are having the worst of it, while All
Manner of Problems begin to mount with Nobody apparently able to Sort
Them Out*

Chapter Seventeen

*In which the Mirror-NBC bid for Channel 5 implodes because of the
Retuning Nightmare and the Tellybrats begin to worry about all the
Screamin' an' Shahtin' going on between Janet and the Mirror Board,
Rachel Purnell finds out about the Ways of Tabloid Journalists, Janet complains about Metaphorical Dicks being placed on Tables, a great many Fibs
are told, Nick Ferrari becomes stranded in the Alien World of Planet Janet,
and the Mirror announces to the world that Knives are Being Sharpened
for Janet Street-Porter*

Chapter Eighteen

*In which L!ve TV is launched and the World is told to Get A Life while
hours and hours of eco-television showing Nothing Very Much are produced and are watched by virtually nobody except Sad television critics who
roundly denounce it all as the Absolute Pits and Janet throws a party which
ends up with a Nasty Incident*

PART III: JANET'S L!VE TV

Chapter Nineteen

*In which L!ve TV comes under Bottle Attack after a muddle over its OB trucks,
The Vision is abandoned and 'L!ve TV' becomes 'Th!rty M!nutes Beh!nd T!me
TV' as the Tellybrats tangle with the ranks of the Horrible Fat Hairy Loony
Australian Slags and the hunt is on to find entertaining Witches, Sex Doctors,
Wankers, Sploshers, Sadists, Masochists, Celebrity Fetishists and Nerds until,
at last, Reality is officially abandoned amid Mounting Hysteria*

puts out a Documentary showing him and Janet at work, and Kelvin is Quite Pleased with it because it makes Janet look as though she has Gone Bonkers and has a Good Title and is the perfect launchpad for a Kelvin PR campaign featuring a great many Cunning Stunts

Chapter Twenty-five 345

In which Kelvin tells of his Adventures in the Land of Media Monsters, demands yet more Cunning Stunts and Gets Them, tries to Save the Channel with the help of some goldfish and The Clangers and unleashes the full force of Uncle Bill Ridley on an Unsuspecting Public, making him Head of Weird

Chapter Twenty-six 359

In which Kelvin makes an Important Speech about the future of Television News, denouncing prevailing News Values as Perverse and A Million Miles Away from the Concerns of Ordinary Folks, and regrets the Constraints placed upon him by the regulators and arbiters of Taste, Decency and Balance, but ploughs ahead anyway with a Plan to hire the country's first Stuttering Newsreaders as Nick sorts out the newsdesk

Chapter Twenty-seven 372

In which the L!ve TV newsdesk hacks are forced to go about their business wearing Bunny-Rabbit costumes, greatly enhancing the range and type of Stunt that can be performed and Boosting L!ve TV's Recognition Rating very satisfactorily, even though nobody is watching and it is, anyway, a Tremendous Wind-Up and talking-point for the Media

Chapter Twenty-eight 382

In which a Great Many Good-Looking Norwegian Girls are carefully examined but L!ve TV misses out on Ginger Spice, Posh Young Ladies are Teased over their Horsy Looks and the female Tellybrats are told to Get Their Tits Out for the Lads, a Dress Code is announced, and a Worldwide search is launched to find some Topless Tarts as Nick and Kelvin go to War against Hypocrisy in the defence of the Common Man and his Bit of Saucy Entertainment

ACKNOWLEDGEMENTS

In the course of writing this book the authors interviewed over a hundred and fifty people, sometimes at considerable length, and had dealings with dozens of others who helped us in some way or other.

None of the main characters in the book – David Montgomery, Kelvin MacKenzie and Janet Street-Porter – granted us interviews, though we had extensive correspondence with them. Nobody in the management structure at the Mirror Group was prepared to be interviewed, and we were twice threatened with legal action from this quarter, even before the book was written, on the basis of questions we were asking. Charles Wilson, chairman of the Mirror Group, threatened us with legal action, backed by the Group as a whole.

On top of this there was a climate of fear which meant that even quite junior people who worked at L!ve TV had to be given assurances that we would not name them or otherwise identify them. Many people pointed out that the *Mirror* is in the habit of 'offering' gagging contracts to current and former employees in a way that we find despicable for an organisation whose business is journalism. The *Mirror* is now a far more tight-lipped and secretive organisation than it was even under the Maxwell regime in the 1980s.

At the same time, we came to realise that we were being 'spooked': that is, one or two people we had spoken to had discussed with senior figures at the *Mirror* the fact that they were going to meet us, and had then attempted to turn the tables to try and find out who we had spoken to.

We were then seized with the fear that we might have been 'set up': fed false information in the hope that we would print it and discredit ourselves, or even present certain persons at the Mirror Group with an opportunity to sue us. The experience of writing this book was therefore not a pleasant one.

Kelvin MacKenzie himself did not threaten to sue, but he sent us a number of extremely angry letters, shouted at us a bit over the telephone, denounced us in strong language to third parties and in the end refused to answer simple factual questions put to him in letter form although, to be fair, we were winding him up a bit.

Our dealings with MacKenzie were dominated by the fact that a few years ago one of us had co-written a book called *Stick It Up Your Punter!*, which profiled the *Sun*'s creator and greatest editor, Larry Lamb. MacKenzie did not like this book, which also described him at some length. But most of all he did not like the idea that other journalists might make money (however modest the sum) by writing about him.

So we wrote to MacKenzie, asking for an interview. He did not reply. The press officer at L!ve TV tried to help, and was at first optimistic (though she could not believe anyone would want to write about L!ve TV). But she phoned back within three minutes to tell us forlornly that Kelvin had told us to 'get stuffed'. She said she would still send us the 'bullshit pack' (press pack) with the standard material boasting about how great L!ve TV is. But this of course never arrived.

By an eerie coincidence a producer at L!ve later that very evening went round to buy the flat of a friend of ours, and promised 'luscious material' if £500 was lopped off the asking-price. The story that the book was happening had spread like wildfire around the L!ve studio, apparently, and people started offering information in return for money. But as high-minded people we never engage in chequebook journalism. And, anyway, how can you believe a word anyone is saying if they are being paid to say it – especially if they have got anything to do with Kelvin MacKenzie?

We then tried to appeal to his sense of humour, writing to him in Norwegian in tribute to one of L!ve TV's many Cunning Stunts, a joke programme called *The Weather in Norwegian*. The following letter was sent:

Kjaere Kelvin
　　Din slask!
　　Hvorfor i all verden vil du ikke gi oss et intervju?
　　Alt vi vil ha, er et par gode saker/anekdoter som vil faa folk til aa smile – uten at de skader noen.
　　Tross alt har vi gjort en hel del for aa forbedre ditt ansikt utad i aarenes loep. Og en tjeneste fortjener vel en saadan i retur?
　　Vi regner med aa hoere fra deg i den naermeste framtid!
　　Sportslig hilsen

　　　　　　　　　　　　　　　　　Chris Horrie
　　　　　　　　　　　　　　　　　Adam Nathan

PS: Hvordan er vaeret i 24. etg?

Which roughly translates as:

Dear Kelvin
　　You plonker!

Why won't you give us an interview?

All we want is a few good stories which will make people smile and do no harm to anyone.

After all the help we've given you with your image over the years, surely one good turn deserves another.

We look forward to hearing from you in the near future. Yours in Sport!

Chris Horrie
Adam Nathan

PS: How is the weather on the 24th floor?

To which he replied (in Norwegian):

Dear Chris and Adam

Your letter puzzled me. Are you planning to write a book about L!ve TV or are you planning to write an article about me?

It was nice of you to ask about the weather on the 24th floor. It will please you to hear that 'the sun always shines on L!ve TV'.

Kind regards
Kelvin MacKenzie

We replied that we were writing about 'both', and proposed that we should either take him out to his favourite watering hole, the swanky Howard Hotel in London, or, perhaps, interview him live on camera in the L!ve TV studio – 'the only location in London where absolute confidentiality can be ensured'.

Much to our delight MacKenzie agreed to an interview and set a date in the future. He then cancelled. We phoned him up but could not get past his secretary until one of us used a bit of harmless subterfuge, posing as the head of a cable TV company and offering to give him a lot of money if he came to work for us. That got him to the phone in a flash. But we were then fiercely denounced. MacKenzie finally said that he would do an interview on condition we paid him a sum which worked out as approximately £100,000 for an hour's chat. We told him that would put him on earnings equivalent to £2.5 million a week – 'We could get Sam Chisholm for that' – but that we would put it to our publishers (who, after a short delay, refused to part with the cash).

After this, and again by chance, we met Piers Morgan, the editor of the *Mirror*, in a journoland pub. We asked Piers, who was charm personified (and praised MacKenzie effusively as the 'greatest tabloid editor in history' as well as giving us a couple of cracking MacKenzie *Sun*-era 'bollocking' stories), to put in a good word for us. But Morgan had anticipated the question and cut us dead in mid-sentence: 'Kelvin says, "Bollocks to you."' He kept repeating this phrase with a broad grin: 'Bollocks . . . bollocks.' Then his mobile phone rang and he had to rush off to rewrite the front page of the *Mirror* because Lenny Lottery had sprained his wrist and he was running the story big. Later we tried to get a mutual friend to line up the interview but were told by our emissary that MacKenzie had been very annoyed: 'What those two know about journalism would fit up a gnat's arse and still leave room for Janet Street-Porter's intellect.'

Eventually, after speaking to about two dozen people, and feeling we had a pretty good grip on the L!ve TV story, we sent MacKenzie a long memo asking him to confirm or deny various points which had been put to us, normally by multiple witnesses. He did not reply, even after several letters, and so we have taken this as a 'non-denial' on many points of fact and a massive overall 'no comment'. Why he should suddenly turn so shy we have no idea.

It was a similar story with David Montgomery. He refused us an interview and wrote anodyne 'no denial' letters in reply, at one point moaning that we were asking too many questions. So we sent a shorter list. This was ignored entirely.

Janet Street-Porter proved to be only slightly less elusive. We planned a friendly ambush on the safe territory of a *Guardian* media 'event' at the National Film Theatre, organised to mark the launch of Channel 5; she was to be one of the main speakers. But we had not factored-in JSP's famous lack of punctuality, and the plan came unstuck when she failed to turn up at this particular sneer-fest, leaving three hundred metropolitan trendies staring at an empty chair. The authors got mildly drunk with a stray Greek media studies student instead.

Janet chose not to reply to all our phone calls and letters until we put a few points of fact to her in writing. There followed a phone call which was a strange mixture of helpful (non-confidential) advice and dire legal threats. This was followed by a letter from her lawyer proposing a meeting to discuss the book if we agreed in return to pay £1,000 towards his fees. At the same time he threatened to place an injunction on the book to stop its publication. It seemed that Janet could not stand the idea of somebody writing about her without her permission. It was all very odd.

Because of the legal threats, and the undertakings we gave to protect the identity of our sources, we are not in a position to mention the people who helped us and have, therefore, as a matter of policy decided not to name anyone at all. This means that the huge contribution made by dozens of people at L!ve TV and the Mirror Group who worked for the channel before and after its launch and 'takeover' by Kelvin MacKenzie cannot be acknowledged in print.

We also spoke to a great many people who had worked with Janet Street-Porter over the years in radio and television at LWT and the BBC. We were helped by numerous people in the cable industry, many of them Americans, and found them to be ten times more forthcoming than the Brits, owing, we suppose, to a greater respect for freedom of expression.

We would also like to thank our agent, Sara Leigh, at Peters, Fraser and Dunlop for all her help, and Martin Fletcher of Simon & Schuster for his encouragement and support especially when, at times, we felt we were being put under extreme pressure by persons who did not want this story to see the light of day.

Most thanks of all go to Clare and Gita for showing great patience in putting up with various domestic horrors resulting from the writing of the book, which was done on a very tight deadline.

PREFACE

The original idea for this book came from Gita Mendis, a journalist at the London *Evening Standard*. In December 1995 the BBC screened a business documentary about L!ve TV called *Nightmare at Canary Wharf*, a fly-on-the-wall account of the launch of the channel, featuring a 'personality clash' between Janet Street-Porter and Kelvin MacKenzie, two of the most colourful characters on the UK media scene. The documentary, Gita thought, was great as far as it went, but it did little to explain the apparently mad way in which these two very different people had come to work at the channel. 'There must be more to it than a couple of big egos clashing,' she correctly guessed, 'It doesn't make sense. Why don't you dig into it a bit?'

The idea had instant appeal to the authors and coincided with a long feature article on the subject which appeared in the *Observer*, full of very promising material about life inside L!ve TV's Canary Wharf base. That was a good start. The author was John Sweeney, a thoroughly Good Egg in the opinion of the authors. (One of us had already done well in the past by nicking his feature ideas and doing them at a greater length.)

Anyway . . . here were two fantastic characters, Janet and Kelvin, born (as we later found out) in the same year (though he looks about a hundred years older than her), who set out on very different careers, one in television, the other in tabloid newspapers, who came together at a crucial moment in the alliance between newspapers and television and chewed each other up amid fantastic drama. As it was later put to us, the whole thing was like *Absolutely Fabulous* (Street-Porter and co) meets *Men Behaving Badly* (MacKenzie and the tabloid boys) on the set of *Drop the Dead Donkey*. This was the story that had everything: characters, drama, billions of dollars, media skulduggery, sex, drugs, rock and roll and punctuation.

At the same time, while L!ve TV itself was small potatoes, the story involved the fate of the *Mirror*, a much-loved national institution which had fallen on hard times but was still an important public company with millions of customers and many thousands of employees and shareholders. As we were soon to discover, L!ve TV was only the tip of an iceberg of intrigue and scheming which led us to look at the war between multinational companies such as Rupert Murdoch's Sky TV and the huge American-owned cable TV and telephone companies, which are fighting it out for domination of the world's media – indeed for domination of a huge slice of the world economy in the coming 'information age'.

We soon found out that L!ve TV is not really a television channel as such, but more a complicated and clever way in which the cable companies ensure the promotional support of the *Mirror* in their deadly skirmishes with Murdoch's *Sun* and Sky TV businesses. There is a lot more to L!ve TV than meets the eye.

On another level we were interested in the way that many of the legendary figures of tabloid journalism in the 1980s, including Kelvin MacKenzie (former editor of the *Sun*) and David 'Monty' Montgomery (ex-editor of the *News of the World*), had followed, along with a host of other more minor figures, Murdoch's lead and moved on from newspapers into 'tabloid television', either here or in the USA. Our thought, frankly, was that these people had to a large degree helped to wreck popular journalism, sucking all the profit and public respect out of it, even unto the point where journalists were less trusted than estate agents and more loathed than traffic wardens. Now they were moving on to do the same to television . . . *like a plague of locusts!*

In the end we tried to write the book on several levels. It is partly the story of L!ve TV itself, a study in what happens when a country with one of the best television systems in the world (however you look at it) is subject to deregulation. On another level it is a business story, dealing with the rise of 'pay TV' in the form of Sky and the cable companies, and the boardroom wars and deal-making this has entailed. And at a third level we have attempted an overview of the British media scene in the past twenty or thirty years, told through the strangely juxtaposed lives of Janet Street-Porter and Kelvin MacKenzie, representing, as they do, two extremes in the spectrum of what might be called, for the want of a better phrase, 'popular culture'.

Chris Horrie and Adam Nathan
Richmond, London, November 1997

PART I

JANET AND MONTY

Chapter One

In which Janet Bull of Fulham and Perivale runs away from home and is transformed into Janet Street-Porter of Chelsea, becomes queen of the alternative art scene, is accused of looking and sounding like a Dalek, writes a book about teapots, dyes her hair purple, becomes a champion of the Derided, gets married twice and invents Yoof TV

'Fatal error! Fatal error!'

Janet Street-Porter is screeching at a hack sent round to her office by the *Guardian* to mark the launch of her latest venture, L!ve TV. As is often the case on these occasions she is straying well away from the point, ranging over many subjects.

'I *shuddernever* [should have never] appeared in peak time. Never! What an *idjut* [idiot] I was.'

Janet is complaining about her public persona. Now pushing 50, she wants to be taken seriously as a big player in the world of British television. Instead she feels unjustly saddled with the knockabout cockney slob-cum-idiot image she developed as presenter on *The Six O'Clock Show* – a lightweight, stunt-driven slot screened primetime by LWT twenty years previously. The programme originally auditioned Derek 'Sid Yobbo' Jameson for the job, but he was too old. Janet Street-Porter got it instead.

At first things did not go well. Three pilot editions were made, all denounced as 'rubbish' by the production team. The third featured a monkey which escaped and ran around the studio pursued by cameramen as the director tried to calm the nervous studio audience. Still, the basic idea, of luring away the BBC audience with a 'fizzy start to the weekend', was strong and *The Six O'Clock Show* went on to become a success, ending up in the top ten of LWT's most successful programmes.

But Janet reckons it nearly finished her. She modestly confesses to having been a 'brilliant interviewer' and a 'natural enabler of others to get their views across'. But the programme-makers wanted her to do pure corn. Naffness abounded. She ended up asking blokes in the street if they preferred wearing Y-fronts or boxer shorts. It was demeaning. It was too lightweight.

So Janet went to see John Birt, LWT's director of programmes, and explained she was unhappy. She loved doing her *other* LWT slot, a late-night chat show in the company of telly intellectuals like Clive James and Russell Harty. That was fine. She liked talking to intelligent people, and she was learning a lot about television production and presentation. But she was sick of being on screen, prime-time. She had done her bit for the ratings. She had even hammed it up, like a pro. Now she wanted an inside job. She wanted to move off the screen and stand behind the camera as a producer. That was where the real power was.

Birt was aghast. Janet was officially 'the nation's favourite cockney', vital for LWT as the perfect foil for 'the nation's favourite scouser', Cilla Black, another Birt–LWT creation. On Friday night the punters got Janet going on *abaht* this and *abaht* that, and then on Saturday night they had Cilla showing them *alorra* this and *alorra* that. No way was she coming off the screen. Was she mad? Why did she want to throw away a brilliant career?

But Janet pleaded. She was depressed. It was all an act. She couldn't keep it up. Really, she was deep and needed fresh challenges. She had been to architectural college and liked foreign films. With subtitles. She was friendly with Zandra Rhodes and had met Johnny Rotten . . .

Birt relented. Janet got her wish and became a producer. The mantle of the country's leading professional game-for-a-laugh gor-blimey-luvvaduck Cockney Motormouth passed to a grateful Danny Baker, a former writer for a punk fanzine called *Sniffin' Glue*, named in honour of the trend for solvent abuse. In 1980, aged 34, Janet set about 're-inventing' herself as a television executive. A Player.

Janet Street-Porter was born in 1946 as plain Janet Bull of Fulham. Her dad, Stan, worked as an electrical engineer for Ealing Borough Council. Her mum, Cherrie, was a school dinner lady, but later became a clerical worker for the council. Her sister, Patricia, in contrast to Janet's celebrity, later became a supermarket checkout girl. The Bulls lived in a cramped terrace house in Fulham, where Janet had to share a bedroom with Patricia. At the time Fulham was a down-at-heel working-class district. It was only much later, in the 1980s, that prosperity and 'gentrification' spread from Chelsea, next door. The Bulls were upwardly mobile. They owned their house, still relatively rare at the time. Janet was not allowed to play with the rougher kids from the nearby council estate, even though the council-house kids (unlike the Bulls) had inside toilets. This seemed strange to the infant style guru, who thought that inside toilets were the height of classy extravagance.

From her very early years Janet was an exceptionally stroppy child, always fighting with her sister and disobeying her parents. She once told a newspaper that one of her earliest memories is of being forced to wear a cardigan she did not like; she got rid of it by dropping it in some dogshit. She went to a primary school just off Wandsworth Bridge Road, where she was marked down as a bright but naughty child. Since her parents took education and social advancement seriously, they made sure that she went on to a local grammar school, Lady Margaret, in Putney. Janet later claimed that she was sent there partly because her dad liked the blazer – an ersatz public-school job with red and black stripes and matching boater.

Janet got on well at school, but she was teased by the other girls, some of whom came from the posher parts of Putney. They imitated her thick cockney accent and ribbed her mercilessly over her sticky-out teeth and beanpole appearance. The school suggested that she take elocution lessons, but the advice gave Janet feelings of inferiority and she angrily refused. This was lucky, since her voice was to be the key to her early success on radio and television.

Nevertheless, as a teenager Janet felt a complete misfit. She hated the way she looked. She was never sent Valentine cards. She considered getting contact lenses, taking 'fattening pills' and peroxiding her hair. She was often miserable, and she took it out on her mum and dad, once loudly complaining that they had picked up the wrong baby in the maternity ward.

Her great height did have one advantage. Even in her early teens she could pass for 18 and this enabled her to go clubbin' around the King's Road in Chelsea, a ten-minute bus journey from Fulham and the very centre of the 'Swinging London' sixties fashion and pop scene. Inevitably there were rows with her parents, and things got worse when the family moved when Janet was 14 to the distant and distinctly non-swinging London suburb of Perivale. She hated it. But the move didn't stop Janet going clubbin'. By the age of 15, she was going out to nightclubs most nights of the week. She had become a 'Mod', a devotee of the resolutely cockney sixties fashion cult made famous by groups like The Who and the Small Faces.

Janet took a Saturday job in Perivale Woolworth's and

spent all her earnings on clothes. She also made her own dresses. She would disappear into her bedroom and re-emerge dressed in plastic and with her hair sprayed silver. There would then be a short slanging match with Cherrie and Stan before she stormed out to the latest Mod night-club.

Janet was engaged to be married in her mid-teens, but her mum made her give the ring back. But boys, really, were just another fashion accessory, she later told a news-paper. You weren't properly dressed at the club unless you had one, were you? And boys were hard to get, weren't they? Especially if you looked like a cross between John Cleese and Red Rum, dressed up like a traffic light and had to chat 'em up with a voice that sounded like Monty Modlyn *shahtin'* [shouting] through a Tannoy. If she failed to pick someone up, Janet would be stranded in the middle of the floor, dancing round her handbag, with the horrible feeling that she was again a misfit and that everyone was laughing at her. She kept detailed diaries about her adven-tures, but they were written in a code so illogical that when she tried to read them in later life she could make no sense of them whatsoever.

Despite this hectic social life, Janet managed to do well at school and even emerged as something of a swot. She took ten O-Levels and three A-Levels and did well enough overall to get into the swanky Architectural Association college in Bloomsbury, central London. She could have gone to university if she had wanted to, but that would have involved systematic study, something Janet was keen to avoid. She was in many ways a natural for art school, but decided against it on the reasonable grounds that most art students were terminal 'losers'.

Shortly before she left school Janet's rows with her parents reached a peak, and at 19 she ran away from

Live TV

Perivale to live with her boyfriend, Tim Street-Porter, the nicely spoken, public-school-educated son of a Lloyd's underwriter, who was establishing himself as a photographer. The couple shacked up in Chelsea in a flat which overlooked Stamford Bridge football ground – from the back window you could just about see one set of goalposts. The flat was equipped with a waterbed (one of the first in the country, it was claimed) with big brass bedknobs, and kitchen furniture made from yellow cardboard. Soon afterwards they got married.[1]

Janet arrived at architectural college in 1965 to find that she was one of only five women in a class of seventy men. She made friends easily and was a compulsive networker. Being an architecture student was brilliant for this. Architectural college was a cut above the art schools, and the students developed contacts not only in the world of art and graphic design but in manufacturing, interior-decorating, set-building and business. Janet plunged into a hectic social life, specialising in organising and attending parties. At the time she was going through a hippy phase, with hair down to her bum. She was incredibly noisy and noticeable and always weirdly dressed in things like silver cowboy boots and luminous jackets. She shocked everyone with her working-class vocabulary of swear words and amazing stories of family feuds in which relatives had not spoken to each other for five years and could only communicate through intermediaries. She liked to read the 'underground press' of the time, including *Oz* magazine and the influential *Suck*, a newspaper produced by Old Etonian 'anarchist' Heathcote Williams,[2] which was described as 'art-porn'. The latter was banned in the UK for a while and had to be smuggled in from Amsterdam. People who remember reading it say it was produced in a way that made much of its content meaningless to those who were not on drugs, but profoundly significant to those who were. Janet was also at one point an avid reader of *Wet*, which was also 'art-porn' but came from California and was said to feature pictures of Japanese sumo wrestlers sweating in Turkish baths and beating each other with sticks.

Janet formed an enduring association with Piers Gough, who was to become one of the leading architects of his generation. Piers was Quite a Character. A lot of the students wanted to do dull things like make office blocks or design motorway bridges. Piers was different. He was, to use a key Janet Street-Porter word, '*innervitiff*' [innovative]. Janet was impressed by the fact that he wanted to design a building for a train station in the shape of the words T R A I N S T A T I O N. He once flooded the college courtyard to simulate the Chicago waterfront, complete with scaffolding, for a Prohibition fancy-dress party. And it was a listed building. Yeah, *Quite a Character*!

Janet spent time at college drawing what she later described as 'groovy' sketch designs for pavilions on Primrose Hill. She was remembered as being very good at this, but hopeless at such things as structural engineering, foundations or drainage. In fact, she was daunted by anything technical and claimed that she could not even fix a three-point plug and did not see why she should. She cheated in her exams by hiding the textbook in her knickers, cunningly concealed under a baggy smock dress. But even using these tactics, and with surreptitious help from Piers Gough, she still failed and dropped out during the second year of her course. It hardly mattered. Her brief status as an architecture student had provided an organised and purposeful way of establishing herself on the '60s fashion circuit, where the ability to stand out in a crowd was all-important. Janet's naturally odd looks, mad clothes and raucous voice were an advantage. She started putting herself about on the 'scene' as a film extra, photographer's model, fashion designer, professional party-goer and 'design writer': anything, in fact, that was glamorous but did not involve any training or much skill of any sort, except self-promotion.

When Michelangelo Antonioni made his classic sixties film *Blow Up*, Janet and 'everybody' appeared in it as extras. Extras were paid good money, and art-school kids were able to bunk off more easily than university students; they were also better at dressing up. They used to go up to Elstree and Shepperton, shivering on the early-morning train, and troop along from the station looking like aliens and shocking the locals. In the film Janet wore red and yellow plastic trousers, a silver coat and a silver wig. She was very pleased with herself until a member of the crew came up to her and started rasping, 'I am a Dalek, I am a Dalek,' in a funny voice and everyone laughed at her.

By this time Janet had become friendly with Zandra Rhodes. She had spotted Zandra at a party sporting blue-black dyed hair and with a black-and-white chequered design on her eyelids, and was thus naturally drawn to her. Zandra was just about to graduate from the Royal College of Art and set up in business selling clothes which were, if anything, even more outlandish than Janet's. And, as it happened, Janet was the perfect ugly-duckling model for Zandra. Janet posed on the opening night of Zandra's boutique in the Fulham Road. The pictures, taken by Tim Street-Porter, were published in a recently launched young women's magazine called *Petticoat*, where Janet was simultaneously making a move into the world of fashion journalism. The magazine's staff included Audrey Slaughter, Eve Pollard (later, editor of the *Sunday Express*), who was beauty editor, and feature-writer Lynne Franks, famous in the 1980s as Queen of the Fashion PRs and said to be the model for Edina in *Absolutely Fabulous*. Pollard's beauty tips were often bizarre by today's standards. 'Apply mascara *heavily*,' she advised. 'No time for mascara? Then slither vaseline over the eyelashes and blink brightly.' Franks's contribution was more wide-ranging. One of her efforts, The Fame Game (a version of the desperate old 'spoof boardgame' magazine space-filler), seemed farsighted: 'The only rule is to have some claim to fame, no matter how small. The game never finishes. Just remember to change your partners now and then!' Some might say that she was still dishing out exactly the same advice twenty years later.

Janet took the dowdy job of home editor, in charge of cookery and housework news. She churned out material of stunning banality, notable mainly for her gigantic by-lines, often printed in shrieking oranges and reds. But elements of the famously direct 'in yer face' JSP attitude were present from her first article, which yelled at readers, 'GET YOUR-SELF A SPACE-SAVING UNIT'. Articles on similar subjects followed, suggesting an obsession with tidiness: 'Cut out clutter with our pop up pages'. 'Are you all bottled up? Use jars and bottles to eliminate mess'. Her advice to 'tidy up all your clutter and put it in a cupboard' was undeniably sensible. This one-woman war on mess was supplemented by cookery news, with Janet taking on the persona of 'The Stupid Cook'. The Stupid Cook's Pin Up Page was meant to be clipped out of the magazine and stuck on the wall, thus contradicting the anti-clutter campaign.

By 1969 Janet was grinding out articles for the FeMail section of the *Daily Mail* as a columnist with a picture by-line juxtaposed with that of Bernard Levin, of all people. She wrote about her time as a film extra and how this had involved spending two days in a Turkish bath with fifty naked women and an Italian film crew. FeMail readers were regaled with her plan to put a 3-D image of the Rolling Stones on her living-room wall. They were told that her mum and dad went on boring camping holidays, and that they scrimped and saved and had no taste or style. She sometimes suddenly dropped the 'plot' and provided a bulletin on her state of mind, physical surroundings or appearance: 'As I write this my hair, at the present moment, is done in shades of brown, blonde and pink.' If Janet became depressed she cheered herself up by airing her tidiness obsession, giving readers advice on how to pack a plastic carrier bag efficiently, or instructions on how to stick stamps on lots of envelopes using a rubber squeegee and a tin of water. ('I'm a bit of a stationery nut. Once I've got all my bits of paper and pens and paper clips together in one place I feel all right,' she later told a journalist.)

In many ways she was a practitioner of 'new' or 'gonzo' journalism, which had developed in the US in the sixties as an adjunct to the drugs and rock music sub-culture, and was now sweeping all before it in the London fashion and pop music magazines. In gonzo journalism the reporter or writer is the star and whatever they are writing about is more or less coincidental. It was a style which only really worked if the reporter was in some extraordinary situation, but Janet applied the approach, apparently instinctively, to whatever she did, no matter how banal. Her first FeMail article gave uncontroversial advice to the nation's housewives, telling them to get a crisp white cotton nightie, which she preferred herself and, she thought, 'scores over blowsy pink nylon lace every time'. This was followed by reflections on a mis-spent youth dominated by working in supermarkets 'to supplement my wardrobe through those expensive days of Mod dressing', and an article in which she proclaimed herself an expert at 'looking really busy for hours on end without doing anything'. A venture into TV criticism seemed anti-prophetic: 'I can't stand plastic pseudo-young figures created entirely by TV and radio to symbolise youth.' She opined that such people were an 'insult to the intelligence of the viewer', and added, 'What turns me off completely are explanatory TV films about students, hippies, or anyone young, coupled with insulting explanatory commentary and hysterically psychedelic camerawork.'

While moving into the mainstream via the *Daily Mail*, Janet kept in contact with the underground scene, which remained the source of her inspiration. In 1972 she helped organise an extraordinary event at the Institute of Contemporary Arts in London called 'The Body', remembered by some as 'a happening'. Janet showed a talent for staging events like this and displayed a natural sense of theatre; her corralling skills amazed some of the others involved. 'The Body' included a boxing-ring with fashion students slugging it out, mannequins flying across the ICA roof in formation, and naked and semi-naked bodies everywhere. Fans included Joan Littlewood, who arranged for the event to be staged as a one-off at the Stratford East theatre. The time had come to move into television.

After limbering up with a few sporadic radio and television appearances, and coincidentally moving to America for six months, Janet landed her first major job in broadcasting in 1973. She was hired by the new London commercial radio station, LBC, to co-present a morning show, together with Paul Callan, a Fleet Street gossip columnist. The show was called *Two in the Morning* and, despite its name, was broadcast between 9 a.m. and 12 noon every weekday.

Janet had put herself forward partly on account of her

voice and the station teamed her up with the suave Callan in a double act. Her role was to be the pert working-class Ms Bossy Boots who put down Callan, the smooth ex-Etonian-style lounge lizard, for the delectation of the listeners. Their routine, normally kicked off by Callan, used to go something like this: 'Hello, Janet, you're looking extremely smart this morning. What's that brooch you're wearing? Is it a tin badge you got in a lucky bag?' JSP: 'Humpf! That's *eck-streeemleeee* expensive I'll 'ave yer know. I went up Petticoat Lane, *dinn-eye*, and it cost a lot of money, *dinnit*.' Callan: 'Oh really, m'dear? Do you mean you didn't find it in a skip as usual?' JSP: '*Awwwwrrrrr*, well *kom-peared*, right, wiv that tatty old suit *yooooovvve gorron* . . . Where d'ya get that from? Tailor blind, was 'e, eh?' And so on until it was time to review the papers or interview their 'guests'. When the couple went off the air during news bulletins, they sometimes continued their banter in a cheerful routine like something from *Derek and Clive Live* – 'You're a cunt.' 'No, you're a cunt.' 'No.' 'Cunt' – turning the producer white with fear that something might escape on to the airwaves. Callan used to tease Janet by ringing the speaking clock and pretending to talk to his agent, negotiating a big deal with the BBC or ITV. Turning green with envy, Janet would pretend not to be interested and then later ask what it was all about, how you got work in television, was it worth having an agent, and so on.

What attracted attention was not what Janet said but the way she said it. Her voice had not mellowed and her accent was a prime example of what linguists were later to define as 'estuarial English',[3] featuring the attention-getting 'glottal stop' and, in her case, the additional irritants of mumbling, slurs and hyperbolic 1970s teenage slang. Janet's catchphrases included a drawled 'brilliant' or 'brill' substituted for 'good', and 'tremendous' for 'big'.

'Completely' or 'absolutely' was used instead of 'very', so in Janetspeak 'very good' became *'kom-pleat-lee, tree-mendous-lee brilliant'*. The overall effect was a 'spaced-out cockney' sound, the female equivalent of Mick Jagger, who was then very fashionable. Janet was ahead of her time, and the change in the standard voice of British broadcasting, spread by her many imitators, and in public life can be counted as one her lasting achievements. LBC got hundreds of complaints about Janet and her voice. The criticism, she complained, was needlessly nasty and, anyway, came from people who had 'clenched-buttock voices'. She told the *Evening Standard* that she was going to ignore the critics and was determined to 'be meself' adding, *'I jus open mee maahf and sey woddeye fink'* [I just open my mouth and say what I think].

Two in the Morning was abandoned after a change in management at LBC; it was decided that the station needed a more newsy approach. Street-Porter and Callan were replaced by Doug Cameron and Bob Holness, later of *Blockbusters* fame. Amid much characteristic *screamin' an' shahtin'*, and even floods of tears when it suited her (she was remembered by senior people at LBC as being 'pushy, ambitious and financially driven') Janet carved out her own solo evening show, but it was not a great success. She spent about a year at LBC, then, to the delight of the capital's buttock-clenchers, moved back into print journalism, writing for the *Evening Standard*, *Vogue*, *Harpers* and *London Life*.

By 1974 Janet was developing an interest in the entrepreneurial side of the media: the business of spotting gaps in the market and organising magazine launches, allowing her to put her networking, 'innovation' and hustling skills to work. After all, what was a magazine launch but a big party? If the mag closed after a while, well, so what?

You just organised another big party and got all *yer mates* to write articles for the first edition. After leaving LBC, she 'did a launch' for Michael Heseltine's Haymarket publishing group and the result was *West One* magazine. Then she did the same for Tony Elliot, the cheesecloth-shirt-wearing owner of *Time Out*.

Time Out had arrived on the streets of West London in 1968 with start-up capital of £7 provided by Elliot. At first it had been a publication for hippies, telling them what was happening and had displayed some of the political overtones of 'underground' publications like *Oz*, *Suck* and *It*. Through the seventies it brilliantly tracked the growing commercialisation of the hippy scene, and by the time Janet arrived it was turning into a goldmine, slowly shedding its anti-establishment political edge and concentrating on the 'Me Generation's' hedonism and limitless consumerism. Like many other alternative magazine publishers, including Richard Branson, who had started out producing a magazine to promote his mail-order hard-to-get hippy LP business, Elliot was becoming a 'bread-head'; millionairedom was not far off.

Janet espoused fashionable left-wing political views at the time, but they were of the ad-hoc 'personal is political' variety, rather than support for a particular party or theory. Her interest in formal, *borin'* politics was slight, but she believed deeply and wholeheartedly in personal freedom and would take up the cudgels on behalf of anyone who was being persecuted for being 'different'. She detested bigotry and narrow-mindedness. Her loathing for the suffocating boredom of 'straight' suburban life knew few bounds and was sincere and consistent, even when it led her to champion causes – such as equal rights for lesbians and gays – that were unpopular, and this no doubt damaged her career prospects. Much of the time she exhibited a sort of kamikaze honesty and openness which offered all manner of hostages to fortune. Later, her refusal to tone down her views made her vulnerable to vicious attacks, especially by the tabloid press.[4]

Janet joined *Time Out* as editor of a spin-off magazine called *Sell Out*, which cut out all the political crap and dealt solely with what was called 'alternative shopping' and 'cut-price, alternative living'. The first issue was billed as a 'survival guide' for living in London. It contained such essential survival information as where to buy a frisbee, how to grow your own herbs (an old Janet chestnut, first warmed up in *Petticoat*) and where to hire a Punch and Judy show. As usual with Janet, much of the content sprang directly from her own activities. There was therefore a 'special feature' on where to buy trendy merchandise on her home turf, Fulham. Around this time, she also, for some reason, wrote a book about the history of the teapot.[5] Tim Street-Porter took the pictures for this piece of Janetesque whimsy.

Sell Out failed to repeat the success of Elliot's main title and closed, though the idea was wrapped into *Time Out* itself to form part the magazine's expanding and profitable love affair with hedonistic 'consumer journalism'. By this time Janet had divorced Tim and married Tony Elliot. Marriage Number Two lasted just nine months, during which time Janet became deputy editor of *Time Out*. The appointment annoyed the magazine's staff and they went on strike partly as a result. By 1975 Janet was on the move again.

Following her early appearances on *The Russell Harty Show*, and in view of her experience at LBC as one of the 'voices' of trendy, young London, she was snapped up by the London ITV company, LWT. Based in a spanking new tower block on the South Bank, LWT was the world centre of trendy television, and in the '70s was known in the trade as 'twenty-two floors of heaving copulation', in tribute to the alternative lifestyle of some who worked there.

From the start Janet Street-Porter the Television Personality was very much the creation of John Birt, another ex-hippy turned mainstream, who had recently joined LWT as head of programmes, and his deputy, Andy Meyer. Both had come from Granada TV in Manchester. Birt was then best known for staging a *World in Action* debate between Mick Jagger and the Archbishop of Canterbury about the legalisation of cannabis (Birt later said he had 'no sympathy with the drug-takers'), and for *Nice Time*, a programme he had devised for Granada. It was presented by Germaine Greer and Kenny Everett and once featured a choir of twelve George Formby impersonators, followed by an orchestra of people who could make tunes by tapping on their heads, and a 'Pick a Vicar' identity parade. In the '70s Birt, like Janet, had been a leader of alternative taste and fashion. He was described in the press as the sort of person who 'would not look out of place behind an electric guitar in front of 5000 watts of solid noise. He is big, hairy and hip. He wears button-through T-shirts and purple cord pants and a jacket with a snakeskin collar. Every inch a product of the rock age from his steel rimmed glasses to his two-tone baseball shoes.' Meyer, who had worked on programmes for 'young people' at Granada, had heard Janet on LBC and decided that she was 'interesting, distinctive, bright and street-wise'. He put her name up to Birt, who took her on.[6]

Birt, a man with a famously mechanistic approach to TV programme-making, was obsessed with the newfangled subjects of 'demographics' and 'audience segmentation'. This meant a new concern with making programmes aimed at particular parts of the public, supplementing the old ITV game of trying to get as many viewers as possible (or as many people as it took to wring the maximum amount of money out of advertisers, which was a slightly different thing).

Birt had worked out that TV shows which achieved high 'penetration' of certain population groups would be more attractive to advertisers than programmes with much larger audiences consisting of just any old body. It was thought that the free-spending 15–25 age group was particularly hard for TV advertisers to reach via big-audience shows designed to appeal to their mums and dads. Birt came up with the idea of making a show aimed solely at teenagers and twenty-somethings. It was to be called *The London Weekend Show* and Janet Street-Porter was hired to front it. The programme was scheduled towards midday on Saturday, after kiddie-vision had finished in the morning and when it was reckoned that the capital's youth had finally dragged themselves out of bed and were ready for a spot of nose-picking on the sofa in front of the TV. The opening credits featured a cartoon sequence of Janet as a happy, gormless figure stomping across the screen in bovver boots.

At first *The London Weekend Show* was a studio-based discussion slot, and featured Janet sitting in front of a gigantic art deco poster with her name on it. As usual she talked mainly about the Amazing Adventures of Janet, followed by *innerviews* [interviews] in which she made herself the star, gonzo-journalism-style, by asking rude questions in her irritating, but attention-grabbing, accent.

The first run of *The London Weekend Show* lasted for fifty-two editions. It branched out and began to feature longer, pre-filmed items. The bulk of the journalism was done by the show's researchers, many of whom went on to become important in the world of television production. Janet's

main role was to write the script and present the show.[7]
But she went further than this, making suggestions for
filmed items and going out with camera crews to do interviews. The show was judged a great succcess and ran for
four years. It was twice nominated for a BAFTA award,
and Janet later claimed that it was one of the foundation
stones of 'youth television' – often called 'yoof TV' in tribute to Janet's accent – which she defined, along with 'youth
culture', as basically a matter of 'wearing dark glasses and
lookin' miserable'.

Janet was doing well at LWT. But the sixties 'youth
culture' from which she sprang was falling apart. She was
now almost 30, and a lot of the pop groups and fashions
that had once been trendy and outrageous had gone mainstream and were getting extremely borin' and establish-
ment-minded. Mums and dads now dressed like hippies,
so it was natural enough that their kids should rebel and
become anti-hippies.

In the art schools and suburban garages a new trend was
being born: punk rock. And Janet Street-Porter, the official
media voice of young London, was well placed to ride the
new wave.

Chapter Two

In which Bill Grundy is humiliated and Janet is called 'the First Lady of Punk' and takes steps towards becoming a sophisticated late-night chat-show host who is then, against her better judgement, lured by the Wicked Bosses of LWT into becoming a Primetime Cockney Chump before disappearing to Australia and returning with a plan to conquer Channel Four and Change the Face of British Television with the help of her friend Jane

In the mid-1970s ITV in London had a current-affairs programme called *Today*. It was no great shakes. Its presenter, the gruff Bill Grundy, had started his career in local television in the sixties with Granada in Manchester and Liverpool, where he had once introduced the Beatles to the viewing millions.

Now, in December 1976, Grundy was sitting on the set of *Today* ready to interview a group of teenagers about the new phenomenon of 'punk rock'. The item was going to occupy the traditional 'And finally . . . ' slot on the show, reserved for lightweight 'believe it or not' material like skateboarding ducks and lovable eccentrics, and designed to send the viewers away with a heartwarming chuckle. It was to go out live and last for a couple of minutes.

The show had already started, and was beaming out a pre-recorded item when the Sex Pistols and sundry other punks were led on to the set. Grundy took an immediate dislike to them. They slouched all over the studio chairs, lolling about, chewing gum and smoking fags. They immediately started winding him up, blanking him, pulling faces and muttering, 'He's like yer dad, this geezer, innee? . . . Nah, he's like yer granddad, innee?'

Bill looked at his script. It said that this talentless shower had just been paid £40,000 (*forty thousand quid!*) by a record company, a huge sum in 1976. It was ten times more than most of the people watching, the early-primetime ITV audience of middle-aged mums and dads, earned in a year. What was the world coming to? Bill decided he would give them a good going over.

The pre-recorded item drew to an end. The floor manager counted them in. The red lights came on. Bill smiled sardonically and spoke directly to the camera in tones of heavy sarcasm about 'the latest pop craze, the punk rockers . . . *Yesss*, here are the punk rockers themselves.' The camera pulled back to show the spotty, bored-looking youths slumped around the crowded studio. 'They are not like those nice, clean Rolling Stones,' Bill continued. 'They are a group called the Sex Pistols and I am surrounded now by all of them.' The camera cut back to Bill, who became more withering than ever. 'Just let us see these Sex Pistols in action.' A clip from Janet Street-Porter's *London Weekend Show*, which a few days earlier had screened a eulogising film about punk rock, was shown. It featured some unhealthy-looking teenagers stumbling about in what appeared to be somebody's basement, creating a tuneless din.

When the clip finished, the camera returned to the studio and Bill began his attack. Did the Sex Pistols think their music ranked alongside Beethoven, Mozart, Bach and Brahms? The youths smirked, 'Yeah, they're our heroes.' And what about people who didn't like punk rock? What about them?

The youths had started to mumble an answer when in the background Johnny Rotten, the head Sex Pistol, who so far had remained silent, said under his breath, 'Well, that's just their tough shit.'

Bill turned on him: 'It's *what*?'

Rotten rolled his eyes and faked contrition. 'Nothing. Rude word. Next question!'

But Grundy persisted. 'No, no. What was the rude word?'

Rotten said, 'Shit' and everyone giggled.

'Was it reeeeally,' the presenter gasped, pretending to be shocked. 'Gooood heavens. You frighten me to death.'

Rotten mumbled another inaudible insult as the camera turned on the striking figure of Siouxsie, of Siouxsie and the Banshees, another punk group featured in Janet's documentary. 'Are you enjoying yourself?' Grundy asked her.

Siouxsie pouted alarmingly and said that she was, adding, 'I've always wanted to meet you.'

Grundy perked up and said, 'We'll meet after the show, shall we?'

There was much 'ooooohhhing' and laughter at this. Steve Jones, the Sex Pistols' guitarist, yelled over the commotion, 'You dirty sod! You dirty old man!'

Bill fell for the sucker punch. 'Well keep going, chief,' he sneered, 'keep going.' There was a pause as Jones thought better of it. But Grundy insisted, 'Go on. You've got another five seconds. Say something outrageous.'

Jones shrugged and obliged. 'You dirty bastard, you dirty *fucker*.'

Bill turned to face the camera and close the show. 'Whaaat a clever boy,' he said.

Jones was heard to yelp in the background, 'What a fucking *rotter*!'

Bill continued, smiling cheerily now, 'Well that's it for tonight. We'll be back tomorrow. So I'll be seeing you soon.' He cast a final glance towards the Sex Pistols, who were looking exceptionally pleased with themselves. 'I hope I'm not seeing you lot again. From me, though, goodnight.'

The next morning the newspapers ran the story big. Three uses of the 'f-word', one 'b-word', two 's-words' ('shit' and 'sod'), plus a live sexual proposition, all in three minutes of television put out on ITV in the early evening, well before the 9 p.m. watershed. That must be some sort of world record. Leading the way was the *Daily Mirror* which filled its front page with the headline 'THE FILTH AND THE FURY', and reported that James Holmes, a 47-year-old lorry driver, had put his boot through the screen when his 8-year-old son, who was watching the show, heard the swearing. 'It exploded and I was blown backwards,' Holmes told the *Mirror*, 'but I was so angry and disgusted with this filth that I took a swing at it.'

The *Sun* ran the headline 'OBNOXIOUS, ARROGANT, OUTRAGEOUS . . . THE NEW KINGS OF POP', and mentioned the fact that the Sex Pistols were about to start a nationwide tour. The paper reported the group's manager, Malcolm McLaren, as saying, 'It is very likely there will be some violence at some of the gigs, because it is violent music,' and 'We don't necessarily think violence is a bad thing.'

Within hours of the Bill Grundy interview almost all the venues on the tour cancelled the concerts, as McLaren had intended. Some said they could not guarantee public safety; others were under the influence of local worthies who had heard about the swearing. In addition, the Sex Pistols' record 'Anarchy in the UK', for which, as Grundy had noted, the group had been paid £40,000 (roughly equivalent to £250,000 at 1998 prices) had been banned from the radio. To make sure this happened, McLaren had hired a team of secretaries to write fake letters of the 'I put my foot through the television' variety to the papers and the BBC.

One or two Sex Pistol concerts did take place, but they were deliberately disastrous. Few people were allowed in, and the gigs were used mainly to allow the group to assault the audience and journalists, spitting and throwing beer cans at them. As a result McLaren was in charge of a pop group which was not allowed to perform and whose records you could not hear. The ultimate triumph of not being able even to buy their records was not quite achieved, though there was a strike at the record factory, with workers refusing to pack the vinyl discs into their sleeves.

McLaren then arranged for the Sex Pistols to vandalise their record company's office, getting them the sack, before joining another record company and then repeating the trick. After Sid Vicious joined the group, they toured the US, and hired session musicians to make an LP called *Never Mind the Bollocks*.

In their two-year life, the Sex Pistols generated many millions of pounds' worth of publicity with McLaren hardly spending a penny. He earned himself a small fortune in cancelled record company and appearance contracts. In 1978, when the Sex Pistols 'caper' was pronounced over, McLaren announced that he had brought to an end the 'Great Rock and Roll Swindle'.[1]

McLaren's impact on the younger generation of pop music operators, fashion designers, 'rock journalists' and trendy television executives was enormous. Here was a man who had succeeded in putting together the equation of youthful rebellion and money-making, by understanding how the media worked, and by producing a non-stop stream of synthetic horror stories and manufactured outrage, tailor-made for tabloid front pages. In essence, his method boiled down to thinking of a publicity campaign first, and then inventing an excuse for putting it into action.

Live TV

This idea, sometimes called 'selling the sizzle, not the sausage', came to dominate the thinking of many in the media world, especially in the 1980s. It was based on an intellectual case that the media, especially television, were tremendously shallow, perfectly suited to shocking people. Eighties media figures like Julie Burchill were to call themselves 'Malcolm's Children', awarding him guru status. He had many admirers and imitators, including Janet Street-Porter. Much later, in August 1995, Janet was given the honour of presenting the keynote MacTaggart Lecture at the Edinburgh International Television Festival. She cited the Sex Pistols and McLaren's Cunning Stunts as being among her main formative influences as a TV programme-maker.

Despite being ten years older than McLaren, Janet was on the same circuit of London art-school graduates and 'street' fashion designers who brought punk to life. She was still a compulsive attender of nightclubs and of boutiques such as McLaren's King's Road emporium, Sex, where the Sex Pistols scam had been dreamt up. Picking up early on the trend, Janet had interviewed Johnny Rotten on the *London Weekend Show*. The encounter was described as a 'scoop' at the time and there was such excitement that the *Evening Standard* described Janet, who had abandoned her slightly fluffy art deco look and was sporting Zandra's designer safety-pins, as 'the first lady of punk'. This was followed up by the special Janet-fronted LWT documentary on punk, which got rave reviews, and which had been featured by Bill Grundy.

Janet became LWT's acceptable, in-house, mass-market punk, the perfect personality to add a bit of street-wise, rejuvenating fizz to otherwise dull chat shows and the like. In 1976 she had taken a sideways move, graduating from *The London Weekend Show* to join media cleverdicks Russell

Harty and Clive James on a late-night LWT chat show called *Saturday Night People*. The programme was officially an attempt to produce a 'gossip column of the airwaves' and it was launched under the slogan 'Malice with responsibility'. The gossip columnist Peter Hillmore was roped in as co-producer, to add an element of waspish wit, as it was put. Janet found it hard going. Harty was already an established star, but Clive James had then done little TV, and was awkward and so nervous that he had to write his gags on the cuffs of his shirtsleeves. The three egos clashed constantly over matters such as camera angles. Janet needed the camera up high because she was so tall, but James complained that this exposed his bald patch. If the camera was moved down, Harty complained that it high-lighted his multiple chins. There was no satisfying them. Worst of all, Janet found that she couldn't get a word in edgeways. She complained to Birt that she 'couldn't 'andle it'; he told her to get her elbows out and get on with it. And there was another grumble. Janet was earning £20,000 a year for her part in the show and complained that she was worth more, and would have been given more if she had been a man.

Saturday Night People was fairly successful and Janet moved on to front *The Chat Show*, the first all-female talk show on LWT, and then *Around Midnight*, another chat show, this time featuring Auberon Waugh as the ultimate upper-class fogey foil for Janet and, to add a bit of controversy, 'Red' Ken Livingstone, then in his undiluted Loony Left phase.

After two years of chat shows, Janet made her 'fatal' move into primetime, as reporter and presenter on *The Six O'Clock Show*, essentially a modernised version of the old Esther Rantzen BBC warhorse *That's Life*, which had always dominated the weekend ratings and so was a major

Live TV

LWT preoccupation. The *Six O'Clock* editor, Greg Dyke, decided to inject a dose of class-based humour. 'I discovered that the working class and the upper class were very, very funny; but the middle class were a pain in the arse,' he compained. 'You couldn't get a line out of them.' He countered the intrinsic po-facedness of the suburbs with the younger and more 'anarchic' feel of 'zany' television (a Birt–LWT speciality) and used Janet to give the show a powerful local accent. *The Six O'Clock Show* became the cornerstone of the LWT schedule.[2]

Janet was unhappy working on the show for many reasons, including the fact that they made her sit at a desk to show off her undoubtedly attractive legs and that, at one point, she was teamed up with Michael Aspel in yet another version of the *Two in the Morning* smoothie vs. punk routine. The difference this time was that Aspel put her down much more effectively. Also, he earned much more than she did, perhaps five times as much, which was naturally a source of resentment. She later told David Docherty, the semi-official historian of LWT, 'I was getting more and more depressed at this hideous cockney character [they were trying to make me become]. It was just more and more removed from reality.' She went to see Birt and told him she needed a change. She wanted to move from being a presenter to being a producer. 'He couldn't believe it. He told me I was throwing away my career.'

But Janet had made her mind up. She parked her LWT career for a while and went to Australia to become a reporter on a current-affairs show called *The Willessee Show* on Channel Nine in Sydney. While she was there, she wrote for the *Sydney Morning Herald*, *Playboy* and the Australian edition of *Harpers*, and also reportedly attended a *Dr Who* convention and developed an interest in watersports. She returned the next year even more determined to become a producer and, after the customary hustling, John Birt gave her a chance. At this point LWT had its eye on the forthcoming launch of Channel Four, the official 'minority' channel which was due to be launched the following year, 1982. (Birt had wanted to be the first head of Channel Four, and had put a lot of effort into preparing programme plans and an application, but the job went to Jeremy Isaacs, later head of the Royal Opera House.) Birt reckoned that Channel Four, which would buy in all its programmes either from independent programme makers or from existing TV companies like LWT, was the perfect vehicle for the ideas about 'market segmentation' and 'niche broadcasting' he had pioneered with programmes like Janet's *London Weekend Show*. He had also set up LWT's London Minorities Unit, which involved much of the same team and was charged with making niche programmes for black and gay Londoners.

Janet was taken on as series producer in her main area of expertise, youth and music programmes. The result was a music-based series called *20th Century Box* which self-consciously mixed in a lot of the style of the punk-rock trend. She lured Danny Baker, then working as an iconoclastic writer (alongside Charles Shaar Murray, Tony Parsons, Julie Burchill, Paul Morley, Ian Penman and Neil Spencer) on the *New Musical Express*, to LWT to front the show. He was, in many ways, a younger, male equivalent of Janet's street-wise punky cockney persona. He was the son of a docker and came from rough *sahf*-east London. After leaving school at 15 to work in a record shop, he had helped launch *Sniffin' Glue*; Janet had met him when she was making her punk documentary. At this point, Baker's main claim to literary fame was that he had coined the term 'Wacko Jacko' after the coup of securing an exclusive interview with monkey-loving American disco sensation

Live TV

Michael Jackson.[3]

Punk had been marked by a shambolic amateurism, a 'disposable youth culture' of bin-liner clothes and safety-pins. It was easy and cheap to get involved, with audience and performers interchangeable. In contrast to the glossy pop music magazines, punk 'fanzines' were often run off on photocopiers, with headlines and pictures cut out of newspapers. The crucial thing was that the music, clothes and magazines had to be produced by *the kidz* and should be free from 'bollocks', meaning professionalism of any sort. The task now was to transfer all this on to the screen.

Janet was well placed to ride the wave of punkish 'alternative' or '*yoof*' television which was to be such a feature of the 1980s, with Channel Four leading the way. The new channel had been set up by statute to cater for people who, until then, had not been well served by the existing channels. This included, officially, the young.

Janet pitched various ideas for LWT-produced shows to Mike Bolland, the Channel Four executive in charge of buying in youth material, but unfortunately for her his philosophy was that programmes for young people should be made by young people themselves.[4] Janet Street-Porter, now 34, was not his idea of a young person. Instead, he commissioned the catastrophic *Whatever You Want*, which really was made by untrained teenagers. Its ratings were later measured as close to zero. Balanced against this disaster was a highly successful music-based series called *The Tube*, which, more than any other, brought into television the genuine DIY feel of punk, with its wobbly cameras, and its stumbling, amateurish, 'no bullshit' presenters (Paula Yates and Jools Holland) who fluffed their lines, argued and contradicted each other on screen and chatted to the cameramen.

Janet teamed up with Jane Hewland, a rising star in

LWT's current affairs department. Hewland had started off on Birt's original LWT stomping-ground, *Weekend World* (known in the trade as '*Weekend Warp*', a dig at his habit of selecting facts to fit a pre-scripted intellectual argument), and had progressed to run the all-important Channel Four-friendly London Minorities Unit. Channel Four bought two series from Hewland's unit, *Black on Black* and *Asian Eye*, which, given the new channel's remit, could afford to be made 'by and for' the minorities concerned, rendering them slightly less vulnerable to the criticism that they were voyeuristic and patronising.[5] Following up on this success, Janet and Jane decided that they had been barking up the wrong tree at Channel Four, going to the wrong commissioning people. They would never get a contract for a youth programme so long as the channel wanted it made by young people; they would never get a music commission, now that *The Tube* was such a great success. What about current affairs?

They booked themselves in to see John Cummins, a Channel Four commissioning editor who was in the market for an *innervitiff* new current-affairs slot. (He had met Janet a few years before when he was a student at Esher College and she was filming an item there, and had been tremendously impressed by her.) Cummins had joined Channel Four at the age of 25 after working as a researcher on *The Tube*. He was toying with the idea of doing a 'factual' version of the hit music show. Luckily, Janet and Jane Hewland were thinking along the same lines.

The two women proposed a programme which would go out late on Sunday morning and would be called *Brunch*. In contrast to conventional current-affairs programmes, which were 'about issues', it would be 'about people'. It would simulate the way in which 'real people' (i.e. Janet herself) talked about current affairs – if they bothered at all – which apparently was to chat about things over 'brunch' on their day off. The programme would redefine current affairs away from male, middle-class, middle-aged preoccupations like politics, towards 'real' concerns such as why nobody was doing anything *abaht* uncomfortable and ill-fitting bras. It would appeal to the young, and stir in a bit of the post-punk DIY chaotic look. It would thus, according to the blurb, 'strip away the ghastly conventions of news and current affairs productions which were dreamt up in the 1950s and '60s' . . . *No more Bill Grundy, right?*

Remarks like these bore the hallmark of John Birt, who after his arrival at LWT had denounced ITV and BBC current-affairs output as old-fashioned. In a paper written in 1971 he attacked LWT's current affairs as having 'a slick but shallow "Oh-I'll-be-home-by-seven-after-a-quick-few-drinks-with-the-lads look"' – whatever that meant. 'With Ulster, the miners and one million unemployed I don't want my truth packaged – I want to *feel* the way it is.' He wanted presenters 'with the mud still fresh on their proverbial boots' and an end product that was 'a bit rough and raw' but allowed people to 'believe television again'.

Originally the idea had been to do a one-hour magazine show. But the two women decided that they would ask for two hours a week, at least. The whole theory of 'alternative television' was that you needed to provide a channel (or something which looked like a channel), rather than a single programme, if it was going to work. They devised their sales pitch, later claiming that they had changed all their plans while sitting in the taxi *en route* to see Cummins. Hewland later told David Docherty, 'We more or less decided in the taxi that we would go for broke' and demand a whole morning rather than just the traditional one or two hour show. 'We were on exceptionally good pitching form that day,' she recalled, and had an answer ready for every objection Cummins might raise: 'We could see the lights going on in his eyes.'

Following the meeting Cummins persuaded Jeremy Isaacs, head of Channel Four, to part with an extra £2.5 million and a large slice of airtime. Isaacs was reluctant, and suggested making five or six one-hour shows to try out the formula before committing themselves. But Cummins was by now a believer and threatened to resign. 'You didn't do five trial episodes of *Channel Four News* or *Brookside* or *The Tube*,' he complained. In its way, Cummins said, *Brunch* would be just as important as those programmes. He explained that it would not only appeal to youth, but would rope in slightly older viewers who were bored with Channel Four's more orthodox current-affairs shows (which he described as 'finger up the bum'-type television). Bravery was the order of the day: 'This is going to be a huge *defining programme* for the channel. Either back the thing and do it properly or fire me.' Isaacs agreed – but warned Cummins that he would be fired anyway if the project was a flop.

Janet and Jane were delighted. They were in business. They dropped the name *Brunch* when another show with the same title was launched during their negotiations. Anyway, now that whole 'channel-within-a-channel' idea had been accepted they needed a different sort of name. Instead of *Brunch [on Channel Four]* they needed a *channel title*. Maybe like the new wave of DIY pirate dance-music radio stations that had sprung up in the wake of punk with titles like the Rastafarian Dread Broadcasting Corporation or Kiss FM. Yeah! A sort of futuristic *pirate* television station! Completely Brilliant. Channel Four was the latest thing on TV. So what about *Channel Five*? No. There'd be a real Channel Five sooner or later. *Channel Seven* – that would be two steps ahead of the game! But *Channel Seven* sounded a bit borin' and British. *Network* sounded better: more funky and American and pirate-like. That was the future, wasn't it? America. Where they already had dozens of channels. *Network-7 . . . Completely Brilliant!* And the effect could be rounded off with the all-important graphics and logo: a satellite dish, giving the impression that *Network-7* was somehow being beamed from outer space by some buccaneering pirate types.[6]

At the same time the title suggested that a brave new world of television had arrived early and that viewers were being treated to a glimpse of the multi-channel future of niche cable and satellite channels that everyone in telly-land was starting to talk about.

Network-7. Yeah! Fantastic! It was gonna be ten years ahead of its time.

Chapter Three

In which David 'Monty' Montgomery ignores the hedonism of the 1960s and leaves his native Northern Ireland to earn a crust working for the Daily Mirror *in Manchester, where he complains in his funny accent about the large number of under-employed drunks on the payroll, is denounced as a creep and a rotter for his pains, resulting in a move to London and a failed plan to take over the* Sun, *which leads him to unleash a tidal wave of steamy Kiss-and-Tell Bonk Journalism at the* News of the World *amid more conflict, denunciations and back-stabbing before he relaunches a newspaper aimed at television-obsessed female yuppies and hires Janet Street-Porter as a television critic*

Nick Lloyd was an unusual figure in the world of tabloid journalism. He was softly spoken, urbane and university-educated. He had joined Rupert Murdoch's *Sun* from the *Sunday Times* in the early 1970s, taking the key job of features editor. Then still in his twenties, he was something of a trendy, holding fashionable left-wing views and supporting movements like CND. He was sympathetic to the new radical agenda of women's rights, gay rights, sexual freedom and racial equality. Partly thanks to his input, the *Sun* had slaughtered the *Mirror* with its much better feel for the interests and attitudes of the younger generation. Murdoch was duly grateful and had picked Lloyd out as a high-flyer, giving him experience as assistant editor of both the *Sun* and the *News of the World* and grooming him for greater things.

In 1979, Lloyd, frustrated by Murdoch's failure to grant him an editorship, moved over to the Mirror Group as deputy editor of the *Sunday Mirror*. But the parting was amicable and it was common knowledge that Lloyd was biding his time, getting a bit more experience as an editorial executive before returning to the *Sun*. At last, in 1981, the editorship of the *Sun* fell vacant. Murdoch phoned Lloyd, telling him he needed to speak to him in person in his private office at *The Times*: he had some urgent business to discuss. 'This is it!' Lloyd thought, and rushed round to meet his old boss.

But he was to be disappointed. Murdoch was offering only the job of deputy editor of the *Sun*. The top job was going to a man called Kelvin MacKenzie, who Lloyd remembered from his time at the paper as only a raucous sub-editor (or 'sub' in newspaper jargon) way down the pecking order – not editor material at all. Lloyd was bemused. What was the phone call all about, then? Murdoch smiled. He said that putting MacKenzie in the editor's chair was a gamble. Lloyd could still end up as editor of the *Sun* if things did not work out. 'I want you back, Nick,' Murdoch said. 'You've got a great contribution to make. I want you to be Kelvin's deputy. You'd make a great team.' Lloyd told Murdoch he wasn't interested. He wanted to be an editor, and he was ready for the challenge. He would stay at the Mirror Group.

MacKenzie's arrival as editor of the *Sun* was bad news not only for Nick Lloyd, but for those members of the *Sun*'s staff who had been awaiting Lloyd's arrival in the hope of promotion. Chief among the pro-Lloyd contingent was the dour, lanky figure of David Montgomery, a fellow member of the new clan of university-educated tabloid journalists. Unlike Lloyd, Montgomery had spent his first ten years in national journalism not on the *Sun* but at the *Mirror*. The two men had met in 1980, when Montgomery moved from the *Mirror*'s northern headquarters, in Manchester, to London to work with Lloyd, who was then spending his year in exile at *Mirror* HQ. Montgomery had become friendly with Lloyd and his influential wife, Eve Pollard. The professional relationship became close and they had much in common. Both Lloyd and Montgomery were outsiders at the *Mirror* in London.

Montgomery had firm ideas about the future of popular newspapers, which he shared with Lloyd and Pollard. In the past ten years, the *Sun* had come from nowhere to overtake the *Mirror*.[1] The reasons were obvious enough. The Mirror Group was overstaffed and, as they saw it, full of lazy, complacent journalists who had lost their competitive edge. At the top level, the paper was led by people who did not understand the younger generation of tabloid-readers. The *Mirror* was stuck in its worthy, male-dominated, Andy Capp, Labour-supporting time-warp. The *Sun* had a much better feel for the younger audience. Once its editor, Larry Lamb, was out of the way, a rejuvenated *Sun* would start soaring away again, and Lloyd and Montgomery would be the people to shape a new paper for the 1980s.

The aim would be to track their own generation – the 'babyboomer' rock 'n' roll generation who were 'aspirational' and 'classless' – and to create a 'modernised' tabloid which would appeal to these people and, importantly, cater for a new generation of liberated young working-class and lower-middle-class women. Montgomery, increasingly out of sorts with the *Mirror*, had left the paper and taken a job as a senior sub at the *Sun*, in readiness for Lloyd's anticipated arrival as editor.

But it was not to be. Instead MacKenzie came and announced that it was his job to push the paper down-market. He launched a reign of terror, shrieking that he was 'the bingo editor' (a reference to Murdoch's costly decision to counter-attack against the newly launched *Daily Star*, which was using newspaper 'bingo' with huge cash prizes to attack the *Sun*'s circulation), and that his mission was to 'drive the *Daily Star* off the streets'.[2] He started combing through the *Sun*'s staff in an attempt to get rid of those who were not ready to follow his lead. 'What are you lot, eh?' MacKenzie would rave at the quaking hacks. 'Eh? *I'll* tell you what you are. Fucking middle-class, middle-aged, overpaid and out of touch. If you don't pull your fucking fingers out, I'm gonna sack the lot of you and bring in some twenty-two-year-olds.' As a protégé of MacKenzie's main rival for the editorship, Montgomery was soon on his way. 'I'm not sacking you,' MacKenzie reportedly told him, 'I am giving you six weeks to find another job. Then I'll sack you.'

Montgomery took the hint and left the paper. Before MacKenzie's arrival, Lloyd had been on track to become editor of the country's biggest-selling national daily, and the future looked bright. Now Montgomery had little choice but to follow Lloyd back to the Mirror Group.

David Montgomery was born in Bangor, Northern Ireland, in 1948 into a family of solidly conservative Presbyterian stock and modest means. His father, who was an orphan, worked for the local electricity board. His mother was a farmer's daughter. Although the family were regular church-goers they were not especially political or sectarian. Young David went to Queen's University, Belfast, in the late '60s and studied history and politics: intellectual commodities which were not in short supply at the time, since Belfast was in the grip of the civil-rights demonstrations and protests that led to the foundation of the

Provisional IRA and the resumption of 'the troubles'. He always dressed smartly, even as a student, and normally wore a tie and a shiny single-breasted suit, which made him stand out in the midst of the long-haired, T-shirt-wearing students of the time. He was unremittingly sober, smiled very rarely and was never seen telling a joke.

Montgomery became the editor of the college newspaper, *The Gown*. He was remembered as a moderate opponent of the civil-rights marchers and a staunch, though not fanatical, Unionist, and was quoted in *The Gown* as joking that he was 'the last bastion of Protestantism' at the university. But mainly Montgomery was interested in keeping out of trouble and making money. He combined his studies with running a news agency, selling stories about the troubles to national newspapers.

As a student editor Monty exhibited some of the characteristics which were to mark his later career in life, including a reputation for sneakiness and a taste for Machiavellian scheming. A long article in *The Gown* described how he had manoeuvred himself into the editor's chair by stitching up rivals at student union meetings. He was described as 'the staff bureaucrat, budding despot and arch-plotter . . . This scheming individual had conspired for years to assume the mantle of authority and so give vent to his biblical yearnings'. The article was illustrated with a cartoon of Montgomery wearing his suit and playing a piano with typewriter keys instead of ivories, with the caption 'Burning the midnight oil'. *The Gown* also accused him of getting a job on the professional local paper, the *Newsletter*, by sneakily selling stories about the students' permissive sex lives.[3]

Montgomery's workaholic approach was clear from the start. Over the two years he edited the paper he filled huge amounts of space, under the by-line 'Dave Montgomery', with stories under headlines such as 'HOW DOES A STUDENT SPEND HIS GRANT?' (an attack on 'the frivolous student who devotes himself to a surfeit of alcoholic pleasure'), 'TEETHING TROUBLES FOR RAG COMMITTEE' and the all-time humdinger 'FIRE DESTROYS SCIENCE HUTS'. The paper's most intriguing story – 'RUFUS IN COMBAT WITH TURD MUNCHERS' – was not his work. He and his colleagues also introduced into *The Gown* a 'cover-girl competition', reminiscent of the *Sun*'s Page Three and featuring busty members of the student cohort.

At the end of his studies Montgomery won a place on the *Daily Mirror*'s sought-after graduate training scheme.[4] At first, he turned down the offer, and he might easily have remained in the provincial obscurity of Northern Ireland had the scheme not needed to keep up its quota of recruits. A junior *Mirror* reporter and former Queen's graduate, who had been in the year above Montgomery at university, was told to phone him and get him to sign up. Montgomery grumbled in his thick Ulster accent that he was making a lot of money from his agency work and didn't want to fold it all to go on some half-baked training scheme in London. But the *Mirror* man persuaded him that the move would get him a job on a national paper with good money within two or three years, whereas it would take six or seven years – if he was lucky – to work his way up through agency work. The training would pay off in the long run. Montgomery did the calculations and agreed to turn up.

Montgomery was, in the main, unpopular with his fellow trainees, and was later remembered by some as a peripheral figure who hung around the fringes of the crowd at the bar, rarely speaking to people, grimly sipping a half-pint of beer. He passed the *Mirror* course and in 1970 started work at the paper's then large Manchester office. From the start Montgomery, who was always known as 'Monty', was remembered as being more interested in gaining and exercising power than in anything else. He specialised in production journalism, becoming a 'sub' rather than taking on the more exciting and glamorous work of a news reporter. On a tabloid, especially, though the reporters got all the glory it was the subs who rewrote the stories, decided how long they should be, put the pages together and wrote the headlines, and therefore exercised all the power. Monty's ambition was to become chief sub – the person mostly responsible for bringing the paper out every night – at a young enough age to have a serious chance of becoming a national newspaper editor one day.

The problem was that the *Mirror* employed scores of subs, and they were the best in the business. It was hard to shine and, even if he could come to the attention of his bosses, he might spend years in the promotion log jam. The pace was crushingly slow for an ambitious young man. Monty reckoned the office was massively overstaffed. On a normal evening subbing shift the pace was very gentle, with most of the work easily completed in an hour or two. Typically, a sub was expected to check and rewrite two or perhaps three shortish news stories, taking a maximum of twenty minutes each – less if the reporter was good at his job – and to deal with one lead article for a page and provide a good eye-grabbing headline. This last might take forty minutes; more experienced subs could work even faster, since they tended to evolve into walking headline pun-machines, able to produce real stomach-churners within seconds of grasping the story. There might be one other story to deal with, or a bit of blurb to be provided for a competition, but that was basically it. A 'good sub' was a man who got through these tasks in under an hour, and that was the day's work. This situation was partly a job-creation scheme, enforced by the unions, and partly to provide slack to keep up the quality and provide the capacity to do a good job on something like a major disaster, when the whole paper would have to be written, designed and rewritten in minutes. On those occasions, the subs worked their socks off with no complaints, but generally, had it not been for the filthy, factory-like surroundings, a casual visitor might have thought he had strayed into a golf club. There was much pipe-smoking, intelligent debate and conversation, crossword practice, bridge-playing, wine-drinking and, on the *Mirror* at least, reading of the collected works of John Dos Passos or George Orwell.

In contrast, Monty kept busy all the time. He pestered the head of the Manchester office, Derek Jameson, creeping around his office door, trying to make himself useful and offering to do extra work. (According to legend, fellow sub David 'Banksy' Banks nicknamed him 'Cabin Boy' because of the way he sucked up to people.) Jameson found this exasperating: 'Not you again,' he would moan. 'Just piss off, will you.' But Monty would be back again the next day. If Jameson didn't give him something to do, he would start badgering the older subs, asking in his thick Ulster accent what the front-page '*splosh*' [splash] story was, trying to find fault and suggesting changes: '*Noi then, wyoi don't we troi toy doi the froint poige thois wyoi?*' Most put this down to an over-eagerness to please born of youthful insecurity, and so he was tolerated, though people told him to get lost if he got too bothersome.

Monty was regarded as an oddball, partly because of his Ulster Unionism and his cold, unsmiling manner. He was disliked by many for his seemingly compulsive sneakiness. He rarely looked people squarely in the face and seemed nervous all the time, as though he was up to something, even when he wasn't. In a profile of Monty later published in the *Guardian*, some of his former colleagues were quoted describing him as 'a dour android with a disconcerting stare'. James Dalrymple (by then a *Sunday Times* writer) who had helped train him was quoted as saying: 'He is the only guy I've ever known who can walk into a room and reduce the temperature by 10 degrees.' Mike Molloy, the *Mirror*'s editor in the mid-1970s remembered him as a 'strange looking, rather quiet chap who, when he did talk, talked only about the minutiae of newspaper production. People always found him a bit eerie. It was as if he had come from another planet.'[5]

Still, he was remembered by some as a good sub-editor in technical terms. But some of his direct superiors did not see it like that. He took on a lot of work, but he had to be watched all the time or he would make changes to the pages without telling anyone: nothing major, just little changes and 'improvements' – which would often as not have to be changed back again when they were spotted.

In 1980, after ten years in Manchester, Montgomery moved to the *Mirror* in London, where he met Nick Lloyd and Eve Pollard and, later, moved to the *Sun*. After MacKenzie arrived as editor, Monty left the *Sun* to be reunited with his mentor, and both men worked for a time on the *People*. Monty was regarded as Lloyd's 'gofer', doing much of the hard work and dealing with the interminable problems in the production department. The relationship suited both parties. Lloyd liked to socialise, whereas Monty's idea of fun appeared to involve wading through a great pile of page proofs and other paperwork. A year later, Lloyd·and Monty moved again. At last they were working for Murdoch, as editor and deputy editor respectively of the *News of the World*, or '*News of the Screws*', as it was known in the trade. Within three years Monty took over from Lloyd as editor. When asked if Monty had stabbed him in the back, Lloyd quipped cheerfully, 'No, he stabbed me in the front.'

In fact, the parting was amicable. Murdoch had given Lloyd the all-important job of organising 'Project X', code for the planned move of all his papers to the union-free Wapping plant. Before taking on the project, Lloyd himself had suggested that Monty succeed him as editor of the *Screws*. Murdoch, though he had never really warmed to Monty, was persuaded. Editorship of the *Screws* meant that Monty had at last reached the top of the tree in Murdoch's London operation, but it also brought him into a tricky relationship with MacKenzie, who was his main rival for Murdoch's attention, affection and support. Murdoch – 'the Boss' – ruled by fear. He had a habit, well known throughout his ever-expanding Empire, of phoning up one of his editors and effusively praising another. The message was clear enough: there were plenty of others who could fill the editor's shoes and do a better job. But then, sometimes within minutes, the 'star' editor would be phoned, slagged off and given the same treatment. The only defence was trust between editors, who therefore needed to talk to each other to work out what Murdoch was up to. What they feared most was not being rung up at all. When that happened, the internal phones would start buzzing: 'Has he called you? . . . He has? . . . Oh fuck! . . . What have I done? I must be in the shit.'

There was no chance of MacKenzie and Monty getting on like this. The personality clash was obvious to anyone who saw them in the same room. MacKenzie used jokingly to call Monty 'the Botty Burglar', not because Monty was homosexual, but because he looked sort of wimpy and was a fastidious dresser and generally very uptight and wore poofy glasses and . . . well . . . was a *fucking pooftah botty burglar* (MacKenzie tended to call any man who took a special interest in grooming a 'botty burglar'). Besides this, MacKenzie took a particular delight in stealing stories that Monty had lined up mid-week for exclusive publication in the *News of the World* on Sunday – especially if Monty had paid a lot of money for the story – and then running them for 'free' in the *Sun*. In the end Monty retaliated by preparing fake front-page splashes to find out who MacKenzie's spies were. Once, he set up a whole raft of leads on a completely fictitious story. MacKenzie took the bait and splashed the story on page one. A hundred thousand copies had been printed before Monty triumphantly revealed his hoax, making sure that Murdoch found out and that MacKenzie got a monumental bollocking.

The two editors had to compete to become top dog in Murdoch's eyes. The key to achieving this was increasing circulation and Monty started to do well, mainly by unleashing the full force of 'bonk journalism', as it became known. The *Screws* had always specialised in exposés of the sexual peccadillos of the rich and famous, but with Monty at the helm the *Screws* took 'kiss and tell' journalism to new heights, paying a standard £30,000 for an account of adulterous sex with a reasonably well known personality (much more was paid for anything kinky). A long queue of bimbos, rent boys, prostitutes and vindictive or merely greedy former lovers thus made their way to Monty's door to get a slice of the action. As a result he was denounced in the columns of the rival *Mirror* as the country's chief 'pornographer'. But Monty did not seem to care. It was sour grapes from a faltering rival. The *Screws* sales graph was creeping up and the extra revenue more than covered the sums being dished out to the kiss 'n' tell specialists, making his position with Murdoch more secure, until the roof started falling in on bonk journalism after the victims began to hit back through the libel courts. A turning-point of sorts was reached with the 1987 Jeffrey Archer case, in which the jury walloped both the *Screws* and, especially, the *Daily Star* for massive damages. In 1986 the *Screws* had turned up a prostitute, Monica Coghlan, who claimed to have met Archer. Monty ran the story, making sure it was carefully written to give the impression that Archer, then deputy chairman of the Conservative Party, used Coghlan's services regularly. But all that was actually said was that Archer had met her once. This was true, and Archer had admitted it.

But then the *Daily Star* picked up the story and embroidered it, claiming that Archer had repeatedly had sex with Coghlan; there was no evidence whatsoever for this. When Archer sued the *Star*, Monty tried to keep his paper out of it. But, realising that the *Star* would summons him to be cross-examined about the original allegations printed in the *Screws*, he agreed to appear in court in the *Star*'s defence. It was his job to make sure that the *Screws* suffered as little damage as possible. However, after a generally ice-cool performance in the witness box, the case was lost and the *News of the World* paid Archer £30,000 in an out-of-court settlement. More expensively, the paper had to pay his enormous legal costs. The Archer affair did Monty no good at all. But by this time there were already developments which would lead him on from the *Screws* to edit a paper even more to his liking.

In 1987 Murdoch bought the loss-making *Today* from the union-busting media entrepreneur Eddie Shah. After a lot of technical difficulties, Shah was on the point of selling the paper and its losses to Robert Maxwell. Murdoch weighed in at the last minute, not so much because he wanted the paper as because he wanted to stop Maxwell expanding his UK operation. Beyond this, the paper was a dead duck. It was positioned in the mid-market, which Murdoch regarded as a killing field, dominated by unshakeable brand loyalty and cut-throat competition between the almighty *Daily Mail* and the ailing *Daily Express*. He was already on record as saying that there was no room for both the *Mail* and the *Express* in the UK mid-market, let alone a third, less well established title.

But *Today* did have one important advantage: it was printed in colour. At the time there were no colour presses in Murdoch's Wapping plant and all his papers were printed in black and white with a smudgy blob of ink for the 'red top' masthead. This state of affairs had resulted in a rare triumph for Robert Maxwell. He had bought colour presses for the *Mirror* and the ability to run colour pictures, particularly of sport, had been a great success. The *Mirror* had put on 200,000 circulation, closing the gap on the faltering black-and-white *Sun*. Murdoch was planning to buy colour presses and so the purchase of *Today* would at least give him some valuable de-bugging experience before introducing colour to the all-important *Sun*. In the meantime it made sense to re-design *Today* as a 'spoiler' against the *Mirror*. In the bleary-eyed muddle of early morning, the chances were that at least some punters would pick up a cleverly edited, tabloid-shaped, all-colour *Today* designed to appeal to younger and less loyal *Mirror* readers, thus taking some of the pressure off the *Sun*.

Monty badgered Murdoch to give him the editorship of *Today*. It was the ideal chance to create the 'modernised *Mirror*' formula which he and Lloyd thought would sweep the popular market. Murdoch indulged him and not only gave him the editorship but made him chairman of News UK, the company which Shah had set up to run *Today* and which became a Murdoch subsidiary when Murdoch bought the paper. Monty was delighted; and by moving into the boardroom he had at last got one step ahead of MacKenzie. It was central to the Murdoch view that journalists, however senior, were basically lazy, vain and, on the whole, stupid as well. It was OK to start out as a journalist, but hacking about was a young man's game. Anyone who was still working as a journalist in their forties without making the move into the boardroom was obviously a mug of some sort.

Monty arrived at his new command, which remained in Shah's old headquarters on Vauxhall Bridge Road, a few miles west up the Thames from Wapping, full of beans. On his first day he tore up all existing plans for the paper and started furiously rewriting everything and planning new sections and regular features. There were a lot of sackings, as was always the case with a change of editor, especially on a Murdoch paper. But as part of Monty's sneaky approach he rarely did the evil deed himself. People were amazed to find themselves scrutinising proofs side by side with Monty one minute only to have a minion from the legal department march up to them with the long brown envelope the next.

Monty gathered the remaining staff together and told them that in future *Today* would be catering for a new audience: 'the children of the Thatcher revolution', as he called them. A new sort of 'classless' young working-class reader who was 'aspirational' and 'style-conscious'. (In the office the polite euphemism 'aspirational' was given its real name: greedy. Montgomery told the hacks that *Today* was a newspaper for 'greedy people'. When he decided to back the Green Party as part of the '80s 'green consumer' fad he updated the message: *Today* was now a paper for 'Green Greedy People', according to one account, or 'Greedy Green People', according to another.[6])

In practice, the pursuit of the new 'aspirational' working class amounted to an obsession with house-price stories. One of the paper's best reporters was given the job of scouring estate agents to find examples of ordinary houses which had doubled or tripled in value and then getting the 'story' from the ecstatic champagne-quaffing householders. It became a matter of policy that *Today* would try to have a house-price 'story' on page one every day.

The thinking seemed to emanate in part from the marketing and advertising people whom Monty had brought with him to the paper. It was noted that he spent an inordinate amount of time talking to advertising agencies and other trend-spotters, who were constantly seen trooping into his office with big black leather portfolios, pony-tails flapping. The standard journalistic view was that these people were snake-oil salesmen who made their living by pretending to have solved the eternal mystery of what made people buy newspapers but, in practice, simply told you what you wanted to hear and charged a fortune for the privilege. But Monty seemed to swallow it all.

Supporting all this was a new and more feminised approach to the paper's features – Monty had decreed that *Today* must appeal much more to women, who were a growing and increasingly wealthy section of the market for popular newspapers. Copying the style of the big-circulation women's magazines and the likes of *Hello!*, wall-to-wall celebrity coverage was introduced. But, in stark contrast to the horrors of 'bonk journalism' lately dished up by Monty at the *News of the World* and the *Sun*, the celeb material was positive and 'heartwarming', earning the paper the nickname '*Toady*'. The general message was always the same. The celebrities were young, fairly ordinary and clearly, in some cases, somewhat thick. Now they were rich and glamorous . . . why not you?

Monty's source for a lot of this material was the burgeoning 'style' and consumer magazines and the new wave of 'lifestyle' supplements launched by newspapers such as the *Daily Express* and many of the Sundays. He simply copied the existing supplements. As a result Monty picked up yet another nickname, 'the Jackdaw', especially after he started directly stealing some of the best features from rival papers. Monty was rather pleased by the intended insult. He placed a stuffed jackdaw above the entrance to his office, complete with a copy of DX, the *Express*'s self-consciously trendy 'lifestyle' section, which he had copied shamelessly.

Since Monty was aiming to appeal to women readers he hired a lot of women hacks (one of whom, feature writer Heidi Kingstone, he later married). An important recruit was Amanda Platel, every inch a *Today* woman from her Gucci shoes to her thrusting shoulder-pads and dripping lip-gloss, brought in as production editor and swiftly promoted to deputy editor despite limited experience. Other senior women journalists whom Monty promoted included Tessa Hilton, Clare Rayner, Jane Moore and Jane Reed, who later became head of PR at News International.[7]

A more famous name was that of Janet Street-Porter, who joined the paper as a TV critic. At the time Janet was riding high on the critical success of *Network-7*, which was designed to appeal to precisely those elusive, aspirational youths crucial to Monty's 'modernised *Mirror*' formula.

At this point, after her previous manifestations as Mod, hippy student, chirpy cockney sparra', metropolitan sophisticate and punk rocker, Janet was playing the role of a female SuperYuppie: just the thing for *Today*. Her column was headed with the inevitable huge picture by-line and was entitled 'JANET STREET-PORTER: *A REALLY WICKED TV COLUMN*'.[8]

Chapter Four

In which life for Janet becomes Completely Brilliant as she becomes a SuperYuppie and drops her guilty feelings about conspicuous consumption, falls in love with the Pet Shop Boys, wows the young with her Infobars and TV executives with her demographics, wins a BAFTA, moves to the BBC at the behest of Alan and Jonathan, wages war on Dreery Old Rubbish, sets up her own mini-channel, is covered in awards and honours, meets Rupert Murdoch and is mightily impressed by him, and toys with the idea of becoming the First Female Director-General of the BBC

Janet Street-Porter was enjoying the eighties. As Monty had realised when he hired her to write for *Today* she was, in many ways, the perfect model for the media's idea of an 'Eighties Woman' – or at least the sort of person Monty's target female yuppie readers might aspire to be. For her part, Janet told people how much she admired 'David' as one of the few tabloid journalists who took *wimmin* seriously, both as readers and as executives. As a journalist he was honest. Unlike the others he did not '*twist fings*'.

And who could beat Janet? She was unique, a one-off. Still young-ish. Upwardly mobile, certainly: the voice proved that. Professional? Well, she worked in the *meedja*, didn't she? Her job, she said, boiled down to *finking what people'll be doin' nex' year 'n' doin' it naaaow*. You couldn't get more professional than that. She wore huge designer Buggles specs and clothes designed by leading designers, drove a flash designer car, drank designer drinks and ate designer food at the Groucho Club, which she had set up with friends in 1984. She went jet-skiing on designer jet-skis and spouted designer opinions on subjects of interest to designers. She was designing her own house and also designing her body. Squeezing into designer leotards, she worked out in a designer gym. She was now married to an *award-winnin' film-maker'* Frank Cvitanovich. She had 'relationships' and friendships with pop stars, architects, fashion photographers, merchant bankers, TV executives . . . and *designers*. When the latest *innervitiff* designer gadgets came on the market – personalised fax machines, mobile phones, bleepers, Filofaxes – she was the first to have one.

SuperYuppie, patron of popular culture, collector of 'street art', alternative *jernerlist*, arbiter of taste, sponsor of talent, queen of the scene, friend to the stars, workaholic, shopaholic – London, Paris, New York, Tokyo, Sydney – Janet was a walking, living monument to *The Life*. Others might dream about it – *sad* fuckers! – but she was prepared to Go For It. She was post-feminist, post-political, post-punk, post-industrial, post-modern . . . You name it, she was post-it. For Janet, the centrepiece of The Life, the thing that *brought it all togevver*, was not a person, an ideology or a religion but an object: her house. In this way, too, she was in tune with the times. In the 1980s houses and related matters, like interior design, DIY and furniture, became a national obsession on the back of a tidal wave of cheap credit and soaring property prices widely regarded by people like *Today* readers as a source of endless free money to which they were entitled for life.

Janet herself had profited handsomely from the property boom. In 1971 she and her then husband, Tim Street-Porter, had bought a former Georgian sea captain's house in Limehouse, which at the time was the absolute pits, the centre of London's filthy, crime- and rat-infested docks. The house was a bit of wreck when they moved in, but that was OK. Living in a wreck was funky and *alternatiff*, a bit like being a *skwotter*. And it meant that the couple could redesign the accommodation to their own liking as they repaired it. As ever, Janet had followed the example of Zandra Rhodes, her inspiration in all matters of style and taste. Zandra had bought her house in the 1960s, about the time she met Janet. The building, near the Westway in funky *Nottin'ill* [Notting Hill], had been in an appalling state, complete with floating sewage in the basement and fungus growing on the stairs: *dis-ghaastin'*. Janet and Tim were invited round for 'building parties', at which they were given dinner and asked to while the night away with a Black & Decker. Since then, Zandra had been through her Shell Period, her Plastic Period, her Ayers Rock Period and her Punk Period – so by now the house was done out in a sort of ex-hippy floating-shell plastic Ayers Rock designer-punk style. Zandra was campaigning to have it turned into a museum and national monument to eccentricity and civilised living.[1]

In Limehouse, Tim, being a photographer, had put a darkroom in the basement and ground floor. Janet concentrated on the living areas. Over the years she had decorated and redecorated the place endlessly, spending all her money on it. She later said that she was *married* to it. The kitchen, at one point, was done out in a leopardskin design. But the main attraction, as far as Janet was concerned, was a windowless 'billiard room' which she redid in the style of a 1930s luxury ocean-liner cabin, with curved art-deco ash and aluminium panels, inevitably designed by Piers Gough, her old architectural college pal. It was stuffed with art-deco furniture and knick-knacks, much of it salvaged from junk shops and restored to perfection at further vast expense. It had a cocktail bar, lit from underneath. The whole thing, really, was like a teenage girl's fantasy version of a bedroom. Janet said it was a 'private nightclub for me an' me friends'. It was always said of Janet, even by her greatest supporters and admirers, that part of her mind was stuck at the age of 14. And Janet herself once described herself in a newspaper article as 'completely self-centred and selfish', with 'the mentality of a spoilt teenager'.

Now that Janet was starting to earn Serious Money at LWT, she decided to sell the Limehouse place and plough the capital into building her own house, foundations and all. A site was found in Islington and she started designing the place with Piers Gough. She was sick of Limehouse anyway. The view of the river was nice, but she was sick of the disco boats playing ancient Rolling Stones records that went up and down all night full of yahooing yuppies celebrating the peak of the Boom. Limehouse was now the centre of a massive redevelopment as 'Docklands', the new commercial district summoned into life by Michael Heseltine and the Tory government. The combined noise and mess was terrible. Hideous office blocks and *'orrible* blocks of luxury flats full of braying yuppies were springing up all over the place. Public transport was appalling 'cos the yuppies didn't care, and The Idiots who did planning permission never got it together to organise a single shop anywhere in her neighbourhood – though they did allow a lot of riverside pubs full of yet more boozie yuppies, brayin' away into the night.

About the only good thing you could say about the redevelopment was that it had left a lot of old factory buildings and warehouses empty, awaiting demolition or refurbishment. This had led to the phenomenon of warehouse parties: groups of enterprising and alternative people took over the empty properties at night, put some heavies on the door and turned the places into temporary 'pirate' nightclubs. Great piles of loudspeakers were assembled on former factory floors, with lighting hung from twisted girders and rusting chains, illuminating the wreckage of lifting blocks, chemical drums, broken glass and exposed wiring. You got yer graffiti artists into spray a few *massiff* 'pieces' all over the walls. Lay on a few smoke machines and back-projected half-speed Fritz Lang movies and there you had it: *Mad Max* meets *Disco Inferno*. Some of these warehouses were as big as aircraft hangars, so, instead of the couple of hundred you got in one of the clubs *Up West*, you could get *fahzands and fahzands* of Ravers in one really *massiff* party, with these really enormous sound systems playing Garage and House music. *Completely Brilliant!* All this was going on while Janet and Jane Hewland were devising *Network-7*, and it provided the perfect inspiration: the warehouse scene was to be at the core of the 'Look' Janet wanted for the series.

Winning the contract to make *Network-7* had given Janet and Jane £2.5 million of Channel Four's money to play with. They had to make twenty-two two-hour programmes, so it worked out at about £120,000 per show – a lot of money, but still the cheaper end of current-affairs production. The first job was to put the key members of the production team together. At John Cummins's suggestion, they asked Keith MacMillan to set up a permanent studio for the series. At the time MacMillan was running a highly successful company which made that central artefact and commercial artform of the '80s, the self-consciously weird pop promo video. His clients included David Bowie and Paul McCartney. He had already amassed a vast fortune and did not really need to work – well, at least not at the wages Channel Four was prepared to pay. He had a farm, he took photos of butterflies and went scuba diving. But he had never done broadcast television before and was interested in the challenge, so he agreed to come on board.

Live TV

A collection of beat-up, rusty caravans was scavenged from a scrapyard and installed on top of a former banana warehouse in Limehouse, to serve as offices and a studio area for *Network-7*. The warehouse itself formed the studio, in which various bits of industrial wreckage were left on show, but painted bright, gaudy colours. Janet wanted the cameras to move about a lot, so the set was equipped with five lightweight cameras which would be carried about rather than mounted. The main lighting was provided by two aircraft landing-lights dumped inside dustbins and a sunbed mounted on a trolley which could be pushed around to follow the camerapersons, who would run about a lot in the style of Anneka Rice's *Treasure Hunt*, a big hit on Channel Four. Two 1000w lights were carried in a shopping trolley, and there were two 500w floodlights (called Archie and Malcolm) which were mounted on mangled bits of old motorbikes and so could be left in shot if required, adding to the overall 'Look', which Janet described as 'Wrecktech'. Cameramen and sound people were often to be in shot, sometimes chatting to the presenters. When in shot, technical people had to wear designer outfits chosen by Janet. The idea was that the camera was there to be used and abused. The production process was on show all the time: it was 'deconstructed television'.

The next step was to recruit a director *innervitiff* enough to organise all the filming, which, in Janet's generalised vision, would be mostly live, or 'recorded as live', at Wrecktech Central and combined with live material from 'the Streets' piped in from mobile Outside Broadcast units (OBs). They tried out one or two directors before settling on Tony Orsten, who was working for Jane Hewland in LWT's Factual Entertainment department. Orsten was 'hot' at the time, having just made a 'safe sex' documentary which had won critical acclaim for the televisual landmark of showing a condom on ITV at 7 o'clock in the evening. The show had caused no end of controversy. He was signed up.

All that now remained was to recruit the on-screen talent. In most cases they were to be young people who had limited previous experience in journalism but who fitted The Look. Leading the way was Magenta De Vine, a striking 28-year-old PR fixer whose real name was the more prosaic Kim Taylor. Magenta, a fruity-voiced walking skeleton who wore Ray-Bans day and night, had spun into Janet's orbit as a PR woman for Janet's then boyfriend, Tony James, who was trying to 'do a Malcolm McLaren', launching a pop 'outrage machine' in the form of a group called Sigue Sigue Sputnik.[2] Janet and Jane assembled the new recruits and set out their 'vision'. It was current affairs – sort of – but it was not gonna be like the normal *dreeery, sad, raaabbish*. It was gonna be completely *diff'rent*. It had to have a lot of *ener'jee*. It would be a lotta fun. *Experimental*. Lots of fast *cuttin'*. A completely *orijunal look*. Eventually it was summed up in a snappy but meaningless slogan: 'NEWS IS ENTERTAINMENT. ENTERTAINMENT IS NEWS'.

The run-up to launch was fraught with tensions. Janet and Jane did not get on with Keith MacMillan, and he soon got pulled into the frequent feuds and temporary vendettas which broke out between Janet and Jane as part of their 'creative' love–hate relationship. One day it might be Janet and Jane ganging up against Keith over a detail of production plans; the next day Janet and Keith against Jane; then Keith and Jane against Janet or, on some occasions, all three against one another.

In addition, the two women argued constantly about the look and content of the show, but would then join forces to argue with John Cummins from Channel Four, to get more money or push the limits of what they were allowed to do. In the four months leading up to the launch, Cummins later remembered being phoned virtually every day about crises ranging from threatened injunctions to seemingly impossible production demands, 'budget issues', 'Jane issues' and 'Janet issues'. The main 'Janet issue' was a long-running feud over the fact that LWT would not allow her to join the board of Sunday Productions, the production company established as a joint venture between LWT and Keith MacMillan's pop video company.

Cummins ended up attending meetings at which MacMillan was sometimes incandescent with rage at the latest 'impossible' Janet-inspired production demand. Jane might be in tears with the strain of it all and Janet would sit there, steely-faced and intransigent, refusing to speak to anyone except through the lawyer she started bringing along with her, and absolutely determined to get her way on every detail – *and this was only pre-production*!

The tense atmosphere was not eased by the weird spectacle of US Army helicopters flying past the Limehouse Wrecktech studio to napalm the nearby Thames riverbank, which had been transformed into the Mekong Delta – complete with specially planted palm trees and disused warehouses decked out in Vietnamese slogans – by Stanley Kubrick in order to film *Full Metal Jacket*. Pre-production slanging matches were thus punctuated by the sound of whooping 'copter blades, machine-gun fire and explosions. But this was all *Completely Brilliant*. Kubrick was the director of one of Janet's all-time favourite films, *A Clockwork Orange*.

The show that emerged was nothing like the one originally pitched. Cummins sometimes felt he had been handcuffed to a roller-coaster: he couldn't confess to Jeremy

Janet & Monty

Isaacs that the whole thing was in danger of spinning out of control, not after the strong pitch he had made in favour of the programme. But somehow they dealt with most of the difficulties and avoided disaster. In retrospect, Janet was admired for sticking to her guns, no matter how much *screamin' an' shahtin'* it took, and insisting that all the rules were broken.

Network-7 went on air for the first time at lunchtime on Sunday, 11 May 1987, and, despite its bumpy run-up, there were only minor problems. The first edition had a story about the fact that the newfangled cash-cards the banks were dishing out could be easily forged, so villains could withdraw cash and charge the transaction to an innocent third party without anyone knowing. The item was shot in the zippy way Janet had decreed, with the reporter charging up and down the street with his cash-card, breathlessly telling the story as he went, instead of just reporting the story over footage of 'guilty buildings' as would have been done in normal *sad* and *dreeery* current affairs. The editorial line was that the banks weren't doing enough to protect victims of phantom withdrawals. But the obvious attraction of the story was to get people thinking they might be able to pull off the scam themselves.

Janet had decreed that no item on *Network-7* should last longer than ten minutes, and she wanted most to last about two or three minutes. She used to wander about, chipping in with ideas and vital bits of Style Information. '*Beverly 'Ills Cop II* – it's gonna be *massiff*. It's got all the key things, innit, brand names, big cars . . . ' or 'I went to see David Bowie at Wemblee – *totally perrfetic*, absolutely *wacko*,' or 'There's a new branch of Next opening in Liverpool *nex'sweek*. It's gonna be amazin', *massiff*. Am tellin' yer, Liverpool Next is the place to be – *absolutelee*.' But it was tough filling two hours in such a disparate way. Subjects

71

like 'youth cancer', army bullying and teenage models with anorexia, jostled with bursts of cartoons and interviews with visiting *slebs* (celebs) in the caravans, and other lightweight stuff.

An early triumph, during the 1987 general-election campaign, was to get the three parties' 'youth' spokespeople in for interviews. Instead of the usual stuff about politics, they were shown a picture of Boy George and asked 'Who's this, then?' followed by 'What's the price of a condom?' and 'What would you expect to pay for a pint of lager in a nightclub?' The politicians had not the faintest idea, showing that they were Completely *Dreery*, their *silly heads* filled with *sad bollocks* like the public-sector borrowing requirement and European Monetary Union, and therefore out of touch with the *real* issues.

To deal with the shortage of material *Network-7* gravitated towards 'themed' editions, which meant that the team needed only one story idea for a two-hour show, but then had to think of fifty ways of talking about the same thing. Halfway through the run *Network-7* went for the 'theme' of marriage, inviting people to get married live on the show. This produced a landmark in the form of the first live televised gay wedding, featuring Shaun and Terry exchanging vows live on TV. The Wrecktech studio was sprayed pink and adorned with flowers for the happy occasion. An attempt at a live OB from an Anglo-Italian wedding in a church, however, flopped for technical reasons, causing yet more *screamin' an' shahtin'*. Another themed or 'issue-based' edition dealt with the death penalty. This cut between a studio presenter re-enacting death by firing-squad, waving about a syringe full of deadly chemicals and demonstrating, *Blue Peter*-style, scale models of gas chambers and electric chairs, and a live interview in America with a real convict awaiting execution on death row. A live phone-in poll revealed that most viewers wanted to see the death-row victim fry. It was later realised that the 'news is entertainment' formula had reached its limits.

But *Network-7*'s main trade mark was to be the infamous 'infobar', a strip along the bottom of the screen displaying an 'infocrawl' of factual information about whatever was on screen.[3] This sort of thing had been done before on television, but *Network-7* pushed things much further. One of the reasons for this was Janet's habit of sitting at the back of the director's box getting on everyone's nerves by keeping up a non-stop commentary on whatever she saw and heard on the monitors. Eventually, one of the producers suggested that her comments be fed back on to the screen, so that she could function a bit like a DJ 'toastin' over the top of the output. *Completely Brilliant!* A member of the production team was therefore given the job of listening to Janet and typing her rants into the graphics machine which put captions on the screen.

Having made this breakthrough, it was a simple step to relegate most of the factual information about any item to the infobar, thus liberating the on-screen talent from the tyranny of having to say who they were talking to or, indeed, what they were talking about. At this point *Network-7*'s 'researchers' took over. Two quick phone calls and a handful of press clippings produced enough information to keep the infobar going like the clappers on just about any subject. The tabloid newspapers had been doing it for years: 'Ten Things You Never Knew About . . . ' So during the gay wedding, for example, the 'ceremony' could be shown without some Idiot Presenter having to ask Terry and Shaun how old they were, where they came from, what they did for a living, and so on. All that *dreery crap* could be scrolled across the infobar, and supplemented by a blizzard of statistical 'factoids' about how many gays there were in the country, when the first gay wedding took place, etc., etc., spiced up with a few wisecracks and announcements about what was coming up next. It was proudly pointed out that by watching one edition of *Network-7* you got more factual information thrown at you than in a *whole series* of *Panorama*. All thanks to the Mighty Infobar.

Network-7 attracted a lot of attention from the other media, where it was hailed as a genuine and fresh approach to current affairs for a new generation (not everyone was a fan, though: the show was satirised by French and Saunders, who gibbered away while pulling the camera in and out wildly and focusing on their teeth. The production team even got hate mail). The audience was seen not so much as 'Malcolm's children' but as 'Thatcherspawn'. This was reflected in its agenda, which had moved away from rebellious punk to the Orwellian idea of 'rebellion through conformity'. Janet herself told the papers that when she had started out in yoof television ten years earlier she had made programmes about unemployment and deprivation. 'Once spending money was almost like saying you had the clap. Now it's the joy of owning a credit card, the joy of wanting something.' The new Cool Consumerism was summed up by the Pet Shop Boys, who had lately replaced the Sex Pistols as Top of the Pops in Janet's affections. Whereas Johnny Rotten had whinged on about people whose 'future dream is a shopping scheme', the Pet Shop Boys' song 'Shopping' had a lyric that went something like 'I've got the brains, you've got the looks, let's make lots of money!'

By being screened at Sunday lunchtime the programme scored a direct hit on the metropolitan elites who, for one reason or another, did not watch television much during the week. The critics liked *Network-7*, and the cheapo, Wrecktech production techniques gave them a chance to dribble on about 'a new grammar of deconstructed television' and much other media-studies-type talk in this vein.

The show was important for launching a new generation of TV 'talent' both on screen and in management and production: luminaries included Charlie Parsons, who later had an enormous success with *The Big Breakfast* on Channel Four. Ten years after the launch of the show, people associated with it were to be found in senior positions throughout the industry. Looking back, John Cummins thought of them all as 'without doubt the most ambitious, on-the-make people you ever saw in your life'. Some, like Parsons, had become millionaires by making *Network-7*-derived programmes. Hewland was to complain that the style had been so comprehensively ripped off that fast-cut interviews plastered with graphics and run over an Acid House beat had become a worse cliché than the 'talking heads' and 'guilty buildings' approach it had replaced.

In conventional ratings terms *Network-7* was no great shakes, pulling in an audience of only about 1.5 million, tops. But the programme's 'demographics' were good. It did reach a lot of the 18–25 age group who were hard for advertisers to reach because they did not watch a lot of 'ordinary' ITV or Channel Four. More important was the show's economics. It was the first programme to 'teach' the advertisers that niche broadcasting could 'deliver' particular groups of viewers, and that made its advertising slots extremely valuable. In addition, *Network-7* was very cheap television by the standards of the time. John Birt, who was in the process of leaving LWT to become deputy director-general of the BBC,[4] said the programme was 'an inspiration' and pointed the way to the future for current-affairs television. He had proved his admiration when halfway through the second series he promoted Jane Hewland (pointedly *not* Janet) to the position of head of features at LWT – maybe placing her on track to become director of programmes one day – largely on the strength of *Network-7*.

Janet claimed most of the credit for all this (Jane gamely admitted that it was inevitable, since Janet was the most famous member of the team), as she had previously done on the *London Weekend Show*, but many of those involved point to the importance of Jane's contribution. One diplomatically described the show as having 'the style of Janet and the content of Jane'. John Cummins, who also played a role in shaping it, thought of Jane as 'the architect' and Janet as 'the interior designer'.

The show brought Janet to the attention of Alan Yentob and Jonathan Powell, who had lately been appointed controllers of BBC 2 and BBC 1 respectively with a mission to inject the channels, especially BBC 2, with more youth appeal. At the time, BBC 2 had a fusty home counties feel: all *Gardeners' World* and Delia Smith. After discussing the idea with Powell, Yentob decided that Janet was just the person to help shake things up a bit.

Janet had already shown that she could be a ratings winner by producing the networked ITV Saturday morning pop-based kids show *Get Fresh* for a couple of years in the mid-'80s. It had beaten the pants off the BBC in the ratings war. This had done nothing to ease growing middle-class worries that the nation's children were being brought up on a diet of rampant consumerism and junk culture, but nevertheless its approach, like many of Janet's ideas, had been eagerly copied by the BBC and others in a toned-down form. Yentob therefore offered Janet an hour-and-a-half slot on early-evening BBC 2 which she could use to develop a 'channel within a channel' aimed at the young, similar in some ways to *Network-7*, but shown every weekday. Janet took the job.

The appointment of someone with no journalistic or television training apart from what she had picked up as she went along, and someone, furthermore, who not only had failed to go to either Oxford or Cambridge, but *didn't even have a degree*, to such an important position naturally caused horror amongst some at the BBC. But the old-timers had too much on their hands coping with John Birt, who at the time, had arrived to begin bombing the citadel of News and Current Affairs, to worry about a more peripheral area like yoof.

Then, a few weeks after her arrival, Janet's credentials were boosted when *Network-7* won a special BAFTA award for originality. Her confidence soared (she was always banging on about '*me Bafter*'), and she began terrorising the BBC's army of conservative male middle managers and announcing that she was going to clear away 'all the *dreery* old garbage that TV is glued up with' and put an axe through the rag-bag of existing BBC youth programmes.

First to go was *No Limits*, which she described as 'a happy, poppy little programme'. It got an audience of 5 million but Janet seemed more interested in its credibility rating, which was zero as far as she was concerned. *Entertainment USA*, another popular show, fronted by *Sun* columnist Jonathan King, was also scrapped. There was a sigh of relief when Janet pronounced *Top of the Pops* safe, saying it was a programme for 'kiddies and their parents' rather than a yoof programme as such.

With the schedule unglued in this way, Janet commandeered two or three hour blocks to be run on BBC 2 on Monday and Wednesday early evenings under the title of *Def-II* ('def' being New York rap slang for 'defiance'). These blocks were to be given the full *Network-7* 'channel within a channel' treatment. Janet even wanted the *Def-II* schedule boxed off in the *Radio Times* listings. *Radio Times* refused, much to her irritation. 'They do it for *Grandstand*,' she moaned.

Def-II rehashed a lot of ideas developed at *Network-7*, few of which seemed to work as well the second time around, especially without Jane's input. Instead of a single multi-purpose 'yoof' programme, Janet was to steadily 'unpack' *Network-7* and create an 'alternative' channel, exactly the sort of thing tellytrendies had always said was needed following the failure of earlier 'ghetto' yoof programmes. Janet's channel would have its own yoof news and current-affairs show (called *Reportage*), yoof entertainment show (*Dance Energy*), and yoof travel show (*The Rough Guide*), together with yoof soaps and yoof sit-coms, all slotted into *Def-II* and held together with over-the-top *Network-7*-type graphics and infoblitzes.

Def-II was set up within four months of Janet's arrival and she was soon riding high and putting a lot of time into office politics and power-base building. In 1989 she was promoted to head of Youth and Entertainment Features, The same year she had a major success producing the annual *Smash Hits* magazine pop awards on BBC 1. To mark her growing importance in tellyland she was given the accolade of organising the prestigious James MacTaggart memorial lecture, the centrepiece of the annual Edinburgh International Television Festival. Controversial as ever, Janet invited Rupert Murdoch to give the lecture. He had recently re-launched Sky television and was something of a hate figure at the BBC, what with his repeated calls for the BBC to be privatised and the orchestrated campaign of Beeb-bashing in his papers. Still, Janet was enormously enthusiastic about pulling off this coup.

People said she looked as if she was 'on heat' at the prospect of meeting him. For the event she wore an amazing creation which she described as a '[get a] result dress'.

Many of the BBC old guard regarded the arrival of the Murdoch-inspired age of 'freedom in broadcasting' and 'multi-channel' television as a dire threat to 'quality' in British television, and thought satellite and cable TV's mixture of ultra-cheap old movies and things like business news in Arabic was the pits. By contrast, Janet was a satellite and cable fan – the logo for *Network-7* was a satellite dish, and *Def-II* had been set up as a self-contained mini-channel, invading the BBC schedules from 'another planet' – and spent hours glued to the screen.[5]

Now, with Murdoch and Sky established, 'multi-channel television' was about to become a reality. *Sad* old rock stars like Bruce Springsteen might whine about 'five hundred channels with nothing on', but Janet was keen. Obviously, sooner or later, the chance would come up to realise what she had always wanted: a whole channel of uninterrupted Janetvision, hitting a niche audience of would-be Janet people, a 'club' on the television. But in the meantime she was doing OK at the BBC. Head of features – same job as Jane Hewland (Janet easily felt slighted when others around her were promoted) but with a much bigger and more important broadcaster. With *Def-II* up and running, Janet began limbering up for the conquest of yet more BBC airtime. She said at the time that she wanted to go right to the top at the BBC and finish her career there, perhaps as the first female director-general.

Chapter Five

In which Rupert Murdoch sneakily moves his newspapers to Fortress Wapping, thus exposing his minions to great danger, builds a mountain of money and nearly loses it all in a premature attempt to conquer British television from Outer Space, brings Mr Sam Chisholm and sundry Antipodean Hard Men to enrich the business and cultural life of the UK, carefully lobbies and flatters the Political Establishment, parts company with David Montgomery along the way and generally sweeps all before him

In January 1986 Rupert Murdoch changed the face of the British newspaper business for good. In a single bold stroke he moved his papers from a collection of dilapidated offices and grubby factories in and around Fleet Street to the hi-tech concrete 'fortress' of Wapping, in London's Docklands. Five thousand workers – mostly printers but also secretaries, accounts clerks, canteen staff and others – had been sacked overnight and replaced by a combination of new computerised technology and cheap non-union labour.

The move had been carried out in great secrecy and immediately brought a massive response from trade unions. A picket was mounted, supplemented by mass demonstrations every Saturday night, aimed at preventing the distribution (which Murdoch had switched from rail to a road-haulage firm, TNT, in which he had a stake, to forestall possible industrial action by the railway unions) of the most profitable titles, the *Sun*, *News of the World* and *Sunday Times*.

Security at Wapping was organised by a former

Rhodesian paramilitary police superintendent who had once been in charge of 1,500 armed men fighting a guerrilla war in the African bush. The 'scab' journalists and others who had made the move were protected by a twelve-foot-high spiked metal fence, beefed up with triple rolls of razor wire, microwave alarms, and remote video cameras, and had to travel to and from work in special coaches known as 'scab wagons' with windows protected by wire mesh. On Saturday nights hundreds of police in full riot gear were used to clear a path through the often violent demonstrators so that the giant TNT lorries carrying Murdoch's papers could power out of the plant through a hail of bottles and stones.

The company had prepared for the eventuality of the pickets breaking into the plant. Assuming that they would wreck it comprehensively and, possibly, set it on fire and murder the 'scabs' cowering within, a series of tunnels had been set up inside the plant leading to a central bunker with heavy steel doors. The plan was that the staff of Murdoch's papers would retreat to the bunker if it looked as though the outer defences were about to be breached. They would lock themselves in and await rescue by the police, army, SAS or US Air Force, as appropriate.

The violent Saturday-night ritual peaked on the first anniversary of the move to Wapping. A crowd of 13,000 fought with 1,000 police leaving 168 officers and scores of protestors injured. But the trucks once again got through. Realising their situation was hopeless, the unions called off the protest. It marked the completion of a total rout of the once all-powerful Fleet Street print unions.

The move to Wapping, with its much smaller and less well paid workforce and new electronic production systems, had brought vast and immediate rewards to News

Live TV

International, Murdoch's main UK company. Within two years profits had almost doubled, to over £145 million a year, by far the best financial performance in any part of the growing international Murdoch Empire. But, after the one-off capital cost of setting up Wapping, these funds were not to be invested, in the main, in the newspaper business. Instead they were used to buy into British television in the form of a new satellite television service: Sky TV.

The idea of getting into satellite television had originated in the early 1980s when Murdoch established a think tank called the New Media Forum within his main company, News Corporation. Obsessed, as ever, with developments in his adopted homeland of the USA, he had decided that newspapers were finished in the long term and that the future was all about television and, maybe, the sort of computer-based communications which were then being developed and which eventually became known as the Internet. The overall plan was that his papers would be run flat out for profit, with the money being invested in television in both the USA and the UK.

The problem was the UK regulations governing media ownership. He needed his papers in order to finance a move into television. But he could not move into television so long as he owned newspapers: Catch-22. One way out of this was to own television in one country (or city in the case of the USA) and newspapers in another. But for the time being he was locked out of British television by ownership of the superprofitable *Sun*, *News of the World*, and *Sunday Times*, very much the commercial engine room of the whole Empire. So in 1982 Murdoch bought a small 'pan-European' cable and satellite channel, which he re-named Sky and ran as an English-language service available mainly on the Continent and in the minuscule number of British homes which, at that time, had access to cable television.[1]

'European' Sky was run by Patrick Cox, a tough-minded businessman who had the advantage, as far as Murdoch was concerned, of never having been tainted by working in British television. Cox had a lot of contact with other Murdoch executives, including David Montgomery, who, from the start, had followed Murdoch's thinking about the eventual need to follow the mass-market audience from newspapers into television. Monty was keen and joined the board of Sky TV.

'European' Sky chuntered along in a small way until 1987 when, despite the fact that it was just about to move into profit, Murdoch got bored with the project and announced that the time was right to move the channel to London and break into the British market – big time. The reason, as he told Cox, was that, to his immense delight, Maggie Thatcher had just been re-elected. Murdoch had the inside track with 'Maggie', especially in the area of broadcasting and media policy (his papers had, after all, helped her to win three successive general elections).[2] She had been thwarted by the likes of Nigel Lawson and Douglas Hurd – Murdoch hate-figures, both – in her attempt to nuke the BBC and privatise its smouldering remains. But she was certain to loosen up the tight media regulation which had been such a barrier to the Murdochian conquest of British television. So why were they piddling about with 'European' Sky, showing repeats of *Crossroads* to bored English travelling salesmen stuck in tacky Belgian motels, when the main prize would shortly be on offer?

The launch of 'British' Sky was announced the following year, after Murdoch had done a deal with Alan Sugar, the bearded home-electronics wizard, to produce the dishes needed to receive the new channel. The venture was a huge gamble, even by Murdoch's standards. The launch cost was estimated at £320 million, immediately mortgaging the superprofits being earned by his newspapers following the Wapping revolution. On top of this outlay, Murdoch soon found he had severely overestimated demand for multi-channel TV in the UK. Most people were happy with what they got on ITV and the BBC. Alan Sugar's dishes piled up in the warehouses and Sky's losses settled at about £2 million a week. Murdoch was soon in deep trouble with his financial backers, and various forms of brinkmanship had to be employed to keep the banks off his back. Even so, by 1990 there seemed every chance that Sky would bankrupt the Empire and sink Murdoch for good. The only bright spot on the gloomy financial horizon was the even greater problems faced by his only satellite competitor in the UK, British Satellite Broad-casting (BSB), which was losing £8 million a week.

Instead of using the cheap and cheerful Amstrad dish system, BSB had gone for a technically superior system needing a 'squarial'. The horrible Amstrad dishes were an instant sign of low social status, whereas BSB's squarials were up-market designer objects. BSB's headquarters, the amazingly flash post-modernist Marco Polo House, across the Thames from Chelsea, was fitted out with granite desks, the stationery cupboard issued Mont Blanc pens instead of ballpoints, and it was said, only half in jest, that the carpets alone had cost more than the whole of Sky's headquarters building, a 'crinkly tin' affair on a desolate industrial estate in Osterley, near Heathrow. More importantly, BSB executives had expensive programming tastes. Their presence in the market for programmes such as films was pushing prices up.

Murdoch began to search for a television executive who could merge Sky with its satellite rival, thus roping in BSB's terrified shareholders to share the losses on the merged venture and keep it afloat until it could start making profits. It was essential that the merger was carried out by somebody who would be utterly ruthless about ending the extravagant ways of Murdoch's putative BSB partners; again, that meant finding someone unsullied by working in British television. After a brief search Murdoch turned up Sam Chisholm, head of Channel Nine in Sydney, Australia, where he was something of a legend for his ruthless management style and golden touch.

Chisholm was a New Zealander who had emigrated to the wider horizons of Australia. He had risen from selling Johnson's Wax furniture polish door to door in the early 1960s to become the company's Australian marketing director. From there he had moved in 1965 to sell advertising at Channel Nine, owned by the Packer family. Ten years later, aged 35, Chisholm was made chief executive at the channel. He at once began shaking up what was then a medium-sized and mediocre outfit apparently going nowhere, and put the ruthless commercialism of his sales background to use in the programming and scheduling departments. Like Murdoch, Chisholm believed Australian television should follow the example of America rather than the British system which had dominated the thinking of the first generation of Aussie TV executives. To the horror of many, he bought hundreds of hours of cheap American imports, and gave the channel an 'aspirational' Californian feel, slaughtering the pretensions of the programme-makers. Channel Nine became a commercial success, smashing competitors who made the error of first deciding what programmes they wanted to make and then scrabbling around in the hope of selling advertising to pay for production.

Chisholm rewarded himself and key executives with vast salaries (another American television trait) and a champagne lifestyle – the station became known as the 'Bollinger Channel' – but demanded much in return. On his desk at Channel Nine he displayed a sign which read, 'To err is human. Forgiveness is not my policy.' Weekly senior management meetings could be gruelling affairs, and executives who Chisholm thought were not pulling their weight – which was just about everyone – were subjected to a bombardment of high-volume abuse. One executive said he had to psych himself up for these encounters by playing 'The Ride of the Valkyrie' as he drove to work. Chisholm was also famed for his 'Friday Night Follies'. Selected executives were called into his office after work and force-fed drink from an industrial-sized refrigerator filled with booze. While the executives let their hair down, voicing all manner of interesting and disloyal opinions, Chisholm would remain sober, taking mental notes and acting on what he heard.

In September 1990 Murdoch flew to Los Angeles to meet Chisholm. The latter had just celebrated his fiftieth birthday (the Channel Nine staff gave him a Harley-Davidson motorbike). He was attracted by the idea of a new and final commercial challenge, working *with* (as he was always keen to point out) rather than *for* Murdoch, one of the world's most famous media moguls, in his hour of greatest need. Chisholm agreed to take over from Murdoch as chief executive of Sky and come to London to sort out the Poms. He made an immediate and massive impact.

Chisholm's mission was to cut costs immediately by at least 10 per cent – even though Sky was already a lean operation – merge the service with its bloated rival, BSB,[3] and then lead an aggressive commercial attack on the rest of the British system. The merger was completed within a few weeks and the merged operation, officially called British Sky Broadcasting (BSkyB) but trading as 'Sky', now had a much better chance of survival.

On the other hand, Murdoch's control of the new company was diluted. He had been sole owner of the original Sky, but BSkyB was jointly owned with BSB's former backers, including other UK media conglomerates like Pearson, owners of the *Financial Times*. Murdoch retained effective control of the new company, as the largest single shareholder, but the presence of other powerful groupings on the board placed Chisholm, as chief executive of the company, in a position of relative strength compared to Murdoch employees, who were entirely dependent on the Boss and the Boss alone.

It fell to Chisholm to sack almost all BSB's 500 staff, a task he started by lining up all the senior managers, eyeballing each one in turn and asking, 'Who are you, and what do you do?' Even though they were for the chop, he told them not to talk to the press: 'Some of you may get a bulge in your trousers when you speak to journalists, but how you act with regard to the press will influence what I do about your termination packages.' He then began working on Sky's programming, cutting the price paid for Hollywood movies, and limbering up for the acquisition of sport. In March 1992 Sky moved into 'operating profit' for the first time, though it was still weighed down with interest payments of almost £3 million a week due to the huge start-up costs and early losses.

From the beginning Murdoch had been sensitive about the political and regulatory environment surrounding Sky. The media-ownership regulations then in force specified that no UK newspaper proprietor could own more than 20 per cent of a UK television station. Murdoch had argued that Sky was not a 'UK' television station but a 'pan-European' one whose signal just happened to be available in the UK. If the government cut up rough, he would close down the Osterley studio, go back to Luxembourg and beam it into the UK from there. But the position was still extremely delicate and tended to make Murdoch dependent on favours from his high-level political contacts. He much preferred politicians to be dependent on him, if at all possible.

The main accusation was that he was not providing consumers with anything new: that Sky was just 'cheque-book television', buying up the more popular types of programme such as American movies and light entertainment on the existing system, and charging people a fortune to see what had previously been provided for 'free'.

Murdoch countered by including Sky News, which he knew would always be a loss-maker, in the subscription price. Great care had been taken to make Sky News a 'quality' service which would appeal to politicians, journalists and other 'opinion leaders'. As the country's first 24-hour 'rolling news' channel, it could be waved about as an example of an entirely new type of television and one which was being provided by Sky, even if nobody (except politicians and journalists) watched it. Crucially, Sky News gave the channel a 'British face' covering British stories with British voices. All Murdoch's UK editors were brought into the lobbying effort on behalf of Sky in the form of ceaseless pro-Sky propaganda in their papers. Some, like Andrew Neil of the *Sunday Times*, were actually drafted to work at the channel.

In the meantime, the cost of getting Sky off the ground was hitting Murdoch hard in the pocket. The search for economies became almost desperate. The loss-making

Janet & Monty

Today newspaper was an obvious target. *Today* was due to move to Wapping, where colour presses had at last been installed for the *Sun* and *News of the World*, in 1991. The decision to move the paper brought to the surface existing tensions between Monty and the senior managers at Wapping. Monty knew that those managers wanted him out and were merely biding their time until the move was over before acting. He also knew that Murdoch thought there were too many senior managers at Wapping and wanted to thin them out.

So, even before *Today* had moved, Monty counter-attacked. He went to the chief executive at Wapping and asked for the managing director's job; then he went to Murdoch's deputy and asked for the chief executive's job and then he went to Murdoch himself and asked for his deputy's job. On each occasion he offered to combine at least two existing jobs, thus saving money. What he did not seem to realise was that all these people talked to each other on a daily basis. They were all sniggering at him behind his back, saying, 'Has he asked for your job yet?' The joke was 'Monty's been talking to God. He asked Him for Murdoch's job.' By this time the whole organisation was fed up to the back teeth with Montgomery, right down to the technical staff, the typesetters, basically all his staff, and the printers. Murdoch was heard to complain about the 'bellyaching from all over the place' he was getting about Montgomery.

Anyway, Murdoch began to wonder if it was worth running *Today* as a 'spoiler' against the colour *Mirror* any longer, now that the *Sun* was being produced in colour as well. Moreover, the rivalry between Monty and Kelvin MacKenzie, reunited under the same roof for the first time in many years (to their mutual regret), began to turn nasty. MacKenzie loathed *Today* as a product, and hated the swarm of 'airhead' lifestyle and fashion journalists Monty had brought with him to Wapping. One of MacKenzie's direst threats at the time was to transfer malfunctioning *Sun* journalists to *Today*, as the ultimate humiliating punishment.

As far as MacKenzie was concerned *Today* was a constant problem, burning up money with the vast advertising campaign Murdoch was paying for out of profits generated by the *Sun*. Monty's paper kept jamming up the Wapping presses, thus delaying the printing and distribution of the *Sun*, and costing readers. He was apoplectic about *Today*'s printing glitches and delays in particular, and roundly denounced Monty to Murdoch, and anyone else who cared to listen. In the Wapping local pub, the Sydney Smith, in front of an audience of *Sun* hacks, Kelvin expertly imitated Murdoch drawling at Monty: 'I don't like your fucking newspaper and I don't like you.'

Monty's relationship with Murdoch became more and more strained. Murdoch had never been really convinced that there was anything behind Monty's 'modernised *Mirror*' vision for *Today*. The paper had been selling around 300,000 copies when Montgomery took over and this increased to around 600,000. Monty naturally emphasised the fact that circulation had doubled, but he was starting from a very low base. Murdoch had provided an enormous advertising budget for the paper and the readers had been 'bought' at great cost. Soon after the move to Wapping Murdoch cancelled *Today*'s advertising campaign and circulation started to collapse.

Monty's response to this was to work out a plan for a management buy-out of *Today*, which would leave him in control of the paper. He prepared the plan in detail, and only when it was complete presented it to Murdoch. Many at Wapping were amazed that Monty thought Murdoch might take it seriously, and his overweening self-confidence caused deep resentment, especially at a time when *Today* was costing News Corp. such a lot of cash.

In the event, Murdoch dismissed the plan within minutes when it was presented to him. After months of anti-Monty goading from MacKenzie and others, the secrecy with which the buy-out plan had been prepared was the final straw for Murdoch. The Boss forced him out of the editor's chair at *Today* and Monty ended up renting an office within the premises of Saatchi & Saatchi and, performing more or less the function of a consultant for Murdoch, began investigating 'city TV', to see if it might be worth Sky's while to get involved.

City-wide TV had been pioneered with some success in North America, where Murdoch was buying up local city stations with names like WNYW (New York) and KTTV (Los Angeles) and linking them together as the Fox Network.[4] It would make a lot of sense, Monty thought, for Sky to do something similar in the UK. Sky's biggest problem was the strength of the existing BBC and ITV national networks, plus the accusation that Sky was both 'foreign' and failing to increase consumer choice. So why not do something that was both resolutely local and entirely different from anything available on the existing channels? The BBC and ITV had regional variations, but these were not truly local, which meant there was a gap in the market for both viewers and, most importantly, advertising revenue.[5]

Murdoch was less than enthusiastic. Monty's plan was risky and would involve Sky in the messy, expensive and unpredictable business of television production which, except for the 'shop window' of Sky News (which cost a fortune, but was great PR and looked highly professional), was unnecessary. Once Sky was in a lot more people's homes, city TV *might* make money as an advertising 'platform', but it – or any sort of news programming – would not persuade people to put a dish on their wall. The world over, there were only three things people would pay for on television: recent Hollywood movies, 'hot' sport and pornography. Porn was out in the British context, so every penny was needed to buy movies and sport. A further investment in city TV, or the replacement of Sky News with cheap and tacky local television, was out of the question. And that was that: no city TV for Sky.

MacKenzie, meanwhile, was cock-a-hoop about Monty's demise. Not only was he gone from Wapping, but *Today*'s new editor was to be his own one-time deputy at the *Sun*, Martin Dunn, a Wapping high-flyer trained up on Bizarre, the showbiz desk. MacKenzie called him the 'handsome munchkin' and 'the Patsy Kensit of journalism'. MacKenzie was soon seen stalking around the *Today* newsroom, slapping Dunn on the back and yelling across the room: 'Now you fuckers are going to see what a real editor is like.'

Chapter Six

In which Janet grows bored of Yoof TV, is pilloried in the public prints by Sad Tabloid Journalists, teams up with Normski, defines Naffness, re-re-invents her image with mixed results, claims that she never tells jokes, wonders if she'll ever make it to top of the tree at the BBC and thinks about moving into the Brave New World of multi-channel television

After a couple of hectic years at the BBC setting up *Def-II*, Janet was bored and on the look-out for new challenges. The most successful programme on Janet's 'channel within a channel' in audience terms was *The Rough Guide*, a travel show fronted by Magenta De Vine[1] featuring *Network-7*-style fantasy consumerism ('Why not take a weekend break in Argentina?'), on-the-hoof camerawork, Acid House soundtrack, relentless infobar activity ('There are no gay bars in Ljubljana' was one deadpan gem) and crass juxtaposition of gruesome and lightweight material. The Argentine edition, for example, cut straight from interviews of weeping mothers of death-squad victims to jovial banter about the price of designer beer in a nightclub.

The Rough Guide averaged around 2 million viewers, but the jewel in *Def-II*'s crown was meant to be *Reportage*, supposedly the first purely current-affairs programme for yoof. The approach was similar to *Network-7*'s: 'News is Entertainment – Entertainment is News'. The show had to *strip away the ghaaaastly conventions* and concentrate on the modern, 'real agenda', defined by Janet as 'cash-cards, credit, gossip and slime'. She wanted 'aspirational television' not 'problem television'. It had to be 'original' and 'optimistic' which, as those involved were about to find out, was difficult with news, which tended to deal with the same subjects over and over again and which was frequently depressing. *Reportage* was nevertheless provided with a flashy studio area, this time based around a 'newsroom' look with a lot of computer screens linked to OBs and highly mobile cameras as well the usual info-bar overkill.

The results were dire in the opinion of many and this was thought by some to be at least partly due to Janet's underestimation of the cost and time needed to do investigative journalism. *Reportage* also had the misfortune to be launched at the height of the argument over 'Birtism', a rigid style of programming being imposed on BBC news and current affairs output by the new deputy director-general, John Birt. This meant that all programme ideas and items had to be written and put through complex approval procedures before they could be filmed. The rigours of Birtism were hard enough for even the experienced reporters on *Panorama* and *Newsnight* to cope with. When it was imposed on the inexperienced (but good-lookin') youths hired by Janet to front the show, the stories ended up looking embarrassingly half-baked. Morale plummeted.

There were additional constraints. The junior hacks were told that they could not interview anyone over 25 or, bizarrely, any person, either over or under 25, who had a beard, because this would not fit with The Look devised for *Def-II*. That ruled out an exclusive interview with Fidel Castro on two counts. Eventually Janet's executive subordinates resorted to the old stand-by of themed programmes. 'Think of items about love,' or 'Do a show about loneliness,' the junior hacks would be told and off they would slouch to find 101 new angles on the subject which did not feature any well-established, newsy or knowledgeable 26-year-olds, such as doctors, politicians, experts and – well, just about everybody you normally filmed when you were doing the news. The *Listener* magazine, the semi-official voice of the BBC, slammed *Reportage* as unwatchable. 'You need to be a five eyed trapezist to keep track of it,' the magazine's critic said, adding that the journalism was often 'disgracefully sloppy or contentless. It looks as if when they make a mess of some item or other, or the story just did not stand up, they just throw a purple patch and a zipper caption over it and hope for the best.' Which was exactly what was happening.

Reportage, and some of Janet's other *Def-II* programmes, attracted the usual grumbles from the general public. She used to listen to overnight complaints on the answerphone and laugh at them. 'Great, innit?' she would sneer. 'With all that's wrong with the world all these *sad* people are worried *abaht* is *wevver* y'can have jokes about sperm banks on the BBC. Unreal, innit?' Perching in her 'penthouse' office near Television Centre, she would tell visiting journalists or the 'Tellybrats' (as she called the young, good-looking presenters and production people she had gathered around herself),[2] 'When a parent comes in the room an' says, "What's that bloody rubbish yer watchin'?" you know y've gotta winner.'

Janet had become a major hate figure in parts of the media, especially the tabloids. They were always running 'The Beeb's gone bonkers' stories and Janet, it seemed, was more grist to their mill. The *Sun*'s television critic Garry Bushell, a great Kelvin MacKenzie favourite, was always on her back. He once wrote that he had seen her crossing the road near Television Centre and contemplated running her over; and the *Sun* had printed her picture next to a picture of a horse and asked the readers to phone in and say which they thought was best looking. *'Weeeerrrll'*, as Janet was apt to say, what could you expect from a bunch of talentless, *sad*, dandruffy, middle-aged paunchy *jernalists* with nothin' better to write about?

The tabloid criticism often had racist overtones due to Janet's latest live-in-lover arrangement. The lucky chap this time was Norman Anderson, better known as 'Normski', who presented *Dance Energy*, the clubbin' show. Normski was black and twenty years her junior. He sprang from the inner-city London electro hip-hop dance scene, and raved away on screen in the unfathomable *yo-comminatyer-live-and-diiiiireckkkt* argot of the rap scene. To prove he was the genuine article, he drove a gold-painted BMW with a million-watt bass booster in the boot which, he claimed, you could hear four blocks away. He also claimed to spend all his BBC salary on training shoes.

After setting up *Def-II* Janet left it to others, notably her 'oppo', Rachel Purnell, to actually run things, while she branched out from the early-evening BBC 2 youth ghetto, spreading her influence across the schedules. She produced a much-derided game show called *Style Trial* and the more successful *The Full Wax* for BBC 1 and the uncompromisingly wacky *P's and Q's*, another game show, for BBC 2.[3]

Janet's ideas for television programmes, which generally came off the top of her head, more and more boiled down to doing one type of television programme in the style of another. So you did a game show in the style of a fashion-cum-lifestyle show (this became *Style Trial*) or you did a fashion/lifestyle show in the style of a game show (this became *P's and Q's*) or you did a sports programme in the style of a fashion show (*Good Sport*) or you did a chat show in the style of a situation comedy (*The Full Wax*). It was simple when you got the hang of it. What you must never, never, *never* do was a current-affairs show in the style of a current-affairs show, or a pop-music show in the style of a pop-music show, because that was not *innervitiff*, and what did you end up with if you did that? *Panorama* and *Top of the Pops*, that's what you ended up with. And they were *Compleeetly Naff*.

'Naff' meant ordinary TV, or people trying to be too professional. Janet lectured the Tellybrats on the subject. There were grades of naffness: simple Naff (almost everything not made by Janet); *Compleeetly* Naff (fairly common) and Totally Naff (rarer, and an example given by Janet was any radio or TV presentation involving Ned Sherrin). The Tellybrats were constantly warned of the dangers of naffness and how to avoid it. For example, *P's and Q's*, hosted by Tony Slattery, was anti-naff. It involved a group of people sitting in a mocked-up baronial hall taking the piss out of people with airs and graces. This idea had, as usual, sprung from Janet's personal experience. Some years before, she had had a noted wine buff round for dinner. She persuaded him to wear a blindfold and taste different wines. Unable to look at the labels, he couldn't tell the good stuff from the plonk. This was *Absolutely Hilarious* and was to be spun out to make a whole series of programmes. One edition was based on the subject of polo, the ultimate snobby activity. The idea was to put polo equipment on a table and get the guests to discuss it in a brilliant and witty way. But Janet declared this was Naff. Not the idea – that was fine – but the way it was being done. She demanded that the polo gear be put on a revolving tailor's mannequin and then, importantly, the presenter had to spin it *'rahnd an' rahnd*, makin' it wobble, and almost knockin' it over as though yer didn't give a toss *abaht* it, an' this stuff didn't deserve any respect, because the *whole idea* was that it was *stewpid* and snooty an' snobby and *didn't deserve* any respect. An' anyway if yer nearly knocked it over, that would *get yer a larff.*' It was little touches like this that made all the difference between ordinary borin' television (*Completely Naff*) and *innervitiff* Janetvision (*Completely Brilliant*).

One intractable problem for Janet was that much of the 'youth culture' she was trying to present on television was explicitly anti-TV,[4] especially the more rebellious movements like rap (much of which amounted to young men screaming about all the crimes and rapes they would like to carry out, or otherwise advocated violence or subversion of a sort which unfortunately fell foul of the BBC and ITV rules on taste and decency). Such Janet ideas might have worked quite well as niche or 'narrowcast' broadcasting, delivered on a channel of their own via cable or satellite. But as television aimed at a broad, mainstream national audience, only rarely did they turn out to be hits.

The all-time stinker of Janetvision was reckoned to be *Style Trial*, a quiz show in which contestants had to guess who owned various objects. Janet had brought in Jane Hewland to help with the programme, but it was a case of the Old Girls' Network going badly wrong. The programme was slammed as self-indulgent and cliquey. It might have amused Janet and Jane to make it, but it failed to connect with the popular audience it was designed to hook in. A further objection was that *Style Trial* was old-hat. Its appeal to 'commodity fetishism' might have worked at the height of the '80s consumer boom, but it went out at the beginning of the deep recession of the 1990s, when a lot of people in the popular audience were struggling with negative equity and job insecurity.

It was a complete flop and became something of an albatross round Janet's neck. *Style Trial* seemed to confirm the view of many at the BBC that outside the youth ghetto Janet was likely to flounder. It was said she simply did not know how to make genuinely popular programmes. Jonathan Powell, controller of BBC 1, agreed that *Style Trial* was 'a bummer' but saw it as a one-off mistake, which was bound to happen when you were being experimental and trying to find new types of audiences, rather than as proof positive that Janet was out of sympathy with the popular audience.

Janet's BBC career was now reaching a turning-point. In her first two or three years she had shaken up BBC 2 through sheer force of personality, as Yentob and Powell had intended. Everything was highly personalised, and people were amazed by her intransigence when she wanted something (right down to the smallest detail of graphics) and by her ability to switch from charm to bullying in order to get her own way. This was fine for building up a department, but keeping things going once she had established a programme-making base was a different matter. She got bored easily, and needed to keep finding new things to do or there was a danger that she might 'implode'.

It was time to move on. The BBC operated an unofficial but rigidly applied 'up or out' policy, which meant that executives like Janet had to keep getting promoted or face the danger of being sidelined and, by various means, slowly pushed out of the organisation. So in April 1991 Janet put herself forward for the vacant post of head of Arts at the BBC, which would have put her in charge of the BBC's highbrow activities such as classical music (including the Proms and opera). The promotion would have kept her on track to join the BBC's all-important board of management, with a chance of becoming a channel controller if either Alan Yentob left BBC 2 or, more likely, Jonathan Powell left BBC 1. This in turn would be a step towards becoming director-general one day.

To stand any chance of getting the Arts job Janet needed to 're-invent herself', ditching the carefully cultivated image of youthful rebellion, and substituting a more mature and thoughtful Janet. She went on the publicity trail, courting media and lifestyle journalists and arranging for profiles to be written in the broadsheets emphasising her more sophisticated side. The hacks noted a distinct change of attitude. Whereas before she had often frankly and rudely asked, 'What's in it for me?' if a journalist requested an interview, now she suddenly became available, targeting the posh papers' media correspondents, inviting them round to the Groucho Club[5] (importantly for the ambitious, Janet was the club's membership secretary) and giving them long interviews, tossing out eminently printable sound-bites like 'I'm not wacky' and 'I'm not thick'.

This exercise in glasnost was accompanied by a similar change in Janet's taste in clothes. When she had arrived at the BBC as head of youth and clubbin', she had boasted that she had made John Birt blush by turning up in a skin-tight rubber mini-skirt. After that she often slipped into a 'little black dress' to make her look half her age when the photographers came round to interview her about the latest *Def-II* developments. But now it was expensive tailoring, executive suits, sensible shoes and moody, enigmatic poses.

Janet was keen to point out that there was more to her than met the eye. She said, for example, that she had done a lot of reading as a sixth-former and had developed a deep appreciation of the philosophical works of Jean-Paul Sartre and the novels of William Burroughs. (If so, she had changed her habits radically by the time she arrived at architectural college a few months later. Fellow students could not remember her reading many books of any sort – or think where she might have found the time to do so.) She was complicated, just like modern culture itself – very much a mixture of pop music and the classics, low culture and high culture, yer *Secret Life of Paintings* ('one of my all time favourite TV programmes') and yer *Wheel of Fortune*. Really, she was a bit like Nigel Kennedy, a mixture of the popular and the serious. Just what the BBC always said it wanted.

Zoe Heller in the *Independent on Sunday*, which at the time was more or less the house journal of senior BBC bods, reported Janet as saying, 'I'm serious. I never tell jokes. That's what I'm like.' Heller was asked by Janet to check this fact with her closest friends: 'They'll tell you.' Her lightweight image was unfair, and *incorrect*. It was all the fault of the press, particularly the filthy tabloids, and of snooty old farts like Richard Ingrams who had saddled her with the 'yoof' thing and made her out to be a moron. After listening to all this, Heller concluded, 'The truth of the matter, it strikes me, is that Janet Street-Porter is her own worst enemy.'[6] Richard Littlejohn, writing in the vile *Sun*, was much more direct: 'Put Janet Street-Porter in charge of Last Night of the Proms and we'll get Normski doing a rap version of "Land of Hope and Glory".'

In the end Janet did not make a formal application for the head of Arts job after being tipped off that she would not get it. The post went instead to Michael Jackson, a much younger candidate and a direct rival who had lately run the trendy BBC 2 *Late Show* arts empire. Jackson was fifteen years her junior. Janet's age was starting to count heavily against her. She was compensated for her failure to land the Arts job by being given a wider role in her existing programming areas, Youth and Entertainment. Her department was expanded to control a budget of £30 million a year, making 270 hours of network television at an average production cost of about £100,000 an hour. This included all the *Def-II* material, together with bought-in series like *How Do They Do That?* (a hit with a rating of 10 million), various quiz shows and celebrity-based documentaries.

But by this time she was cheesed off with the BBC. Like others she had to put up with the upheavals introduced by her former patron John Birt. Janet was not against Birtism as such. In fact, she had been something of a Rottweiler for the key Birtist idea of 'producer choice', the internal market for use of BBC resources which Birt brought in – and which was being fought to the death by most other executives in Janet's position – and gamely joined in some of the nuttier aspects of Birtism, such as executive training and game-playing initiatives. In the run-up to 'producer choice', BBC executives were obliged to go away to hotels for the weekend and, supervised by swarms of management consultants, take part in 'exercises' in which they practised buying and selling their own production resources. (This once involved the senior management of the BBC bartering scissors, glue and pieces of paper with each other with the objective of making paper-chains. On another notable occasion, Janet assumed the role of an independent producer-cum-hustler trying to sell programmes to the corporation in competition with her own real-life department.)

Now, though, Birt had announced a major reorganisation of 'production resources' into 'centres of excellence'. This meant that Janet and her Youth department had to move to Manchester. No Way! She didn't mind going Up North at weekends to stay at her country cottage in Yorkshire and indulge her hobby of hill-walking and ramblin'. But she was *not* going to reverse the equation and be based Up North, commutin' down to London, like some sort of . . . commuter. FORGET IT! She was a trend-spotter. She *had* to be in Soho with other trend-spotters, otherwise how could she do her job? In Manchester she would be off the circuit. All they had up there was *sad* football supporters and Bernard Bleedin' Mannin'. There was a couple of groups, but mostly they hung about in Soho like everyone else. They didn't *really* operate from Manchester – how could they? And there was another point. She had just spent a small fortune building her own house in central London, and had only moved in recently.

In 1987 when she was about to make the move from LWT to the BBC, Janet had moved out of her house in Limehouse, put her vast collection of art deco and other trinkets into storage and moved into a flat where she had lived for two years while supervising the construction of a new purpose-built monstrosity on a bomb-site in run-down Clerkenwell. The land had had no planning permission but she bought it anyway – the act, she sportingly confessed, of a person who was 'a hundred and one per cent nuts'. Her old pal Piers Gough was engaged to build the house of her dreams, based on the theme of a post-modernist pirate castle.

Dealings with Islington Council over planning permission had been predictably difficult, since a lot of people thought the place would be an eyesore, especially the planned bright-blue glazed tiled roof, deliberately mish-mashed brick design effects and jutting 'papal balcony' which was to look out over the street and was based on a fantasy of Janet waving to swarms of admirers thronging in the streets below. The building also had a fish motif, with the roof tiles acting like scales. There were other references as well. There were cast-concrete tree trunks, acting as window sills, meant to represent Janet's love of the countryside. The spiky metal fence represented her personality.

In the end Janet had got most of what she wanted, but she had lost out on one very important point. She had planned to fly a gigantic skull-and-crossbones flag from the flagpole on top. The flag was apparently the idea of Tony James, the Sigue Sigue Sputnik guitarist who was Janet's boyfriend at the time and who gave it to her a present. But it was soon in tatters and, after complaints, the council suggested she take it down (*fuckin' sad bureaucratic pisspots!*). Despite this setback the house, which Janet described as a 'sculpture', was a shrine to Piratical Street-Porterism. When asked by a newspaper to list the most stylish things in the whole of world history, she nominated her house top of the list, followed by her Land-Rover Discovery – much better, she opined, than a Range Rover, which was 'just a big taxi'. (Janet's taste in cars had changed over the years, in tune with her husbands. Friends remember that when she was married to Tony Elliot, and deeply involved in the ex-hippy scene, she was the proud owner of a 2CV. In her SuperYuppie phase she had a flash sports car which, she said, was a substitute for having children.)

Janet said her house 'was her best friend'. She was not going to leave all that behind and get some *dreery*, *ghaaastly* flat in bleedin' Didsbury. Officially she did move to Manchester, but in reality she operated from London. The Tellybrats, however, were mostly sent up north. There was relief, on the part of some, that they would be getting away from Janet, with all her moods and tantrums. But this soon evaporated when the army of secretaries, implementers and production-controllers began commuting between London and Manchester, often accompanied by an unannounced Janet on a lightning mission to shake up the department.[7]

With things not going her way at the BBC, Janet began preparing to jump ship. Changes in the nature of broadcasting meant that the BBC was likely to play a much less dominant role in the future, anyway. Lots of new possibilities were springing up. The booming independent sector, ushered in by Channel Four, had been boosted by new regulations forcing the BBC to buy in a quarter of all its programmes from the independent production companies. Sky had been relaunched the previous year after the merger with BSB, and the age of 'multi-channel television', which Murdoch had predicted in his Janet-organised 1989 Edinburgh lecture, seemed to be dawning. For a well-connected woman like Janet there were, in the words of her favourite Pet Shop Boys record, 'lots of opportunities'.

Chapter Seven

In which Monty dreams of becoming The British Rupert Murdoch by setting up a Network of City TV stations with Janet's help but is frustrated by a great many Short-Sighted and Smooth-Talkin' Americans, takes over the Daily Mirror *instead, picking up the nickname 'Rommel' ('because Monty was on* our *side'), tries again to get City TV off the ground but is pipped at the post by the* Daily Mail, *but at the same time manages to make friends with some Very Important People in the cable industry who, at last, want to Do Business*

Alan McKeown was a well-known figure on the independent production scene.[1] He ran a clutch of programme-making companies under the banner of SelecTV. He was responsible for supplying one of the Birtised BBC's few hit situation comedies, *Birds of a Feather*. But his interests were far wider than that. McKeown had lived in the United States, commuting between London and Los Angeles where he lived for a while with his wife, Tracey Ullman, one of the biggest stars on the American NBC network. In the early '90s he was back in the UK, re-organising his business and trying to find a way to become a broadcaster. He was looking trimmer than usual: thanks to a course of liposuction paid for by his wife as a birthday present. 'It was a relief to get rid of all those prawn cocktails from the 1960s,' he told people.

McKeown's visits to London were one long round of power lunches and meetings with the new and avidly courted aristocracy of 'commissioning editors': the people who controlled multi-million pound chequebooks for buying in programmes for ITV, Channel Four and, increasingly, the BBC. Alan was always full of entertaining stories about how things were going on in the States, where television was panned as down-market and horrible, but where television executives earned maybe ten times as much as their counterparts at the BBC or ITV.

One of Alan's best yarns was the saga of Glen Jones. In the '70s Jones had been a penniless odd-job man in Denver, living in a Volkswagen campervan, fixing fences, clearing gutters and putting up television aerials: a difficult job because TV reception was poor in the Rocky Mountains. One day Jones had the brainwave of putting a big aerial on top of a conveniently located mountain and running a long cable down to the houses. Reception improved and he started getting a lot of customers. 'Y'see Glen is very tall,' Alan would chuckle, warming to the story. 'He was the only bloke . . . right . . . who was prepared to climb up the mountain and fix the aerial every time the wind blew it over.' Then McKeown would deliver the punchline with all the panache of one of his sit-com writers: 'And that guy today is worth seven and a half billion . . . not *million* . . . seven and a half *billion* dollars.' Senior British TV executives, like those at the BBC, struggling along on maybe £70,000 a year, would be agog: '*Whoooww!* You're kidding. Seven and a half *billion*?' Nope. He was not kidding. Jones had sold his cable business to Bell Cablemedia and cleaned up.

McKeown would fill in the detail from his personal experience, explaining that when he had first moved to the States he had paid $150 for a cable subscription, and there had not been much on it. Now he was paying about $2,000 and he was by no means untypical. There were – what? – 50 million households in the USA. Say only half of them signed up, each paying their $2,000. Well, work it out for yourself. The cable market was worth *hundreds of billions* every year. And that was just the beginning. Once you 'punched the wire' into people's homes, they kept ordering more and more stuff, spending more and more money. 'Down that wire will come all the information of the new age,' McKeown would intone, 'the telephone, shopping, the Internet . . . it's a dream.'

But not yet. Not in the UK, at least. Britain was lagging far behind in the cable revolution. It was not for want of trying. Big, mostly American, telephone and cable companies with baffling acronymic names were burning some of the billions they had made in the States digging up the streets of British cities bringing the gift of cable television to the masses. By the early '90s the cable operators had already sunk around £7 billion into the technology and it was predicted that by 2000 they would have put in another £3 billion, bringing the system within reach of almost everyone in the country.

The trouble was that people were just not buying it. Why should they, when there was virtually nothing on cable that was not already provided by the BBC, ITV or Sky? Nothing, that is, of interest to anyone but the utterly demented. OK, there was business news in Arabic for the Arabic community, non-stop Country and Western videos, spurious 'sports' channels mainly featuring morons from the American Midwest driving lorries with unfeasibly large wheels; and so on. One of the great mysteries of modern economics is why anyone would invest £10 billion to ensure the distribution of material which, in general, was of far less use and interest than the information printed on the back of a bus ticket.

Still, men like McKeown were determined to do something about this sad state of affairs. David Montgomery, former editor of *Today*, was plunging into this brave new world as well. And Janet Street-Porter, becalmed at the BBC, was surveying the scene with increasing interest. All three were shortly to come together at the Mirror Group, with a plan to get in on the ground floor of British multi-channel television.

For the time being, Monty was leading the way. After leaving *Today*, he had hired an office in the headquarters of Saatchi & Saatchi and he was making contact with all sorts of people in the TV industry, including Janet Street-Porter, in an attempt to set up a British version of Fox, Murdoch's successful chain of American city TV cable-distributed stations. Fox worked by linking local affiliates which produced local news but for part of the day screened programmes produced at Fox TV headquarters in New York. The purpose of the national material was to give each local station a much stronger 'branded' identity than any of them could achieve on its own. The idea was similar to a franchise business like McDonald's in which the hamburgers are made at each 'affiliate' but according to a national formula backed by national advertising. In the US Fox had deliberately chosen a young, funky, alternative image, designed to set it apart from the existing middle-of-the-road networks and to appeal to groups like blacks, gays and the young who were not well served by the big networks.[2]

In other words, the Fox formula was remarkably similar to both *Network-7* and, especially, *Def-II*, whose perplexed critics noted that the channel-within-a-channel 'rolling' format looked as though it was made with commercial breaks in mind. Really, the heavily branded and resolutely hip *Def-II* could be moved into a cable system and function in exactly the same way as Fox's national 'spine' with only minor modifications.

Janet was in many ways the perfect choice to head a

Live TV

British version of Fox-style City TV. In 1987, when *Network-7* was starting up, she had also worked as a consultant at LWT with the job of putting a bit of pizzazz into local news and current-affairs programming. This was useful experience, but more important was her track record in creating cheaply produced 'alternative' television for niche audiences, and for generating outrage and publicity. In full conspiratorial mode Monty was soon telling figures in the industry that Janet Street-Porter was seriously considering leaving the BBC in order to join his venture.[3]

Monty's problem was not programming or the advertising revenue (his own research had convinced him that there was a huge market for truly local television advertising which ITV was unable to tap) but distribution. He had talked to Sky about taking a sub-lease on one of the transponders on the Astra satellite used by Sky, but they wanted too much money for the use of their encryption and subscriber-management systems. The potential advertising revenue was substantial but Sky had a stranglehold on distribution and would have taken every last penny, leaving Monty with a very small potential margin in return for the vast risk of getting into television production.[4]

Instead he turned to the cable operators, but he found that they were divided and a nightmare to deal with. In London, for example, his city TV station would have required half a dozen distribution companies to co-operate (different and sometimes hostile companies own the cable system in different parts of the capital) and they had not, at that point, even linked up their systems so that the same signal could go out across the whole of London at the same time. Even if he could get them interested, each company had a local monopoly and could dictate harsh terms in return for allowing him on to the system.

Monty's main problem at this time was that they would only offer him very short-term contracts. The insecurity of the venture, more than anything else, made it difficult to attract investment or secure the loans he would need to meet the large start-up costs each city station would require. The idea was aborted for the time being.

But Monty's investigations had not been a complete waste of time. Far from it. His attempts to find finance for city TV led him to meet Lord (Clive) Hollick of the MAI financial services group, and the two men worked together during 1991. Hollick decided that he could not help with the city TV idea. Instead, the following year he steered Monty towards Mirror Group Newspapers (MGN), with a plan to install him as chief executive. Once Monty was in charge of the *Mirror*, his city TV idea would be much more attractive to the cable distribution companies, who knew that if MGN-owned city TV was on their system the *Mirror* itself could be hooked in to promote subscription to the system as a whole. This was extremely important, since the cable industry's own marketing was dire while its main competitor, Sky, had relentless promotional support from the *Sun*. Once Monty controlled the *Mirror*, most of the cable companies, instead of trying to charge him a fortune to distribute city TV, might be very keen to do business.

The position at the post-Maxwell MGN was bleak, but not entirely disastrous. In the months after Maxwell's death the *Mirror*, *Sunday Mirror* and *People* had all started to do well. Set free from Maxwell's constant interference, the Group's titles put on circulation and began closing the gap with the *Sun* and the *News of the World*. Things were going so well that the board had even authorised bonus payments and a small pay rise for the journalists.

The *Mirror*'s long-serving editor, Richard Stott, had

patched up the business and started work on a management buy-out. He and other senior figures, including the *People*'s editor, Bill Hegarty, and Charlie Wilson, the former *Times* editor brought into the Mirror Group by Maxwell, had a series of meetings with a merchant bank aimed at raising the cash to pay off the bankers and gain full control of the group. Rival bids were in the offing from Tony O'Reilly, the Dublin-based chairman and chief executive of Heinz; from Conrad Black, the Napoleon-worshipping owner of the *Daily Telegraph*; from the D.C. Thomson group, of Dundee, owners of the *Beano*; and from a consortium headed by Lord Hollick. None of the offers was high enough to interest the bankers, though Hollick did buy enough shares to play an influential role in the crippled company – he played an important part in installing Monty as MGN's chief executive in 1992. (The appointment was approved by John Talbot, the administrator put in by the banks after Maxwell's death to manage the ruins of the Maxwell empire in the interests of its creditors.)

Monty had to give the MGN board assurances that the *Mirror* would not, once in his charge, descend into 'sleaze' in pursuit of readers and profits. This objection was easily dealt with. His stint on the *News of the World* was now well behind him and he could point to the way he had run the squeaky-clean *Today* as an example of the way forward. The debate lasted for just an hour before the board voted, with a majority of only one, in Monty's favour.

News of the appointment reached the *Mirror*'s staff indirectly. Board member Joe Haines (who had written a famous article in the *Mirror* calling Monty 'a liar, a thief, a hypocrite, a bigot and a pornographer') resigned the minute he heard of it. His resignation statement, in which he complained that the board had not been told in advance that Monty was to be brought in, was put out on the news wire services – and picked up by the hacks on the *Mirror*'s newsdesk.

The paper's editor, Richard Stott, was aghast. What was the board up to? Only a matter of hours before, they had been negotiating with him over a possible management buy-out by the paper's staff. Now the carpet had been pulled out from under their feet. It was a bolt from the blue. Bill Hegarty was also dumbfounded. He had spotted Hollick and Monty deep in conversation in a Soho restaurant, the Gay Hussar, a few days earlier. He had wondered what they were up to, but thought no more of it. Now he knew.

There was equal amazement among the staff of the *Mirror* and its sister papers. When the news was confirmed, they stopped work and began to gather in the newsroom. Some of them had worked with Monty years previously when he was a lowly, and unpopular, production journalist on the subs' desk in the *Mirror*'s Manchester office. Others had been with him more recently at Wapping, where he had been seen as the ultimate Murdoch *apparatchik*: cold, ruthless and, above all, secretive and sneaky. As a boss he was as nasty to work for as Kelvin MacKenzie, though it was said he was a stiletto blade whereas MacKenzie was a battleaxe.

A delegation went to see the chairman of the board, Sir Robert Clarke, to ask him to reconsider. Clarke told them it was too late: the board's vote had been taken. Hearing this, the *Mirror* staff took their own vote, deciding by 278 to 4 not to co-operate in any way with Monty until he had given assurances that there would be no sackings, that he would not interfere in the day-to-day editing of the group's papers and, in particular, that the *Mirror*'s 'social stand' and support for the Labour Party would be maintained. Under threat of strike action Monty issued a statement in which he said that 'the editorial independence of our newspapers will be preserved and vested in the editors, with continuing support for the left-of-centre tradition of all titles', and that 'I have definitely got no plans for job cuts in editorial departments, nor has the board considered any.' In addition, he gave an assurance that 'all editors will remain in place'. But the protest continued through the night in the form of a sit-in.

The next morning Monty appeared for the first time in the *Mirror*'s editorial offices. He swept through the newsroom and marched up to Frank Murphy, the journalists' union representative. Monty put his arm round Murphy and insisted that they went to the canteen for a little chat. 'Anyone would think I bite the heads off babies,' Monty moaned as the two men sat eating breakfast. Murphy explained that a lot of the staff at the *Mirror* had taken jobs mainly because they had wanted to get away from him at *Today* and the *News of the World*. So what did he expect? Monty told Murphy that he was serious about the assurances he had given. The protest was called off but Murphy warned that there would be instant strike action if he broke any of his promises. Stott was likewise persuaded and asked his staff to accept the appointment and get on with their work as normal.

Normality, however, did not last long. Montgomery soon began to explain, with apparent earnestness, that when he had said that 'all editors will stay in place', the words had been used 'strictly in the present tense'. Likewise, when he had said, 'I have definitely got no plans for job cuts in editorial departments', this too had been true: he had had 'no plans' when he said it. Now he did have plans.

The first major figure to go was Richard Stott. Monty asked Stott to meet him at Claridges Hotel in central London to discuss 'affairs of world importance'. Over breakfast, Stott was summarily dismissed. 'There is nothing wrong with Richard,' Monty then told the papers, 'but he represented a culture of decline at the *Mirror* that existed before, during and after its takeover by Robert Maxwell.'

There was shock not only at the dismissal but at the fact that it had been arranged in secret, without consultation, warning or any apparent reason. But that was the way with Monty. The difference between Maxwell and Monty, senior *Mirror* people decided, was that while Maxwell had been a compulsive liar, Monty was compulsively sneaky. When Maxwell told you something you knew it was a lie, so you knew where you stood, but nobody ever got close enough to Monty to know where they stood. Hearing about all this, Monty's old mentor, Nick Lloyd, told the papers, 'The old *Mirror* habits will die now – the drinking and the long lunching and all the boyos having a good time. The fun *Mirror* is over.'

After quickly consolidating his control over the *Mirror*, Monty turned his attention back to his city TV idea. The *Mirror* needed to expand its way out of trouble. Above all, it needed a bold move into television, following the example of Murdoch and most of the other UK newspaper groups. There was no chance of getting *Mirror*-owned and -produced city TV programming on to Sky, since MGN and News Corp. were deadly rivals. If Monty's plan for a city TV network was to happen at all, it would have to be distributed on cable.

In early 1993, a few months after Monty took over at MGN, a cable opportunity presented itself. A group of six cable operators in London overcame their internecine warfare to form a consortium called the London Interconnect Group, headed by John Sheridan, a smooth-talking Canadian who ran a cable company called Encom. Each of the individual operators had a patchwork of unconnected franchises in different parts of the capital.

Some were interested mainly in telephones. The idea was that if they could link their systems together they could offer big discounts to heavy local phone-users, such as big companies with several offices dotted around the City. The link also meant that cable TV programmes could be bought and marketed centrally and pumped out across the whole London cable system, instead of each company buying its own programmes and putting them out to a few thousand subscribers. It all made great sense.

The problem was that, at this point, virtually all the channels available to the cable companies were made by Sky, where Sam Chisholm had proved adept at playing the companies off against each other, offering better terms to one than to another, soaking every available penny out of them or even, worst of all, threatening to refuse to give them the channels at all if they did not play ball.

As Sheridan used to explain in his soothing Transatlantic tones, 'We are in a dependency *sitooashun* here, and that's *rilly* not a comfortable position to be in, especially when . . . *ha, ha, ermmm* . . . yer dealing with *our old friend Rooopert Merduck.*' So the idea emerged of London Interconnect developing its own cable-exclusive channel as a way of reducing dependence on Sky. The consortium had first contacted London News Network, the joint LWT–Carlton ITV television news operation for London, to see if it would provide a continuous cable news channel for the capital. That had not worked out but then Monty's financial fixer, Richard Horwood, who had been talking to the London cable companies for a while, got wind of the idea and fixed up a meeting.

Sheridan explained the cable business's plight. 'It's not *just* a cable *exclusive* programmin' *sitooashun* we're dealin' with here, David, it's more of a *mull-tie-fassited tellacoms sitooashun* we're dealin' with here. We *rilly godda* keep the *tellacoms* boys on board here.' The cable companies squab-bled all the time: no wonder Sam Chisholm was running rings round them. Some were interested mainly in phones, others in television. Some were floated public companies with shareholders to consult; some were in private hands and were more prepared to take risks; mostly they were run by engineering specialists, who knew how to dig up the streets but did not understand programming.

Chisholm at Sky held the initiative, Sheridan complained. And he was giving the cable companies a hard time – *a dependency sitooashun*. Sheridan had just been investigating the possibility of setting up a pay-per-view movie channel on cable, in competition with Sky. This had been a nightmare. In contrast to the 'Balkanised' cable companies, Chisholm could bring the whole weight of the Murdoch Empire into play with just one or two phone calls. Sam was in Hollywood pounding his meaty fist on the desks of studio heads, freezing cable out, before the companies could even agree which hotel to meet in to start discussing how they were going to negotiate. The position would remain hopeless, Sheridan and others realised, unless the cable companies learnt to work together and exert some sort of collective leverage against *our old friend Rooopert Merduck*.

Monty outlined his idea for a London city TV channel called London Live. It was just the ticket. It would run on all the local London cable stations at the same time. Even if few people watched it, as seemed likely at first, it would give them experience in working together, and this could lead to bigger things. The *Mirror*, once it had a financial stake in cable subscriptions, would hype the idea of connecting to the cable TV system, thus countering the *Sun*'s ceaseless pro-dish propaganda.

Sheridan listened politely, but he was worried. 'David'

was a *rilly* impressive *business guy,* but what he was offering *programmin'-wise* was . . . well, *kinda blurred.* Monty was vague about who would be involved on the creative side. Enigmatic as ever, he kept saying he was in contact with people who were 'right at the top of the tree, *tree-mundusslee expoirianced people'*, who would come on board once the project got the go-ahead. But not before. The editorial plans were hazy as well. There was going to be a live element to it, a *nooos* element and some light *enner-tainment.* What he was promising seemed to change from meeting to meeting. That did not inspire the *kinda comfort level* that the members of Sheridan's consortium were looking for.

Instead London Interconnect turned to Associated Newspapers, owners of the *Daily Mail* and *Evening Standard.* Associated, led by the former *Mail* editor Sir David English (inventor of 'talking-point journalism'), were just as keen to follow Murdoch into television as Monty, and for similar reasons. Associated offered to produce for Sheridan a cable-exclusive channel to be called Channel One. Associated's plans were much more definite: a combined news and entertainment channel based on a tie-up with Alan McKeown's SelecTV.

McKeown had been approached by Associated's Roger Gilbert, who offered him a 20 per cent stake in the London cable channel. The plan was to build a schedule around repeats of SelecTV's vast back catalogue of hit shows. This would be mixed with live news bulletins using the *Evening Standard*'s expertise and other cheap and cheerful studio-based materials like chat-shows. Was McKeown interested? You bet! Sheridan and London Interconnect went for the Associated bid, leaving Monty mightily pissed off. The big attraction for Sheridan was not so much Associated's better programming plans and SelecTV's involvement as the fact

that the *Daily Mail* and – in particular – the *Evening
Standard* were in a much better position to promote cable
in London than the *Mirror* was. The *Mirror* was read by far
more people than the *Standard* in the country as a whole,
but the *Standard* was read by far more people in London,
especially people – such as stockbrokers – who used the
phone a lot ('*strongly engaged in tellacoms traffic*'), which
meant better 'demographic fit' with the market for *high
den-sidy tellacoms use an' enhanced tellaphone services*. In other
words, the *Standard* would be a highly effective way of
telling everyone in London that wonderful cheap phone
lines were available to people who signed up with cable
TV.

Sheridan offered to pay Associated 25p per month per
subscriber to the cable system, regardless of whether the
subscriber watched the channel or not. This meant that
Channel One's income was entirely dependent on the
number of subscribers to the cable system as a whole.
Associated's newspapers were therefore duly roped into
promote cable TV and phone-line subscriptions, as
intended. Quality-control arrangements were put in place
to allow the cable companies to veto and stop paying the
25p per month fee if the channel did not come up to
scratch.[5]

Once the deal was signed McKeown went to dinner with
Sir David English to discuss progress – or so he thought.
Instead, to his amazement, Sir David told him that he was
going to make Channel One a full-time rolling news channel and reruns of SelecTV programmes would not be
required. It was going to be a great success, Sir David said,
and would 'roll out' from London to cities like Bristol and
Liverpool, eventually covering the whole country.
McKeown, he went on, had made a smart move getting in
on the ground floor with his 20 per cent stake in the

venture. There would be big losses at first, of course, but as cable spread, well, one day . . .

'Hang on!' McKeown said. 'No way! Look, we have just got the franchise for an *entertainment* channel. Not *news*, mainly. We've got the programmes. Everything's ready to go.' But Sir David was adamant: news was the thing. McKeown thought this was bonkers and told him so. There was no way SelecTV was going to blow millions setting up a news channel which nobody would want to watch. He wanted out. Sir David obliged, paying McKeown £1 million for his stake. Channel One, now an entertainment-free zone, steamed ahead and became available to London's small band of cable subscribers eighteen months later, in November 1994.

The loss of the London Interconnect channel was a blow for Monty. For the time being it left him empty-handed before stock-market analysts and share tipsters hungry to know when MGN would follow Murdoch into television. But there were still possibilities. Monty was already talking to his old News Corp. contact Patrick Cox, now head of the American network NBC's European activities,[6] about a joint NBC–Mirror Group bid for the forthcoming Channel 5 franchise. And the city TV concept was far from dead. Monty might have lost London as a possible franchise, which was a problem, but all was not lost. Adam Singer, UK head of the mighty American cable operator Telecommunications International (TCI),[7] the largest single cable company in the UK, had monitored the bidding for the London Interconnect franchise carefully. Now he started talking to Monty about possible co-operation outside London.

In 1992 the cable companies, led by TCI, had come together tentatively to set up a consortium to make cable-exclusive programmes to compete with Sky. The consortium, called Cable Programme Partners One (CPP-1),[8] in turn launched a cable-exclusive channel called Wire TV. The idea was that Wire would start off in a very low-key way, but that it would give the cable companies some experience in co-operating with each other. In the longer term, it could be developed into a brand of 'family' channels like Sky. It screened a mixture of cheap American imported drama, supplemented by ultra-cheap, live studio-based material, such as chat shows, during the daytime and a ragbag of sports programmes at night.[9]

But Wire TV had not prospered, despite the heroic efforts of those involved. By 1993, just as Monty was licking his wounds over the failure to get London Live off the ground, the cable companies were ready to offload the channel. David Montgomery was to be a very willing buyer.

Chapter Eight

In which Janet makes Der Vampyr *and wins yet more honours and awards but does not become controller of BBC 1 or BBC 2 or anything else for that matter and so meets her old friends in the Independent Sector and considers joining them but thinks again and takes a new job at the BBC for a few months before moving to Mirror Television to be united with Kelvin MacKenzie – of all people – in the launch of L!ve TV, and a Mirror-owned version of Channel 5*

There's never anything decent on the telly over Christmas and New Year. This is because the advertisers realise the punters are skint after the annual shopping binge and so there's no need for ITV to push the boat out to get an audience. The BBC follows suit, saving its diminished resources for the ratings wars later in the year.

Christmas 1992 followed this pattern: *World Darts* on BBC 2. Compilation editions of *It'll Be Alright On The Night* on ITV. Repeats of *Porridge* on BBC 1. Adding to the gloom this time was ITV's *The End of The Year Show: The Best from . . . Thames*, marking the demise of the London weekday ITV station and its replacement by Carlton, 'the C-word of British television'.

But anyone surfing this ocean of seasonal tedium and nostalgia would have eventually found something very odd on the screen: the spectacle of conspicuously wealthy and good-looking young City commodity brokers, male and female, ripping off their lustrously expensive Paul Smith suits and power-dressed shoulder-pads, romping around in a Docklands loft-apartment while warbling like canaries; diving into the duvet for a spot of furious shagging accompanied by the sound of a pack of ravening wolves and great spurts of blood.

Pop out to kitchen, get another curling turkey sandwich, come back to the sofa and the scene has changed to a Satanic mass on the floor of the Saatchi & Saatchi art gallery. The camera cuts between a giant fishtank containing a pickled shark (Damien Hirst: *Completely Brilliant!*) and grisly close-ups of singer Omar Ebrahim's gaping cakehole, as he gargles with blood and sinks three-inch fangs into the neck of an innocent virgin, all accompanied by more falsetto singing, demonic operatic *Haaa Haaars* and *Hoooraahhhs* and more wolf noises.

Janet Street-Porter had fought long and hard to get what became *Der Vampyr* on to the screen. She had first had the idea of doin' a 'television opera' in about 1980 when she was still at LWT, planning to move from being a presenter to become a producer and executive. Now it had come to fruition, just at the time Janet was making her pitch to get out of the ghetto of yoof TV and move up the BBC hierarchy. After all it was High Culture, done with a popular touch. It was definitely *innervitiff*. With opera, you had good tunes (*look at Ness'n'dorma* and *Pav'rotti*), ludicrous plots (just like the soaps) and plenty of nineteenth-century Helena Bonham-Carter types trussed up in corsets, all bonkin' away like rabbits.

Janet made herself producer of the project and brought in opera expert David Freeman as a consultant, telling him to find a suitably obscure work ripe for the 'opera as soap opera' treatment. She wanted a work featuring 'young, glamorous people as its central characters' and a daft plot that could be worked up as a five-part series. After a few false starts Freeman turned up Heinrich Marschner's *Der Vampyr*, an early-nineteenth-century Gothic Horror job. This was perfect. Vampirism was an intrinsically sexy

subject, with bonking, violence, horror and horny aristocrats all bundled up in one bloodsoaked package; and very
fashionable at the time. Francis Ford Coppola *himself* was
doin' a $40 million Hollywood remake of *Dracula*. Then
there was the whole issue of blood-mixin' and AIDS. The
next step was to bring in an opera director, Robert Chevara,
to work with Nigel Finch, the film-maker Janet had
persuaded to co-direct the series.[1]

The original plot was updated from aristocrats to
yuppies in the City who, in the middle of the 1992 recession, were a hot topic. They sort of sucked the blood out
of the economy, didn't they, preyin' on each other and
everyone else and leavin' them drained and dead? And so
the original Vampire, Ripley, wakes up in a sewer after two
hundred years of undead sleep. Naturally he becomes a
City commodity dealer. All goes well until the Devil offers
him the ultimate incentive package: he must kill three
women, one per day, in order to stay on earth. If he does
not do this he will fry in Hell for ever.

Charles Hart, who had worked on Andrew Lloyd
Webber's *Phantom of the Opera* was brought in to do the
words. The result was heavily redolent of the Gold Blend
advert. 'I'd invite you in for coffee, but all I have is gin,'
crooned the female victim. 'I never could resist tempta-
tion, so I might as well come in,' boomed Mr Vampire.

Der Vampyr was a bit of a disappointment in ratings
terms and was panned by some opera experts as being too
much like a soap, and by soap commentators as being too
operatic (the *Guardian*'s critic described it as looking like
'a docklands carnival sponsored by *Der Sun*'). Despite
falling between these two stools, *Der Vampyr* earned Janet
a Prix Italia to join the other awards crowding her mantel-
piece.[2]

Not that it did her much good. Janet's campaign to

become one of the top executives at the BBC was stalling seriously. In December 1992, a few weeks before John Birt was due to move up from director-general designate to be crowned director-general proper, Jonathan Powell left his job as controller of BBC 1 to take a job at Carlton. His departure left the controllerships of both BBC 1 and BBC 2 vacant, since the BBC 2 chief, Alan Yentob, announced that he was interested in moving over from BBC 2 to replace Powell at BBC 1.

Janet, later claiming that she had been invited to do so by the BBC's managing director of television, Will Wyatt, made an application to be a channel controller in March 1993.[3] The personal publicity machine was cranked up again – just as it had been at the time of her attempt to land the position of head of BBC Arts – helped by the fact that *Der Vampyr* was being screened over Christmas and had got people in tellyland talking about her again. It was all to no avail. Control of BBC 1 was taken by Alan Yentob and BBC 2 went to Michael Jackson, who two years earlier had pipped Janet to the job of head of BBC Arts. Now he had beaten her again. Janet was left out in the cold and she was, according to people who knew her at the time, 'devastated'.

The media had done her in again, she reckoned, this time revealing that she was not even a BBC employee and was paid via her private company as a tax-avoidance measure. John Birt had done the same thing, causing an enormous stink and much sneering when it was discovered that he was claiming substantial tax relief for his famous collection of Armani suits: Armanigate!

The BBC issued the standard soothing statement saying that she was not bothered about the setback and would be staying on as head of Youth and Entertainment. 'She is very happy here at the moment,' the corporation fibbed, adding, 'She has no plans to leave.' In reality Janet was already looking for a way out, and had been for a while. There was her behind-the-scenes contact with Monty about his plans for a city TV cable channel – if it ever got off the ground – and she had other options as well.

In the autumn of 1993 Janet was talking to people at Chrysalis TV, the thrusting independent TV company headed by Mick Pilsworth, an old friend of Janet's from LWT, and Tony Orsten, the former *Network-7* director. They discussed the possibility of Janet's moving from the BBC to take an executive job with Chrysalis.

Pilsworth had first met Janet in 1979 on his first day working for LWT and they became friends. When she moved to the BBC in 1988, Pilsworth was working for McKeown's SelecTV, where he became managing director. He had pitched Janet some ideas for *Def-II*; they had not worked out but he still did some work for her, mainly organising concerts and helping with the live coverage of youth events in the early 1990s. Now he was very keen that Janet should join Chrysalis: she was the perfect person to get involved with the company's burgeoning interests, which included a move into making and selling primetime programmes to the terrestrial stations and to Sky and cable.[4] The two of them talked about many things, and Janet mentioned her past involvement in the *Mirror*'s bid for the London Live franchise and the plan to launch a national version of the same thing in 1995.

In the end she turned him down, saying that the *Mirror* plan was more of a challenge since it involved creating an entire national network rather than being a programme producer, which would have been her role at Chrysalis. She had more or less made up her mind up to go to the *Mirror*, but decided to stay on at the BBC for the time being, so as to have a secure base while she looked at all her options.

Janet & Monty

In December 1993 Janet made a sideways move at the BBC. She left her job as head of Youth and Entertainment and became head of independent commissioning in Light Entertainment. At Youth and Entertainment, she had been the head of her own operation and had dealt directly with the channel controllers, which was the key to the complex internal politics and status game at the BBC. She would now be working in a more junior position, under the direction of David Liddiment, head of the BBC's Entertainment group. The job itself involved wielding a multi-million pound chequebook and buying in material from independents,[5] although all spending had to be authorised by Liddiment and, in the case of really big contracts, by Alan Yentob, the new channel controller.

Janet stayed in this job for ten months before leaving to join Monty at the *Mirror* and start work on the launch of 'L!ve TV', the putative national cable channel which he had finally got off the ground after much wrangling in the cable world. At roughly the same time Monty had also started working with the American NBC channel on a strong-looking bid for the Channel 5 franchise, up for auction in about eighteen months' time. Janet was naturally interested in this as well, seeing herself as a potential programme controller for the new channel.

Her move to L!ve TV was announced on 21 September 1994. She told the trade press that she wanted the new job because, at last, she would have the opportunity to start a new channel from scratch. And she would be her own boss. That was a big attraction. 'I won't have a network controller, I'll work directly to David Montgomery,' she said. 'Cable is exciting. It's brilliant at being local, empowering people, delivering live programmes, getting at things happening on the street. We have the funds and we're going to change TV.'

L*i*ve TV

Janet's friends went on record to say that the BBC was losing a great talent. Moving to a tiny cable channel was a step down in the world, in some ways, but her chances of getting to the top at the BBC were now slight and so the move made sense. At least at L!ve TV she would be in control. She would not have to report to the 'grey, unattractive, sexist men' she had complained about at the BBC.

But then, within days of announcing Janet's arrival at Mirror Television, the company announced a second 'bombshell' appointment: Kelvin MacKenzie, the greying, unattractive and wildly sexist former editor of the *Sun* was going to be managing director of Mirror Television – and, therefore, Janet Street-Porter's boss. There was general amazement. It would be hard to think of two less likely characters working together. Judging from the coverage she had got in the *Sun*, it could be fairly assumed that MacKenzie, if he thought about her at all, hated Janet Street-Porter and all she stood for. Janet, for her part, loathed the *Sun* with a passion and had, anyway, announced that she would report directly to David Montgomery, and made it clear that the main reason why she was joining up was that she would have no boss. Now she would be formally answerable to, of all people, *Kelvin MacKenzie*. She explained this apparently odd state of affairs by saying that she and MacKenzie would be working on different projects within the company. As she saw it, there would be no need for them even to meet all that often.

Soon after her arrival at the *Mirror*, Janet had lunch with Nigel Haunch, former chief executive of the now defunct cable-exclusive Wire TV channel whose 'band' slot on the cable system L!ve TV was taking over. The meeting was at the Ivy, one of the most fashionable restaurants in Soho. Haunch was deeply impressed by Janet's ability to get a table and then by her panache in arriving half an hour late, as was her habit, without any apology or explanation. He had hoped to persuade her to keep on as many of the staff of Wire as possible. Janet was dismissive. She wanted nothing to do with Wire. She was going to start from scratch and didn't need any advice on what to do, thank you very much. Since there was nothing much else to discuss, Haunch started asking her about MacKenzie, and how it was that she had ended up working alongside him.

Janet let him in on Monty's latest thinking. The takeover of Wire was only part of the plan. L!ve TV was gonna grow into a group of channels, to rival the various Sky channels. On top of this they were going to put in a bid for Channel 5 in conjunction with NBC and there was a good chance they would get it. There was plenty of room for both the former *Sun* editor and herself. She would be doin' L!ve TV and the daytime stuff on Channel 5. And Kelvin would do the sport. He knew all about sport, Kelvin did. And he had big plans. Between them they would cover most of the important programming areas. It all made perfect sense. It was not a problem.

Chapter Nine

In which Kelvin MacKenzie grows weary of editing his beloved Currant Bun and makes an Unexpected Move to become Managing Director of Sky TV where, at first, he Makes All the Right Noises

''Ere! Where's the fucking sumo wrestler? Tell 'im 'e's dead, the fat cunt!' Kelvin MacKenzie is unhappy. Definitely unhappy. He has just heard that Sky TV's news editor has refused to run an item that he, Kelvin MacKenzie, Probably Britain's Greatest Post-War Tabloid Journalist, former editor of the World's Biggest Selling English Language Daily Newspaper *By Far*, personally, by himself, has set up. Kelvin, eyes bulging, spit flying, is bowling down the corridors, yelling at the top of his voice.

'The fuck-ing Harkess story is going on the fuck-ing screen whether Fryk-fucking-berg fucking likes it or not, *the fat fucker*!' Failing to find his prey, MacKenzie – MacFrenzie! – turns on a gaggle of hapless Sky News minions. He glowers at them and draws breath. Stabbing his finger at them all the while, he explains, 'Alan Clark is a *story*! Yoooou knowwww, a STORY!' The minions stare back blankly. Kelvin is exasperated. 'Look – *fuck me* – this woman's gonna say how big his *fucking prick* is! Right there on national-fucking-television! No one's got that, have they? *A FUCKING STORY!!!*' They are still blank. 'Oh fuck it. Fuck off.'

It is May 1994, in the middle of Prime Minister John Major's imploding 'Back to Basics' morality campaign. Former Tory minister Alan Clark's recently published *Diaries* contained the thinly disguised revelation that he had slept with Valerie Harkess, wife of Judge James Harkess, and with both her daughters. Stung by this, the Harkess family decided to counter-attack.

The family have turned up in England to accuse Alan Clark of exposing his private parts to the girls years before, when they were teenagers. 'He showed his willy to us constantly,' daughter Josephine had already told a newspaper. 'He just sort of got a kick out of it.' The *News of the World* is running the 'kiss and tell' story big – and Judge Harkess has threatened to horsewhip Clark. But Kelvin has topped them. He had lined up Valerie Harkess to appear live on Sky. And yes, she is ready to prove the allegations according to normal tabloid fashion by reference to anatomical details known only to those who have seen the kiss and tell victim in the nude.[1]

But Sky's news editor, a 22-stone New Zealander called Ian Frykberg, who does indeed look a *bit* like a sumo wrestler, is trying to stop him. Frykberg, mortified by what this sort of thing could do to the reputation for professionalism and responsibility he has painstakingly built for Sky News will be over-ruled. The story will run. But Kelvin is not happy – *Definitely Not Happy*.[2]

The row over the Harkess story took place in late May 1994, when Kelvin had been at the channel for four months, but there had been similar rows almost daily. On his very first day at Sky the story of Stephen Milligan, the Tory MP found dead wearing women's underwear and with an orange in his mouth, broke. It was the perfect *Sun* story. Kelvin swaggered into the Sky newsroom, sleeves rolled up, and started organising the coverage as though he was still at Wapping. All this was taken as charming eccentricity at the time, since when he arrived he had seemed keen to get on with people and find out how the place worked.

Things had turned nastier during a memorable spat over an exclusive interview with Barbara Windsor's ex-husband, Ronnie Knight, who was serving a seven-year sentence for receiving stolen money. Frykberg refused to run the story at the top of the bulletin, above the day's political and international news. Kelvin would have restructured the bulletin himself, but did not know what buttons to press. Instead he ended up shouting at Frykberg over the newsroom Tannoy. Another time Frykberg refused to run an interview with Lady Bienvenida Buck about her affair with Sir Peter Harding, the Chief of the Defence Staff. Using his position as managing director, Kelvin commandeered Sky One, the light-entertainment channel, to show a lengthy and specially produced version of the rejected interview. After the Harkess incident Frykberg left the channel in disgust, causing morale to plummet and Sam Chisholm to consider acting against Kelvin.

It was in many ways amazing that MacKenzie should make the move from his beloved 'Currant Bun', as he called the *Sun*, to the uncharted waters of the television industry at the comparatively late age of 48, and it was widely predicted that he would not last long at Sky. Kelvin Calder MacKenzie was born in October 1946. His parents, Ian and Mary, then lived in Camberwell, London, and were both journalists on the local weekly newspaper, the *South London Observer*. When Kelvin was a boy the family moved to the more up-market Dulwich, where he attended Alleyn's School.

Aged 17, MacKenzie got a job on the *South-East London Mercury*, where he learnt the basic skills of newspaper reporting. He soon became bored with local journalism, and left to join a news agency run by Dan Ferrari. As it happened, Ferrari's son Nick was, much later, to play an important part in the creation of L!ve TV.

MacKenzie soon made it to Fleet Street and the national press. His progress from then on was rapid, and included a spell at Rupert Murdoch's *New York Post* and, back home again, the night editorship of the *Daily Express*. Then, in 1981, he became editor of the *Sun*, and with that he found his element.[3]

MacKenzie did well enough at the *Sun* until towards the end of his reign, he made a series of catastrophic errors. One of these ended in a £1 million libel payoff to Elton John. The Elton John saga began in February 1987, when the *Sun* splashed across its front page the headline 'ELTON IN VICE BOY SCANDAL: STAR'S LUST FOR BONDAGE'. MacKenzie had assured his boss, Rupert Murdoch, that the story was completely sound, and there was nothing to worry about. In fact the story was completely untrue. The *Sun*'s sole source for these stories – about Elton John attending orgies featuring perverted sex and drug abuse – was the unsupported and unreliable evidence of a homosexual prostitute and self-confessed con-man. The star responded with a flurry of libel writs, and a ferocious legal battle seemed likely.

In November 1988 an out-of-court settlement was agreed with Elton John's lawyer, Frank Presland. The *Sun* had to pay out £1 million damages and print a grovelling front-page apology under the headline 'SORRY ELTON!' (which was duly done). MacKenzie wondered how to break the news of the loss to the Boss, and decided to fax him in Los Angeles. After what seemed like seconds, the Murdoch 'hot line' in the editor's office started ringing. His news editor was ushered out of the room: 'I'd better deal with this myself,' Kelvin mumbled. Half an hour later he emerged from his office, white as a sheet and holding his head in his hands. 'Fucking hell, mate, that was the bollocking of a lifetime,' he said. 'Fucking hell. There'll have to be some changes.'

Although MacKenzie liked watching TV sometimes, he had nothing but contempt for most of the people who worked in and ran the business. British television was a pile of trendy piffle: toffs swanning around country mansions in eighteenth-century costumes, bollocks about termite hills in Africa, unwatchable pop-music shite, and Loony Left current-affairs programmes, punctuated by only the occasional flash of brilliance such as *EastEnders*, *The Bill* and repeats of *Carry On* films.

But for some reason Murdoch – the Boss – had decided to get involved, as Kelvin knew to his cost. At first Sky had lost an absolute fortune and the *Sun*, still one of the most profitable parts of the Empire, had been more or less looted to pay for it. It had all been so unfair. There he was flogging his guts out, *day in, day out*, while budgets were slashed, expenses cut and mobile phones taken away just so a load of media luvvies – many of them women, some of them openly homosexual (shirt-lifters! pooftahs!!) could fanny around earning big wonga trying to be Bernardo Bleeding Bertolucci.

No, something was not right here. But then again . . . the Boss was never wrong. 'He's cleverer than a barrel full of monkeys,' Kelvin would explain earnestly, forehead furrowed, to anyone having difficulty following Murdoch's twists and turns. Yep! There was a trick here somewhere, with this dish business. But Kelvin was fucked if he knew what it was. He could see *parts* of it working. Charging for films and football – that made sense. But Sky News? What was that all about? Kelvin had puzzled long and hard over this question. It appeared to be some sort of televisual equivalent of the *Guardian*. *Newsnight* meets Mogadon – hours and hours of gobshite about Parliament and foreign affairs. Nobody wanted that sort of stuff – *did they*? What was the point?

At the *Sun* Kelvin had prided himself on avoiding foreign coverage of any sort, no matter how big it was playing in other papers or on telly, unless he could think of a free publicity angle for the paper. For instance, just days after the revolution which overthrew the Romanian dictator Nicolae Ceausescu, Kelvin ("'Ere! I've 'ad an idea!') got one of his photographers to blag his way on to a 'no press' emergency aid flight carrying medical supplies and baby milk, by promising a contribution to the relief effort from caring *Sun* readers. In fact all the snapper had with him was a catering-size box of Smarties and a few old copies of the *Sun*. After being given, along with the others, the red-carpet treatment at Bucharest airport, he set up shop in the bar, bartered most of the Smarties for local plum brandy, dished out copies of the paper and paid a girl to pose outside in the snow pretending to read the *Sun* while keeping her illicit Smarties out of view and beaming broadly. The resulting picture was printed alongside some lies about how millions of Romanians were queuing up to read the *Sun*, now that they had Western-style democracy and press freedom. That was the Eastern European revolution more or less sorted out. That was how you dealt with foreign stories. You had to get the readers involved. On a human level.

Apart from Sky News's obsession with Boring News about Foreigners Nobody Has Ever Heard Of, there was another thing about Sky. The Boss, for some Machiavellian reason best known to himself, had put the sex 'n' technology-mad Andrew 'Brillo Pad' Neil in charge. That hadn't worked out, and Neil had been sent packing to Yankland. With Brillo out of the way, the much more interesting figure of Sam Chisholm had become chief executive of Sky in 1990. Under Chisholm's influence, Kelvin began to warm towards the new world of multi-channel television.

Not long after Kelvin's move to Sky, he had bumped into Roy Greenslade, previously his number two at the *Sun* and then his rival when Greenslade became editor of the *Mirror*. Greenslade asked him what he was doing mucking about in the world of television. Kelvin puffed himself up to mock the pomposity of the hated television 'luvvies', and said, 'What you've got to understand, Roy, mate, is that television is a "hot" interactive medium.' Greenslade was puzzled, and said, 'If anyone had said that to you six months ago you would have said "bollocks".' Kelvin winked. 'Yeah,' he said, 'but I'm into it now.'

Kelvin and Chisholm had met in 1990, shortly after the New Zealander arrived in London. They liked each other immediately and became drinking pals, since both had a taste for the high life. Kelvin loved Chisholm's endless fund of filthy jokes and robust, no-nonsense approach to business and humanity in general. Chisholm found Kelvin strangely un-stuck-up (for a Pom), with a brilliantly cruel and vicious sense of humour and plenty of funny Murdoch stories, plus a hatred of the British Establishment to match his own.

They agreed on the main point: the British media was stuffed with useless elitist, stuck-up, toffee-nosed pooftahs who were ripe for the taking – financially speaking. They were often seen together in haunts like the Savoy Grill and the Howard Hotel, cutting an odd figure like a couple of overgrown schoolboys in expensive but badly fitting suits, Kelvin roaring away telling war stories. 'So the Boss is on the phone, right, Sam, and he says, right, "*Kilvin, are y'rilly sure this Friddie Starr character acturely ate this f'kin' hamster?*" So I says, "Yup, Boss," and the Boss says, "Huh. And yer tellin' me that's the most *impordant nooos in the wholla Grade Bridden t'day*?" and I says, "Yup, Boss" . . . no, no, listen . . . and he says, "Right," he says . . . ' and Chisholm is rolling around like a neckless human cannonball, helpless with mirth.

From his vantage-point at the *Sun*, Kelvin had watched Chisholm's progress at Sky with more than a passing interest. In less than four years Chisholm had managed to turn Sky from a loss-making enterprise that threatened the very existence of the Murdoch Empire into one of the UK's largest profit-makers, becoming one of the best-paid executives in the country as part of the process. His salary, topped up with bonuses and share options, was said to be worth around £4 million a year by 1993. Kelvin was impressed.

Though the two men were friends, the relationship was far from equal, and it got less and less equal as Sky forged ahead and the *Sun* remained stuck in the circulation doldrums. Unlike Chisholm, Kelvin was, at the end of the day, *just a wage slave*. Big wages, yes. Quarter of a million a year. But, still . . . a hired hand who could be dismissed by Murdoch at will. Kelvin reckoned he worked as hard as Chisholm did, and had made a contribution of similar importance to the success of the Empire. Without the *Sun* and the profits he had made for Murdoch in the '80s there would have been no Wapping. And without the Wapping move, which Kelvin had played such a central role in making a success, there would have been no Sky.

Kelvin had always wanted to make serious money, but he was pretty hopeless at it. He had dabbled in the stock and property markets, but these ventures had come to grief in the recession of the early '90s. With his wife, he had attempted to launch a chain of local newspapers in Kent, but that had not worked out. Yet all around him people who he reckoned were not half as clever or hard-working as himself were coining it. Look at Old Monty! He was only a humble sub from the *Mirror*, who hadn't made the grade at the *Sun*, had gone on to get the whole tabloid press politically crucified by unleashing bonk journalism at the *Screws*, and had ended up ploughing it at *Today*. Now he had taken over as chief executive at the *Mirror*, was pulling a huge salary, and had grabbed himself share options worth millions. All over TV-land nonentities were cleaning up on the share-option front as ITV companies merged with one another. No. It wasn't right. He was being taken for a mug. He wanted to become a player. It was time to move on.

At the same time, Murdoch was starting to see Kelvin, once his favourite editor, more and more as a liability. In 1991 MacKenzie had passed an important landmark: ten years as editor of the *Sun*. He was increasingly moody, sometimes telling cronies that he was on 'borrowed time' as editor. Then, perking up, he would announce that the only way he would ever leave the *Sun* was 'in a wooden box'. His mission when he was brought in in 1981 had been to drive the paper down-market to fight off the threat from the *Daily Star*. He had accomplished this and the *Star* was now dead in the water. After the fuss over tabloid intrusion, all the papers, including the *Sun*, had promised to clean up their act. They were becoming boring and the punters were walking away. In fact, the *Sun*'s sales were so bad that Murdoch had agreed to a costly price cut and a TV advertising campaign to see off a renewed threat from the *Mirror*. The price-cut ads entailed a rare TV appearance by Kelvin, who appeared tying a struggling Murdoch-like figure into his executive chair to stop him cancelling the 'recession-busting' price cut.

Kelvin had endured almost daily 'bollockings' from

Murdoch for more than a decade and the strain was starting to tell. One reason for the mounting severity of the
bollockings was Murdoch's increasing years. He was turning into a 'grumpy old git', common enough in the elderly
but made worse in his case by constant transcontinental
travel, which had destroyed his body-clock and left him
in a permanent jet-lagged foul mood. He took a great many
jet-lag pills and these too seemed to affect his mood. After
a telephone bollocking from Murdoch, which might come
at any time of the day or night, at home or at the office,
Kelvin would complain, 'Rupert's been taking his Angry
Pills,' or 'F'kin hell, the Boss has been on the Gorilla
Biscuits again.'

At the same time Kelvin was slowing down a bit, and
his health was far from perfect. The story circulated of how,
a few years previously, he had keeled over during a lunch
with Eve Pollard. It was said that he had blacked out, and
then, when he came round, had accused her of trying to
steal his chop. Afterwards he bounded back into the newsroom announcing at the top of his voice that he had nearly
died and demanding to see his obituary. When it was
explained that it did not exist he offered a cash prize to the
reporter who wrote the best one. The prize went to an
effort that started, 'Here lies Kelvin MacKenzie – and lies,
and lies and lies'.

After this Kelvin reportedly went on a health drive. He
was already an anti-smoking fanatic and had never taken
to drink, which he could not handle anyway. He often
disappeared in the afternoon officially for a spot of jogging,
swimming or squash. Mysteriously, however, he continued to get fatter even after he signed up for the Wapping
Weight Watchers. He joined the secretaries' aerobics in the
gym, jiggling up and down obediently until he was dripping with sweat. The no-smoking, moderate-drinking

regime was supplemented by a large bowl of fresh fruit eaten in the office before the first harangues of the day. He ate little else all day, unless he had a business lunch, and made do with decaffeinated coffee and weak milky tea. But there were frequent lapses from this regime.

Early in 1993 things between Kelvin and Murdoch had got so bad that, after a particularly devastating bollocking, delivered face to face in Murdoch's office, Kelvin had simply stood up and walked out, sending in his resignation by fax from home and then refusing to take Murdoch's phone calls. He then disappeared from his home, and it was a few weeks before he was tracked down by senior managers and persuaded to return. 'I've gone too far this time,' Murdoch reportedly told Gus Fischer, a senior Wapping manager, while asking him to lure Kelvin back. Murdoch had even apparently promised Fischer, 'I'll change.'[4]

Murdoch pondered what to do with MacKenzie for a while, and discussed the problem with Sam Chisholm and others. 'It's time for Kelvin to move on,' Murdoch mused, 'but I don't know what to do with him.' He could just pay him off. But there were dangers in this. Kelvin might be ill and slowing down a bit, but he was still a formidable operator with a few good years in him: there was no chance that he would retire. Besides, he knew the game plan for the *Sun* in great detail, and had a network of contacts throughout the rest of the Empire. Any other popular newspaper group would be eager to snap him up. Murdoch needed to 'park' him somewhere for a couple of years, until he was past his sell-by date.

This was Murdoch's normal way of saying goodbye to senior people: 'kicking them upstairs' or finding them a fresh 'challenge' elsewhere in the Empire. It reminded some of the British Empire at its height, when troublesome senior civil servants were never sacked but might end up being 'promoted' to become governor of the Falkland Islands. In Murdoch's case it was not quite as cynical as that. If the person did well in their new role they could, in theory, still move up inside the organisation. In practice, this was rare. More typical were the cases of Larry Lamb and Andrew Neil.

Lamb was the man who had created the *Sun* and made it a national institution, building up its circulation in the '70s. He was promoted to become 'editorial director' of all Murdoch's papers for a while, before being shown the door. Neil suffered a similar fate with the dreaded 'move to work in American television'. In his book *Full Disclosure*, he described himself as 'a blossom' who was 'decapitated' by Murdoch the minute he came into full flower at the *Sunday Times*.

Now it was Kelvin's turn. He had already been offered jobs in television in America, but had turned them down. Chisholm came up with an answer: 'Well, I'll have him.' Kelvin could join the management team at Sky. At first Murdoch thought this was one of Sam's little jokes. 'You must be f'kin mad,' he said. But Chisholm was serious. And Kelvin was by now keen to make the move into television.

Sky needed a 'British face', Chisholm believed, to answer the lingering political feeling that it was an alien and essentially Aussie–American intrusion into British life. If they put Kelvin into some sort of figurehead position this would solve two problems at once. They could pay him a lot of money to keep him loyal, and he could look around Sky, study every detail of its operations, and learn about the Bigger Picture at News Corp. Then, after a year or two, they could look at the position again and decide what he should do next. Murdoch, who still thought Kelvin was a 'political pygmy' and told him as much, was persuaded, if not convinced.

Kelvin's move to Sky was agreed in the summer of 1993, and was due to take place towards the end of January 1994. He behaved strangely in his last six months at the *Sun*. A couple of years before, the slide in circulation and the *Mirror*'s onslaught would have driven him into a frenzy. He would have been running laps round the newsroom floor, shrieking at people and egging them on to 'fight fire with fire'. But that summer he instead seemed preoccupied and strangely distant, often content to leave the running of the paper to his deputies, Stuart Higgins and Neil Wallis. Whereas he had always famously been the first man into the office and the last one to leave, he now seemed to be taking it a bit easier. People wondered if his health problems had suddenly got a lot worse. Quite often he would disappear in the afternoon and return late in the evening to make wrapped, anxious phone calls, or not come back at all. He was not 'on the case'. It was all completely out of character.[5]

Others reckoned that Kelvin's strange behaviour was partly due to personal circumstances. He had split up with his wife, Jacqui, and gone off with a much younger woman (he was caught in a Caribbean love nest by a reporter hired by the *Mail on Sunday*, which gleefully splashed the story and snatch picture under the headline 'GOTCHA KELVIN!'). When he returned, he told one associate that he was going back to both Murdoch and Jacqui and remarked, 'Well, at least they know all your faults. You don't have to hold in your tummy in front of them.'

After this distinctly odd period, Kelvin announced his move to Sky as managing director, and said goodbye to the staff of the *Sun* at a party in a City wine bar with a karaoke machine. Inevitably he launched into an imitation of Frank Sinatra singing 'My Way'. He jokingly announced that his job at Sky would be to 'out-boob the Beeb'.

There were mixed feelings about his departure. The secretaries, who called him 'Kellypops' and almost mothered him, reminding him to pay his bills and helping to buy his clothes, were sad to see him go and wondered what life would be like under his successor, Stuart 'Higgy' Higgins. The new editor was advertised as a 'safe pair of hands' after the turbulence of the MacKenzie years. Higgins, who many thought suffered from a charisma bypass, had risen through the ranks of the *Sun* newsdesk, weathering the constant bollockings. (At one point Kelvin, enraged by the way Higgins simply soaked up criticism and kept smiling, had made him pose in the paper as 'Higgy the Human Sponge', who could soak up any amount of abuse. Readers – the Folks! – were invited to 'let off steam' by phoning his direct line on the newsdesk and screaming at him, which they did in large numbers.)

And so Kelvin arrived in the alien world of television. According to the plan, he was supposed to leave journalism behind and become Sam Chisholm's warm-up act as the 'British face of Sky'. He was meant to take things easy, stay well away from Sky's day-to-day output, especially Sky News, learn about the business, eat a lot of expensive lunches with politicians and other bigwigs and get ready to move into the News Corp. boardroom. And to begin with that is what he did.

At this point Kelvin's knowledge of the television business, as he cheerfully confessed in one of his favourite phrases, 'would fit up a gnat's arse'. He later said that he knew less about the operation than the tea lady, because at least she knew her way round the building. At first he 'made all the right noises'. He asked people to explain how Sky worked, how decisions were made, where the power lay, carefully and respectfully listening to the answers and asking for more help and information. People told him it would take years to learn it all. He would reply in a friendly way that he was going to learn it all in six months.

Kelvin's normal way of operating in any media situation was dominated by sizing up the opposition, identifying their weaknesses and declaring all-out war on them. That was what he had done at the *Sun* where, every day of his thirteen-year editorship, a single thought had dominated his way of working: how can we smash the opposition? So it was natural enough for him to size up the opposition to Sky as his way of understanding how it worked. But Sky was different. Since Chisholm had pushed through the merger with BSB, Sky had had an effective monopoly in British pay television. He later told a journalist that so long as Sky had this monopoly running it was simplicity itself. There was no skill or intelligence involved: 'a black rat' could do it.

But in 1994, coinciding with Kelvin's arrival, Sky was starting to face the first stirrings of a serious competitive threat. It came from the cable companies, who, until then, had been completely under Sky's thumb, forced to distribute its channels over their systems on very unfavourable terms because there was no other saleable programming available.

All that looked as if it was about to change. The cable companies, especially the big ones able to draw on the vast funds of their American parent companies, were starting to demand a partnership with Sky. They still wanted to run Sky's channels, and were prepared to pay a good price. But so far Chisholm had been able to 'screw' them by threatening to withdraw supply of the channels if they did not pay fees which, basically, extracted every single penny out of them and left them with just about enough margin to stay in business.

At first the cable companies had tried to reason with Chisholm, pointing out that they had invested some £10 billion in creating a cable network which was ideal for distributing Sky's programming. Satellite dishes were a deeply inferior way of getting the programmes into people's homes. The dish itself was ugly and an embarrassment to the more middle-class type of punter, and its signal was nowhere near as good. Cable had far more bands, and so could carry a lot more channels. There was scope for growth. And it was fully interactive: you could have two-way services like home shopping without having to use the phone. In addition, interactivity meant you could introduce pay-per-view more easily and more quickly.

In short, Sky's dishes were a vulnerable and somewhat poxy technology. They fell apart within three to five years and needed replacing. There was the horror of 'churn': people not renewing their subscriptions when the dish went on the blink. The biggest technological weakness of all was the Astra satellite itself. Eventually, possibly within a few years, its orbit would start to decay. Murdoch might be able to pull strings to get media regulations changed, but not even he could arrange for the law of gravity to be repealed. In contrast, cable, once it was in the ground and 'punched' into people's homes, stayed there, like the connection to the gas or water supply. This was the way things were done in the United States, where Murdoch's operation concentrated on making the programmes and the cable people distributed them. They both shared the spoils evenly.

Chisholm listened to the cable people's pitch: Well, Sam, what about it? Come on. Be reasonable. Think of the long term. Give us a margin we can live with, and we will finish laying the cable network and win a lot more subscribers for Sky than you'll ever get with your dishes. What do you say?

Chisholm then thought about this carefully and told them, basically, to go and fuck themselves. They needed him. He did not need them. And as for the long term, well, in the *long term* we're all dead. Murdoch had gambled his entire future on Sky. Sky had established a monopoly because they had the balls to get into pay TV before anyone else. They were now fully entitled to the superprofits they were reaping. They were a just reward for risk-taking. Chisholm had gobbled up BSB and now he was going to crush the cable companies too.

The cable companies reacted in two ways. First they tried to force the government to investigate Sky's pricing policies and monopolistic practices. This did not get them very far, at least not at first. Murdoch's political contacts were impeccable and the power of his newspapers could be used to counter any direct legislative or regulatory threat. At the same time the cable companies started to develop cable-exclusive channels which they could run on their systems in competition with Sky, so that Chisholm's threat to withdraw supply of his channels was counter-acted – a bit.

At first the move into programme and channel production by the cable companies was very modest. TCI took over the 'channel-packaging' company Flextech and started to develop it, not so much to compete with Sky, but to provide leverage. Then there was Wire TV, the cable-exclusive general sport and entertainment channel set up with minuscule resources by the CPP-1 consortium.

This activity failed to make Chisholm take the cable people seriously. He headed off the threat by means of divide and rule. Chisholm offered to buy the new TCI-Flextech channels such as Bravo and The Children's

Channel and put them on satellite as Sky Multichannels, thus re-establishing his monopoly over programming and distribution.

Faced with Chisholm's continuing intransigence, the cable companies decided that they would have to make a direct attack on Sky's main business, the premium movie and, especially, sports channels. They would develop cable-exclusive rivals with huge budgets at their disposal to compete with Sky to buy 'hot sport' including, perhaps, even Premier League football itself.

In 1993 Wire TV had been divided into two parts. During the daytime it still ran as LiveWire, and consisted of very cheap programming. But the evening slot, from 7 p.m. onwards, was re-designated SportsWire. In January 1994 TCI, the leading member of the SportsWire consortium started to make large sums available to SportsWire so it could buy important sports rights, developing it into a serious competitor to Sky Sports.[6]

SportsWire's first move was to buy up World Cup cricket. TCI paid £7 million, which was well over the odds, and passed the cost on to the consortium. The effect of this was to advertise to the sports world that TCI was ready to spend. 'Leave Sky,' they were in effect saying, 'and come over to cable, and we will double or triple your money.' The loss of World Cup cricket to cable rattled some at Sky. It was evidence that the company was under full-scale attack. Money was no object. Whatever Sky could bid, TCI could easily outbid using funds provided by its US parent company which was bigger, even, than News Corp.

There was worse to come. A few weeks after the cricket deal, cable pulled off another coup, joining forces with the BBC in a deal to screen Wimbledon. The cricket and tennis would enable SportsWire to fill its own channel, planned for launch on 1 May 1994. Thus by the time the Premier

Live TV

League 'bidding-period' opened in June 1995, the cable companies would have a credible channel up and running, ready to carry the football.[7]

Everyone at Sky knew this threat had to be taken seriously. The question was: how should they react? Chisholm wanted to take a hard line, locking up all the sport in watertight contracts, paying whatever it took to buy the rights when they came up, or keep the ones they had – at any cost. There should be no concessions, no talks. As a result of Chisholm's actions the cable industry and Sky were heading towards a multi-million – maybe multi-*billion* – poker game over sports rights. They were on the threshold of what every person involved in pay TV anywhere in the world fears more than almost anything else: a bidding war.

From Mayfair to Massachusetts lights began shining in the beady eyes of the agents who sold the rights to screen sports. Sky (pocket depth: £4 billion) and TCI (pocket depth: £10 billion) were squaring up to fight each other to the last penny to secure the services of their clients. Any day now it was going to start *raining money*!

Chapter Ten

In which Kelvin is courted by the cable bosses and comes to fear a Bidding War and so decides to take a firm line when the Sports Agents turn up asking for more money, but then makes a Rather Serious Mistake over boxing, falls out with Sam Chisholm and leaves Sky TV

As chance would have it, Sam Chisholm was away in Hong Kong much of the time in early 1994, just when the cable companies were rolling their SportsWire nuclear missile on to the launchpad. It therefore largely fell to Kelvin MacKenzie to deal with the problem on the ground, just when he was starting to have arguments over the direction of Sky News. Frykberg, the news chief, was a Chisholm man to the core. The whole thing was getting out of control and heading for a big showdown.

Kelvin thought Chisholm was wrong. It was *madness* to take on the cable companies and risk a bidding war. Sam was still riding high on the merger with BSB – playing the Invincible Monopoly Monster, thinking he could *crush* the cable companies, just as he had crushed BSB two or three years earlier. *Wrong!* Kelvin, with fresh eyes, could see that Sky would have to cut a deal with the cable companies. Otherwise both sides would be sliced up by the Sports Agents, a gruesome lot as Kelvin knew from his dealings with them at the *Sun* – they had squeezed hundreds of thousands out of the papers by making them compete for things like exclusive interviews with 'hot' sports stars. If the Agents got two *pay-TV* operations fighting with each other, well . . . there would be only one winner: the Agents (*greedy fuckers!*).

And so Kelvin started to put out feelers to the cable companies. He wanted to form a united front against the Agents and, yeah, maybe look at the upside of co-operating and looking after each other's backs in the future. He started to return cable executives' phone calls. *Good sign!* Chisholm rarely did that. This turn of events was noticed at once in the cable industry. *There seems to be a change in direction at Sky. They seem to want to talk to us. Maybe they've seen the light!*

The cable companies started carefully courting Kelvin. A full-scale Lunch Offensive was organised. They found him highly receptive. They liked him. *Kelvin* wanted to do a deal. He wanted Sky and cable to go into the future hand in hand, working pay TV and making undreamt-of millions. A battle between Sky and the cable companies made no sense. There needed to be a new alliance, with both sides working together . . . and with Kelvin MacKenzie in charge of it all.

John Sheridan, the Canadian head of the Encom cable group, was *kinda lookin' forward* to seeing Kelvin MacKenzie, the British tabloid legend. A meeting had been arranged at a swanky Chelsea restaurant one evening in April 1994. Sheridan's car crept through the West End traffic and as he approached his destination he was amazed to find the place surrounded by gangs of hysterical teenage girls. *Hnnnnmp! Well whadthahell's goin' on here?*

Sheridan parked his car, cut a path through the crowds – *Muss be some kinda teenybopper sitooashun* – and negotiated his way past the ranks of security guards – *but it's s'post t'be morrova bizniz sitooashun* – ending up at Kelvin's table. The managing director of Sky Television was there, obviously *havin' fern* and lookin' *purdy neeet* but also *kinda ridiculous*, sitting next to the members of the pop group Take That. *Crazy Guy!*

Not much business was discussed that evening. It was more of an ice-breakin' *sitooashun*. Kelvin wanted to talk, and, Sheridan thought, he was not the first or only cable company boss Kelvin had been consulting. Kelvin was ... *kinda smart*. He was seeing all the big players and trying to come to terms, to ward off the evil of a Bidding War. Sheridan himself was a Big Player. His company, Encom, and the consortium he led ran the biggest cable operation in London, one of the most important in the UK and one with well-advertised expansion plans.

The Take That encounter was followed up by more friendly chats. Sky had to realise that the cable companies were serious, Sheridan thought. They had been fighting each other, so far. But they were *po-tenshul pardners* for the future. Cable was in the UK for the long haul. They were not there just to be – what? – well, to be screwed for short-term profit by Sam and Rupert. 'You guys haven't liked us in the past,' Sheridan told Kelvin at one of their meetings, 'but we're both gonna be around here in the *Yookay*. *We godda have a relashunship that kinda . . . works.*'

Kelvin appeared to agree. Sheridan could see Sky's argument that it had deserved a bigger return than the cable companies to begin with, because Murdoch had taken all the risks in getting pay-TV off the ground in a country which, frankly, seemed perfectly happy – for some strange reason – to be able to watch hours and hours of premium sport, movies and other expensive material for next to nothing on the BBC and ITV. True, Murdoch had broken the BBC–ITV monopoly and the punters were starting to cough up. But it no longer made commercial sense for Sky to push its business partners' business to the brink of extinction, or to make them revolt and bite back.

Again Kelvin appeared to get the point, and he listened

carefully. He was a *purdy smart guy*, Sheridan thought, not like Chisholm. The two men talked about many things: a better deal on programming for the cable companies; investment in each other's businesses; the direction of programming; whether to try to compete with the terrestrial channels in areas like *nooos* and *enner-tainment* as well as premium sports and movies.

And on the main point, Sheridan assured Kelvin that he had no intention of getting into any sort of 'bidding war' over rights to sports or other programmes. He was happy to leave the programming to Sky – unless Chisholm kept trying to screw the cable industry. That could end up in a *purdy serious sitooashun*.

Over the late spring and summer of 1994 Kelvin was also in contact with some of the top people at TCI. He became friendly with Adam Singer, head of TCI, Bruce Smith, the American TCI executive mainly in charge of sports rights, and Roger Luard, head of TCI's UK programming arm, Flextech. Kelvin hit it off with all of them, especially Luard who, like himself, was something of a wag.

The TCI boys took the same sort of line as Sheridan and Encom. But, coming from this quarter, there was more of an edge to it. TCI already had a *bit* of leverage against Sky as the suppliers of the channels for Sky Multichannels, one of Chisholm's most magnificent monopolistic marketing scams. More importantly, they were the main movers behind SportsWire, which was limbering up to make a direct competitive attack on Sky's all-important pay-TV sports monopoly. Also, TCI had a money pipeline to their headquarters in Denver and a lot of expertise in buying sports rights.

Could Kelvin persuade Sam to see sense? After all nobody wanted a *Bidding War*, did they? There would be *blood all over the carpet* if that happened. Time was running out. The bidding-period for Premier League rights was just about a year away. What was it to be? Competitive bids from SportsWire against Sky? Did Sky *really* want that? The football authorities were no longer the rank amateurs and suckers they had once been. Now they were *Utterly Ruthless TV-Rights-Mongers*. If the two pay-TV operations competed against each other, Rick Parry, the Premier League chief would *play them like violins*. He would go for a *billion* – and *get it*!

But, if Sam could just be *talked round*, if he could be *Made to Face the New Reality*, TCI would stand to one side, cheer on Sky from the sidelines, and block any competitor from going on cable. Sky would get the rights at a *reasonable* price and then produce and provide Sky Sports to the cable operators *at a price they were comfortable with*. That way *we get richer* and *you stay rich* and *everybody's a winner*.

As the cable companies saw it, Kelvin was persuaded. There needed to be a Change of Direction at Sky. Really, the idea of cable versus satellite was last year's game. What was needed was Big Boys (TCI and Sky especially) against Little Guys. The chances of hanging on to an absolute monopoly for good were zero. It had been good while it lasted, and Murdoch had been more than handsomely rewarded for his original investment and risk-taking. The choice for Sky was now this: do a deal with the Big Cable Companies, and form a sort of joint operation with them, or else have the Big and Small cable companies (together with the *Mirror* and the *Daily Mail* and the Office of Fair Trading and the Labour Party and God knows who else) gang up on Sky in a huge Anti-Murdoch crusade. Did Sam *really* want that? Did *Rupert* really want that? And a *Bidding War* as well? Did he? Because that was what Sam was risking.

After his early fact-finding talks with the cable people,

Kelvin's demeanour at Sky changed remarkably. The humility of his 'fact-finding' and 'listening' phase evaporated. Within just a few weeks the meek Kelvin MacKenzie who liked and respected Sam Chisholm, and who had come to sit at his feet and learn How Sky Worked, was replaced by the more familiar figure of Kelvin MacFrenzie – super-confident, aggressive, and utterly convinced of the correctness of his views. He began swaggering about denouncing his new television colleagues to the newspapers as a 'bunch of parasitical pansies', and started to pick fights with Chisholm and his supporters inside the organisation.

That did not go down too well, especially as it coincided with MacKenzie's recruitment of Richard Littlejohn, an old pal and former *Sun* columnist, to Sky as a nightly chat-show host. Littlejohn's budget was huge in Sky News terms – it was put by one source at Sky at £2 million – and his salary was in the region of £400,000, which was reckoned to be an insane sum of money to pay a man who, while clearly an extremely talented broadcaster, had no previous television experience and no existing audience that might follow him to the channel.

After SportsWire's success in getting World Cup Cricket and Wimbledon, the first major potential confrontation between Sky and the cable companies came in July over the rights Sky already held to screen boxing matches featuring Lennox Lewis.[1] In March 1994 Lewis had defeated the American fighter Phil Jackson in a bout screened on Sky TV. He was lined up to fight a much-hyped 'grudge match' with Riddick Bowe later in the year. If he won the Bowe fight, as then seemed possible, Lewis would be in line to fight Mike Tyson, with the world heavyweight championship at stake. Better than this, the anticipated Lewis vs. Tyson fight would be ideal for the launch of pay-per-view if, as seemed likely, the technology was ready by then.

Picking up on the rumours that a bidding war was about to break out, Lennox Lewis's specialist TV-rights agent, Chester English, phoned Kelvin to see if he would pay more money to keep him from defecting to SportsWire. English was surprised by Kelvin's reaction: instead of discussing more money, he replied by demanding a cut of 20 per cent on what Sky had already agreed to pay under the terms of Lewis's 1992 contract. He seemed confident that SportsWire would not outbid anything that Sky was offering.

Frank Maloney, Lewis's main agent, phoned Kelvin to find out what was going on. He found him to be extremely combative and confident. Kelvin aggressively repeated his demand for the 20 per cent cut and added, 'If you can get somebody else to pay you more than that, you can fucking well go to them.' Maloney, scandalised, said he and Chester English would do just that. Kelvin then sent Maloney a letter, again repeating his demand for a 20 per cent cut in Sky's fees and enclosing an article from the London *Evening Standard* which said that Lewis was overrated. A couple of paragraphs which claimed that Lewis was not even British were circled with a crude scrawl. 'I agree with this,' Kelvin had scribbled in the margin, yet again repeating his demand that Maloney should accept less money if he wanted Lewis to stay with Sky.

After this Maloney and English decided that Sky had folded the contract, leaving them free to go to SportsWire. English phoned the Denver headquarters of TCI, the main financial backers of SportsWire, and secured an offer of about £5 million for four forthcoming fights, including the Riddick Bowe bout and the putative megamatch with Tyson. After this Maloney again phoned Kelvin to warn him that he was ready to take Lewis to Wire unless Sky honoured or improved the existing contract. Kelvin told him to 'stick your contract up your arse'.

Maloney and English therefore signed Lewis to SportsWire, whose executives were delighted. They had been sizing up Lewis for a while and were prepared to pay more than Sky for his services. The problem had been that so long as Lewis was contracted to Sky they could not get him at any price. Now that Sky had folded the contract, he was theirs.

Lewis's first fight against Riddick Bowe was hyped hugely by SportsWire and the cable TV companies, which now started selling considerable numbers of subscriptions, gaining momentum for the anticipated showdown with Sky over the Premier League. But even this was not the end of Kelvin's dealings in boxing rights. His loss of Lewis was regarded by many at the time as a costly mistake, but his signing up of the fading boxer Chris Eubank looked like madness. Kelvin had agreed to pay £10 million for eight Eubank fights. Almost everyone in the boxing world was amazed by this switch round. It was likened to trading Premier League football for Scottish League Division One.[2]

Sam Chisholm, returning from setting up Murdoch's Star channel in Hong Kong, came to London, surveyed the wreckage and went berserk. There was an enormous row between Kelvin and Chisholm at a board meeting and both men turned to Murdoch for backing. Murdoch shared Chisholm's 'hawkish' views on dealing with the cable companies, and chose to back him.

After this Kelvin realised that he would never now become 'King of Sky' and that his rise in News Corp. was blocked. This meant a bleak future. So he walked away from Sky, saying that he no longer liked the people there and that he could stand it no more. He later told a journalist that while he was at Sky he was 'learning about television' and that he left because 'I did not wish to continue working with somebody there so I chose not to work with them. I didn't take a pay-off. And that was that.' The fact that he took no pay-off meant he was free to move anywhere else he liked.

More perplexing was the fact that his departure involved the voluntary surrender of an extremely valuable Sky share option. After Sky's flotation in December 1994 the value of these shares, he later (on the brink of tears) told associates at the Mirror Group, where he was then working, would have earned him a cool £1 million. Some of those associates remember his horror in December and January 1994, when he would look at the Sky share price and wince with pain every time the price moved up again, working out on the back of an envelope how much more he had lost and cursing his own hot-headedness in resigning after his rows with Chisholm and others.

Still, once set free from Sky, Kelvin found that he had plenty of admirers and potential employers in the cable television industry. Shortly after this he wound up at Mirror Television, at the same time working closely with the SportsWire people, preparing to re-launch the channel as the Cable Sports Network: a full blown competitor for Sky, complete with a workable plan to buy the Premier League rights.

Chapter Eleven

In which Monty worries about his Share Price but finally realises his Dream by launching a version of his City TV idea which is to be called L!ve TV and at the same time puts the Mirror *at the disposal of the cable companies to promote cable subscriptions as part of a Somewhat Convoluted plan to capture the Premier League football rights from Sky with a series of arrangements which are Very Crafty and bear the hallmark of His Sneakiness, and is then joined at the* Mirror *by Kelvin*

David Montgomery is sitting on a small stage flanked by Mirror Group Newspapers chairman Sir Robert Clarke, managing director Charlie Wilson and other elegantly besuited executives and moneymen. It is April 1994, the end of Monty's second full year in control of the *Mirror*. He has just reported that, since his arrival, there has been a surge in profits, mainly the result of sacking 600 people, combined with the much cheaper accommodation now occupied in Canary Wharf and the fortuitous repayment of £30 million of previously missing Maxwell pension money. He is looking pretty pleased with himself. 'If it is in order, *Moister Churmoyn* [Mister Chairman], we will now take questions from, erm, the, er, the *flerrrr*.'

An old lady, who has looked agitated throughout the proceeding, shoots up her hand. Her name is Ester Allen. She explains that she is 70 years old and had been a munitions worker during the war. She proudly announces that she has been a *Mirror* shareholder all her life and that she is to appear in the paper's forthcoming edition commemorating the fiftieth anniversary of D-Day.

Mrs Allen at last comes to the point. 'What I would like to know is why it is that the price of my shares sometimes goes up, and at other times they go down. Nobody seems to know why. Perhaps the chairman could explain that, please.'

Stunned silence. The ranks of professional share tipsters (known as analysts) and institutional investors who, with their advice and decisions, control the process which so mystifies Mrs Allen, titter.

Clarke leans over to the microphone and, as sympathetically as possible, explains, 'Well, the price usually goes *up* when there are more buyers than there are sellers. Then, erm, the share price will tend to go *down* – and we hope this won't happen too often, ha, ha – if there are more sellers than buyers.' There is more smirking as he adds, 'But I confess it is really more of an art than a science. Erm, does that answer your question?'

Mrs Allen seems satisfied, but asks, 'Well, then, can you tell if more people *are* going to buy shares, then, because if they are I would like to buy some more if you are saying that means the price is going to go up.'

That brings the house down. Sir Robert cuts through the mirth, casting nervous glances at the assembled analysts and tipsters: 'We certainly hope so, Mrs Allen, ha, ha, ha. Yes, we *certainly*, erm, hope so.'

Sir Robert had more reason than most board chairmen to hope that the company's share price would go up. He had been put in place on the board by the banks, which had turned the huge debts Robert Maxwell had left them with into shares. These were fairly worthless when Monty took over. Now, two years later, the shares as a block were on track to reach the magic valuation of £200 million. At that point, if they so wished, the banks could sell the shares and at last get their money back.

Monty had a special interest in the share price as well. When he was appointed he had been given the right to buy

Mirror Group shares at the low price of 61p each as part of his salary package (this was in addition to his chief executive's salary of £350,000). He was already starting to dip into this share option whenever the price moved up a bit, earning him up to £500,000 a year on top of his wages.

During Monty's first couple of years at the *Mirror*, the all-important analysts and serious financial journalists had been generally supportive. The company could only recover after the ravages of the Maxwell era and Monty had clear and well-advertised plans to cut costs and boost profits. But now the analysts were starting to have their doubts.

Cost-cutting was a one-off, like the 'windfall' of the returned pension money. There was no future in popular newspapers, it was reckoned. Between them the *Sun* and the *Mirror* had lost – what? – a *million* readers over a decade. The next wave of profits, needed to keep the share price moving up (or, more to the point, stop it slipping back down again), could only come from expansion into other areas. In response to this pressure Monty had recently bought the troubled *Independent* and was taking an axe to it. That was good news. But the *Indie* was still a loss-maker.

Moreover, since the shock and rapid sackings associated with Monty's arrival in 1992, there had been further ructions at the group. In March 1993 Lord Hollick, the man who had brought Monty to the Mirror Group, resigned from the board. He had been unhappy since the beginning of the year about Monty's habit of keeping things secret from the board, but had waited a while to see if any notice was taken of his criticism. In his resignation statement he said, 'I have for several months voiced my concerns about a number of governance and policy matters which I believe to be important to the long-term commercial and editorial success of Mirror Group Newspapers. Unfortunately it has not been possible to resolve these matters and I have therefore tendered my resignation. I wish MGN every success.'

What the Mirror Group really needed to do was to follow Rupert Murdoch's example and make a move into television. BSkyB had made a huge loss at first but now, just a few short years later, Sky was approaching a stock-market flotation which would value it at £4 billion. Once the stock markets got a bee in their bonnet that a certain type of share was likely to go up in price (*sexy! hot!*), every-one in the sector tended to benefit. So if Monty could arrange a similar move into television his share price might ride on Murdoch's coat-tails as the dealers piled in (*synergy! fit!*). If not, if the *Mirror* missed the bus . . . Oh dear, Mrs Allen: *sell! sell! sell!*

Fortunately Monty's long-term ambition to move into television was about to come to fruition. He had been talk-ing to the cable companies and they were about to sell (in fact virtually 'give') him a ready-made channel, Wire TV, which was already being transmitted over the country's cable networks. With a bit more investment and the estab-lishment of local affiliates, Wire could easily be turned into L!ve TV, a British version of Fox, according to plan. Janet Street-Porter, then still at the BBC, was ready to join the new network, to set up its 'distinctive' national 'spine'.

In addition, Monty had hired Nick Ferrari, who had lately been running the news operation at Fox TV itself in New York. He had also signed up Terry Lee, a specialist in the technical side of cheap, rolling television production, who had recently been involved in setting up Associated's Channel One in London. The final key member of the team was Richard Horwood, managing director of Mirror Television. He was an expert in mergers and buy-outs, which was just the sort of background needed for L!ve. Mirror TV was planning to develop its local 'affiliates' as joint ventures with local newspaper groups such as the *Birmingham Post*. MGN would either buy these groups or set up joint holding companies with them. Horwood's experience would be invaluable.

A deal was worked out. Monty agreed to pay a nominal £1 million for Wire TV. Its main asset was the channel's national subscription agreement with the cable distributors which Mirror TV, as the new owner, would inherit. This involved the participating CPP-1 cable companies (who between them accounted for about 95 per cent of the national cable network) paying 25p per month for every subscriber they signed up. This deal would provide Mirror TV with an income of about £3 million a year to begin with. But income was set to rise sharply as the network of cable subscribers spread. By the year 2000, if independent predictions of cable growth proved correct, all those extra 25p subscriptions would add up to £15 million a year.

The cable companies were using what they called a 'warm-puppy strategy'. This meant getting people to connect the wire to their homes fairly cheaply, a bit like buying a cute puppy for Christmas. The beast would then grow and grow, meaning that subscribers would buy more and more premium-rate movie and sports channels pay-per-view services and the like, until it was a monster which devoured all their disposable income. But in 1994 the puppy was still *very* small.[1]

The *Mirror* reckoned that if it started putting out L!ve TV in 1995, it would make a total loss of £30 million over four years as the cost of making the channel outstripped subscription income. By 1999 subscriptions would have grown and profits and advertising revenue would start rolling in. By the year 2003, if all went according to plan, the debts accumulated in the early years would have been paid off and L!ve TV, if it could keep its costs under control and the cable companies agreed to keep distributing it, would become a licence to print money. In return for this remarkably generous deal, the *Mirror* would promote subscriptions to the whole cable system, thus providing the necessary promotional counterweight to Sky.[2]

In the summer of 1994 there was every sign that the number of people subscribing to cable, as opposed to buying a Sky dish, would, after a slow start, begin to increase dramatically. This was mainly because the cable companies were starting to develop their own cable-exclusive sports channel to run alongside L!ve TV and compete with Sky, where Kelvin MacKenzie was still managing director.

The figures used by Mirror TV to work out the budget for L!ve TV were based on the assumption that cable subscriptions would more than triple between 1994 and 1997 to reach a total of 4 million, and then move forward again in 1997 to 5.3 million in 1998 before starting to level off. All predictions for cable growth were over-optimistic in the early 1990s, but the figures Mirror TV was using were about double the average of independent analysts at the time. According to those around at the time, the reason for this optimism was that Mirror and TCI felt certain that they were going to get the Premier League on to SportsWire, or get Sky to provide the Premier League coverage to cable on better terms. If that happened the 3 million or so dish-owners who bought Sky solely or mainly to watch football would switch to cable overnight and this would account for the leap from 1 million to 4 million subscribers which was contained in Mirror TV's business plans.[3]

Furthermore the Mirror Group was so certain that the

L!ve TV

Premier League would be captured from Sky that, as part of the purchase of Wire TV, they agreed to give the cable companies subscribing to L!ve TV a 'subscription holiday' from June 1995 until September 1996, when the first Premier League matches were due to be shown. Even the launch date of L!ve TV was tied into the football deal, although the reason was highly technical. SportsWire had to be up and running as a channel in its own right before the Premier League bidding-period began in June 1995, in order to show the football authorities that it worked in technical terms and was just as good as Sky. This meant moving the existing evening-only SportsWire service off the general Wire channel and on to its own 24-hour channel, leaving a huge gap in the evening. This was where the Mirror Group came in. It would replace Wire with its 24-hour L!ve TV service.[4]

The deal between Monty and the cable companies to transform Wire into L!ve TV as a means of securing the all-important promotional support of the *Mirror* and its sister papers for SportsWire was concluded in the summer of 1994, just as Kelvin MacKenzie was manoeuvring his way out of Sky amid talk of personality clashes.

Then, after a few weeks, Kelvin turned up at the Mirror Group where, to general astonishment, it was announced at the start of October 1994 that he was taking over from Richard Horwood as managing director of Mirror Television and would be working with Janet Street-Porter on the launch of L!ve TV, as well as developing a *Mirror*-backed cable sports channel.

After the shock of his move to Sky TV in January 1994, his arrival at the *Mirror* was the second Kelvin 'bombshell' in a year.[5]

Chapter Twelve

In which Kelvin receives an offer of £36 as a fair-minded valuation of the worth of his reputation but turns down the cash, becomes the Great Marketing Genius of the cable industry, shows off Kevin Keegan to some unimpressed Americans, tries to persuade the Cable People to give him a Great Pile of Wonga to launch his very own Sports Channel but is frustrated by yet more Machinations of cable politics, and warns the General Public to expect some Big Surprises

'Do you know who you are talking to? I'll tell you who you're talking to! . . . I'll tell you who I am . . . You want to know who I am? . . . I'm The Million-Pound Libel Lawyer!'

The cultured voice of Frank Presland, the feared libel lawyer who helped Elton John win £1 million from Kelvin MacKenzie's *Sun*, is booming across the editorial office of *Business Age* magazine from a speakerphone. He is starting to lose his customary cool and reserve. The assembled hacks crack up, but quickly control themselves. They are trying to keep him on the phone for as long as they can, and annoy him as much as possible.

In September 1994 *Business Age* had run an article saying that Kelvin had been sacked from Sky TV because of the way he had handled the purchase of rights to screen boxing matches featuring Chris Eubank. Kelvin was insisting he had not been sacked but had resigned. He said he had heard about the *Business Age* article while he was playing golf. His golfing partners had teased him about it – thus proving that irreparable damage had been done to his reputation. He had turned to Presland.

Business Age had refused to take Kelvin's action seriously. Presland nevertheless invited them to his office and asked them how much they were prepared to pay to compensate the former *Sun* editor for the hurt and damage they had done to him. Anil Bhoyrul, who wrote the article, and *Business Age*'s editor, Tom Rubython, turned out their pockets, counted up their money and plonked £36 on the table. 'Will that do?' they asked.

Presland was not amused. They should go away, think about it and make a better offer. And so, a few days later, they were back on the phone. The *Business Age* team had upped their offer – from £36 to £36 *plus* the guarantee that they would put a picture of Kelvin on the front cover of their magazine, showing him walking his dog, so that people would see how nice he was. 'I will put that to my client,' Presland had said. But the offer was rejected. *Business Age* then countered by offering to cut the grass in Kelvin's garden.[1]

This behaviour, known in technical legal language as a 'wind-up', continued for some time. Each call made a substantial addition to Kelvin's legal costs. At one point *Business Age* upped the ante by counter-suing Presland for slander. The case lumbered towards a court hearing, with the *Business Age* and other hacks licking their lips at the prospect of Kelvin paying hundreds of thousands in legal fees for the privilege of being grilled in the High Court in the Strand day after day. *Business Age* was defending itself without lawyers and therefore had much smaller costs. The magazine was ready to drag the case out as long as possible. It started issuing subpoenas to all sorts of people, including Rupert Murdoch, thus adding to the costs (which are normally paid by whoever loses the case in the end).

On the Friday before the case was due to be heard in

court, *Business Age* was approached by Kelvin's lawyer, George Carman, who told them that his client was ready to settle to avoid going to court. 'Look, boys,' he said, 'we don't want a big media circus here. Why don't you give us £30,000 and we'll shake hands.' The *Business Age* hacks were now involved in the familiar game of libel poker. They could pay the £30,000 to get rid of the case or, even though they were sure their story could be justified, take a chance that a rogue jury might whack them for a million after a trial. The equation for Kelvin was similar. If he lost he would have to pay the costs of the trial, which would be enormous. The hacks held their nerve.

By 12 noon Carman had dropped his asking price to £10,000. Still the *Business Age* team did not bend. By Friday mid-afternoon, with only minutes left, Carman said it was all over. Instead of *Business Age* paying, Carman was offering £10,000 to compensate the magazine for its legal costs if it (a) withdrew the allegation that Kelvin had been sacked and (b) drafted an apology to be read out in court. *Business Age* agreed to apologise but haggled the sum Kelvin's side was required to pay up to £50,000.

MacKenzie turned up at court on the Monday expecting to meet the World's Media on the steps of the court and triumphantly read out the apology. But there was hardly anyone there. *Business Age* had arranged for the settlement of the case to be reported in the Sunday papers and it was not a story any more. Kelvin struck a lonely and bemused figure on the steps of the High Court. Later on *Business Age* splashed £5,000 of the £50,000 settlement money on a riotous 'thank you, Kelvin' party. But *Business Age* had got it wrong. Kelvin had resigned from Sky before moving over into cable TV with the Mirror Group. He had not been sacked.

* * *

Kelvin's arrival at the Mirror Group as managing director of Mirror Television in October 1994 came as a complete surprise to almost everyone in the organisation, including Richard Horwood, the managing director whom Kelvin was replacing. Naturally enough, Horwood was reported to have been 'disappointed' by the move.[2]

The whole thing, on the face of it, was a puzzle. Kelvin had never expressed anything but hatred and contempt for the *Mirror* and everything it stood for. Monty had sworn to the *Mirror* board that he would not steer the Mirror Group's papers in the direction of circulation-boosting 'sleaze'. Yet MacKenzie was a tabloid sleaze merchant if ever there was one. Monty had assured the board that the group's papers would remain loyal to Labour. Yet here was a man who loathed Labour and whose proudest claim was that his paper, the *Sun*, had won the 1992 election for the Conservatives.[3]

MacKenzie was being hired to head the Mirror Group's TV activities, yet his track record in television amounted to six unhappy months at Sky, littered with incidents like the loss of the Lennox Lewis boxing rights and the arguments over Sky News. With a television CV like that, MacKenzie might have thought himself lucky to get a job running a local cable station in Siberia. Yet at the Mirror Group he was to be given a starting salary of around £250,000 a year (which was to increase steadily until it reportedly reached about £400,000 a year), a seat on the Mirror Group board and responsibility for the group's television activities which, Monty thought, were the key to its future, even its survival.

As managing director of Mirror Television, Kelvin would outrank Janet – whom Monty had spent years trying to recruit to his television ventures – and his sudden arrival as her boss, when to Janet the whole attraction of the

Mirror Group job was that she would at last be her own boss, was bound to cause problems. A personality clash seemed inevitable, and that might threaten the stability of the whole operation.

But he did have his admirers. After Kelvin left Sky he was in contact with his new cable friends almost immediately. He had failed to become king of the hill at Sky, but he clearly thought he might still be able to become King of Cable. He thought that the mainly American executives who ran the UK cable operations understood little about British public taste and, divided among themselves, had failed lamentably to market cable effectively or to capitalise on Sky's weaknesses. He accused them of giving up in the face of Sky's dominance and spending all their time on the golf course, working on their handicaps, before returning to the States to be demoted. There was huge potential, he thought, especially in the area of sport.

Kelvin considered taking a job with the leading cable company (and main mover behind Sportswire) TCI and he visited TCI's international headquarters in Denver, Colorado, several times. He also apparently considered going to work for Flextech, TCI's main programme- and channel-making company in the UK. He was already friendly with Adam Singer and with Bruce Smith, the American TCI (and TCI subsidiary TeleWest) executive who had bought the Lennox Lewis boxing matches when Kelvin tore up Sky's contract with Lewis. And he was on very close terms with Roger Luard, the colourful head of Flextech.[4]

Kelvin was popular with the cable companies' executives for two main reasons. First, many of them had watched his career since his days at the *Sun* and regarded him as a marketing genius. The way he had promoted Sky with the *Sun* was a major reason why dishes had taken off and cable had stalled. The cable companies had put tremendous effort and large sums of money into building up SportsWire during 1994 and were seriously contemplating a bid for Premier League football the following year. But none of this would be much good without the kind of promotional support which the cable companies believed Kelvin could organise for them. Second, and just as important for some, his time at Sky meant that he had learned a lot about the pay-TV business in general and had gained this experience at Sky, the market leader.[5]

So Monty took him on as managing director of Mirror Television. This was a neat arrangement, which seemed to suit all concerned. Kelvin could become a major figure in cable programming and the *Mirror* would provide the perfect platform for his marketing skills. Kelvin himself would cement the relationship between the Mirror Group and the cable companies, which Monty was desperate to develop so that he, at last, had some form of distribution for his television ambitions. It would mean Kelvin working with Monty in a theoretically subordinate position (which was humiliating), but the importance of the cable connection would give him a lot of power in the Mirror Group boardroom.[6]

And so Kelvin's appointment was announced to the world. His first major move was to convene a meeting of all the cable companies to unveil a masterplan for joint national marketing of cable. The cable executives, eager to meet the towering marketing genius Adam Singer had told them all about, waited with baited breath. After a few preliminaries Kelvin pulled back the ceremonial curtain, so to speak, and revealed the slogan that would save them all:

GET SMART! GET CABLE!

He then asked for a modest £30 million, in return for which the *Mirror* would organise national publicity around this theme. The cable operators turned him down, eventually deciding to waste a smaller sum on a series of adverts featuring Dawn French which, in the opinion of most people, merely succeeded in making everyone even more confused about cable TV than before.

At the same time Kelvin started negotiations to make the Mirror Group a part-owner of SportsWire (the idea being to change its name to the snappier CSN – Cable Sports Network) in addition to its ownership of L!ve TV. This would entitle the Group to a one-fifth share of subscriptions to CSN, which would be worth a fortune if it managed to get the Premier League in the bag. Negotiations and arguments over how much control, or size of stake, the Mirror Group would have continued for some months.[7]

Kelvin moved into supersalesman mode, drawing up detailed dummy sports pages of the *Mirror* with mocked-up headlines and graphics saying things like 'ARSENAL vs. MANCHESTER UNITED: TONIGHT ONLY ON CABLE TV' and showing them to people in the cable industry. Armed with this, he tried to get the companies to give the Mirror Group upwards of £500 million so that he could buy the rights to the Premier League for a Mirror-owned football channel to be available on cable.

To this end he called a special meeting of the CPP-1 shareholders – the consortium of cable companies which owned SportsWire/CSN – ending up with a presentation at a hall in Camden (giant stretch limos were arranged for the cable chiefs). Baffled American executives, who did not know the first thing about 'soccer', as they called it, were treated to a surprise visit, complete with fanfares and glitz, from Kevin Keegan (*Who is this guy?*) before Kelvin revealed his latest brainwave. The Mirror-led Premier League channel would go out under the title of . . . GOAL!

But they didn't buy it. Confusion in American minds was intensified by a rival bid presented in more modest fashion by the executives from the now defunct Wire TV who thought that it was too ambitious to go for the Premier League in competition with Sky. They reckoned the cable companies should settle for the Endsleigh League, buying it up and calling it the Cable League. But all this was soon to become academic. Over at Sky, Chisholm was alarmed. SportsWire/CSN, which he had at first contemptuously dismissed as a 'minor nuisance' had built up a head of steam and looked like becoming a serious competitor for Sky Sports.[8] It was unlikely that they would be able to grab the Premier League, as Kelvin dearly wanted to do, but they could, at the very least, mount a serious counter-bid and push the cost through the roof. As figures in the cable industry later put it, he 'put out a white flag'. Nobody wanted a bidding war – 'a bloodbath' – which would benefit only the football clubs, which were already awash with cash.

Chisholm contacted Murdoch and obtained permission to strike a deal with some of the cable companies (which was ironic because that was what Kelvin had wanted to do the previous year). If they allowed him a free run at the Premier League bid, so that the football remained on Sky Sport, he would supply the channel to them wholesale – together with other premium channels like Sky Movies – at a reduced rate. The cable operators could then sell Sky Sport, and Sky Movies, to their subscribers at a good profit.

The deal was worked out by Chisholm and Adam Singer in London, very much along the lines that Kelvin had been after, and was then approved in the US by Murdoch and by John Malone, the head of TCI. In the end there were few problems. Murdoch was used to co-operating in a very similar way in the much larger and more important American market. TCI and its TeleWest subsidiary (and one other CPP-1 member, Nynex) promised not to carry any competitor channels to Sky (either sport or movies) over their cable networks, by far the largest in the UK. SportsWire/CSN became a dead duck overnight. A cable-exclusive movie channel being developed under the title of Home Box Office suffered the same fate.

This was a relief for Chisholm, but the cost to Sky was vast. The reduced rates for supply would cost Sky hundreds of millions over the ten-year period of the agreement. At the same time, Chisholm lost the powerful threat of withdrawing Sky's premium channels at short notice if the cable companies did not agree to his terms. This threat had always terrified the cable channels, who, basically, had nothing of any real value to sell – apart from Sky's premium channels. Now the threat was lifted and they could sleep again at night.

Singer emerged from the negotiations covered in glory in his own circle, but hated by many of the other cable companies, whose executives claimed they had been led up an expensive garden path and then stabbed in the back. He and others in the TCI orbit explained that they had never wanted to run a competitive sports channel, if it could be avoided. The whole thing had worked as a feint, a clever diversion in the tussle between cable and Sky, organised 'to get Sam Chisholm's attention' and to make him reduce his 'crippling' prices and moderate his 'draconian' behaviour. The £20 million TCI had invested in sports programming was written off and some rights owned by the channel, such as World Cup cricket, were sold back to Sky at a massive discount (TCI had paid £7 million for the cricket; it now sold the rights on to Sky for around £1 million). The battle had gone right to the wire. The 'sweetheart deal' was signed with just days to go before the year-long bidding-period for Premier League rights opened in June 1995.

The rise and fall of Wire TV – its division into SportsWire and LiveWire, of which the latter was sold cheaply to the *Mirror* as the basis for L!ve TV, and the destruction of SportsWire once it had served TCI's purposes – left a trail of recrimination and bitterness in its wake.[9] With the exception of Nynex (the second biggest cable operator in the UK) the other members of the CPP-1 consortium which had owned Wire were not party to the new 'sweetheart deal' and were therefore left high and dry, at a deep disadvantage to TCI with its cheaply obtained Sky programming. There was a flurry of legal activity and complaints to the Office of Fair Trading accompanied by furious denunciations and counter-denunciations in the trade press.

'Watch out,' Kelvin had warned in a statement marking his arrival at Mirror TV in October 1994, 'this company is into cable in a big way. Be prepared for some huge surprises.'

But now the Mirror Group would have to scale down its ambitions, for the time being at least. By now the Mirror-led bid to run Channel 5 had been aborted for technical and financial reasons, so all the Group had left was the L!ve TV cable channel, the national 'spine' of Monty's original city TV idea worked up with Janet Street-Porter.

PART II

THE LAUNCH OF L!VE TV

Chapter Thirteen

In which Janet is reunited with her Implementers, who advise on how to use a Chicken to get the best out of her, and meets Nick Ferrari of Piranha Fish fame, before getting down to the nitty-gritty with the customary Screamin' an' Shahtin', deciding to push the Infobar to greater excesses, and succinctly articulates the Whole Concept of L!ve TV with great clarity as

'!'

'The thing about Janet – how can I put this? – the thing is . . .' A former colleague of Janet Street-Porter, now installed at L!ve TV, is giving an informal briefing on the subject of How to Get On With Janet.

'Well, really, the best thing, to be perfectly honest, is to lock her up on her own in a room for three days, throw her the odd chicken to keep her alive, and get her to pass her programme ideas out under the door.' Her ideas were *fantastic* when they came good, the sage explained. 'But she does need her *implementers*. What you need to do with her, to get the best out of her, really, is to make sure she's surrounded by *good people* – people she trusts – so they can pick up on her ideas and run with them. Then she's *great*. No really, *Really Fantastic*. But otherwise, well – *ha!* – you could just run into a few problems.'

L!ve TV was now under way and to make it all happen Janet brought in Rachel – *Raych* – Purnell, one of her key *implementers* at the BBC, to fill the key post of director of programmes. Their relationship went back the best part of a decade. Soon after Janet's arrival at the BBC, Rachel, then a producer on *Open Air*, a daytime programme, had been called into a committee meeting to discuss progress on *Def-II*. She had been full of trepidation. Janet struck her as an amazingly fashionable and ferocious character, and she was a bit scared of meeting her.

The meeting started and Janet turned to Rachel and asked her if she wanted to run the *Rough Guide* series, an *innervitiff* travel programme which would involve the drudgery of people flying around the globe on expense accounts, swanning *abaht* in the most exciting and romantic locations in the world, meeting any *interestin'* local *slebs* [celebs], trying out the bars, restaurants, beaches and other attractions, and then flying back again to pick up a big salary cheque. Dirty work, but somebody had to do it. Was Rachel int'rested, at all? Rachel gulped. Well, yes she was, really. The appointment was made, and the two women hit it off.

Rachel turned out to be adept at handling Janet and putting up with her frequent tantrums. She kept calm in crises and was especially good at handling the personal side of Janet's professional life,[1] which enabled her to explain away and smooth over her boss's phenomenal rudeness towards other members of the production team. What generally happened was that Janet came up with nutty ideas and Rachel explained why they wouldn't work. There would then be a lot of *screamin' an' shahtin'* before a compromise was reached and the operation moved forward.

Rachel's relationship with Janet had had its ups and downs over the years, but she always remained fiercely loyal, and deeply grateful for the way in which Janet had provided her and others with their big break in television. So when Janet phoned her with the offer of a job at L!ve TV she was happy to come along and help out. At first

Janet had suggested that Rachel should be head of features, working under Nick Ferrari, a former *Sun* and Sky News hack who was the Mirror Group's resident TV production expert before Janet arrived. But after a bit of wrangling it was agreed that Purnell and Ferrari would be placed on an equal level in the power structure, as co-directors of programming.

Nick Ferrari had started out in national newspaper journalism on the *Sunday Mirror*, where he met and married Sally. Nick then joined the *Sun* as a cherubic young reporter on Bizarre, the showbiz section. He had the advantage of being the son of Dan Ferrari, who was the founder of a news reporting agency in south-east London and, as it happened, one of the few men in British journalism whom both Kelvin and Murdoch liked and respected.

Young Nick turned out to be a wily operator. Despite his tender years he started dishing it with the best of them, becoming a hero in Kelvin's eyes by managing to get himself beaten up by Elton John's security guard during the star's 1984 wedding in Australia. The *Sun* had reported the nuptials under the headline 'GOOD ON YER, POOFTER!'. The next day Ferrari gleefully reported that, after reading this, the guard had yanked him out of his chair, ripped his shirt, dragged him across a hotel lobby, hit him in the face and slammed his head against a lift door.

Ferrari was soon mentioned in dispatches again, this time for putting one over on John Blake, the original editor of Bizarre, who had since defected to the *Mirror*. Blake was planning a big exclusive interview with the toothsome '80s pop sensation Bucks Fizz, who had come to grief in a coach smash. This was a big story, and all the papers wanted an interview. The group were recuperating in Mauritius and they invited Blake, in conditions of great secrecy, to fly out and interview them. There was a twist. In return Blake had to agree to be filmed asking his questions, hamming it up a bit so that the material could be used in the group's latest video.

Blake turned up as planned and was being filmed doing his interview sitting next to a swimming-pool in the middle of a lagoon when, suddenly, the production was halted by a voice screaming, 'Oi, Blakey! Oi! Over here!' It was Nick Ferrari. He had hired a canoe and paddled it across the lagoon. 'Oi! Blakey, I've got *every word*!' Nick shook with laughter and nearly fell into the sea as he waved about his rifle microphone and recording gear. Having made his point, he paddled away again at top speed.

The action then moved to the hotel, where there was a brawl as Blake tried to get hold of the tape. To cap it all, Neil 'Wolfman' Wallis, then of the *Daily Star*, turned up, making a three-way scrap. Nick took a particular dislike to the photographer Wallis had brought along with him, and put a piranha fish in his bathtub with the intention of having the snapper's dick chewed off. The photographer and Blake took their revenge by throwing Ferrari's shoes into the piranha pool, but the *Sun* man astonished everyone by wading into retrieve them. After this there were multiple late-night fire-extinguisher sorties. At one point Ferrari sprayed Blake in the face with a fire extinguisher which he thought contained water. In fact it contained suffocating carbon dioxide gas, and at first Blake thought he was going to die. However, after a few days gasping for breath, he said he did not really mind. It was all good clean fun.

Ferrari returned to London, mission accomplished. Blake's Bucks Fizz exclusive had been properly 'spoiled' and he was now well and truly 'a made man' – Kelvin code for a hack who had pulled off an outrageous stunt at the expense of the opposition. Kelvin loved the way Ferrari was giving Bizarre a harder, newsier edge, moving it away from cheerful PR nonsense, and steering the stars on to the front page by revealing the nastier details of drug abuse and sexual deviancy, something Blake had always avoided doing.

Bizarre had become so important to the PR people that the *Sun* had come to regard certain acts as 'theirs'. One of these was the group Culture Club, featuring Boy George, whom Blake had helped hype to a string of chart hits in the early '80s. George had been so grateful that he even dedicated one of his records to 'John Blake and the Big Value *Sun*'. Ferrari's formula was simple: Blake and the *Sun* had built a lot of these people up. Now, if there was a story to be had, the *Sun* would knock them down again.

He went to work on Boy George. The usual Blake-style 'news' about hairstyles and record launches was replaced by headlines like 'JUNKIE GEORGE HAS EIGHT WEEKS TO LIVE' over stories dealing with the star's heroin addiction. Following on from these innovations the *Sun*, though not always Ferrari personally, began to put other TV and pop stars through the mill on a more or less weekly basis. This was all great, circulation-building stuff for a tabloid and, at first, fairly cheap and easy to do. It was only later that the stars and celebs began to counter-attack with a tidal wave of libel writs – and won (as in the *Sun*'s great Elton John Disaster).

In November 1987 Ferrari, then aged 27, moved to work for David Montgomery when he was promoted to features editor of the *News of the World*'s magazine, *Sunday*. Ferrari had been something of a protégé of Murdoch's – partly because of the Boss's friendship with his father, which went back a long way – and when Sky News was launched in 1988 Murdoch made him the channel's news editor. But, like many hacks from a print background, Ferrari found it hard to adapt to the world of moving pictures, where a great story in newspaper terms might not work visually. His period there was undistinguished. He was remembered for his trick of obtaining exclusive interviews by getting the Sky cameramen to pretend they were from another, and more widely watched, channel (*Rat-like cunning!*) and for an unfortunate episode when he arranged for a Rottweiler to appear live in the Sky studio.

Nevertheless, he moved on to head the news division of Murdoch's Fox TV network in New York, where his mission was to help organise 'rolling news' and, more generally, to act as Murdoch's on-site spear-carrier and learn how to do 'tabloid TV' properly. At the time, Fox was producing *A Current Affair*, an attempt at the American genre of 'reality television'. Its most famous episode had shown a home-made video of a convicted murderer twisting the head off a doll, while telling jokes about strangling women. Fox also made *America's Most Wanted*, which featured a non-stop horror show of reconstructed 'real-life' rapes, murders and stabbings, all lovingly filmed using freeze-frame and 'slo-mo'. Ferrari enjoyed his time in American tabloid TV, where the news philosophy was 'If it bleeds, it leads'. He played the role of the Brash Brit to the hilt, specialising in scam stories of one sort or another and driving his boss, an Australian nicknamed 'the Pig', round the bend. Murdoch's Australians were meant to be the nutters, the Yanks thought, but the Brits were the real risk-takers. Ferrari was soon on the move again after his wife, Sally, suddenly became seriously ill and needed to return to London at once.

At this point, Monty had just taken over the *Mirror* and

when Ferrari returned to Britain, Monty hired him. Monty thought Ferrari, whose work he knew from the *News of the World*, was just the person to help out with editorial plans for his 'British Fox' idea. Because at that time Monty did not have a budget for Mirror Television, Ferrari was officially hired as a senior editorial executive on the *Mirror* itself. But the idea was that he would work mainly on the television side of things, producing sample material for presentations to the cable companies and business partners. With Ferrari to do the news and Janet to do the trendy lifestyle and showbiz stuff, Monty had put together about the best editorial team to do 'British Fox' that was available. The arrival of Kelvin MacKenzie, in addition, had come as a complete surprise to Ferrari, as it had to everyone else as the Mirror Group, despite the fact that the MacKenzie and Ferrari families had stayed on close social terms after Ferrari had left the *Sun*.

Now that Janet had brought in Rachel Purnell, Ferrari was forced, in effect, to stand aside. In theory he remained 'co-director' of the channel, on an equal footing with Rachel, and there was an arrangement whereby they were supposed to alternate week by week being in control of the channel's content, when it went on air. But in reality, Rachel and Janet were calling all the shots, at least to begin with.

Rachel's first move when she arrived was to take the brief that had been worked out in outline by Janet and Monty and lock herself in a room with Nick Ferrari and Ruth Wrigley, the woman hired to organise Outside Broadcasts. All she knew to begin with was that the channel would be live, it would have celebs and it would provide a national 'spine' for a series of local city TV stations that Monty wanted to set up in places like Birmingham, Liverpool and Glasgow. After three days

Live TV

Rachel emerged from the room clutching lots of big pieces of paper containing the outline plan for L!ve TV.

Following Monty's instructions, Rachel and Janet decided that L!ve TV would have a 24-hour-a-day 'rolling format' with no programmes as such, but based around the Canary Wharf 'Entity' with, crucially, Outside Broadcast camera teams in vans. These 'OBs' would be sent to trendy locations such as nightclubs and feed back live footage which could mixed with whatever was going on in the studio. Output would switch seamlessly from one nightclub to another, back to the studio and back to yet another nightclub. The schedule, it was decided, would consist of three blocks (known as 'shoulders'). Each shoulder would be made with what was described as an 'editorial kit' consisting of a mix of OBs and short pre-recorded items, all linked with live chat in the studio. Producers were to be appointed to take charge of the shoulders on a rota across the week.

The first shoulder would run from 9 a.m. to 4 p.m. and was supposed to appeal to 'home alones', which was PC-speak for housewives. Then there was the all-important night-time block, from 9 p.m. onwards. This was the time when cable could come into its own, especially after 11 p.m. when people came back from the pubs and started surfing the channels looking for something eye-catching. The official watchword for the night-time slot was 'mainstream weird', whatever that meant. Later, when the Tellybrats arrived to make this masterplan work they were told that night-time was the 'take your breath away' slot.

The daytime and youth slots were to be the same every weekday, with some variation at weekends, but the night-time slots were to have a different theme every day. Tuesday and Friday were designated as 'love' nights, where all the material had to be linked by the theme of bonking. Wednesday was 'weird night' and would be devoted to the paranormal. Monday was 'advice night', meaning differents sorts of phone-in. Thursday was generally ignored (despite being 'giro night' for many people with enough time on their hands to spend many hours watching cable television). There was a move to make it 'dangerous night', but it ended up as 'reality night'.

Saturday was to be 'active day' and was to be dominated by live weddings (events which Janet loved and were, she would explain, one of the main reasons she had so many husbands) during the day, together with 'cult sport' meaning things like underwater chess or celebrity dwarf throwing or any other rare material which had not been hoovered up by Sky. Saturday evening was, of course, to be given over to clubbin', punctuated by 'people news' (*sleb* gossip lifted from magazines). Sunday was 'lazy day', when the idea was to have an OB unit spend a day with a *sleb*, following them to, for example, a flea market in the morning and then filming them cooking and eating their lunch. It was proposed that Sunday morning should have a sex theme because 'Sunday mornings are the one morning of the week when our target audience have sex.' The draft schedule notes started at 9 a.m. and referred to the viewers: 'They're in bed *doing it*. Only sexy items will tempt them to watch the box because that is what they have got on their mind.' Ideas for 'inserts' (*sic*) into the schedule included '10 places to have sex without the kids knowing' and '10 things to tell the kids when they catch you bonking', together with 'female sexual fantasies' plus 'Take A Bath With . . .' videos in baths with people 'fantasising about their fantasy star' and, for good measure, a phone-in entitled 'Who fucked up your weekend?'. Even more exciting than this was 'Down at JSP's', a programme featuring Janet eating her dinner: 'We're in the lucky position of having a celebrity as our MD . . . so we will have a weekly lunchtime show where Janet Street-Porter cooks for a bunch of "star" friends. It'll be informal, chatty, lively, fun and naughty because the conversation has no boundaries . . . ' There was also mention of showing 'old movies' on Sunday, but there was no budget for this.

Vast attention was given to the logo for the station. Ideally this would become a well-known trademark like the Coca-Cola symbol and would one day come to be worth a fortune in its own right. The person chosen to develop the L!ve logo was Georgia 'George' Cooke, who had worked with Janet's old LWT pal Jane Hewland and also on *Def-II* at the BBC. Cooke was told that the overall 'Look' of L!ve TV depended on 'hot reactive colours'. Puzzled by the exact meaning of this, she brought in some books of colour samples. The two women sat down next to each other with Janet flicking crossly through the pages: 'Nah, that's Crap [flick] an' *that's* crap. [flick, flick] 'Orrible, innit? [flick] *Urrrughhh*. [flick, flick, flick] Nah, s'all *Com-Pleeetlee* Crap.'

After several sessions like this, Cooke decided to take charge by presenting Janet with an intellectual case in favour of using various shades of blue. Janet was not best pleased. 'Cut the bullshit,' she snapped. 'I want something nobody has ever seen before.' After more *screamin' an' shahtin'*, Janet grumpily settled on a combination of orange, purple and pink. Attention then turned to the graphics themselves. These, Janet said, had to be 'modern, clean and functional'. Apart from that, the graphics used to introduce programmes all had to look similar or hang together, giving a coherent 'Look' to match the continuous nature of the output.

Cooke went away to ponder this and came back with all sorts of ideas. Her own favourite was a series of 'icons' or 'pictograms' (*Gilbert and George!*) which told stories in their own right. So for the breakfast-time output you would have a little stylised picture of a milkman, and for night-time a wolf howling at the moon, or something (*not* a cup of cocoa). The pictures would all be different, but the over-all style would be the same. Janet was annoyed: 'I fuckin' *hate* icons. It's a fuckin' *visual cliché*. I *toooooooold* you, I want it *modern* an' I want it *clean* an' I want it *funkshernal*. Keep it Simple. *Puleeeeze.*'

By now time was running out, and Janet kept on reject-ing everything. Cooke picked up on all the talk of using the graphics to 'punctuate' the output. One of the purposes of the graphics, Janet would explain in her ratty way, was to place a 'full stop' (this was said by way of exasperated metaphor) to show where a shoulder of programmes ended. Why not take her at her word? They settled on punctuation marks for the graphics. The station's main identity logo was to be a huge

!

The exclamation mark was 'hot' in the magazine world at the time, in the wake of *Hello!*, and one of Janet's edito-rial models for L!ve TV was '*Hello!* magazine on Acid'. A straight rip-off of the title was not possible, but the chan-nel could at least use the all-important '!'. The 'on acid' aspect could be achieved with a psychedelic treatment of the crucial punctuation mark. To achieve the effect, and make the viewers even more edgy, the exclamation mark was to be animated so that it looked sort of crackly and radioactive and was constantly fizzing, strobing and spark-ing with electrical energy (*David Lynch! Completely Brilliant!*). It was designed to crash violently into programmes, in mid-item if required, as though somebody in charge of output at the station had accidentally stuck their finger in an electric socket or had a sudden infusion of cocaine, or as though the broadcast was being interrupted by an urgent message from outer-space aliens, or all these things. Either that or the telly was on the blink. (The exclamation mark, as it happened, was also the international warning symbol used on road signs to indicate an unspecific but serious upcoming hazard. At some deep psychological level, L!ve's viewers might be persuaded to keep their eyes on the screen to avoid being buried in an avalanche.) The punctuation theme was pushed further with stroboscopic quotation marks, psychedelic commas and throbbing full stops which would blast their way on to the screen to break up items within shoulders.

This approach encompassed all Janet's style obsessions, including the infobar with its stream of *completely ironic* factoids, which Janet and Jane Hewland had introduced on *Network-7* and then flogged to death on *Def-II*. This time she was determined to push the infobar even further. The entire bottom third of the screen was going to be a 'billboard area' where Janet or one of her deputies could 'talk' directly to the viewers about what was happening on screen. For instance, if there was a studio guest Janet could stand in the director's box and dictate infobars along the lines of '*He looks funny, dunnee?*' or '*This is getting boring, innit? Never mind, there's something better coming up inna bit,*' alongside more general information and news snips about an entirely different subject. So the viewers got two channels for the price of one.

Kelvin and Ferrari watched all this from a distance, with a mixture of perplexity (*fucking lazy Groucho Club art-school ponces!*) and genuine contempt for the time, attention and money being lavished on the graphics. Kelvin knew that any attempt to intervene would lead to the mother of all tantrums from Janet, so he restricted himself to mild sneering and teasing. He would sidle up to the design team and ask them what they were earning. Then, 'Fuckin' 'ell. Did you hear that, Nick? Forty fuckin' grand for farting about with a comma. We're in the wrong game, mate!' It was all a long way from the *Sun*'s logo, which had been drawn in ten minutes by Larry Lamb using a red felt-tip pen (to his later regret, he then sold the copyright to Murdoch for £1). At the *Sun*, there had been in-house designers known in old-fashioned newspaper terminology as the 'art desk'. Their job was to run a service operation, creating short-order visual jokes to support headlines, such as the famous graphic turning England football manager Graham Taylor's head into a turnip. But they had no say in the overall look of the paper, which was deliberately 'designed' to look like a mish-mash thrown together in a hurry, and the key elements of which had not really changed since the 1930s.

Kelvin's own artistic activities had so far been restricted to drawing little stick-men on the *Sun*'s page proofs. (He once drew a stick-man picture of TV 'critic' Garry Bushell, identified by his beard, sitting on the toilet, to indicate that he thought Bushell's column was shit.) His view of all art, including graphic art, was the standard lower-middle-class suspicion that anything short of nineteenth-century portraits or landscapes was a con. His favourite painting was, he claimed, *The Crying Boy*, a mass-market Woolworth's job of the Green Lady school, which was perfect for his target audience of proud ex-council-house freeholders. It was a creation he had repeatedly featured in the *Sun* as part of a series of scam stories.

The modern art scene was shot through with Loony Left charlatans on fat Arts Council grants making so-called sculpture out of piles of bricks or, in one (true) story, a performance artist being paid to wander around East Anglia balancing a plank on his head. Janet was very thick with these sort of people, of course – loonies and shirt-lifters, a lot of 'em. Now Janet and her designers had taken weeks to come up with their jittery exclamation mark. It was crap, of course – what could you expect? But there it was.

Journalists were, in general, very careful about the use of the exclamation mark, which in sub-editing and head-line-writing jargon was known as a 'screamer'. The unwritten rule was that you never used a screamer unless the sentence to which it was attached was actually being screamed (as in 'Help!').

On the other hand the screamer was often very useful for tabloid headline-writing. The effect of using it is to soften what was being said, or turn it into a joke, to flag the presence of a pun (the *Royal Wee!*) or otherwise signal, 'This is bollocks, folks!'

Chapter Fourteen

In which Janet finalises The Look, recruits some Tellybrats as Human Special Effects, telling them that they have a Bright Future so long as they never ever wear beige, comes up with ideas for what exactly they should put On Screen and advises others on the same topic, but strikes people as Distant and Distracted because she is off working on Mirror TV's spluttering bid to run Channel 5

'There's gonna be no beige. No beige – *ever!*' Janet is wandering about on the half-built 24th floor of the Canary Wharf tower,[1] airily explaining her Vision to a crocodile of potential presenters and production staff – *wannabe Tellybrats!* – who have answered an advert in the *Guardian* and have turned up for an interview. It is explained to them that soon this will become the studio base for L!ve TV. The *Mirror* and its sister papers have lately been installed elsewhere in the tower. But this floor, set aside for Mirror Television, is for the time being a building-site.

The original *sad* corporate conformist raspberry-pink carpets, grey and cream walls and speckled suspending ceilings have been ripped out, on Janet's instructions, revealing the innards of the building, the perfect starting-point for post-modern interior design. Janet wanders about, waving at apparently useless and randomly assembled lumps of chrome, protruding plug sockets and piles of hideously clashing luminescent pink, green, yellow and purple carpet tiles. Expanses of 'acid' colour are starting to creep across the recently plastered walls. People tend to stick close to the inner walls round the lift shaft, well away from the huge plate-glass windows which, without blinds, do not look capable of holding anything in. Some, walking across the cluttered floor, suddenly remember where they are in relation to solid earth, turn white as a sheet and grab hold of something to steady themselves.

'It's all gonna be fitted *aht* in chrowwme . . . architechural lightin' . . . yer industrial look . . . very nineties. And *NO* beige. Ever,' she says, apparently expecting a round of applause. 'Wow! No beige! That's Terrific!' the visitors echo, hoping to make a good impression and catch her attention. All the while they keep one eye on the floor to avoid stumbling over cables or planting a foot in a bucket of Evostick. At this stage wires are still dangling everywhere. A vague fear of sudden death by electrocution is thus added to the vertigo.

Janet wandered about as though in a trance, trying to describe the picture of the finished studio – *The Look* – which had already taken shape in her imagination. To help her with The Look, she had brought in David Connor, the trendy creator of the Atlantic Bar and Grill, a fashionable eating-place in Soho. Connor, who came recommended by Piers Gough, was one of several interior designers who had been asked to put in bids to create the L!ve TV studio. The brief was that it was going to be a combined office-cum-TV-studio. Connor knew relatively little about the normal constraints of designing a television studio, which was useful because, in the end, Janet had decided that there would be no 'studio' as such. Instead there was to be a multi-purpose space – an 'Entity' or 'Facility', as she called it – which would break all the traditional divisions between office space, technical areas and studios spread throughout the 24th floor.

The idea of having the production staff in shot was not new. Normally, though, there was a glass screen between presenter and production, which gave the appearance of the presenter being in a working newsroom but, in reality, was the same as putting them in different rooms. Janet wanted to do it for real, without a glass partition. You could do anything, anywhere: you could present programmes from the reception area in front of the lift *if yer wanted*, interview *slebs* in the cluttered little area where secretaries made coffee *if yer liked*. The receptionist's desk near the lifts could double up as a cocktail bar for the many L!ve TV parties which were to be broadcast as an essential part of the output. Every part of The Entity was to be on show, with only one exception: a 'padded cell' replacing the traditional greenroom. This was to be a sanctuary beyond the reach of the camera, an area where *slebs* could be entertained, fed and watered, or could *chill out*. It was all Completely *Innervitiff*. A Totally Different Concept of Programme-Making.

Having established the multi-purpose Entity concept, Janet was mainly interested in the colour scheme, which would have to blend in with the station's graphics. Connor spent weeks painting bits of plasterboard in different shades and hanging them up so Janet could have a look at them. The idea was that the walls would become 'plains of bright colour' painted and repainted quickly and cheaply with Dulux, thus avoiding the expensive need to change scenery or build sets. Janet denounced Connor's first efforts as 'tragically tasteful' but the two never really fell out.

Different areas of The Entity would have different colour schemes so that different sorts of activity could take place. If you were doing an interview on a sort of yellowish topic with a purple person, you could balance that by doin' the interview against a lilac wall. If the subject matter was more orangey, and the interviewee was greenish, there would have to be a powder-bluish area. And so on. It all made perfect sense.

In addition, the Dulux could be quickly painted over to match the changing seasons, or changing colour fashions, or a combination of both. In line with the colour scheme for the studio design, the first 'shoulder' of the day's schedule was to be colour-coded bright yellow and the general idea was 'sunshine TV'. The second, from 4 p.m. to the 9 p.m. 'watershed', would be designed for 'youth' – the idea here was a straightforward rip-off of Janet and Rachel's *Def-II* material at the BBC, though the shoulder was to run longer – and was colour-coded orange. Sport, which did not really exist on L!ve TV, would have been colour-coded Green.

With the overall Look of the graphics and colour scheme sorted out, attention turned to the next visual Special Effect: the on-screen 'Talent', who would be the next generation of Tellybrats. The Talent (either at Canary Wharf or on location with an OB unit) would be wired up with the latest easy-to-use, lightweight cameras and, according to The Vision, they would look something like Madonna or Michael Jackson on stage, rushing about equipped with those Completely Brilliant wireless head-mikes pioneered by the Thompson Twins: *Blade Runner* meets Directory Enquiries.

It was central to the Janet method that you did not waste money hiring stars. Some of the people who were to appear on screen at L!ve had worked in television before, but many were to be drawn from the vast army of mostly clueless twenty-somethings who wanted to do 'something in the media'. Janet would then be able to mould this unpromising clay into the Stars of the Future. (After all Malcolm McLaren had created the Sex Pistols out of a bunch of spotty oiks he had caught trying to pinch things from his boutique in the King's Road, hadn't he? None of them had any so-called skill or so-called talent.) Looked at in this way, it was essential that the on-screen people were as inexperienced as possible, thus giving Janet a clean sheet of paper to work on.

And so an advert was placed in the *Guardian*, prompting a predictably enormous response. The *airheads* and *wannabes*, as they were derisively described, were invited to Canary Wharf in batches, given a tour round the place and then put through a lengthy selection process. One group of applicants was given a written exam, with Janet setting questions along the lines of: 'Say Princess Diana was visitin' Docklands. How would you get her to appear on L!ve TV?' That one had the assorted bimbos and good-lookin' hunks who made up the bulk of applicants sucking long and hard on their Garfield pencils.

Those who made the grade were then asked to look at that morning's papers and produce a 'running order' of what was most important to L!ve TV. Trivia predominated. One applicant, who had researched a bit more thoroughly than the others what she was getting herself into, spotted a fellow hopeful squinting at the *Daily Telegraph* foreign pages. Taking pity, she warned the *Telegraph* reader off, and helpfully directed her to the showbiz pages of the *Daily Mail* instead. At the end of this process Janet looked through the running orders perfunctorily. In essence, some thought, this was a 'negative' test to smoke out any crypto-*sad* people who were interested in things like politics or news in the conventional sense of the word, but who had got dressed up in rave gear in the hope of getting a job. Many fell at this hurdle and trooped mournfully towards the lift door.

Then the real business began. The applicants were herded together and addressed in turn by Rachel Purnell,

Live TV

Nick Ferrari and Janet. This triumvirate struck many as odd. There was Janet, beanpole thin and decked out in a power-dressing suit which would not have been out of place on a bank manager, except for the fact that it was bright crimson and was mismatched with a pair of skin-head bovver boots. She said little, to begin with. Rachel, in contrast, was short, stocky and swathed in baggy black clothes and yammered away ten to the dozen, with Janet sort of snorting in response from time to time. Then there was Ferrari. *Where had they dragged him up from?* He was overweight and waddled about, puffing and panting, obviously trying to be *hip* and *happening*, but failing badly in his pastel Ralph Lauren shirt with big sweat patches under the arms. The two women seemed to be ignoring him as Rachel came to the end of her monologue and introduced Janet to give the main spiel.

Janet went into full Power Mode, arms folded, head nodding, feigning boredom, her voice drawling with supercool sarcasm (sort of '*Huh! so you wanna be media stars, then, do yer? Huh! well, I'll show yer a fing er two*'), her accent dropping *dahn* a few notches on the social scale, to show she *reely* meant business. It was emphasised that L!ve TV was completely *innervitiff* . . . happening . . . breaking the mould . . . the future of television . . . going to parties . . . never mind the bollocks . . . training on the job . . . ' The tellybrats were warned that if they came on board they would have to work very hard, and that not many of them would make it. At one point Janet nonchalantly mentioned that on-screen reporters could expect to earn around £40,000 a year, which caused a rustle of interest round the room and made Ferrari's jaw drop to the floor.

Next, Janet introduced a number of Fun Young Guys in Wacky T-Shirts, as one applicant thought of them, who were bristling with technical equipment. She then disappeared, taking Rachel with her and leaving Ferrari wandering about, looking lost. The Fun Guys came over as though they had just had a heavy session on laughing-gas. It was all happy-clappy and 'Right! Let's make a movie!' in the style of *Blue Peter* presenters. The interviewees were given a few minutes' rudimentary instruction in camera operation, after which Janet re-emerged, impatient but still supercool, and said, 'Right, enough of that. I want you to go *aht* and get me *sumfink* I can put on L!ve TeeeVeee. *Y've got arf'n'aahr,*' and she folded her arms again, spun on the spot and marched off in a power haze.

The wannabes scampered out of the building, desperate to get hold of anyone they could on the mostly deserted streets of Docklands. The more experienced tried to do this in a businesslike fashion. One, Rebbeca Pike, did a proper piece on the Death of the Yuppie. Lightweight, yes, but Proper. This included such things as non-*innervitiff* techniques as balance, a timed script and some reasonably thoughtful commentary. The piece was denounced by Janet as exactly the sort of stuff – *the usual borin' crap* – she did not want. Ms Pike did not get the job and, instead, went on to work for *Today* on Radio Four.

Another applicant, a good-looking young blonde called Imogen Edwards-Jones, who was after her first job in television, did much better. Up to this point Ms Edwards-Jones's main claim to fame was having humiliated herself on *The Word*'s 'I'll do anything to get on television' slot, the 'zoo TV' stunt which got the programme-makers (Planet 24, also makers of *The Big Breakfast*) into trouble with the television authorities. Previous 'I'll do anything' stunts included a man pulling weights across the studio floor with his penis, volunteers going out on to the street and kissing genuine tramps, and a man who drank a pint of his own vomit. Imogen had submitted to having plastic surgery performed on her lips, live on television, bringing the house down but leaving her with a permanent pout.

Faced with the problem of impressing Janet, Imogen decided to do a 'piece' on Britain's Best-Dressed Woman. But instead of agonizing over this thorny question, she simply went up to people and persuaded them to shout, 'Cilla! Cilla!' at her camera. Janet thought the result was Completely Brilliant, by far the best. A combination of Edward-Jones's genuine 'I'll do anything' attitude and this piece of cheap and effective television-making got her a job towards the top of the list.

Another Good-Looking Young Woman, Julia Bradbury, did a piece on Chris Evans joining Radio One, which scored maximum points for subject matter, and another piece on the Canary Wharf building itself. This was not so hot but showed that she looked good on camera and could talk pleasingly for a long time without saying much – a vital qualification for L!ve TV. Also, she worked quickly, and had the material edited and ready to broadcast by 7 p.m., whereas less successful applicants were still there pointlessly toiling away until midnight. Bradbury was offered a job on the spot, helped by the fact that her application was supported by Mick Pilsworth, Janet's friend at Chrysalis TV, where Bradbury had previously worked.

The Talent may have had £ signs in their eyes after Janet's mention of £40,000, but Ferrari intervened, phoning up the successful applicants and bargaining salaries down below £30,000 – still above the odds for people with so little experience. Finding wannabe TV presenters was easy enough, but luring more experienced and scarce production and technical people from secure and well-paid jobs elsewhere in the industry was more of a challenge. There was a pool of production people available, in the form of the staff of Wire TV, which L!ve was about to replace on the cable networks. Steve Timmins (Wire TV's programme controller) and his clutch of forty 'cable missionaries', who had brought the channel out for two years, had pulled off the unique trick of making at least something which could be shown on the screen within a budget of less than £2,000 an hour. As a result, they claimed a mass of valuable experience gained from their own early cock-ups and underestimation of the difficulties involved in the enterprise. This was indeed a different world from Janet's experience at LWT and the BBC, where programmes costing fifty times as much were considered cheap.

All kinds of different skills were needed to make 'microtelevision'. But Janet was not interested. Despite a vague agreement, at the time of the takeover, that L!ve would retain as many of the Wire TV staff as possible, Janet did not so much as interview a single one of them.

This was not altogether surprising. She had met Timmins – just once – during the takeover, at the Shepherd's Bush Hilton near BBC Television Centre, and had treated him with utter contempt. There he was, this *sad* little man from the sticks, who probably thought his native Bristol was trendy (*Wrong!*). An ex-hippy, probably, like a lot of them down there, in his stupid hi-tech cottage with a satellite dish on top and his poxy studio in a *dreeery* provincial shopping-mall and his linen jacket and his cheesecloth shirt and his beard. Yeah. Collar all buttoned up but no tie, like a lot of the ageing male trendies at the Beeb who thought it was clever to look like Mark Knopfler. Fashionable? Yeah. In 1985. And here *he* was tellin' *her* about his phone-ins and flower-arrangin' and competitions and local opt-outs, traipsin' round bleedin' Bromsgrove and Ipswich in his pathetic yellow van, givin' out leaflets and Darth Vader masks in shoppin' centres like a cross between a team of double-glazing salesmen and New Age bleedin' travellers. Yeah. Thanks. But no thanks. Yeah.

With the Wire people ruled out, Janet might have been in a position to head-hunt among her former protégés at *Def-II*, but there were relatively few takers. She had her admirers at the BBC, but she had not been popular with many of the rank and file who worked with her, particularly in her later years. At first she had a habit of 'love-bombing' younger recruits, telling them they were wonderful and would go a long way and, in the process, promoting them too quickly into positions where some found it difficult to cope. Then, later on, she had a crackdown and effectively demoted many of them. That had left a bad taste. She often said, in a very general way, that she wanted to help people with their career plans, and that her door was always open. In practice it was difficult to get past the picket-lines of her secretaries and personal assistants. Also, she struck many as moody and could be difficult to work with. The BBC security guards became expert at judging her mood and, taking pity on the Tellybrats, would phone the fifth-floor office to warn them she was in the building and on her way up. Everyone would then scurry to their desk in an effort to look busy. (Janet's leaving do, a typically attention-grabbing affair held on the roof of her office, had been an unemotional event. Janet made a stilted speech of thanks, but there were no tears and, frankly, few signs that anyone really regretted her departure. People just guzzled the free food and wine and then cleared off.)

Rachel from *Def-II* was in place, of course, and so was Darryl Burton, who had been part of the small army of in-house BBC middle-manager 'implementers' which had surrounded Janet at the BBC, with the particular role of nursing Janet's enormous taxi bills and other expenses claims appropriate to her woman-about-town lifestyle and operating methods. Burton had joined L!ve TV early on and was to play a vital role in juggling with the station's budget day by day. Janet seemed to regard him as a sort of human cash-dispensing machine. When anyone at L!ve asked for money, Janet would tell them to go and see 'Lill the Till', her nickname for Darryl.

With Sky and the BBC largely ruled out as a source of recruits, and with few in ITV likely to be interested, the word about L!ve was spread among graduates of the 'Network-7 Academy of Excellence', meaning those people who had worked with Janet at LWT and were now spread out through television, making Network-7-derived Janetvision of one sort or another. They had by now done very well for themselves and were scattered about in a number of suitably swashbuckling independent production companies, notably Planet 24, which was headed by ex-Network-7 'entrepreneur' Charlie Parsons and Bob Geldof.

The chances of getting any of the original Network-7 people involved was slight, since this would have been a big step back for most. However, a new generation of less well established people, schooled in infobar appreciation by the likes of Parsons, heard about L!ve on the grapevine and some were keen to work with the Genuine Article. L!ve was able to recruit a number of people from The Big Breakfast, which, after its initial success, was going through a difficult period and was not the happiest of ships. The main problem seemed to be the style of Parsons and the Network-7 originals, some of whom had believed all the hype about their being 'the future of television' and all that, and had grown as 'difficult' to deal with as Janet herself. Geldof could be a moody sod as well. Life for lower-grade people at Planet 24 was often unpleasant, not to say humiliating. (The story was told of a senior producer who dropped a pile of files one day and, instead of picking them up himself, phoned a menial researcher and ordered her to come into the office on her day off to pick them up.) So at least some people were willing to come over to escape second-hand hi-NRG rampant egomania and experience the Real Thing at L!ve, so long as attractive salaries were available.

And so, throughout the spring of 1995 more and more people joined L!ve TV from a variety of sources, and the staff list started to creep towards 180 employees, the absolute maximum allowed in the budget. Janet began calling regular Friday afternoon staff meetings, attended by the growing throng. The meetings tended to be dominated by exhortations and promises of various sorts, rather than by detailed instructions about what to do. In general, the assembled troops were told they were lucky to get the chance to work with 'legends' like Janet, Kelvin and, less plausibly, Nick Ferrari.

It was pointed out that they were going to get extensive 'multi-skill' training for free. Most of all, it was pointed out that they had joined the exciting new hire-and-fire Meritocracy of the Modern Media, where losers did not last long. They were going to make a Totally New and Wicked Type of Television for the Next Millennium. The Rule Book had been thrown away and there was no room for passengers, but with A Bit of Luck the rewards for Self-Starters who did not sit around on their Fat Arses but who were Hungry, Really Hungry, and could Put Energy on the Screen and generally Cut the Mustard Again and Again, Day In and Day Out, like Chris Evans in his Early Days, were Instant and Quite Literally Limitless, and overnight fame and fortune could be earned Purely on Merit and if people worked very, very hard and Always Delivered No Matter What because they were Team Players and had Got What It Takes because, after all, there were plenty more where you came from so shut up and Get On With It because it's gonna be like One *Massiff* Party anyway and what have you lost if things don't work out? *Nuffin*, that's what.

By comparison with any 'old-fashioned' (the Orwellian phrase insisted upon by Rachel to describe normal television) operation, L!ve TV's complement of staff was tiny. Until recently the BBC had employed 25,000 people, and they all moaned that they were having nervous breakdowns because of low staffing-levels. Even Sky, where Murdochian slave-ship conditions were the norm, employed 6,000. So from the start it was clear that each employee at L!ve would have to do the job of at least 500 people.

To help with this task Monty and Richard Horwood had invested heavily in the latest computer technology which, it was true, replaced a lot of the craft jobs, in areas like editing and control of transmission, previously done by humans. But this presented its own problems. The Talent, in particular, would have to be trained up. In many cases this would mean moving from having no television or journalistic skills at all to becoming 'multi-skilled', the new jargon for people who could do any job in the station, missing out altogether the intervening stage of being merely 'skilled'.[2]

There was editorial training and technical training on cameras, but nothing about how to use an autocue or anything like that, because those pieces of equipment were not going to be used. Eventually, everyone realised that the only skill that really mattered was the extremely hazardous one of ad-libbing straight to camera for hours and hours while continuing to look cheerful and neat. The only real official editorial guideline was that 'L!ve TV is a happy place where the sun always shines', which was odd for a station which planned to capture most of its audience in the middle of the night as the clubbin' channel.

The job of training the Talent fell to Tony Orsten, the director brought into launch the channel.[3] Orsten had previously worked with Janet on *Network-7*. He now organised the latest generation of Tellybrats into small seminar groups which ran on a strict timetable, like school. Orsten felt he had to start at a fairly basic level, using a marker pen and a whiteboard to explain the basics of script-writing: 'Start with an intro: who, what, where, when. Then the story, and then' – miming a boxer's uppercut – 'hit 'em with a punchline.' The Talent grimaced and made copious notes, later abandoned. Essential matters such as the law of libel, the constraints of the regulations on such things as taste and decency, together with the normal legal requirement to get 'release forms' (permission from people being filmed, so that they did not pop up later and claim copyright or otherwise cause problems), were briefly mentioned but, often as not, seemed to go in one ear and straight out the other.

Janet would turn up at the training sessions from time to time, to give a masterclass on the finer points. Questions which boiled down to 'What do you want us to do, Janet?' were often answered with snappy but unhelpful slogans. 'Make it cheery, not sneery,' she would say, or 'Just enjoy yerself. Make it like *Hello!* magazine' – demonic grin, chuckle, punchline – '*on acid*.' At one of these sessions the hapless trainees were told that if they ever had to interview a middle-aged man they should stab him with a Biro to make him shut up. That would be Completely Brilliant, *ack ack ack*!

Beyond this there was constant advice and discussion about The Look and what to wear. Janet regarded herself as a sage on this topic. Once one of the production staff, hanging about near Janet's office noticed a pair of Puma Gazelle training shoes on her desk. Thinking she was out, he opined that the shoes were out of date and that no genuinely trendy person would be seen dead wearing them. Unfortunately Janet was not out, but was in fact lurking within earshot. She burst forth and raged, with a trembling lip, 'People like you come and go. Soon you'll be '*isstree*. But, unlike *yoooo, Pooma Garrzel* [Puma Gazelle] trainers are Com-Pletely Classic. They will be around *f'revver.'*

After these fundamentals had been attended to, the training branched out into simulations of Actual Situations which might occur when the channel went on air. The Talent had to act out imaginary scenarios whilst being filmed by imaginary cameramen. It was obvious that Orsten and others were deciding who would make the best presenters. Behind a façade of jolly japes and cool self-deprecation, the Talent were competing furiously for the best presenter slots and so hammed it up as much as possible during the simulations.

At first these were organised around people pretending to be obvious things like rock stars or supermodels. But that got borin' so one of the male presenters stripped down to his underpants and pretended to be a ghost being interviewed on a programme about the paranormal. This was followed by a wannabe-female-presenter acting out the role of a lisping infant schoolchild (kneeling down and putting on a silly voice) so that another wannabe-female-presenter could practise the essential skill of interviewing a 6-year-old. The interviewer was chided by Orsten for being too aggressive, and the session dissolved in hilarity.

Nick Ferrari also got involved in the simulations, and required another female presenter to dress up as a 'celebrity sex beast' so they could all practise interviewing her about her sex life. The presenter obliged by wearing an amazing, gravity-defying uplift bra. Ferrari was impressed. 'Your tits are so high up,' he observed, 'you could lick your own cleavage.'

The Talent, paraded school-assembly-style before Janet at the Friday meetings, were told that, for the most part, they would have to generate their own material. This was a disappointment to those who had visions of merely turning up, reading a script and looking gorgeous. In fact they were being expected to perform as journalists or TV researchers, which was hard work, calling for exactly the sort of training, experience and contacts many of them lacked. The Talent were not told in any coherent way what sort of material was required or where to get it. Instead Janet, and even Ferrari (joining in the fun), would yammer on about 'deconstructed television' or advise them to specialise in material which was 'Relentlessly Upbeat and Youth-Driven'.

They were told that 'ideas are the Lifeblood of This Television Station', but usable ideas seemed to be in very short supply all round. Janet was sometimes more specific, in an irritated way, but her programme ideas came by way of off-the-cuff examples, rather than any sort of agenda. 'Say the Motor Show was on,' she would explain with studied boredom. 'Go to the Motor Show. Get an idea. Like, er, yeah, "more an' more wimmin are into four-wheel-drives"' – coincidentally, Janet had just invested in such a vehicle – '"Why?" Dig into it a bit. Find *aht* why wimmin like to have these *huuuuuge* tanks to drive *abaht* in. Ask a few of 'em. It's not s'*differkult*.' But what if the Motor Show wasn't on? What then?

The Talent were sent packing into their small discussion groups and told to engage in 'brainstormin' sessions' with Rachel or Ferrari, or even with Janet herself. Janet would start off by drawing four circles on a piece of paper: 'Right. Those are yer four hours in yer programmin' block.' Then she drew two lines across each circle, dividing it into quarters. 'And there's yer ad breaks. OK? Now just go away and think of fings to put in 'em.' Then she would disappear. The result was that a lot of people sat around The Entity with rulers, geometry sets and rubbers, endlessly drawing pie-charts and filling up the hours with the first thing that came into their frequently empty heads.

Most ideas for slots and items fell into two categories, the asinine and the impossible. The more memorable gems included 'Things I would do if I was prime minister', 'How I dress to annoy my mum' and 'What I hate about my car'. Impossible (and possibly illegal) ideas included 'The Dangerous Report – every day we do something completely dangerous and weird'; 'Challenges – we stop people in the street and make them do things'; and the less well formed 'Could we do a medicine spot by filming in a kind of *Peak Practice* sort of place and then cutting it like a soap opera?' to which the obvious answer was 'Er, no.'

To move things along Janet organised an editorial 'awayday' to brainstorm yet more ideas. She circulated the results with a covering memo which read: 'It is important that our output is tailored to appeal to the right audience at the right time, within our broad plans to be *hip* and *youthful* (like me! *NOT!*).' But her suggestions and hints for daytime output were still relentlessly vague: 'You have got to make it work as radio,' the Tellybrats were told. Then there was the inevitable stricture to 'make it hip, more in touch than the BBC', supplemented by the innovative suggestion to 'do something for small kids'. There was undoubtably sensible advice for the newsdesk, who were reminded to 'phone up newsmakers' from time to time. The main new idea for weekday night-time output was 'naked yoga'. Ideas put up by others included 'Fuck or Die', a 'challenge' programme in which a contestant had to pick somebody up on camera; this idea later mutated into *Desperate and Dateless*, which was to become one of the mainstays of the early months of L!ve TV on air.

Janet would pass judgement on the quality of the ideas emerging from the brainstorms. Much, in her opinion, was 'borin'' and 'crap' unless it had some more or less direct connection with whatever she was doing in her life at that moment. One Tellybrat hit the target with the idea of 'doing something about reflexology'. Janet was enthusiastic: 'Yeah! Now yer talkin'. That's exactly what we need, lotsa alternative people. Yeah!' And she launched into a lengthy account of a visit to her friend Lynne Franks's house the previous evening, describing the way in which Franks had lain naked on the floor while 'this Russian woman pulled all 'er negative auras out. *Everybody* uses 'er – 'er muvver even does Colonel *G'ddarrrfeee*!' Minions were despatched to track down the Amazing Russian Aura Woman.

Soon after the takeover of Wire TV in February 1995 the launch date for L!ve had been set for 12 June. This was a very tight deadline and had been dictated by the Mirror Group's priorities as a whole, including the optimum date for the proposed – but doomed – dedicated Mirror football channel MacKenzie had been working on. Many of Janet's problems and the difficulties with L!ve came from this too-tight deadline and the lack of preparation time, a factor over which she had little or no control.

The drawing-up of business plans and the recruiting of senior staff had taken a couple of months, so the countdown did not really start until 1 April, when the outline schedule of the channel was decided – or *'frozen'*, in Janetspeak. And there was another problem. At this crucial time, Janet was deeply involved in putting together Mirror TV's bid for Channel 5. She was trying to keep several plates spinning at once.

Chapter Fifteen

*In which Patrick Cox loses out on Breakfast TV and many
people curse the Franchise Process while Cox looks around
for Other Opportunities and is reunited with his old
Wapping Pal Monty and joins forces to bid for Channel 5,
is delighted that Kelvin with his Gut-Wrenching
Promotional Instincts has come on board and even more
delighted when Alan McKeown signs up, leading to Janet
being sidelined, an Enormous Row and a split right down
the middle of the management of Mirror Television*

It is 9.40 a.m., 16 October 1991. Sir Paul Fox, lately of the
BBC, and Patrick Cox of NBC Europe, together with a
gaggle of advisers, accountants and general bag-carriers
cluster nervously round a specially designated fax machine
in a corner of the ITN newsroom in central London. A
camera is trained on them to record for posterity the
impending moment of drama. The machine begins to click
and whirr. Fox, Cox and the others twist their necks into
unnatural positions to see what the long-awaited message
says. The upside-down letterhead of the Independent
Television Commission emerges first. Fox pulls the document off the machine and reads it quietly to himself. The
others peer over his shoulder.

Bad news. Six months' hard work has been wasted. The
chance to break into the lucrative breakfast-time television
market has been lost. There are sighs and handshakes.
What a shame. It was a close-run thing.

Fox was the chairman of Daybreak Television, a consortium bidding for the ITV breakfast television franchise.

Daybreak consisted of Cox's NBC, ITN, Carlton TV and the *Daily Telegraph*, and was financially backed by the construction company Taylor Woodrow.[1] Daybreak's offer of £33.26 million for the franchise had been pipped by a rival bid from Sunrise TV, later renamed Good Morning TV, led by LWT and backed by the Disney organisation and the Scottish ITV company, STV. Daybreak had got their sums wrong by a tiny fraction and had been outbid. The team dispersed, empty-handed, cursing their luck and their pocket calculators.

A few miles across central London, the mother of all parties was starting as LWT celebrated not only gaining the GMTV franchise, but the retention of the station's own licence to run the weekend ITV service, one of the most profitable in the country. The champagne corks also popped for Carlton TV, which had won the weekday franchise for London, replacing the venerable institution of Thames TV. (The new Carlton service in London was at first dismally bad – hence its nickname of 'the C-word of British television'.)

Others were in more sombre mood. At the Camden headquarters of the incumbent morning-franchise-holder, TV-AM, there was much bitterness. The station was led by Bruce Gyngell, often said to have been Mrs Thatcher's favourite broadcaster after he pulled off an 'electronic Wapping' and became the first to break the power of the television trade unions. The loss was ironic. Gyngell was exactly the sort of person Maggie had originally intended to bring into the ITV system by way of the franchise. Now his business had been ruined: 'death by faxecution'; Maggie sent him a personal letter of condolence. Elsewhere it was reported that Harry Turner of Television South West, which had lost out to the upstart West Country Television, said that, on reflection, it would have been better if his bid to the ITC had consisted of just two words: 'Fuck off.'

The 1991 'blind bid' auction for regional and morning ITV franchises was to be thought of evermore by most people in tellyland as an unmitigated disaster which had made a few people very rich at the expense of the health and quality of the service. The companies had been forced to bid huge sums, in many cases, and prune programming budgets to find the cash to pay for the bids. At the same time, it had geared the entire industry towards 'accountancy television', bringing to the fore the hard-nosed financial strategists who had planned the successful bids, and pushing further into the background the programme-making people who had previously run most of the ITV network. Yet more money was taken away from programme budgets to pay for multi-million-pound bonuses in the form of share options needed to keep key executives in place during the bidding process, stopping them defecting to rivals.

NBC was locked out of ITV for the time being, so Cox looked for other ways to break into British television. There was the launch of NBC Europe (later modestly renamed the NBC SuperChannel) on cable, but that would remain small potatoes until the cable industry as a whole started to grow. Instead, Cox began sizing up the unknown quantity of Channel 5, the new national service proposed by the same legislation as had brought about the franchise auction. The government's idea was that Channel 5, which was due to come up for auction in the mid-'90s, would compete with the ITV companies for advertising, putting them under even more financial pressure.

Little was known about Channel 5 at first, except that it would be very hard to get off the ground in competition with the existing channels, especially ITV and the newly populist Channel Four, and in competition with the new force of satellite. There was also a technical 'nightmare' lurking in the background: the Independent Television Commission (ITC) was insisting that whoever won the franchise retune the nation's video recorders at their own cost. A third problem was that the costs of the most important types of popular programme, including sport, movies and light-entertainment repeats, were set to go through the roof as satellite and cable entered the programme-buying market.

Cox was convinced that Channel 5 could succeed only if it went all-out for the younger ITV audience, establishing some sort of identity and loyalty with them before they, as predicted, steadily switched over to satellite or disappeared to surf the Internet. Billboards and other advertising media would not be enough against that kind of opposition. Channel 5 would need the sort of relentless promotion that the *Sun* had given Sky when the satellite service was getting off the ground. Even then, Cox knew, it would be a uphill struggle.

The deadline for Channel 5 bids had been set for May 1995, but serious plans would have to be formed, at least in outline, much earlier than that: by summer 1994 at the latest. The more Cox looked at the potential audience and ad-revenue figures, the more he was convinced that he needed a tabloid newspaper partner to help promote Channel 5 to the mass audience. The *Sun* was, of course, out of the question, and anyway Murdoch was likely to make his own bid for Channel 5. So a link-up with Montgomery's Mirror Group, also keen to get into TV, seemed one way to go.

Fortuitously Cox had known Monty since the early 1980s, when they were both involved with Sky, and later they had discussed Monty's original city-TV plan for London, but Cox had been unable to get involved with that. Now, with Monty firmly in the driving seat at the Mirror Group, they started talking about a possible bid for Channel 5.

Talks between Cox and Monty began in the summer of 1994 but nothing was firmed up. Cox and Monty were both playing the field, weighing up possible partners. Then Kelvin joined Mirror TV and that clinched it for Cox.[2] He was an enormous fan of Kelvin and of what he thought of as the ex-*Sun* editor's 'sheer gut-rending, instinctive promotional ability'. MacKenzie knew the target Channel 5 audience Cox was after like the back of his hand and had proved it by tickling their fancy more effectively than anyone else for more than a decade. That was the thing about MacKenzie. People who judged him by the standards of conventional journalism misunderstood his game. Kelvin was *showbiz*. Really, he was like one of those old-fashioned 'barkers' the Victorians used to have outside seaside Palaces of Varieties. What he had in effect done with the *Sun* was stand there in front of a big billboard displaying half-naked girls, waving a Union Jack and shouting, 'Roll up, roll up, folks! See the A-mazin' hamster-eatin' pop star! . . . Housey, housey! I'm giving away lotsa luvverly Lotto lolly – I must be *mad*, sir! Only 20p, madam! . . . Step this way, folks, and Scoff at a Toff . . . Roll up, roll up! Try yer luck, sir! Kill an Argie and win a coconut!' He always drew a big crowd. And that was what Channel 5 needed. Cox was adamant. It was essential that the *Mirror* had him in place if NBC was going to put serious money into a Channel 5 bid.

Janet's role in the Mirror Group's bid for Channel 5 was more complicated. She had arrived at the same time as MacKenzie. By the start of 1995 she had set out her Vision for L!ve TV, and had left her implementers (people like Rachel Purnell and Tony Orsten) to get on with it. She turned her attention to programme plans for Channel 5. Cox admired her as a creative talent and an ideas person, but some things about her worried him. She started working alongside the NBC people whom Cox had brought over from New York to sketch out a schedule, based on all the work that had been done for the breakfast-time ITV franchise a couple of years before. But Janet quickly fell out with Caroline Vanderlip, who led the NBC programming team. Vanderlip, who had previously worked at NBC's New York headquarters and who had launched NBC's cable channel, left the bid team, took up a better offer from another company, and went back to the States.

Cox was not too fazed by this. He had been in television long enough to know that 'creative people' could be 'difficult'. But he still had his worries about Janet. She was 'brilliant' of course. But that, in a way, was her weakness, at least as far as Channel 5 was concerned. As programming chief she would not have as much cash as ITV to play with, but they would still have to give her a lot of money. What would she do with it? Janet's great claim to fame was that she was an innovator. Great. But that meant taking a gamble. She might come up with something fantastic that nobody had thought of before and make everyone a fortune. But with innovation came risk. NBC did not like risks. Neither did General Electric, the vast American multinational which owned the channel. And neither did the stockbrokers who valued GE's stock as worth more than any other company in the world because . . . well, because it did not take risks.

Janet was a great signing for L!ve TV, Cox thought. Perfect for the central programming of some sort of British version of Fox, if that was Monty's game. The Mirror Group had done well to get her. She had done wonders for their profile in the TV business already. That was clever, too. But, apart from the innovation thing, there was concern about her 'feel' for the existing and primetime audiences, especially the more conservative viewers. She had experience in these areas, it was true, and had done well supervising series like *Men Behaving Badly* and *How Do They Do That?*. Her involvement in *The Six O'Clock Show* way back had shown that she could grab the attention of a mass audience. But her record was mixed, especially when it came to originating new programmes.

Her forte, as Cox saw it, was daytime and late-night niche programmes, which had been great for BBC 2 and even better for cable, but he was convinced that Channel 5 had to win in primetime, at least one night a week, if it was ever to get off the ground, even with the promotional backing of the *Mirror*. For NBC the only programming issue was whether they spent all their money on programmes to win the ratings battle against ITV on one whole night in the week, or whether they attacked ITV for an hour or two every night. There just would not be enough advertising revenue to pay for anything else. All the channel's money would have to be spent on about ten hours of ITV-crunching soaps, light entertainment and movies every week. The remaining 150 or so weekly hours would be surrendered to ITV. You couldn't just run the test-card, but . . . well, frankly, you might as well.

Any remaining doubts Cox might have had about the shape of the consortium, and Janet's role in it, evaporated when Alan McKeown of SelecTV joined up, bringing with him a vast catalogue of repeatable light-entertainment hits such as *Birds of a Feather* and *Lovejoy*.[3] With Kelvin and McKeown on board, backed by NBC's money and the *Mirror* to advertise it all, the bid would have a 'headlock' on the target audience, Cox thought. It was in with a chance, definitely. The trade press started saying it was the strongest bid.

McKeown heard on the circuit that Cox had teamed up with the *Mirror* to mount a bid. NBC, he thought, was a 'powerhouse broadcaster' which, as chance would have it, employed his wife, Tracey Ullman, as one of its leading stars. The *Mirror* readership was a perfect 'fit' with the audience for *Birds of a Feather* and other SelecTV gems. And McKeown knew of MacKenzie not only as the former editor of the *Sun* but as a friend and associate of Adam Singer and Roger Luard, two of the leading figures in the network of TCI companies which aimed to dominate British cable television. NBC's deep pockets and experience of daytime scheduling, his own catalogue of sit-coms, and the marketing power of the *Mirror* looked like a winning combination. He wanted in, and he was welcomed with open arms.[4]

When McKeown joined the bid team he went through programme plans devised by Janet. They were based around a modernised daytime Richard-and-Judy-style show, to be broadcast from the Canary Wharf 'Entity' she was creating for L!ve. This was to be followed at 5 p.m. by a live news and 'lifestyle' programme using a lot of OB units. More live programmes were planned for later in the evening, together with studio-based Janet-style chat and game shows. McKeown was not impressed. The material was too similar to that which Janet had been turning out at the BBC: game shows about fashion, fashion programmes about game shows, that sort of thing – 'silly "pet-trick" shows', as he thought of them. All very trendy, but nothing with mass appeal. This stuff wasn't going to be viewed by anybody except a small group of people in the trendier parts of London, and by the rest of the media. Some of it, McKeown thought, was even more esoteric than Channel Four. McKeown thought Janet was 'a real bright girl' and that the programmes she made had 'real flair' but . . . it was a *very particular type of programming*, wasn't it? She worked best doing the sort of shows that interested her and which reflected the people she found interesting and hung out with.[5]

When the management team met to discuss Janet's schedule, it was suggested that additional mass-appeal material be bought into restore the balance. Cox, as guardian of NBC's cash, was not having any of that. 'Woooaah,' he said, 'wait a minute,' and he turned to McKeown. 'Alan, say your company works for us twenty-four hours a day; tell us how much programming you can produce. We can use it all. *Then* we can work out what to do with the rest of the schedule.' Janet's programme plans were mostly pulped and the search began to find a new director of programming to take her place. It was antici-pated that she would react badly to this, but Monty had no choice if he was to keep Cox and, especially, Alan McKeown on-side.[6]

The change made sense for Monty for another reason. While Janet was sitting in on the Channel 5 planning meet-ings, Monty now had over a hundred people on the L!ve TV payroll sitting on the 24th floor of Canary Wharf. The launch date was looming and there were already all sorts of problems. Rachel Purnell and Nick Ferrari were deputis-ing but they needed Janet there if they were to make any real headway. Monty became more and more insistent: Janet had to get upstairs and sort it all out.

Janet did not take kindly to this advice, and the Channel 5 bid meetings became a battleground. The meetings normally involved about twenty people, all strait-laced executives and money people from NBC and the Mirror Group and their accountants and advertising agencies: plus Janet and MacKenzie, who turned the otherwise boring and formal gatherings into a non-stop stand-up comedy show. Janet would be there, sitting with her back to the door and yammering on. Kelvin would tiptoe into the room walking with exaggeratedly quiet steps, his finger to his lips, mouthing 'shhhhhh' and winking at them all. Janet, unaware of this, would yammer some more, and all the accountants had to bite their lips to stop themselves cracking up. Kelvin would then position himself behind her, stick out his top teeth and start miming to her words, nodding his head from side to side in a passable imitation of Ken Dodd and making 'blah, blah, blah' gestures. Eventually, Janet would sense that the executives were not listening to a word she was saying: '*Wasssamatter wiv yer?*' At which point Kelvin would mince forward rapidly and say, 'Hello, my little petal, how are you today?' and give her a peck on the neck, causing Janet to yelp, '*Fahk off, Kelvin! Just grow up, will yer!*'

Kelvin would then take his seat on the other side of the boardroom table, eagerly lean forward, brow furrowed in *extreme* attentiveness, nodding with excitement and enthusiasm as Janet made her points and hanging on every word, with lots of appreciative uhmmmms and 'Ahhhh! yes, *now* I see it.' '*Kelvin! Will you stop doin' that. It's perfetick. Just grow up will yer, f'chrissake.*' MacKenzie would then switch to extreme boredom, whistling, tossing paperclips in the air, starting up conversations with the person sitting next to him, and trying to goad Janet into addressing him directly. Eventually she would fall for it and say, 'And what I'm saying, right, is that, looking at the *demergrafficks*, we are not gonna make it Blokevision – *all right, Kelvin?* It's not gonna be fucking Blokevision, because Blokevision has no place—' 'All right, love, all right,' Kelvin would respond with patronising gallantry. 'We won't make it Blokevision. I promise. But I don't think

Tampax TV is gonna do the trick either. So no Tampax TV – right?'

In the end, the job of telling Janet she was being replaced as director of programmes for Channel 5 fell to MacKenzie. He was managing director of Mirror Television. No matter what she thought about his lack of TV expertise or the implied relationship of equality between them, he was the boss. And so he took her off the bid. He did not even tell her who was going to replace her. The name remained a secret, to be placed in a 'brown envelope' and given to the ITC as part of the bid, never to be revealed to the world unless the bid was accepted.

The obvious tension between Janet and MacKenzie so far siphoned off into rude and non-stop, but fairly harmless, personal banter now exploded for the first time. There was a huge shouting-match, which was widely reported in the press. It was said that Janet was on the point of resigning from the Mirror Group as a result. This did not happen and a bland official statement was issued noting that 'creative tension is inevitable' and adding the enigmatic comment that 'Mirror Television is setting up a multi-million-pound business, not a playgroup.'

Chapter Sixteen

In which the Talent start to Find Life Difficult at L!ve TV but reckon that the Poor Sods on the technical side are having the worst of it, while All Manner of Problems begin to mount with Nobody apparently able to Sort Them Out

On 1 May 1995 the 24th-floor Entity was completed, and on-screen Talent, sundry other Tellybrats and the technical staff moved into begin dress rehearsals. In typical skinflint fashion, the Mirror Group had based the whole operation on a single floor, which meant that some 180 staff were supposed to work there. Now that Janet had commandeered the entire floor for her multi-purpose Entity, these staff had nowhere to work and were crammed together in nooks and crannies, thus creating additional and considerable excess body heat. Summer was coming. On warm days the fug on the 24th floor was unbearable and the Talent, sweltering directly under the lights in their tight-fitting Lycra outfits, were in danger of looking like something out of a deodorant advert.

Janet dealt with the overcrowding problem by announcing a policy of 'hot desking'. This was a typically trendy management idea, much in vogue in the sorts of advertising and architectural offices Janet admired. The fact is that most people spend, say, only 20 per cent of their time at their desk. The rest of the time the desk is redundant and could therefore be used by somebody else. So if you have a hundred people in the office you only need, say, twenty desks. In theory there will always be a desk free – unless, of course, everyone decided to sit down at the same time, in which case there would be chaos. But that never happens, right, so there was no need to worry. For the rest of the time people would be involved in a game of musical chairs, hopping from one desk to another, thus boosting internal communication and creativity all round. Completely Brilliant. Some said that Janet thought desks were 'a male power trip' and were unnecessary at L!ve TV. Except for herself.[1]

Janet had a fairly large office, though it was partly open to the rest of the studio. It was dominated by her desk, which was moulded out of solid plastic waste of many colours and was reckoned to have cost a huge sum. The office had an internal window, a bit like a serving-hatch, connecting her with her PA's office next door. Janet called this *'me shahtin' 'ole* – I jus' push it open and start *shahtin'.'*

In line with The Look and The Vision, Janet had arranged for the main studio cameras to be mounted on a track leading from the windows past the 'newsdesk' and ending up near her own office, which, of course, was gonna be on show since she was *by far* the Biggest Name the channel had, so why not use it? Shoulder-borne cameras would give more wobbly access to the rest of The Entity and everything would be linked up so that the director in The Box could leap about like a DJ for up to six hours at a go, switching every few seconds from camera to camera inside The Entity and blastin' the

!

graphic on to the screen and then going out to OB cameras in a nightclub and back again to another part of The Entity and then out again to another OB at a film premiere or somethin' and cutting out of that if it got too borin' an' sprayin' more graphics an' infobars all over the screen, an' *screamin' an' shahtin'* at everyone an' bein'

Massively Innervitiff.

There were just one or two problems with all this. Although The Entity looked good – like a nightclub as intended – there was nowhere anyone could frame a shot. The huge plate-glass windows, which it had been thought would provide a brilliant backdrop, were actually another nightmare. At night they acted as giant mirrors, full of glare, and if they ever came into the picture reflected back the cameraman. They had to be covered up with blinds, which meant the groovy City of Lights background vista was lost. That vista had been the location's only real advantage, and its loss meant they might have well been broadcasting from a shed in Ipswich (which, frankly, would probably have been easier for the staff and studio guests to get to, given Canary Wharf's lack of transport links).

Canary Wharf, while state-of-the-art when it came to accommodating office workers, was not well suited to use as a TV studio. The computer-controlled air-conditioning could not be adjusted to deal with the immense heat generated by TV studio lights: the programmers had never imagined that anyone would want to put banks of TV studio lights into a space designed to be used by insurance underwriters.

Then there was the fact that the whole Entity was going to be used as a normal office and a studio at the same time. If the lights were bright enough to allow filming to take place, they would be too bright for people to sit at desks and use computers. But if the lights were turned down, so that people could see their screens, it became too dark to film. At first, as rehearsal began, the lights were left on at full blast all the time, making The Entity unusable as an office and, to Janet's presumed delight, pushing the style obsession to the point where people arriving on a sunny day would put their Ray-Bans *on* when they got into the office and started typing away.

Then it was decided to link the lighting to the director's box so that a computer could turn the lights up in a particular part of The Entity as the cameras approached. So, as people struggled away at their screens writing scripts or, more likely, encyclopaedic memos moaning about the mounting technical and editorial problems they were facing, they would suddenly be engulfed in a pool of blinding light, heralding the arrival of a jogging lycra-clad presenter yapping away into a camera held by a crablike cameraperson walking backwards at high speed. This spectacle would pass, leaving the victim blinking at their screen. Then, just as their whirling pupils re-dilated, *Wham!* the lights went up again. The camera crab and attendant yapper were making the return journey. This might happen as many as ten times in an hour, resulting in a wave of migraines and eye-strain-related medical problems.

The lights were bad enough, but then there was the problem of noise. A lot of TV studios in the past had office workers in view, making phone calls and *looking* as if they were in the studio. Background hubbub could then be carefully mixed into the soundtrack to achieve the required effect. Then there were the American cop shows like *Hill Street Blues*, in which an office was featured with phones trilling pleasingly in the background. That was obviously part of Janet's thinking about The Look. This effect, too, was entirely artificial. At L!ve people were making real phone calls on screen, complete with such things as swearing, screaming at photocopier repair men who had not turned up, taking personal calls (and perhaps bursting into tears) and so on. The presence of the cameras meant that people had to whisper or hiss through gritted teeth, 'I can't talk now, I'm on national television.' Not that it was easy getting to a phone in the first place. Under the hot-desking rule, nobody had their own extension and, as a result, phoning in from the outside world, or returning calls in any sort of organised fashion, was impossible.

The worst phone problems occurred when there was live music in the studio. Janet and Rachel had planned to have live groups and other ear-splitting activity taking place in The Entity. Delicate phone calls could be interrupted by 1000 watts of audio dynamite exploding on the other side of the 'office' at any time, bringing all work to a halt. There was just enough soundproofing to keep out the background drone from passing aeroplanes and helicopters, but the soundproofing was otherwise pretty basic, especially between the floors, and nowhere near what would have been needed for a 'real' television or sound studio. But this fact had somehow slipped everyone's attention.

During the first live music rehearsal a furious little man from the Swiss bank which occupied the floor below forced his way into The Entity, blinking at the array of acid green and purple walls, nightclub accoutrements, lolling Tellybrats, amplifiers, blinding lights, drumkits and electric guitars. One minute he had been sitting in the calm of his office, buying and selling Eurobonds, the next he couldn't hear himself think! His phone was jumping up and down on the table! What was going on here? Were they running some sort of rock music club? Live music was restricted to after normal office hours.

Naturally, The Entity conformed to basic health, safety and fire regulations. But, reasonably enough, things like these were not near the top of Janet's creative agenda. According to plan, and in line with normal cheapo daytime television practice, there would be a lot of L!ve cookery featured on the channel. Obviously a permanent kitchen studio set was out of the question, on account of not being multi-purpose. So the idea was to have a mobile kitchen 'unit', a bit like a hot-dog stand, which could be wheeled about to do cookery demonstrations. Unfortunately, the 'unit' kept setting off the smoke alarms. Mobile industrial ventilators had to be brought in, but this added to the noise problem. And so flambés and traditional Christmas puddings remained off the editorial agenda.

Because everything on the 24th floor would be on camera, everything had to conform to The Look. Janet was adamant about this. So, for example, instead of buying a job lot of normal robust formica desks, she ordered at vast cost weirdly sculpted metallic affairs which, since they had been created as designer objects to be displayed in the sort of Fantasy Apartments featured in *Hello!* and never actually used, seemed to fall apart the minute anyone touched them.

The computers on the desks represented a major threat to The Look. They could not be dispensed with entirely, so Janet had them sprayed khaki, purple and orange, thus invalidating their warranty and maintenance contracts and reducing their resale and accountancy value to zero. Ordinary wastepaper baskets were also, naturally, out of the question. Instead Janet invested in huge matt black and silver designer objects of limited practical use. There was a constant problem with mess, which was not allowed – even unto a carelessly discarded newspaper or rogue piece of paper – despite the fact that this was 'a living, working space'.

The visual house-style was rigidly and almost fanatically imposed. The trademark '!' appeared everywhere in The Entity, either on its own or written into signs such as 'L!brary' and 'To!let'. Coffee-making and -drinking were a major bone of contention. When Darryl Burton noticed that stray coffee cups were invading The Entity, he simply closed down the minuscule coffee-making area and said it would not open again until people tidied up. Caffeine was the absolute minimum stimulation aid the Tellybrats required, and they rebelled by sealing him into his office with gaffer tape. But Burton, who struck the Tellybrats as being a bit of an East End hard man, did not relent. For a couple of weeks they had to troop down 24 floors and hunt about in Canary Wharf whenever they needed a pick-me-up.

Coffee cups and newspapers were one thing, but most of all Janet didn't want a load of unsightly humans appearing on screen and fucking up The Look. A secretary who, on a warm spring day, came to work in a chintzy Laura Ashleyish chiffon dress was bitterly denounced for dressing in 'jumble-sale rubbish'. Janet talked grimly about introducing a compulsory dress code. This never happened, as such, but Janet occasionally zeroed in on individual sartorial offenders. One good-looking but inexperienced female presenter was gravely summoned to Janet's office for a little chat. What had she done wrong? Had she screwed up in some way? Would she get the boot? Janet launched into a highly personalised critique of her dress sense: 'Look, darlin', you've got *massiff* potential, right? But you just can't go abaht wearin' *them* clothes on *this* channel. And that *'air* – you gotta do something about the *'air, perleeeeeze*. Get it sorted.'

The idea was that eventually all 180 staff members would be sent to a stylist for a make-over by a woman who had previously been involved in creating the Look for Upside Down, a manufactured 'boy band' popular among the nation's 10-year-old girls and, frankly, homosexual men. The make-over campaign was not entirely successful and some of the older production bods, such as the bearded Tony Orsten, were declared Hopeless Cases and had metaphorically to sign a pledge never to appear on camera. Which was fine with them.

Naturally the Talent tried to please Janet by dressing as trendily as possible, but this had its own dangers. One person turned up wearing a pair of loafers in bright orange. Janet was ecstatic: '*Com-pletely Brilliant!* Where'dya get 'em?' It was explained that they were made by Patrick Cox. This was even better: Patrick Cox (no relation to Patrick Cox of NBC) was the most Completely Wicked footwear maker in the whole of London. It was time for an on-the-spot Janet Decision. Patrick Cox orange loafers were declared compulsory for anyone who might come within camerashot. Many pairs were bought. Shortly after this a joke memo, attributed to Janet, circulated, saying that everyone had to go and get a L!ve TV tattoo. It was ignored, but nobody was entirely sure if it was real or not.

By now the on-screen Talent were starting to sweat a bit. But it was reckoned that the Poor Sods who were setting up the technical production side of the channel were having the worst of it. The Entity was being equipped by Terry Lee, the independent consultant who had advised Monty on his unsuccessful bid for London L!ve. The technical brief was vague, but from the start it was agreed that L!ve TV would use a system of rapid, 'non-linear' editing.

The idea of rapid editing made a lot of sense for a station with relatively few staff which planned to be on air 24 hours a day. It meant you could use the same footage over and over again, editing it in different ways. If, for example, some footage of a fashion show was thrown into the central computer, all the editing terminals could fish this material out and edit it in different ways, so you could do a 'news' item about the show, then another item about the dresses, another about the celebs who were there, another item about shoes and then, maybe, lash bits of it together with other footage to create an item about careers, or what-ever. It was a way of using the same few minutes of footage to make hours and hours of output. There was no waste at all. Rachel Purnell called it 'eco-television': everything was to be endlessly recycled.

To make all this work L!ve bought a digital editing system called Avid, which was becoming the standard edit-ing system throughout the television industry, replacing the old analogue editing systems based on video-tape. Under the old system the cameras recorded everything on tape and then an editor cut everything together on what amounted to a stack of video-recorders, taking a bit from one, then a bit from the second and third machines, and building it all up on to a master tape ready for transmis-sion. Avid did the same job. But instead of using tape the footage from the cameras was changed into a series of files on a computer, whose vast memory could cope with all the footage coming from multiple cameras in The Entity, from the OBs and from other sources. Editors and produc-ers would get footage out of the system, merge it with other footage and graphics, edit it all 'inside' the computer's memory, and transmit it immediately.

Avid was great for making very short items which could then be wiped. Also, it was much easier to use than the older systems, which required years of training and a lot of skill and patience. Since it was faster, far fewer editors and operators were needed and, importantly, they could learn on the job as part of multi-skilling, thus keeping the wages bill down – even if the result was a lot of amateur-ish crash and 'scratch' editing, with the output screen suddenly goin' blank in between shots and that Completely Brilliant electronic *kkkkrrrskrrrrzzzkkkk* noise happening for a few seconds as the studio presenter handed over to the OB reporter and then *zzzxooommpskr-*

rrrzzzkkk back again to the studio. This was exactly the sort of 'punk' and 'DIY' and 'disposable' television Janet liked to make, so she was a great fan of the system. She was said to have been the first person at the BBC to use Avid, excitedly having one of the earliest versions installed in her office, where she played about with it for hours.

Five Avid editing suites were ordered. In a normal television operation these might have been used independently to make a series of programmes to be put out one after the other. To make Janet's vision work, all five would have to be linked together by an enormously powerful central computer (called a file server) so that up to five editors could dip into the material on all the suites and edit the live output simultaneously. But Avid was not designed for this – not at such short notice.[2]

The production team tried to explain the difficulties to Janet and pleaded with her to change The Vision to something more conventional so that the system could cope. This did not get them very far. Janet had created The Look. That was her job and she was brilliant at it. It was up to the techies and implementers to make it happen. She tended to treat the technical team at L!ve as an outside company, just as she would have done at the BBC where the production department was at the end of a phone and she was the 'client'. With one or two exceptions, her experience at LWT and the BBC had persuaded her that the technical people in television had to be pushed very hard. To get anything Half Decent you had to do a lot of *screamin' an' shahtin'* an' refusin' to water things down an' compromise because what did you end up with On The Screen if you compromised? A watered-down compromise, that's what. *Great, innit?*

Janet's approach had caused a deep divide in the technical staff. Some of those from a more conventional background could not stand the sight of her. They had been trained over the years to do things 'properly'. Building a studio inside an office – with no lighting rig? *It'll look like shit.* Using different bits of the screen for different output? *She's fucking bonkers!* Then there were those whose background was in electronics or computers, rather than 'conventional' television. They listened to her going on and on, and might think, 'She's mad,' but when they stood back and stroked their chins . . . Yeah, maybe if you plugged this in here and that in there and connected up this to a box containing that . . . yeah. And if you got on the Net, had a look for a company that made the right thingymajig . . . yeah . . . perhaps. It might work. Or it might blow up. Who knows? In the meantime Janet and Rachel forged ahead on the assumption that the Avid server problem would be sorted out in time for the launch, and the system would work as advertised.

MacKenzie, as managing director, might have been expected to get a grip on production problems. But he was not in a position to do so. One day he was taking VIP visitors on a tour round the directing gallery, growling authoritatively about what it all did, but essentially making it all up. Afterwards he bumped into a member of the technical team. 'Here,' he said, waving expansively at the rows of White Man's Magic, 'you'll have to tell me one day what all this stuff does. To tell you the truth, I haven't got the foggiest.' MacKenzie had been brought up in a world of typewriters where the most advanced type of technology was carbon paper, but when the *Sun* went over to computerised production after the move to Wapping, he had embraced the new technology with enthusiasm. He called the individual journalists' newfangled computer terminals 'the scamulator machines' and he loved the speed and centralised power the system gave him. But he remained ignorant about how any of it worked.

While the techies were working round the clock trying to rewire the Avid, rehearsals, the need for which was becoming increasingly urgent, would have to take place without fully using or testing the editing system. This was bad enough. But there was a second major technical problem. The OB units which, according to The Vision, would provide over 60 per cent of the material for the channel, were not working, and there was little prospect that they would until well after the launch date.

The plan had been that the OB vans would be ready many weeks before launch, so that there would be time for rehearsals. The vans had been ordered from BT, and the idea was that BT would make and own them and lease them to L!ve TV. Then, as a cost-cutting measure, it was decided that BT would install the communications equipment linking the vans to Canary Wharf, but that L!ve itself would install the TV equipment, bought from a third source. The effect of the decision was that responsibility for creating the vans was divided between BT, L!ve and the TV equipment supply company. This led to endless arguments between the three parties about who was paying for what, with each saying they couldn't do their bit until the others did their bits, and much passing of the buck.

Mike Spinks, L!ve TV's head of technical operations, was on the phone to the equipment suppliers right up until two days before the launch. When they refused to guarantee delivery, he angrily slammed down the phone in mid-sentence, jumped into his car, drove at top speed to their Luton headquarters and resumed the high-decibel conversation face to face. In this way L!ve got the vans just in time for the launch. They were not fully finished and had the wrong type of equipment, but, as Spinks pointed out, banging the table, they had to have something – *anything*. They could work on the finer points once the vans were on the road.

All the time the clock was ticking away and budgets were in danger of being busted all over the place. The techies refused to believe that it was all supposed to work for £2000 an hour. They knew that what they were being asked to set up would cost a *lot* more than that. And it wasn't even working yet. The problems were starting to spin out of control.

And there didn't seem to be anyone at L!ve TV who could sort them out.

Chapter Seventeen

In which the Mirror–NBC bid for Channel 5 implodes
because of the Retuning Nightmare and the Tellybrats
begin to worry about all the Screamin' an' Shahtin' going
on between Janet and the Mirror Board, Rachel Purnell
finds out about the Ways of Tabloid Journalists, Janet
complains about Metaphorical Dicks being placed on
Tables, a great many Fibs are told, Nick Ferrari becomes
stranded in the Alien World of Planet Janet, and the
Mirror announces to the world that Knives are Being
Sharpened for Janet Street-Porter

Patrick Cox slumped in his executive-class seat on the
flight from back from Hong Kong to London, wrapped in
thought. The NBC chief had just spent a gruelling time
in the soon-to-be-ex-British colony trying to find a way
into the Chinese television market, the biggest in the world
and, some time after the year 2000, scheduled to become
by far the richest and most important. It was April 1995.
Murdoch was there already, of course, developing Star TV,
the Far Eastern version of Sky. And where Murdoch went,
others, including Cox, were sure to follow.

But now, as he floated at 30,000 feet, Cox was preoccupied by a problem much closer to home. The bid he was
putting together with Mirror Television and Alan
McKeown's SelecTV for the Channel 5 franchise was in
trouble. He poked lethargically at the keys of his laptop.
The figures were all there. Programme costs. At least £200
million to get the station on air. Franchise fee. Another £20
or £25 million to beat the opposition in the forthcoming
auction. Advertising revenue. You'd need to take at least

10 per cent of the whole UK audience away from ITV to get the advertisers to pay for it all. More if you wanted to make a really decent profit.

Could it be done? There was a problem. Ideally you would have to get virtually the whole population of the UK to buy a new aerial to receive the new channel. No chance of that. Maybe you give the aerials away? Murdoch had effectively given away a lot of Sky dishes at first, as Cox remembered well. *Nightmare*. All those installation teams piling into council estates and clambering around on tower blocks. Then you would have to send teams to retune everyone's video to make sure the signal from the new channel didn't interfere with existing channels. If you didn't, or if something went wrong, you would have to compensate people. That meant *unlimited liability*.[1] Would they have to retune people's Sky boxes as well ? Would Sky, *would Sam Chisholm*, let them do it? Hmmm. A lot of variables.

And there was another problem. Could the retuning be done in time? It looked as though Channel 5, without aerials, would be available in only two-thirds of homes by the time of its scheduled launch. Maybe less. Whole urban centres might be missing. A *lot* of variables. It meant that to get your 10 per cent national share you would maybe have to get a 20 per cent of the ITV audience in homes that could actually receive the new channel. Could you really capture nearly a quarter of the ITV audience with maybe a tenth of the programme budget? With no sport and not many decent movies?

The target audience had a lot of choice about what they watched. Channel Four was competing for the same 'young ITV' audience: *Brookside, Friends, The Big Breakfast, The Word* . . . minority channel, my arse! Everyone was after them and they were difficult to reach. They had dishes, a lot of them, with the *Sun* telling them what to watch on Sky. They used the Internet more than anyone else. They went down the pub. They rented a lot of home videos. They used their telly to play computer games. They even went to the cinema. Yep. A *helluva lot* of variables.

A couple of hours later Cox was driving through the London traffic, heading towards Canary Wharf for a meeting about the bid. His jet-lag was so bad that he missed a red light and almost crashed. But the more he turned over the familiar numbers in his head the more sure he was that NBC would have to pull out of the bid. It just wasn't worth the risk.

The mood was grim as Cox, Monty, Kelvin and McKeown gathered in the *Mirror*'s boardroom. All the partners had been looking at the same figures and were about to come to the same conclusion. The latest technical reports on the retuning problem painted a bleak picture. The first estimate had been that the operation would cost £50 million, but the figure kept going up every time the technical people looked at it. The key thing was the cost of the individual visits to do the retuning. It depended on how many videos could be retuned in an hour, and that was almost impossible to predict. The estimated cost of retuning had now reached £120 million and was still heading north. Even then you would only get into two-thirds of homes, tops. The accountants were asking for a definite figure for the retuning, but the technical bods simply wouldn't commit themselves, some of them saying, 'Whatever you think this is going to cost, double it.'

For Cox and the others it was a simple equation. The more it cost to do the retuning, the less you could afford to bid for the franchise. Cox tapped the latest figures into his laptop. Even if they held the retuning cost at £125 million, the most they could afford to bid would be £5 million. He shook his head and told his partners, 'We'd love to do it. But it won't fly.' Monty and Kelvin agreed. There was only one issue left to resolve. The team's accountants had worked out that the consortium would have to bid around £22 million to win the franchise. If they put in a bid of £1 million or £2 million, which was all they could afford, they would lose. Cox thought it was better to throw in the towel than be classified as losers, which might reflect badly on the NBC stock-price. McKeown, who in many ways had the most to gain from Channel 5, thought they should go ahead and bid anyway. The partners agreed to sleep on it. But when they gathered again it was decided to abort the bid.[2]

The collapse of the Mirror Group's bid for Channel 5 was followed, a few weeks later, by the 'sweetheart deal' between Sky and the two largest UK cable companies, TCI and Nynex. This had led in turn to the collapse of SportsWire, the more important 'sister channel' to L!ve TV. MacKenzie had been spending a lot of time negotiating the Mirror's position in relation to the consortium that owned SportsWire and helping with early preparations for a potential joint cable-industry–*Mirror* bid for the all important Premier League. Now that Channel 5 was a nonstarter and SportsWire was a dead duck, he had very little to occupy him, or justify his salary, other than L!ve TV.

Back in the autumn of 1994 Janet had told people that she would have no problem getting on with MacKenzie because he would, mainly, be doin' the sport. Mirror TV had big plans and the organisation would be big enough to accommodate them both. It was almost as though they would be separate channel controllers, MacKenzie heading the sports channel and Janet running the lifestyle channels, with Monty standing above them at the next level up in the management structure. It was not critical, therefore, that they got on with each other.

But now Mirror Television was left only with L!ve TV, a minuscule cable channel. MacKenzie and Janet were bound to clash over who would have control of the channel, which was the Mirror Group's only going TV concern. At the same time, the collapse of the Channel 5 bid and, especially, the decision about SportsWire, had a catastrophic effect on Mirror TV's financial projections. On the assumption that football would be mainly on cable, the finances of L!ve TV were based on a sudden surge of cable subscriptions, scheduled to take place in 1996 when the Premier League matches started appearing on cable and people sent their dishes back. The surge had been written into the L!ve TV business plan as a bankable fact, so certain was MacKenzie that he could swipe the football rights from Sky. But without the football the number of subscriptions to cable would be much lower than previously anticipated.

The collapse of SportsWire, as a result of the 'sweetheart deal' between TCI, Nynex and Sky, drove MacKenzie into a rage. A crisis-ridden Mirror TV board meeting was held, at which he roundly abused TCI chief Adam Singer as 'a traitor', who had led the Mirror up the garden path. The Mirror Group had been conned, along with all the other cable companies. L!ve TV would still go ahead but it would now have to be a very different sort of channel.

Immediate budget cuts were demanded, to try and match the new and much lower levels of predicted income from the Mirror Group's share of cable subscriptions. At the same time MacKenzie became even more morose about his personal position. Instead of cleaning up as the King of Pay-TV with cable he had been *well stitched up*. His morning ritual of tracking the Sky TV share price and moaning about all the cash he would have made from his share options if he had 'kept his head' and stayed with Murdoch became even more heartfelt.

The problem for L!ve, meanwhile, in terms of cutting the cloth to meet the much lower expected levels of income, was that a lot of money was already committed in terms of building and equipping Janet's Entity. So all the cuts would have to fall on the operating budget, meaning an instant freeze on spending and, above all, a strict cap on the number of people who could be employed. The effects of the new 'scaled-down' L!ve TV were first felt in June, just as the station was due to come on air.[3] At first, at least as far as the Tellybrats (who never had the slightest inkling of what was going on in the boardroom) were concerned, L!ve TV had been a great, fun place to work. Janet's talk of TV revolution was exciting and flattering. Everyone was new, so there had been no time for the normal resentments and office vendettas to build up. Janet had arranged for photographs to be put up on a noticeboard so they could get to know each other. Everyone at L!ve TV was very friendly; many of them were young, astoundingly good looking, exceptionally smiley and delighted to have been taken on. The only thing they knew for sure about L!ve TV was that it was to be 'a happy place where the sun always shines'.

The Tellybrats' main point of contact with management and, generally, work of any sort, was Tony Orsten, who was training them. And he was an *absolute sweetie*. Janet, when they saw her, was full of beans, going round tellin' everyone that they would shortly become stars like her previous Tellybrat creations, and she seemed, when in a good mood, to think even the most asinine programme idea was Completely Brilliant. Millions were being spent to provide them with the very latest in television technology and the studio itself was a sight to behold, despite all the problems.

Then the pressure began to build and the effects of the spending freeze and Janet's precarious position began to be felt. The first serious crisis had come when Janet was taken off the Channel 5 bid. The fact that she was considering leaving was widely reported in the press, creating great Tellybrat unease. This coincided with an enormous bollocking given to Rachel over The Vision for L!ve.

The row boiled up when Rachel was giving Monty and Kelvin a progress report. Monty was antagonistic from the start, and seemed to be spoiling for a fight. He started a discussion about how to film a fashion slot on location at Top Shop. Monty said that they should just film the clothes and put that straight out on the channel. Rachel did not agree, and told him so. An item like that, she said, would have to fit in with the rest of the output. There would have to be something 'going on'. The raw material would have to be edited and re-edited on the Avid system, and properly structured, or it would not work.

Monty begged to differ, it should go straight. But Rachel held her ground. She was the telly production expert here. She knew what she was talking about. That was the way you did it – The Vision. It was different from editing a newspaper. To her astonishment the normally ice-cool Monty exploded at this show of insubordination. How dare she contradict him! She was not at the BBC now! Things did not work like that in newspapers! The editor and proprietor always had to be obeyed, no matter what!

Rachel had heard about the newsroom 'bollocking' process from Nick Ferrari, who had warned her that things were very different in the world of tabloid newspapers. But she had never imagined that such treatment would be dished out to her. She couldn't believe it! It had nothing to do with how you filmed an item any more. It was a ritual display of macho power. Monty kept hammering away. Every time Rachel tried to defend herself he went for the jugular, leaving her speechless and close to tears. To her surprise, MacKenzie who had been looking on silently, stepped into the argument on her side. He told Monty to ease off, and said maybe she had a point: they could talk about it another time.

Rachel went back to her office where, a little later, MacKenzie phoned her to apologise on behalf of Monty and the company. He explained that this was the way in newspapers. It did not mean that they thought any less of her. OK? Rachel was perplexed. In tellyland everyone had to be a luvvie and be nice to each other even if, behind the scenes, they were stabbing each other in the back. Otherwise nothing would get on air. But when she told others about the incident they assured her that this sort of thing was normal. The really amazing thing was not the bollocking, but the fact that they did not treat her like that every day.

These ructions had caused much demoralisation on the 24th floor. To set matters right Monty called a general meeting of all L!ve staff. He gave a pep talk, saying that rumours and talk of a 'rift' between Kelvin and Janet were untrue and were to be officially ignored. People were flabbergasted by the sheer audacity of this fib and the coolness with which it was delivered. How could he hope to get away with it? Many people had seen Rachel coming back from meetings day after day close to tears and muttering bitterly, 'They have no idea. They are trying to destroy us.'

By this time Janet had issued a strict edict in the form of a memo addressed to 'Everyone' that nobody should talk to the press about L!ve TV's internal doings. 'Please can I remind everybody that it is of the utmost importance that

L!ve TV

ANY contact with the press – print or broadcast – must go through our Publicity Manager, Charlotte Ashton. This is a very sensitive time for L!ve TV/Mirror Television and any leak/off-the-cuff remark/so-called joke/inaccurate statement could be damaging.'

In public MacKenzie said (most of the time) that it was true that Janet could be 'difficult' but that this was 'not a problem' because a lot of creative people were like that, and really, he thought she was terrific and he admired her very, very much. At the same time he was privately telling his cronies, 'Janet Street-Porter is a fucking nightmare. That fucking woman will be the fucking death of me.' Janet and her people were 'on another planet', he moaned with genuine exasperation: 'Planet Janet'. She was 'light years away from the interests of Great Swathes of the population'; more interested in impressing her snooty friends in the Groucho Club than in giving the Great Swathes what they wanted.

Janet, too, struggled to maintain the public façade of unity. She would say that things between her and Kelvin were 'fine', side-stepping questions by adding that she really did not see that much of him. She was getting on fine with Monty, too. That was official. Although relations between Janet and Monty were strained following her exclusion from the Channel 5 bid, she loyally toed the line, even telling one media journalist how much she liked Monty on a personal level. The hack, who had followed Monty's career for years, was sceptical. People sometimes said they admired Monty in some ways: that he was a ruthless competitor in the mini-Murdoch mould, that he was highly effective at cutting costs and sacking people, that he was a man to be reckoned with. But he had *never* heard anyone say that they actually liked him. Janet explained away this odd preference by saying that he was intelligent and that she liked all intelligent people.

In reality the management of L!ve TV was now split right down the middle. Two entirely different factions existed at L!ve TV. All the power was in the hands of Monty, Kelvin and the Mirror board lurking on the resolutely normal 19th and 20th floors of the tower. The 24th floor was Janet's domain, the amazing multi-coloured Planet Janet, the lurid and brightly illuminated carnival of hot-desking and deviancy, flashing exclamation marks, scarlet television monitors, nightclub furniture, khaki computers, purple carpet tiles, inter-racial fraternisation and feminism. Planet Janet was dominated by distinctly Amazonian women, staffed by experienced JanetSpawn from places like Planet 24, and supported by a legion of Janet wannabes drawn from the worlds of youth culture, pop music, clubbin' and PR. The inhabitants of Planet Janet included exotic types rarely or never before seen in large numbers in the ranks of an organisation like the Mirror Group, such as black people, lesbians and openly 'out' homosexual men.

The main exception to the general style was Nick Ferrari, positioned by Kelvin and Monty as co-director of programmes to keep an eye on Rachel. Ferrari struggled to find his feet on Planet Janet as the sole representative of the more mainstream *Mirror* tabloid culture. Quite apart from the sort of people he had to deal with, he had difficulty coping with the endless, open-to-all-comers meetings which were the hallmark of Janet and Rachel's post-feminist management style. He was more used to brief editorial conferences, at which a select band of executives (like himself) cowered before a tyrannical editor (like Kelvin) and were furiously and efficiently bollocked for the previous day's cock-ups and then accepted the orders for the day without question. The whole thing could be horrible, but at least it lasted for only a few minutes.

Janet and Rachel had organised things differently. Equality meant everyone was to be valued and 'included'. Everyone had to have their say about everything, on the grounds that if ten people pondered a decision it would be ten times better than if it was taken by one person alone, even though, in the end, Janet made all the important decisions anyway. Ferrari was naturally uncomfortable with these arrangements. He had to attend meetings in a room full of women and gay men orchestrated by Janet and Rachel. At one of these meetings, out of forty-three people present thirty-six were women. And of the tiny and barely tolerated male minority, at least half could be reckoned to be gay. Many of the women disliked Ferrari personally. Rachel had once drawn a joke flipchart diagram entitled 'How L!ve TV works' on which he had a box all to himself labelled 'Pond life'. His other nicknames were 'Mr Blobby' and 'Jabba the Hut'.[4]

Once the meetings started, Ferrari was lost. The idea behind 'meetings management' was that a new and more feminine, sisterly and co-operative way of working could be developed. Alas, this was not to be. Out of sheer exhaustion, if nothing else, individual gripes springing from the unresolved technical problems with the studio (*Nothing works! Absolutely nothing works!*) and sporadic needlematches arising from Tellybrat competition to get the best presenter slots (*Actually, that was my idea!*) were incubated into a single gigantic shouting match during which everyone seemed to be on the verge of a nervous breakdown. Ferrari mostly just sat there, looking uncomfortable, staring out of the window and occasionally smirking (*Wait till Kelvin hears about this!*). After several hours, he would meekly ask, 'So, to sum up, what have we resolved here?' As often as not he would be shrieked at for his pains

(*Shaddup, slimeball!*) and the fight would continue for another three hours.

In contrast to the gay- and women-friendly world of Planet Janet there was the resolutely straight environment of the Mirror Group boardroom, dominated by the puritanical Monty, an uptight Presbyterian Ulsterman, supported by MacKenzie. The board was almost exclusively male, middle-aged, straight and white.

Janet had difficulty getting on with the board. She didn't like too much formality and hated the way they concentrated on the downside, always banging on about why things couldn't be done, instead of why they should. She told a newspaper, 'Very few forthright wimmin have got to the top. There's a lotta clever wimmin around, but they don't sign up to corporate culture. Wimmin have a built-in bullshit detector. I mean, I can't sit around at meetings listening to this utter crap poured out by men justifying their own existence.' If one of the men on the board started showing off she would sometimes wave about a sign she had made with the letters 'DOT' in her scrawly handwriting. 'DOT' stood for 'Dicks On Table', the sort of pointless display of power inflicted on Rachel during the great Top Shop filming rumpus.

As the launch approached it became increasingly difficult for Janet and Kelvin to keep up the love-and-harmony façade in public. Things turned nasty at a promotional-cum-advertising sales conference at Canary Wharf. Dozens of local newspaper executives turned up, mainly interested in the chance to meet the legendary wisecracking Kelvin MacKenzie. He lived up to the occasion by introducing Janet as 'the brains behind L!ve TV', and then adding, 'Now, you all know what a fucking big liar I am.' That brought the house down. Good old Kelvin! Janet stormed out, saying that the people there were anyway only '*sad* journos from the sticks' who were 'dripping with dandruff', leaving Horwood to glad-hand them and lead the tour round The Entity. According to one report, Horwood handed out business cards with his name and the legend 'Consultant, Mirror Television' on one side and, on the other, an advert for a restaurant he owned in the West End. One executive told a newspaper, 'All these young presenters were supposed to convince us to put in a million quid so that our local advertisers would buy space on L!ve to sell their greenhouses. There was just a huge credibility gap.' Janet and Kelvin were also required to tour the country, selling more ad time and preparing the way for the network of local stations which Monty still saw as the key to the operation. They refused to travel to these meetings together and went in separate cars, rarely arriving at the same time. At least once MacKenzie went into his spiel without bothering to wait for Janet. She turned up later and denounced what he had said as incorrect, and they started bickering.

After this less-than-perfect introduction of L!ve TV to regional business persons, it was time to unveil the station to the public at large through a PR blitz aimed at national newspapers, television and radio. L!ve's in-house PR chief, Charlotte Ashton, had decided to organise a 'press launch' for the channel in May 1995, a month before the channel was due to go on air. With all the technical problems in the background, there was still a worry that the channel would look diabolically bad once it was up and running for real. By having the 'press launch' before the 'real launch' the hacks, suitably loaded up on champagne at breakfast time, could be shown the most watchable few minutes of material from the hours of rehearsals, and Janet could tell 'em (with fingers crossed) that this is what it would all be like, supplemented with sound-bites and buzz phrases.

The Launch of L!ve TV

L!ve TV was 'TV with *attitoood*,' Janet said. 'We've thrown away the rule book. We've gotta simple *ee-foss* [ethos], OK? If it's live we'll be there, right . . . Wot? . . . Yeah . . . Nah, it's not tabloid television, *not at all*, not *dahn*-market, not *dreery-sneery* TV, not *snoopy* TV. It's *selly-braay-tree* [celebratory] TV. . . . Wot? Who'll watch it? Lotsa people. They'll graze it, dip in and out, like you do with MTV. You think, "I fancy a bit of music," so you think, "Let's turn on MTV for a bit." Well, L!ve TV is like that . . . the factual version – a Reality Version, of MTV if yer like. . . . Yeah, Wot? . . . Me and Kelvin? *Aahhhh*, well! Yeah, *ack ack ack* . . . No seriously, it's just not a problem . . . Nah, really, we sorted it all before we both came 'ere. Sorta cleared the air. We're both strong perser nalities and we're quite capable of defendin' ourselves, I can assure you, *ack, ack, ack* . . . Yeah? Wot? . . . No . . . Yeah, *aspirational* . . . Like I said, *cheery* not *sneery*.'

Monty failed to turn up to the photocall and that made the photographers grumpy. Eventually he had to be dragged up to the 24th floor, where he posed in a characteristically dour and expressionless way. He didn't say much about Janet's vision for L!ve and instead concentrated on saying that the station had a small and fixed budget. His most positive comment was that the Mirror management knew what the costs were, and he added, 'It's not the sort of thing that can run out of control.' Then MacKenzie turned up and it was Janet's turn to get grumpy – Ashton had to work hard to keep them apart, so that they did not start slaggin' each other off. Janet stayed at one end of the room, near the TV display, resplendent in a shrieking scarlet power-dressing suit (designed, as she pointed out to one inquisitive hack, by Joseph and purchased from Harvey Nicks) with MacKenzie as far away as possible, next to the booze and nibbles at the other end of the room. The mutual loathing could not be entirely disguised, and both were in a foul mood. A radio reporter asked Kelvin for an interview and was told to go and 'fuck himself'. Undaunted, the reporter went to the other side of the room to grab a few words from Janet. When he asked her to say something to test the sound level on his machine, she spat, 'Fuck, fuck, fuck, fucking cunt.'

But, overall, the launch got a lot of positive coverage for what was, after all, a carefully designed non-event. Leading the way was the *Mirror* itself, which ran an enormous double-page spread hyping the new channel under the guise of a 'frank' interview with Janet, headed 'IF I WAS A BIMBO I WOULD NOT BE RUNNING A TV COMPANY WORTH £30 MILLION'. In passing, the article reported Janet scoffing at the idea that she had fallen out with MacKenzie. 'Utter rubbish,' she said. 'We still have an on-going frank exchange of views because we come from different media backgrounds and we are very opinionated people. But we haven't fallen out.' The article passed the opinion that 'now Janet Street-Porter has become the first woman to run a national television station, the knives are being sharpened with relish'.

The *Mirror*, as L!ve's sister paper, was in a position to know.

Chapter Eighteen

In which L!ve TV is launched and the World is told to Get A Life while hours and hours of eco-television showing Nothing Very Much are produced and are watched by virtually Nobody except Sad television critics who roundly denounce it all as the Absolute Pits and Janet throws a party which ends up with a Nasty Incident

'Where's Rhodri? Has anyone seen Rhodri?'

Tony Orsten, chief director at L!ve TV, is fidgeting about in the control box, scanning a row of monitors, beads of sweat blooming on his forehead, rows of knobs and switches at his fingertips. He glances up at the clock. Four minutes to go. L!ve TV is about to be launched on an unsuspecting world by presenters Donna Bernard and Rhodri Williams. Donna is in place, bum planted on the edge of a desk, looking tense and gawping into the camera. Orsten's eyes skip from screen to screen. No Rhodri. 'Oh shit! Where is he? Has anybody seen Rhodri?' Orsten leans over the desk microphone: 'Rod. *Rod!* You twerp, where are you?'

A thickset young man with sideburns ambles into view on monitor three. Rod's head is down, for he is concentrating on a mumbled last-minute rehearsal of his lines. He is loyally wearing his Janet regulation orange shoes matched with a pair of yellow, mauve and orange checked trousers.

'Sorry, loves,' says Orsten. 'Rod's on camera three. You OK, Rod?' Rod, still preoccupied, nods. Less than a minute to go. 'Good luck, everybody,' chirps Orsten. 'Enjoy it. And remember, if you look upset and nervous – like me! – it

251

just won't work.' Rod, head *still* down, smiles and shrugs. Orsten studies the clock. Twenty seconds. His voice bursts through the tense studio silence, addressing nobody in particular. 'Remember, everybody, lots of life, so let's be lively, let's enjoy it. Ten, nine, eight . . . '

The channel is finally live. Rhodri starts rushing round The Entity, followed by the camera, pointing to this and that with jerky movements. 'This is not about dull sofas or studio sets, we are a revolutionary channel,' he gabbles, before handing over to an equally mobile Donna in the manner of a relay-runner passing the baton. She yaps away, displaying her nerves, ending up in Janet's office, gibbering on about the fantastic view.

Back in the directing box, Orsten is also leaping about, directing a sort of ping-pong match between the two presenters, arms like windmills, establishing the required style of rapid editing. 'Aaaaand (*two, three*) . . . cue Rod . . . Aaaaand cue Donna. *Gooooood* . . . aaaand . . . camera three!!! *Whateryoudoin'!!?* . . . Sorry, loves. OK, that's better. Annnnd cue Rod . . . *That's fine*. Annnnnd cue Donna. Annnnd . . . ' He is planning to keep this up all morning. There are about fifty items to be directed, some of them stored in the memory of the Avid wonder system and ready, in theory, to go out at the press of a button. The top fifteen items are already displayed as a list of titles on the Avid's control screen. While Orsten conducts the Rhodri and Donna ping-pong match his eyes flick across the banks of computer screens and monitors: feeds from the three patched-up OB units, cued-up bits of pre-recorded film on one monitor, ready-to-run adverts on another, the computer screen lists of graphics bursts, sound stings and other material. Beside him an assistant is typing away, bringing to life the relentless viewer-hectoring infobar on the bottom of the output screen: *get a life . . . get l!vetv . . .*

coming up, l!vetv at disneyland . . . if it's live we are at it . . . get a life . . . get l!vetv . . . coming next . . . people news on l!vetv . . . stay with l!vetv . . . get a life . . .

The problems start after about five minutes. Rhodri, already winded but manfully facing up to another three hours and fifty-five minutes of Entity-jogging before his 'show' comes to an end, rushes up to Julia Bradbury, who is sitting on the so-called 'people newsdesk'. The linking graphics are lost and this causes everything to grind to a halt. Orsten goes bonkers. The output screen goes dead for eight seconds, an eternity in terms of live television transmission. The infobar typist is still at it ten to the dozen: *coming later . . . buzzin' with bouncing bhavesh . . . get a life . . . get . . .* But there is no point. These pearls of wisdom are not making it through the overloaded system and are being typed into a cybervoid.

The graphics are dumped. This brings Rhodri and Julia back on to the screen but – '*I don't believe it!*' – Julia's lapel radio mike is dead. For a few moments Rhodri conducts an excited, but one-sided conversation with a mute Julia. 'Rod, her *mike* isn't working,' Orsten informs Rhodri via his earpiece. 'Just lean over a bit so she can talk into yours, will you?' Obediently, Rod leans over – '*Yep, that's it, love*' – and the viewers are treated to the odd sight of Julia talking to Rod's shirt. Orsten pulls back from the desk: 'Will somebody *pleeease* get her a new mike!' This order is issued, BBC or LWT style, to nobody in particular. But the various technical bods in the box mumble dejectedly. 'We haven't got any mikes, Tone.' says one. 'And, uh, even if we did have, we haven't got anyone who can take it over to her,' says another.

For cost reasons L!ve TV has only four mikes – of which only three, evidently, are working – and the plan is to hand them over when presenters are due to appear on screen.

L¿ve TV

In 'old-fashioned' television there would always be a few junior production minions, known as 'runners', hanging about to deal with snags like this. But at L!ve TV there are no runners. Or, more accurately, all the runners have been promoted to become key technical operators who, at this moment, have their hands full. 'OK, stay calm,' Orsten urges. 'We'll be OK. Right, what's next?' A glance at a misleading running list reveals the probable answer: 'OB from Disneyland.' *Oh shit!* The infobar grinds on . . . *dreams come true at disneyland . . . get a life . . .*

Most of the coalface work is being done by Orsten, with Rachel Purnell in overall control. Janet hovers about. In an ideal world she would be able to help out by doin' a spot of DJ/MC toasting on the infobar, dictating her state of mind and subjective reaction to what she was seein' on the output screen to the infobar typist. But things were less than ideal and the infobar had to be turned off from time to time because it was bunging up the rest of the already overloaded system. Really, the technical people would have liked to turn it off for good. It was a *fucking nuisance.*[1]

Anyway, Janet had done her bit earlier in the day, before the 9 a.m. lift-off, meeting a clutch of underwhelmed reporters and photographers who had gathered to mark television's latest Moment of Destiny. Janet had again put on her scarlet power-dressing Joseph suit and had done a repeat cliché-ridden performance of the pre-launch 'press launch' a fortnight before. An accomplished media manipulator, polished by the likes of Lynne Franks, she responded to all questions with pre-prepared sound-bites. Q: 'Janet, how are you feeling today?' A: 'Live TV's *ee-foss* will be witty, stylish and lotsa fun.' Q: 'Janet, how are you getting on with Kelvin MacKenzie?' A: 'Fine. But whatyv-gotta understand is . . . well, I know it sounds corny, but the L!ve TV look is kinda modern. You know, kinda bright, fresh, youthful? And friendly, yeah. "Cheery, not sneery" is 'ow I put it. Yeah, "*cheer-ree*, not *sneer-ree*", goddit?' Q: 'Janet, do you think Britain should rejoin the exchange-rate mechanism of the European Monetary System?' A: 'Yeah, well, like I was sayin', if yer tune into L!ve you'll never quite know what to expect . . . We've got three OB trucks. If we've gone live an' it's workin', we'll stick with that and we'll ditch the studio stuff. We'll be, like, taking people to all the parties they're not invited to. Startin' t'night, wiv our own launch party. So tune in – an' see the staff get wasted, *ack ack ack*.' This time, though, for reasons which were clear to nobody, she was stumbling around carrying a piece of polystyrene sculpted into a gigantic

!

Back up on the 24th floor 'deconstructed' People News is under way with Rhodri, Donna and Julia peering at a computer screen, reading unprocessed newspaper articles from the display, stumbling constantly over their words, as Orsten keeps up the 'Cue Donna . . . Cue Rod . . . ' ping-pong routine in The Box. They attempt to be *tremendously amused* by everything everybody says and, unaided by autocue, are ad-libbing like mad, trying to fill up airtime. Much is made of a newspaper report alleging that younger women are now having sex less frequently than of late – *Bad luck, girls!* – and the fact that Richard E. Grant is to be the main judge of a nappy-changing competition. By now the infobar has been put on a repeat loop to save on manpower. So has Rod's patter, which amounts to non-stop self-promotion for the channel and little else.

'We'll be out and about in London catching a celebrity off their guard,' yelps Rod, bursting with excitement. 'Like this.' And the screen is filled with a pre-recorded item

Orsten has managed to fish out of the Avid, featuring a reporter galloping down Portobello Road behind an unco-operative Paula Yates. 'Where you off to, Paula?' yells the breathless Tellybrat, poking a microphone in the back of her neck. 'The office,' Paula replies. 'What's in yer bag, Paula?' Paula doesn't even turn round. 'Not telling you,' she says. This triumph, L!ve TV's first scoop, was repeated throughout at intervals of about twenty minutes.

At 1 p.m. Rhodri and Donna, entirely knackered, handed over to Simon London, an energetic young former *Sun* and *Mirror* showbiz reporter. He had been picked out as a potential high flyer and given the awesome task of filling up six and a half hours of L!ve TV, in two shifts, five days a week. The channel's editorial 'blueprint' described him as 'the link-meister' and 'the mother of all highlights'. He was officially 'cheeky, informed, curious, witty, everyone's best friend, never threatening, often wicked, challenging and easy to get on with. He's laddish, but in the nicest possible, impish, slightly guilty way . . . like a naughty, eager puppy you'd like to take home with you but, as you can't, you see his home and social life on the home videos he shoots every day. He's never bored.'[2]

His slots were called *L!ve with London* and he was to function like a VJ, video-jockey, on MTV. But instead of music videos he would be introducing gobbets of recycled footage from earlier in the day (or, after launch day, the previous day and night's output), together with free celebrity promo material, recycled OB material, competitions, phone-ins, vox pops and other stunts. All this was described in the 'blueprint' briefing as 'hours of balanced and seamless transition between Simon's antics, comments, high jinks and jokes and pre-recorded material'. Importantly, his slots were to have a big element of audience interaction, including the idea of viewers sending in their own 'talent videos'. Other regular features included 'the weather watch phone-out', in which he would phone travelling salesmen at random and ask them what the weather was like where they were; a 'book of the day' slot featuring lightweight titles you could read on the toilet and entitled *A Book at Bogtime*; a 'moustache of the week' competition and *Phone Simon's Plants*, in which viewers would be encouraged to ring up and talk to a cactus he was growing in a corner of The Entity.

But by now, on launch day, the technical problems were mounting, and this made London's job particularly difficult. He, above all others, depended on the Avid working according to plan and doing its recycling and sequencing job, but the machine was overloaded. Pre-recorded items came out in the wrong order, so he would excitedly announce that L!ve was going to Disneyland, Paris, and then Paula Yates would come up on the screen again, perhaps with sound, perhaps without. Sometimes graphics crashed on to the screen while London was in mid-sentence. Sometimes he would introduce an item and the screen would go blank, and then cut back to the studio to reveal London and various production bods mumbling away, flicking through great piles of paper unaware they were on air. The infobar was now only sometimes relevant to the rest of the action on the screen. It was looping out-of-date '*coming next*' messages, although these were never really out of date because anything which remotely worked or looked OK was copied by the Avid and endlessly recycled in line with Rachel's concept of 'eco-television'.

On top of the technical difficulties, the audience-interaction aspect of London's show was handicapped by the fact that there was no audience to interact with. As the *Mirror*'s PR endlessly pointed out L!ve was 'available' to about a million cable subscribers.³ But in fact L!ve was 'available in cable homes' only in the sense that staring at the wheels going round on the electricity meter was an activity 'available' to anyone hooked up to the national grid. It didn't mean that people would look at it. And nobody had actually asked for L!ve TV, as such. It was just there. Like the electricity meter. All other things being equal, no more than a couple of thousand people were likely to be watching L!ve TV at any one time. It was entirely possible, as people surfed the channels, that the audience figure dropped to zero. The infobar was, at last, loaded up with the station's phone number, but there were so few callers that the scarce production staff were cunningly deployed to phone from the other side of the office, putting on a variety of funny and implausible voices and pretending they were genuine viewers. Even then they could not bring themselves to claim the Wet, Wet, Wet concert tickets – the biggest gun in L!ve TV's arsenal on launch day.

Link-meister Simon London handed over to music presenter Bhavesh Hindocha at 4 p.m. and collapsed in an exhausted heap. After a brief production-department muddle, 'bouncing Bhavesh' burst on to the screen, yelling: 'Ultimate Chaos in the House!' It was his way of turning the day's technical problems into a talking-point. *'Comin' at yer . . . phat and funky . . . woooowah I am telling yoooo . . . Chaos in . . . Therrrr! . . . Howwwse!'* Bhavesh's slot was called *Buzzin'* and promised to treat viewers to 'what's hot in the world of sex, soap and style', even though the 'blue-print' had it down as a tea-time show for schoolchildren. A third dimension was added by Bhavesh himself. He decided to turn the slot into a black music programme featuring groups that couldn't get on television anywhere else. Video snippets were shown, with Bhavesh doing the links: *truly massive . . . comin' at yer . . . in the house*. Then, after a while, the resident Tellybrat film reviewer wandered on to camera to discuss the latest PR film release clips. 'Yo, Julia! Howya doin'?' asked Bhavesh, gesticulating like a New York crack-dealer. 'Buzzin', buzzin',' Julia replied, nodding like mad. '*Cool, reely cool*,' Bhavesh replied, also nodding and still gesticulating furiously. They continued like this for a long time before Julia started wittering on about Bruce Willis's performance in *Die Hard with a Vengeance*, which she thought was all about 'bein' tough in a cool kinda way'.[4]

After an hour and half of this, 'Bouncing Bhavesh' handed back to Simon London for his second shift of the day. It kicked off with his personal 'video diary', which linked the gobbets recycled from earlier in the day. These were now considerable and included 'the best of *Buzzin'*' as well as the Paula Yates sensation. London padded out weather bulletins with phone calls to travelling salesmen asking them if it was raining where they were, and, in addition, to London's mother. There was much excitement as his dinner was delivered from the *Mirror* canteen and he ate it in front of the camera and then washed up and tidied up The Entity for a bit, while the infobar came back to life: *get a life . . . get l!vetv . . .*

At 9 p.m. Simon London handed over to 'The Night-Time Posse'. This part of the schedule was described by Janet as 'the take your breath away slot' and, according to plan, would have a different theme each night. The themes included 'Weird Night' and 'Love Night' and these sounded ominous to the official guardians of the nation's televisual morals. But on launch night itself there was no theme as such, because, as Janet had promised the media hacks, L!ve TV was gonna use three multi-camera OB units to cover its own launch party, or parties, which were to take place at nightclubs in London.

Janet had put tremendous effort into the organisation of these events, using a 'celebrity booker', said to have previously been A Big Cheese at Radio One, to organise suitable entertainment and get *slebs* to turn up. The trouble was that the booker never seemed able to attract anyone but C-list people. This infuriated Janet, who called him 'the non-celebrity booker'. Looking disgustedly at his list, she had sighed and issued a definite instruction. 'If you can do one thing right, it's book the fucking Peggy Spencer Latin American Formation Ballroom Dancing Team. I saw them at the Pet Shop Boys' party and they were *faaaannntassstic*. So *book 'em*. They're in the phone book.'

But the Big Cheese found Peggy Spencer elusive. Instead he booked a sub-sub-Spice Girls act consisting of six teenage girls from a comprehensive school in Essex, who turned up wearing boob tubes and mini-skirts, who could not dance in time and who sang out of tune on a karaoke machine. (Janet started *screamin' an' shahtin'* and the Cheese left L!ve TV shortly afterwards.)

Apart from the missing *Come Dancing* effect, the problem with Janet's party was that 1,500 people had found their way on to the guest list. This was more than the likely total viewing figure for L!ve TV at certain times in the day and, more importantly on the night, twice the capacity of the nightclub where Janet herself would be starring. The staff and presenters turned up early, rubbing shoulders with sundry fashion models, rock groups and C-list celebrities, filling the place up with their friends and leaving a long queue on the pavement.

When the OB producer turned up she found a group of stilt-walkers and other entertainers, including a costumed Superman lookalike, standing on the pavement next to a bunch of furious VIPs – among them Monty and

Kelvin and their pals such as Roger Luard of Flextech. The venue owners raged at the producer, accusing her of irresponsibility and saying that the OB cameras and the overcrowding were creating a fire hazard. They threatened to close the whole thing down, thus bringing L!ve TV's output to an abrupt halt, unless she cleared some people out. At the same time the locked-out *slebs* were shrieking at her to sort things out. The producer pushed her way in and found Janet, who had set herself up in a special VIP compound, where she was drinkin' with the grotesquely attired Zandra Rhodes (whom the bouncers had let in, mistaking her for Janet herself), her friend Mick Pilsworth from Chrysalis TV, and the *massiffly fan-tass-tic* Neil Tennant of the Completely Brilliant Pet Shop Boys.

The producer asked what she should do. Janet told her to boot out the L!ve TV staff and their mates to make room for the real *slebs*. Darryl Burton was told to get a pile of petty cash and set up shop in a pub across the road, and the Tellybrats were told to go to the pub, where he would buy them unlimited quantities of drink, peanuts and crisps. The next step was to get rid of the bands who had performed, to make room for *slebs*. They too demanded cash up front and were sorely upset at not being allowed to stay.

The *slebs* eventually got in. But, all in all, the producer was having a miserable time. Apart from all the grief she was getting from the venue owners, from Janet, from the disappointed Tellybrats, from performers and from arrogant, irritated *slebs*, she had the small task of directing six cameras attempting to film in a packed and darkened room and getting a signal back from the OB trucks to the Avid system in Canary Wharf for live transmission. Things got worse when members of a novelty grunge cabaret act bounded on to the minuscule stage, powered up a chainsaw and started juggling with it. The chainsaw immediately bounced off the low ceiling and hit the cameraman, nearly killing him. Everyone laughed, assuming (incorrectly) that this was part of the act. Minutes later a female member of the group started rubbing the chainsaw between her legs, showering the audience with sparks from her metal knickers. Then she slipped and the sparks were supplemented with showers of blood. More incorrect laughter. The OB producer had to administer first aid to a three-inch laceration in the young woman's crotch though, strangely, the performer said she didn't mind and had actually quite enjoyed the experience. She was paid off and sent to casualty in a cab.

The next day the critics delivered their opinion on the first day of L!ve's output. The *Mirror* thought that it was great. The *Sun* and the other tabloids generally ignored it. But the broadsheets were universally hostile. Tony Orsten, reading through the almost hysterical criticism, shrugged. 'Surprisingly,' he told people, 'I didn't think it looked *too* bad.' But the *Daily Telegraph* thought L!ve TV was rubbish and, above all, boring. The channel featured 'mind-numbingly tedious interviews', the paper complained, and the presenters came over as morons: 'Their language is riddled with dropped aitches, glottal stops and crude Americanisms; the tone is invariably flippant and lightweight; and the intellectual content almost nil.'

The *Guardian* agreed. 'The race is on,' the paper said, 'to create the worst cable TV channel in Britain.' L!ve was amateurish rubbish like 'an endless audition tape by media trainees'. The paper rounded on Simon London's personal 'video diary', which had kicked off on launch day by featuring Simon and his flatmate, Boyd, in heated discussion about how to change channels with their remote control: 'You get better entertainment when you're asleep. There's more intellectual stimulation printed on the paper napkins at Burger King.'

The *Guardian* finished its hatchet job by asking, 'Can British TV sink any lower than this?'

PART III

JANET'S L!VE TV

Chapter Nineteen

In which L!ve TV comes under Bottle Attack after a muddle over its OB trucks, The Vision is abandoned and 'L!ve TV' becomes 'Th!rty M!nutes Beh!nd T!me TV' as the Tellybrats tangle with the ranks of the Horrible Fat Hairy Loony Australian Slags and the hunt is on to find entertaining Witches, Sex Doctors, Wankers, Sploshers, Sadists, Masochists, Celebrity Fetishists and Nerds until, at last, Reality is officially abandoned amid Mounting Hysteria

It is approaching midnight on a warm Saturday night in the summer of 1995. L!ve TV has been on air for a few weeks. Huge numbers of young people, many of them drunk, are teeming through the streets of London's West End in search of excitement. Thousands converge on Leicester Square, where, in reality, there is not all that much going on.

Except that on this evening there is an OB unit fly-parked on the corner of the Square. It has the words 'L!ve TV' emblazoned in huge letters on the side. It sways slightly when the breeze catches the hydraulic mast mounted on the roof of the van. The mast is cranked up to maximum extension so that the communications dish atop it can point in the general direction of the satellite linking it to Canary Wharf. From time to time the area around the van is flooded with bright light as filming takes place.

The van acts like a lighthouse and magnet to the swarms of young drinkers, many of whom are *en route* to trendy nightclubs, and fancy themselves as TV stars in the making. L!ve TV? Never heard of it. But what does that matter? This could be the Big Break. *Hello, Mum!* Soon a large crowd is gathered round the van. The crowd, in turn, creates the impression that something interesting or exciting is happening, attracting more drunk or bored people, and so on *ad infinitum*.

The van door is open. There is so much electronic equipment inside that the heat is unbearable. The OB producer is crouched, staring intently at the monitor, pressing buttons and listening to directions coming over the airwaves from the director's gallery on the 24th floor of Canary Wharf. The producer is in a bad mood. The gallery people say they don't like the footage he is sending them. Can he get the cameraman to reshoot? Can he frame the shots a bit better? Can he tell the cameraman to find some better-lookin' people?

The producer loses patience. Don't they fucking realise that nothing, *absolutely nothing* works? There are only three of them of here. There's a semi-trained cameraman. There's the driver, who's got one eye on the lookout for traffic wardens and clamping teams, and the other on the over-cranked-up satellite mast, making sure the van doesn't keel over. And there's himself, trying to hold everything together. He's been cooped up in a metal box *sweating his bollocks off* for six hours without a break, with no assistance at hand and nowhere even to take a piss. It is the middle of the night. He's knackered. There's nothing going on that's worth filming. He can't even talk to the cameraman from the van. There's no cable connecting them. The one they've given him *isn't fucking long enough*. Instead he's taking whatever he can get in the form of videotape and sending them that.

'Yeah, but . . . ' says the director in the Canary Wharf gallery, 'but it is absolute *dogshite* – Janet's doing her nut.' The OB producer explodes: 'Look, *fuck you*! What I'm sending is what you're gonna get. That's your fucking *lot*. Have you fucking *got* that?' The gallery director replies, 'Well, if that's your attitude, *fuck you*!' The OB producer re-replies, 'No! I'll tell you what – *fuck you*'. Gallery: 'Oh fuck *yoooooo*!' OB: '*Fuck, fuck, fuckity fucking fuck yooooo!*' At this moment the sole editorial control of L!ve TV consists of two people shouting 'Fuck you!' at each other over a satellite link.

During this creative exchange, a semi-drunken yobbish figure pops his head through the open door of the van: 'What you doin', mate? . . . Can I be on the telly? . . . Where's Chris Evans, then? . . . What channel is this on, then?' The OB producer has been putting up with this for hours. Unlike 'old-fashioned' telly, L!ve TV has no production assistants and planners to sort out parking, get permission to film or organise the roping-off of the operation to keep out the general public. The OB producer has been straining to remain patient and polite all evening. But now, after the interchange with the gallery, he has lost it. 'Look, pal,' he sighs, 'just *piss off*, will you.' The semi-drunk looks startled but disappears, muttering under his breath. But minutes later he is back with a gang of his mates, who start yelling abuse, banging on the side of the van and rocking it from side to side, making the already unstable mast sway alarmingly.

The producer gets straight on the line to Canary Wharf. 'The lights are going off in thirty seconds! We are under attack! If the lights stay on for a *second* longer somebody's gonna be killed. That's your lot!' The cameraman jumps on board and the doors are slammed shut. The rocking stops and there are a few seconds of relative calm before a hail of bottles arrives broadside as the dish mast retracts. The van moves off, horn blaring, creeping through the crowds before speeding away to safety.

After several incidents like this the L!ve TV management

grudgingly arranged for bouncers to ride shotgun on the OB trucks. Not that it did much good. Switching on the lights anywhere in the West End, in the middle of milling crowds of disappointed, bored and cantankerous drunks turned away from celebrity nightclubs, had much the same effect as erecting a large luminous sign saying, 'Look here! Millions of pounds' worth of unprotected electronic equipment. Please come and steal or vandalise it!' or 'Cleverdick TV Luvvies at work. Come and stove our heads in. We deserve it!'

Moreover, as often as not the presence of bouncers proved even more provocative. On one occasion, a scuffle between drunks and L!ve TV bouncers outside a salsa bar in Wardour Street, Soho, led to another full-scale bottle attack followed by a huge ruck between drunks, police, L!ve TV bouncers, a group of cleaver-waving chefs and kung-fu experts from nearby Chinese restaurants, and rival teams of bouncers from several nightclubs. At one point a passing troupe of Hari Krishna missionaries was also swept up in the mêlée.

The problems with the OB trucks stemmed from a failure of communication between Janet, Rachel and the editorial people on the one hand, and Spinks and the technical people on the other. The Vision decreed that L!ve output should switch seamlessly from The Entity to multiple parties and locations around town, with good-lookin' Tellybrats using the latest lightweight cameras and leaping about with head-mikes. Few people on the editorial side ever bothered to ask, 'Will this work?' They had been told by Monty that L!ve would have OB trucks, three of them. They could use them how they liked.[1]

The snag was that L!ve had inherited the OB arrangements between Wire TV and the satellite company,

Intelsat.[2] And these were not very suitable. Intelsat was low down on the horizon and the signal it could manage was fairly weak, which was why it was cheap. It was fine if you were going to 'uplink' from a satellite truck in a place where there was a direct line of sight between the van and the satellite – for the best signal of all, you wanted to be on top of a hill in an open field. The techies had imagined that L!ve would be doing something similar. Since L!ve was using Intelsat, they reasoned, the editorial people must be planning to do most of their OBs from big open spaces (with no buildings in the way), which was where OBs were normally used: theme parks, or the Scene of a Major Disaster, or football matches or whatever. Maybe racecourses or golf or something – MacKenzie was keen on sport, wasn't he?

Not until too late did the techies find out that, following Monty's instructions, Janet and Rachel planned OBs, usually multiple OBs, from the West End almost every night. This meant that the satellite trucks were virtually useless, because in the West End you'd be parked in narrow streets surrounded by tall buildings, and the only clear line of sight was straight above your head. Unless you could work out a way to bounce a signal off the Pole Star, there was No Way a satellite truck could get a signal back. To do city-centre OBs, they would need microwave trucks, which were much more expensive and would take six months or so to commission from scratch, but which could bounce the signal off buildings in a zigzag pattern until it reached Canary Wharf.

The bad news was reported to Rachel and Janet. There was then frenzied and heroic activity to find a way round the problem – it dominated the work of Ruth Wrigley, L!ve TV's OB specialist, at a time when she should have been thinking more creatively about the content of the channel. In the end she and Darryl Burton managed to find a solution of sorts. They arranged to use BT's videocommunications 'plug-in' points around London to get the signal back, and, at the same time, BT undertook to supply other equipment to L!ve TV until the 'proper' vans became available.

The other solution involved parking in relatively open spaces, such as Leicester Square or Pall Mall, cranking the mast up to maximum height and hoping for the best. But this created another conundrum. If you parked in a narrow street next to a Soho nightclub, you might be able to get the signal back to the truck from the camera via a long cable connecting the two. But then, often as not, you would not be able send the signal from the truck to the studio. If you parked the truck in an open space such as Hyde Park, you could get the signal back to Canary Wharf but you would need a two-mile cable linking you to the cameraman in Soho.[3]

With all these difficulties it was quickly realised that The Vision would not work in practice, at least not quite in the simple-minded way Monty had specified and Janet and Rachel had designed it. Genuine 'live' OBs were abandoned. Instead, the trucks went out and parked in open spaces with line of sight to the satellite. The cameraman/presenters would then go off and film for half an hour or so and then run back to the truck with video cassettes of undirected footage showing the presenters pretending to be live (carefully not letting any clocks appear in shot). The cassettes were then clunked into a machine and sent back to Canary Wharf, where the material was put on the channel accompanied by the infobar harmlessly lying that what was on screen was happening at that very moment. Using this system, the OB trucks, bought at such vast cost and with so much hassle, were to all intents and purposes redundant. The cassettes could have made the five-mile journey from the West End to Canary Wharf by motorbike messenger at a cost of perhaps £10 instead of making a pointless 72,000 km detour via outer space, using satellite trucks costing millions.

With the abandonment of 'genuine' live OB transmission, the trucks could be parked out of the way and it became easier to venture into the West End, in a way. After this the worst job for the OB people was reckoned to be *Desperate and Dateless*, the live element of Tuesday and Friday nights which were designated 'love' (i.e. sex) nights. *Desperate and Dateless* was based on the prototype 'Fuck or Die' slot dreamed up in the pre-launch brainstorming sessions, crossed with an existing Australian format, described as a version of Cilla's *Blind Date* but proceeding directly to the snogging. The idea was that L!ve would introduce unattached young people to each other, and then follow them around all night as they attempted to bed each other.

The routine was therefore simple. The OB van would fly-park as close to Soho as was safe and possible. A camera-and-sound person, producer and presenter would go into whatever was currently thought to be the most notorious pick-up joint and set up shop in the corner. As the punters arrived, the producer would grab them, especially any good-lookin' single women (who were at a premium), offer them a free bottle of champagne by way of reward for taking part, and take a polaroid picture. The snap was then placed on a noticeboard.

At 9 p.m., when L!ve switched to its night-time sex theme, there would, according to plan, be a dozen or so pictures on the noticeboard. At this point the presenter, normally a woman, would unleash the surprise element of the show. With a camera in hot pursuit, she would dive into the crowd of drinkers, asking for a punter who wanted to be on television. Volunteers were dragged over to the noticeboard and, with varying degrees of reluctance, shown the polaroids, asked to comment on the pictures and, with much jolly, giggly risqué banter from the presenter, nominate the one they fancied most. Then came the pay-off. The presenter cried, 'Well, hey, we are gonna introduce you to her [or 'him'] *right now!*' and, with the camera still in pursuit, dragged the volunteer back into the crowd to find the lucky girl (or boy). Then it was the presenter's job to get them to kiss. The idea was that they would chat each other up, live on TV, with the camera returning from time to time to see how they were gettin' on.

The problem with all this, which like a lot of L!ve TV ideas looked *faaantaaastic* on paper, was that most people were extremely reluctant to join in. Many had arrived for a quiet night out, and the last thing they wanted was a camera crew pestering them. There was a world of difference between an invited studio audience, who might cheerfully engage in this sort of ritual humiliation on a show like *The Word* in the highly controlled environment of a TV studio, and a group of randomly assembled drinkers in a pick-up bar. Some signed up for the polaroid board and took the bottle of champagne, but simply told the presenter to 'Fuck off' when she later returned with their 'blind date'. Sometimes the polaroid people managed to get off with somebody before the L!ve presenter barged in with her volunteer. Things could turn very nasty then, and a two- or three-person OB team could find themselves backed against the wall facing dozens of drunk and disgruntled punters.[4]

After a few unsuccessful outings to the West End it was decided to switch the location to an infamous Australian bar in Covent Garden, on the muddled grounds that the Aussies had come up with the *Desperate and Dateless* formula in the first place and the more well-founded idea that they were, as a group, much more gung-ho, randy and game for a laugh than the shy and uptight Brits. This proved to be the case, but the fact presented its own problems. The team found many of the Aussies unbelievably uncouth, especially the women (the 'horrible, fat, hairy, loony Australian slags', as the team fondly thought of them). The Slags volunteered for the stunt with enormous gusto. It was no longer a matter of dragging blushing volunteers reluctantly through the crowds and goading them into performing a giggly and chaste kiss for the cameras. As often as not the Slags took matters into their own hands, grabbing the presenter and dragging her up to some good-lookin' sport, on whom the Slag then leapt, sticking her tongue down his throat before diving towards the fly buttons on his 501s and yelling, 'D'ya want me to give him a blow job as well?'

This material was sent back ('This is all you are getting. You sort it out if you don't like it.' 'Fuck you!' 'No, fuck *you!*') to the 24th floor, where it was mixed with whatever activity had been arranged to take place on the 'love' theme in The Entity. One source of inspiration here was the 'zoo television' cable channels in the States, led by New York's Manhattan Cable which featured a lurid stream of DIY polymorphous perversity provided by the Big Apple's many bondage enthusiasts, transvestites and other exhibitionists. Rachel had been taken with a regular item on Manhattan Cable which featured a 'sex doctor' helping people overcome their hang-ups by getting them to take their clothes off, lie on the floor and follow his detailed instructions on how to do foreplay. This was far too 'raunchy' for British television, so for L!ve a milder version was organised with a 'sexologist' directing two writhing students in a sleeping-bag. The 'sexpert' gave instruction like a po-faced latter-day Bernie the Bolt: 'Up a bit . . . right a bit . . . Is *that* working? . . . Does that do *anything at all* for you? . . . OK, try again.'

This was supplemented by pre-recorded features on a sexual theme. One reporter was sent out to interview people on street corners in Soho. When this did not work out he phoned Rachel to say nothing was happening, and ask what he should do. As was often the case with Rachel, the reply was along the lines of 'Just do, you know, *some-thing* – you know, *anything* . . . It's *easy peasy*.' The reporter obliged by befriending two gay men, who invited him back to their flat for a long, frank and detailed interview about sado-masochism. The interview was sent back and edited into a ten-part series on S&M and bondage, punc-tuated with a cheap, repeated cutaway shot of a fly swat whacking a piece of bare flesh. Rachel saw the results and collapsed in laughter, tears rolling down her face. She was just recovering her composure when another producer burst into her office and announced, 'Hey! I've got the Wicca Witch to come on: She's *faaantaastic*. She's gonna sing Simon and Garfunkel songs.'

The fly-swat sado-masochism series was soon supple-mented by another regular 'What's your perversion?' slot dealing with entertaining peccadillos, based on the premise that there's nowt so queer as folk. A producer was detailed to look through a stack of hard-core porn videos to see if there was anything original and adaptable for 'love night', and came up with a long list of barmy parasexual activi-ties.

First up was 'splosh' sex, which mean getting a thrill out of seeing nude people who are covered in mess of one sort or another. The splosher phenomenon, the producer thought, could be passed off as 'journalism' by showing clips of the video, then gettin' some splosh fans into The Entity to explain why they liked it, and then, maybe, gettin' them to do a bit of live sploshin' for the edification of the viewers. But, basically, he thought, an investigation into sploshers was a brilliant excuse to show pictures of pretty girls with liquid chocolate or whatever dribbling over their breasts.

The producer found a splosher couple, who arrived at The Entity game for anything. There was a short interview, establishing that sploshing was 'just good clean fun', that it did not harm anyone, that it was nobody's business what they got up to in private and that it was a lot healthier than, say, smoking cigarettes. After this the couple was led over to a row of labelled vats of custard, porridge, rice pudding, mayonnaise and baked beans. 'Right, then,' said the presenter, 'show us what this is all about.' The presenter had expected they might stick a finger into the porridge and do a bit of suggestive licking, accompanied by some more flirty, jokey, sexy chat: 'Is mayonnaise hornier than rice pudding?' – that sort of thing. Instead, in front of the live camera, the woman ripped her dress off and started rubbing great handfuls of baked beans and custard over herself, concentrating on her breasts and on her crotch, which was covered only by a g-string (later described as 'skimpy'). Her partner meanwhile developed an immediate, enormous and highly obvious erection. The cameraman, lacking experience in this sort of situation – *never work with children, animals or sploshers* – went in for a close-up of the woman's crotch, ignoring the producer's screams in his earpiece: 'For fuck's sake, get the camera *out of there*! This is going out *live*, you stupid fucker, you can't take pictures of her *fanny*! Cut *away* from that. Cut *away* from it – *imm-ediately*!'

Fortunately, the ITC weren't watching at the time. Or

if they were, they did not say anything. But L!ve TV's lawyer, who did an internal monitoring job trying to stem the complaints before they arrived, saw it on video the next day and sent a memo to the producer saying that it was quite legitimate, probably, under the ITC code to show this sort of thing but asking 'was it necessary for the camera to linger *quite* so long in the crotch area and for it to record *every* baked bean as it dropped from her g-string?'

The Tuesday and Friday sex-theme nights were separated by 'Weird Night' on Wednesday, which was supposed to deal with supernatural phenomena but, as often as not, ended up showing more sex-related material such as body-piercing, with tarot-card readers, witches and wizards specialising in casting phone-in spells and mixing phone-in 'love potions' from herbs bought from the Sainsbury's spice rack. Featuring the occult on television was fraught with all sorts of problems, not least the ITC rules, which were at least as strict as those dealing with sexual material. The combination of the two was a definite No-No and so the regulators were sent into a spin by 'the pierced witch', an early Weird Night guest in The Entity who wanted to have her belly-button pierced for the umpteenth time live on television, complete with blood and everything. In fact the woman, who struck the technical team as horrible, mad and spooky, had a great many rings and chains through far more private parts of her anatomy and wanted to show them off as well, but was not allowed to do so. Weird Night slowly gravitated to towards being 'weird sex night', featuring interviews with porno 'stars' talking about clips from their work and 'weird food', which was splosher-type activity involving, on one memorable occasion, the son of an enormously famous and virtuous TV personality eating his dinner off the nude belly of a hired 'glamour model'.

L!ve TV also produced an extremely risky item for screening late at night: a sort of consumer guide to the use of prostitutes. Actresses were hired to reconstruct the daily grind of working girls, using such devices as performing simulated 'blow jobs' on chocolate bars. Unfortunately one of the actresses involved turned out to be the genuine article and the story of how a L!ve presenter, a fairly posh and squeaky-clean minor celeb, had got involved with this sleazy activity found its way on to the front page of the *Sunday Sport*, complete with a video still. There was a theory that the story had been leaked by somebody at L!ve in order to get Janet, who did not see the item when it was broadcast, into trouble. MacKenzie intervened, giving the producers – who had made the item on their own initiative – an almighty bollocking. L!ve's lawyer, Neil Pepin, seemed more worried that the ITC would complain that the brand name of the chocolate bar was being given 'undue prominence'. It was, of course, a Mars Bar.

Monday night was originally intended to be a phone-in 'Advice Night' with, according to the editorial plan, 'alternating panels of washing machine mechanics, vets and astrologers'. But this did not work out, owing to the lack of viewers and, therefore, callers. The old scam of phoning up from inside the building was used for a while, until everyone got fed up with it. Monday was thus redesignated 'Cyber Night', a variation on the *Desperate and Dateless* formula. It was based in 'cyber-cafés' and featured spotty male nerds (extremely desperate, terminally dateless) chatting to L!ve's glamorous 'sex beast', Imogen Edwards-Jones, about not very much. This was despite the fact that Janet hated the Internet and thought the people involved, mostly men, were beyond the pale. 'It's like CB radio in the seventies,' she would moan, 'strictly for wankers'.[5]

L¿ve TV

The wreckage of Advice Night was moved to Thursday
to fill the gap left by the implosion of 'Reality Night', which
the Tellybrats had fondly imagined could be filled up with
live OBs from London's hospital casualty units and police
station charge rooms. When the obvious impossibility, not
to mention illegality, of this was realised, L!ve TV officially
dispensed with 'Reality' altogether.

Chapter Twenty

In which Transvestites and Time-Travellers invade The Entity for a Saturday Night In and Janet becomes Very Depressed as Kelvin begins to denounce the Filthy Perverts and Bum Bandit Mafia surrounding him while Skulking About with a Worrying Smirk on his Face

Technical director Mike Spinks more than once considered walking away from L!ve TV. It was a nightmare. More than almost anyone else he was caught up in the daily – no, the *minute by minute* – crises caused by trying to keep on air a 24-hour station run by a split management team, on a budget one-tenth the size of 'conventional' television, with a gummed-up Avid editing system, wrongly specified 'live' non-live OB trucks, a semi-trained and inexperienced editorial staff, a near-total mismatch between the editorial Vision and the facilities to produce it, the malfunctioning infobar, Janet's tantrums, Kelvin's glowering . . .

But he could not walk away, any more than an airline pilot can resign thirty seconds before his plane crashes into the side of a mountain. You just had to stay there and, well, do what you could. He took each day – no, each *hour* – as it came and made the best of it. At the end of the week, on Saturday night, he would at last drag himself away, struggle home from the nowhereland of Canary Wharf and collapse into bed, thinking, 'Another week without it all falling apart. How did we get away with that?'

So Spinks was not entirely pleased when at around midnight one Saturday evening his mobile phone rang, summoning him back to The Entity. 'Sorry, Mike. Look, mate, we've got a problem. There's . . . well, we've got a transvestite in the main control room and he, or she, or whatever you call it, she's . . . he's been pissin' about with the main computer and we're not really sure . . . '

Spinks, half awake, screwed up his eyes. 'A *what*?'

The caller chuckled. 'Yeah, this bloke dressed up like a woman – not bad lookin' actually, heh, heh, heh. A transvestite – *you* know. It's that fucking "Dinner Party" thing they do . . . Anyway, sorry, mate, but the place is in a right state. I think you're gonna have to come in and take a look at it all.'

Spinks put down the receiver and moaned. *Oooohhh noooo!* The 'Dinner Party' was part of The Entity's output during the all-important *Saturday Night In* slot,[1] the official clubbin' night with a semi-official and explicit gay TV aspect to it. As if things weren't bad enough, swarms of unknown Party People would arrive at The Entity from God Knows Where, pile into the free booze in the 'padded cell' hospitality room, and then start wandering about the fully open-plan studio-cum-office-cum-production-area with nobody to keep an eye on them. There was a constant fear that the Party People would be sick over the computer, start toasting on the infobar, electrocute themselves, or nick the cameras or something.

Janet took a deep interest in the Saturday-night output, which was wittily called *Saturday Night In*.[2] The title was *ironnick*, a play on the word 'out' as in 'out of the closet'. She had set out some ideas for the style and content of Saturday night in a memo written after an editorial 'away-day' brainstormin' session. Saturday night, the memo said, should 'lift-off' after the 9 p.m. watershed with a 'Gay/Talent/Party Time' theme. There would be 'Gay news' and 'Gay fashion' and the memo pleaded for more 'Gay suggestions', and advised everyone to 'get raunchier after 11 p.m.'. A separate memo, not from Janet, suggested

a Saturday night 'cottage watch', with an OB outside a
public lavatory in the style of *Badger Watch*.

Saturday Night In used the usual mix of OBs and activity in The Entity which was anchored by a gay agony aunt
and drag queen called Ivana. Her/his catchphrase was
'I'm Ivana and I always come up trumps. Call me now and
I'll put you straight, even if you're not!' and the infobar
eventually displayed the phone number, out of sync with
the action. As the night wore on the 'Dinner Party' guests
would arrive and interact with Ivana and other regulars
dotted about The Entity, including a character called Terry
Tarot, who read their fortunes. On the first Saturday the
main attraction had been a psychic-cum-hypnotist who
specialised not only in regression to previous lives but in
'progression' to future lives.

The psychic managed to send one of the presenters into
a trance, transporting her into the distant future, where
she found herself in a world where people did not have
bodies any more but just sort of floated about in the ether.
This act went on uninterrupted for fifteen minutes, with
the zonked-out Tellybrat giving dreamy bulletins from the
year AD 2 billion: 'Wowww! I can see all these kinda . . .
woowww . . . kinda tiny sparkly lights . . . and it's all kinda
bright and floaty . . . oooohhh . . . wooowwww . . . it's
really beautiful . . . .yeah! wow! . . . a-mazing.' Afterwards
the rest of the team congratulated her on giving such a
convincing performance. But the young woman, who
struck them as an exceptionally spaced-out person at the
best of times, disabused them. Voice still quivering, and
distinctly wobbly, she explained that it had not been a trick.
She *really, really* had been floating about in the future and
it had, indeed, been amazing and beautiful. (News about
the near future, such as next week's football pool results
or lottery numbers, was not forthcoming.)

After this warm-up act the dinner party itself swung into action. The slot was hampered by having a budget of only £200 to feed and inebriate up to a dozen people. Food was prepared in the *Mirror* canteen and had to be warmed in the microwave and brought up in the lift on a trolley. At first the canteen staff were paid overtime to stick around until the early hours. But this was cut out as an economy measure and the production team, which consisted of just three people, responsible for four hours of live output, soon discovered that the glamorous new world of 'multi-skilling' included going around with bin bags and washing dishes at 2 a.m. Janet helped in attracting dinner-party guests to begin with, but the supply of *slebs* willing to trek out to Canary Wharf and sit in an office block eating cold, greasy chips for four hours on Saturday night (when they could be at a real party) soon dried up. 'We take you to the parties you haven't been invited to' soon became 'You stay away from the parties you wouldn't be seen dead at'.

Inevitably, a few weeks into the run, the production team found that they had, in practical terms, nobody at all for that Saturday's show. The producer decided to play an ace he had been keeping up his sleeve: a promise he had secured from the editorial team at *Loaded* magazine to 'do' a dinner party at short notice. Warned about the budget horror, the Lads came with their own copious supplies of lager (et cetera) and, by the time they turned up, were already well pissed. One of them immediately threw up in the hospitality room. Then, as a group, they took an instant dislike to the presenter (*Pooftah! Wanker! Dickhead!*) and started throwing their alleged food at him. During the first ad break, the presenter told them to behave themselves. They told him to 'Fuck off' and decided to leave, trying to push over the table as they went.

The director in the box got an excited message in his

earpiece: 'The *Loaded* lot are leaving. They're really cheesed off. Don't come back after the break, whatever you do. There's only empty chairs!' The cameraman was instructed, at some personal risk, to follow them out to the reception area, where they were featured shouting abuse and flicking V-signs as the lift doors closed. The presenter then ad-libbed for two hours, showing edited highlights of the *Loaded* departure over the infobar which, as usual, was out of sync: *coming next . . . Loaded drop in for dinner! . . . get a life . . . get l!vetv . . .* [3]

The gay aspect of *Saturday Night In*, coming as it did on top of the increasingly kinky and gay flavour of the Tuesday and Friday 'Love' nights and the decidedly pervy Weird Night, had come to the attention of Kelvin MacKenzie. And he was not happy. Definitely not happy. As managing director of Mirror Television, he played no direct role in day-to-day programming, leaving that to Janet and, beneath her Rachel and (in theory) Nick Ferrari. But he monitored the output from time to time and he was Not Happy. He had taken a particular dislike to Ivana 'I'll put you straight', the gay agony aunt, and moaned to Janet who, clearly, was coming under more and more pressure from the Mirror management. At first MacKenzie had respected Janet's dignities and not intervened directly. He was busy anyway with his continuing efforts to get involved in the much more important area of exclusive cable sports. But as the weeks passed MacKenzie was more and more in evidence.

One of his first interventions in L!ve programming was spurred by the fact that the channel had broadcast pictures of gay members of the invited studio audience kissing passionately. This had been broadcast at 11 p.m. and was therefore OK ITC-wise. MacKenzie saw it on a videotape of recent output a few days later. He flipped and, having resisted the urge for many weeks, stormed into the 24th floor and burst in on a Tellybrat planning meeting, demanding to know who was responsible: 'It's bad enough having fucking queers, but I'm not having them *doing it*. It's absolutely *revolting*. It's stopping here. And it's stopping now.'

The guilty producer piped up: 'Would you have had any objection if it had been two leggy lovelies giving each other a quick snog? I don't think so.' And, horror of horrors, the gang of gays and women started *laughing at him*! His writ did not run here. It was Planet Janet! MacKenzie turned a shade of purple – *steam coming out of his ears* – and seemed to be about to go on the attack. But he checked himself and thought better of it, and retreated. He skulked back to his lair, muttering, *F'kin' perverts . . . f'kin' queers*.

The presence of so many women at L!ve TV was bad enough. Kelvin thought women were, on the whole, naturally stupid. But sometimes you needed stupid people on your team, to write the stupid stuff in the paper for stupid readers, also mostly women. So they had their place, women did. Fair enough. But if they ever had to do anything difficult or important, they would fall to pieces. Except Maggie Thatcher. But she was more like a man, anyway – everyone said so. No. It was not a matter of being sexist – that was bollocks, that was. It was just the natural way of things. They could be annoying, women could. Like Janet. Extremely annoying. Even the more normal ones sat around in the office preening themselves and doing their lipstick and fiddling about with their handbags. They did not wear nice clean white shirts and ties, like proper journalists needed to. But how could they? They were women. It wasn't their fault, was it? Annoying, yes. But basically they were harmless in the end.

Gays – *shirt-lifters* – now they were a different cup of

cocoa. Gays could band together. Some of them were clever. You had to be careful. They were devious by nature. You had to watch yourself. Was it true, all them gays on the 24th floor? It couldn't be true, could it? All them perverts? Ferrari was delighted to supply a report from the front. The narcissistic nightclub culture at the centre of Janet's Vision for L!ve was homosexual from top to bottom. Many of the main operators were gay and those who were not tended to be 'stray' (meaning *straigh*ts who pretended to be *ga*y). Gay men had always played an important part in Janet's life. Her admiration for Neil Tennant of the Pet Shop Boys knew few bounds and her greatest formal success in television, the Prix Italia-winning *Der Vampyr*, was a typically camp effort made in conjunction with a gay director, Nigel Finch, who had since died of an AIDS-related illness. And Janet, when explaining her vision for L!ve TV to the trade press, had flagged a gay connection. The two big media successes in recent years, she had said, were *Hello!* magazine and 'a proper respect for the power of the pink *pahnd*.' So that was it, then. The formula for media success. *Hello, Duckie!* magazine. On Acid.

Kelvin's worst fears seemed to be confirmed by some of the output of the early rehearsals. He was once seen staring transfixed with lip-curling horror at a monitor featuring a black transvestite sitting between a mirror and a bowl of fruit and talking in a strange, lisping voice about how to get the maximum sexual thrill out of putting on lipstick. This was followed by an item featuring two particularly limp-wristed gays staging a camp and bitchy domestic quarrel on the subject of cooking and eating baked beans. 'Oooh, I'm a pig, me,' said the first gay, to which the other replied, 'Oooh, that's good. Let's have a cup of tea.'

Fear and loathing of gays was something of an obsession with MacKenzie. Not only were gays horrible and deviant, but they were a menace. He had picked up from Murdoch the idea (based on his supposed experience in dealing with film executives in Hollywood) that homosexuals were a determined and conspiratorial group who were secretly plotting to take over the world's media or, at least, lock Murdoch out. Yep. There was a deep gay conspiracy whereby PR agents and gay DJs and journalists worked together to promote the work of fellow gay performers. It was obvious, wasn't it? Kelvin would complain that 'genius' non-gay performers like his pal Jim Davidson were being frozen out by a bum-bandit mafia. As for the Pet Shop Boys, it means *what*!!?

So far Janet and Rachel had managed to shield the L!ve team, including the gay contingent, from contact with Kelvin. But Janet had become deeply depressed about the whole venture and the 'knives' that the *Mirror* had said were being sharpened for insertion into her back were now being prepared for use. The Vision had not worked out properly because of all the technical problems and, although bits of it looked OK, overall it was deeply compromised. The fact that the infobar was not working drove her to distraction. The Mirror management's determination to keep the staffing level below 200 meant that there was nobody to operate the infobar, when it could be made to work. Staff shortages and tight budgets were also destroying Completely Brilliant programming ideas like the Dinner Party.

Janet would arrive in The Entity and march rapidly past all the staff, make a beeline for her office, eyes on the floor, arms tightly crossed, ignoring everyone, and slam her door behind her. Within minutes she could be heard shrieking, 'What the *fuck* is that doing on *my* channel . . . Get that programme off my fucking television station! *Naaaow!*' She would then march back out again, head down, heading at a brisk clip for the latest meeting with the senior Mirror TV management for another session at which she would be asked to do the impossible, as she saw it, with the resources available to her. An hour or two later she would return, this time walking more slowly, kicking imaginary tin cans and muttering, 'I'm depressed, I'm so fuckin' depressed.' Later still, people would hear a monumental primal scream from some part of the open-plan Entity, sometimes followed by crashin' and bangin' noises as she threw things round the room. Work would stop and the Tellybrats would stare at each other or make 'she's flipped' gestures. She would then come rampaging through the studio screamin' at techies and production people in particular or, well, just screamin'. (Her own independent production company was called Screaming Productions; not without reason.)

Still, people were sympathetic and tried to get on with things as best they could. They knew she had a big ego; they also knew she was getting it in the neck from the Mirror board. She was never really nasty with it, just autocratic and strangely whimsical. At least they were not dealing directly with MacKenzie, who, it was known, was apt to sack people instantly and without mercy.

There were occasional sightings of him, and it was reported that he had an amused 'you-bunch-of-tosspots-are-going-down-the-pan-and-nothing-can-save-you' smirk permanently fixed to his face. But for the time being, apart from his outburst over the gay kissing episode, he was keeping well out of it.

Chapter Twenty-one

In which 'Hello, Duckie! Magazine on Acid' turns into 'Hospital Radio on Diazepam' as it is realised there is often Absolutely Nothing Happening in the Whole Country causing Monty's Vision to collapse and Many at L!ve TV to start thinking about Jumping Ship

L!ve TV had been on air for a few weeks now. Many had thought that, after the inevitable glitches of the launch, things would settle down and go more smoothly once the channel had been through a few cycles of programming which would shake out all the bugs. But things were not working out like that. Nothing seemed to get better and none of the multiple problems afflicting the channel seemed to get sorted out.[1]

Most people who thought about it could not see the channel continuing in this form, and there was a strange air of unreality about the place as people waited for the roof to fall in (metaphorically). People said that the pyramid on top of Canary Wharf tower was emitting 'bad vibes' that made everyone slowly go crazy. It was noted that if you read the word L!ve backwards it spelt out Ev!l.

On top of this, for some reason a camera crew from BBC 2 was creeping about, poking their noses into everything and obviously waiting to film the impending disaster. Some of the staff openly wondered if they were making a television version of *Spinal Tap*, capturing all the follies, bitchiness, absurdities and egomania of media luvviedom in one day-glo package. L!ve TV? What's it like? *Absolutely Fabulous* (Janet and Rachel) meets *Men Behaving Badly* (MacKenzie and Ferrari) on the set of *Drop the Dead Donkey*.

The documentary crew was headed by Hugh Dehn, a journalist whom MacKenzie had known at the *News of the World* but who had since moved to the BBC, where he made business programmes. Dehn, working under the overall direction of Robert Thirkell, a leading BBC documentary-maker, was granted an amazing degree of access, and even allowed to film senior management meetings, on the grounds that L!ve TV needed all the publicity it could get. Even so, this was an abrupt turnaround in MacKenzie's attitude to such activity. A crew from BBC TV News had once turned up in the *Sun* newsroom to film a few seconds of background footage, having been granted permission by News International's powerful PR department. MacKenzie went ballistic and tried to have them thrown out. The BBC people held their ground, brandishing official letters of authorisation, signed in blood. MacKenzie nevertheless hovered around menacingly as they captured a few innocuous wideshots, and he made sure they were booted out the minute they had finished.

This time it was different. He didn't actually welcome the BBC crew with open arms, but he did not stand in the way. He even agreed to be filmed himself. Janet also consented to the filming, but smelt a rat from the start. She had an argument with Dehn, which led to him having less control over the project, and insisted on dealing directly with Thirkell, who was much more her cup of tea. Thirkell and Dehn started filming just before the launch of L!ve and soon came to the view that the channel was going to go belly up. They were astonished by the ferocity of the spats between Janet and the management and, in the end, reckoned they had been able to catch only about 1 per cent of the arguments. They decided to play the story as a simple personality clash. A lot of the background, such as how Kelvin and Janet had ended up working together in the first place, remained a mystery to them.[2]

In the heady early days around the time of the launch, the cameras' presence added an air of glamour to the world of L!ve TV, but as time passed many people began to find it creepy to be filmed and this added to the all-encompassing sense of paranoia.

Apart from moments of convulsive laughter at the absurdity of the Whole Situation, all the staff, except the most airheaded juniors, were by now extremely ratty with each other and many were afflicted by deep insecurity. Some senior executives suspected, in all seriousness, that their offices were being bugged, and many felt sure Ferrari was spying on them and providing unflattering reports to the sinister, sneering Grey-Suited Ones on the management floor.

Some of the on-screen Talent, especially the more inexperienced, were having fun in this weird and wonderful world. They were sustained by the powerful ego-boosting drug of appearing live for hours and hours 'on the telly'. For them, it was all a bit like spending a few extra months at college, but much better paid. At least they could put any decent moments of output on their electronic 'showreel' CVs and then move on to a 'real' television show (which a great many did at the first possible opportunity). Even the most junior Tellybrats, though, were knackered from weeks of unrealistic rehearsals which had done precious little to prepare them for the reality of what was to come.

The more senior people were mortified by what association with this rolling disaster might do to their reputation and future employment prospects. They started composing plausible 'it wasn't my fault' scenarios in their heads and looking for a way out. Lack of cash and low staffing levels were affecting the output, not just the more expensive or ambitious material such as the 'Dinner Party' slot, but all aspects of programming. The cheaper and simpler Entity-based daytime programming was also very thin, and things were not going according to plan.

Once the channel went on air the supply of 'event-driven' material supplied by the PR people soon dried up. The trendy presenters, lacking contacts and clout, found that they were excluded from the pick of the showbiz parties. Still, some of the Talent were having a great time trying. Armed with a specialist bulletin listing the day's film premieres, charity events, shop and restaurant openings and other celebrity doings, they could go to anything they fancied. It was a bit like being an autograph-hunter for a living.

Armed with cameras, and doing their lipstick on the Tube, they would turn up in the West End and try to muscle in alongside what they thought of as 'the big boys': ITN film crews and the paparazzi, who, because the Talent were young, naive and good-lookin', and because L!ve TV was not regarded as competition, would chat to them and sometimes let them push towards the front of the pack. Until the celebrities appeared, that is, at which point they would, as often as not, be shoved to the back of the pack as the real business was conducted.

According to the Montyvision plan, L!ve TV presenters would be invited by eager PR people to mix it with the stars at events such as the opening of Planet Hollywood ('Oh, there's Sylvester Stallone. I'll just have a quick word.'). In reality, the PR people regarded them as a nuisance. At first they were tolerated, on the grounds that anyone pointing a camera with an OB truck attached added an air of glamour to any celebrity event. But very quickly familiarity bred contempt ('Not you lot again!'). Sylvester Stallone at Planet Hollywood was replaced by

Sharon from Ilford at the 'launch' of Top Shop's new window display. Finding themselves excluded from any real activity, the Talent went for shop or restaurant openings in a big way. The material was dire, but at least the PR people let them in. Staff at L!ve TV were soon joking to each other that the station would go to the 'opening of an envelope'.

But there were problems even with this. The PR people wanted their pound of flesh: free publicity in return for filming rights. The Tellybrats, lacking journalistic experience and desperate to keep in with the PR people, would oblige by filming what often amounted to lengthy adverts. If they did so, they were slapped down by the ITC regulators (who were not very interested in L!ve TV as such, because it had so few viewers, but were worried about precedents being set in the tricky area of 'advertorial').

The ITC's senior programme officer specialising in cable, Guy Phelps, had complained on L!ve's very first day about an OB from Disneyland in Paris. He thought that there seemed to be no reason for showing the footage, 'beyond the wish to join in the fun at Disneyland', and that the broadcast quickly degenerated into an advert for the place: 'Just to go there and show the rides and say how good they are really is just promotion and is not acceptable. Unless you can find some justification for these sorts of items they should not be continued.'[3]

The Tellybrats were also warned about this by L!ve's in-house lawyer, Neil Pepin, but carried on regardless. What else could they do? There was a simple choice, do deals with pluggers or, much of the time, have no material at all. So off they went to trendy shops and restaurants, sampling the wares and saying how Completely Brilliant they were; there was no concession to balance. Three days after the launch Guy Phelps of the ITC was becoming a daily correspondent, even though he was watching only a random sample of the output. In a regular feature on video releases broadcast from the Virgin Megastore, the way the cameras lingered on the Virgin logo was condemned as an advertisement for the shop. Weeks later he was still sending memos, now referring 'the old problem of undue prominence'. He complained about a live OB from Tower Records showing the 'Tower Chart' which, he said, 'not only gave the store publicity but also allowed it to demonstrate its keen pricing'. An item on shoe designer Patrick Cox (maker of those Completely Brilliant orange shoes) was a problem, Phelps thought: 'the presenter really did little but invite Mr Cox and his clientele to say how wonderful his shoes are, and at some length. The result did give the impression of being a promotion for the cobbler and his (no doubt) wonderful shoes.'[4]

But that was the problem. L!ve rarely had any stories. According to The Vision, it really was meant to be a long series of plugs for Completely Brilliant things: 'cheery, not sneery'. Many of the Tellybrats, drawn more or less from the world of Absolutely Fabulous, would not have recognised what a journalist would have thought of as a story anyway and would have been reluctant to criticise or investigate anything put in front of them, even had the PRs allowed them to do so. Which they didn't. But the bottom line was that, unless they got permission to go to a restaurant or shop plugging session, they would have nothing, absolutely nothing, to film.

Once, in desperation (and regressing to the hilarious high jinks of Orsten's make-believe training sessions), one presenter persuaded a L!ve sound technician to pretend to be a stoned rock star while she interviewed him. Another time, a live OB crew bumped into 'Victor Meldrew' in Leicester Square, where he was attending a charity do in a cinema, and eagerly asked for an interview. 'I don't *believe* it!' the actor complained. 'You've already done me three times this week.' Monty's belief that he could get 'something for nothing' by hiring a load of kids to run around London with cameras was not working out. Instead of being '*Hello, Duckie!* magazine on acid', the channel was in danger of ending up like Hospital Radio on Diazepam.

Underlying these problems was the simple fact that while live OB broadcasts were specified to take place all day, every day, there were many points in a typical 24-hour schedule when absolutely nothing of any interest was going on in public anywhere in the country. Faced with the reality of this simple fact, one reporter gamely turned up in Leicester Square one fine Tuesday afternoon, appeared on camera with thin clusters of aimlessly milling tourists in the background, cheerfully shrugged her shoulders, and announced that since there was nothing happening ('as you can see') she was going shopping. The camera duly recorded her trooping about Knightsbridge and flicking through racks of clothes.

The 'nothing happening' problem was particularly severe on mornings in the early part of the week. One Monday the producers checked the diary and found that the only thing happening in the whole of the UK was a prize-giving cattle show just outside Leeds. The presenter, dressed in her customary lilac clothes (and with personal hairdresser and make-up artist in tow), grumpily trekked up north, where she anchored the day's OB output: 'Tell me, just what *sort* of cow is this, then?' – at least the ITC could not complain about *that*. But then Janet saw the output and charged into the director's box: 'What the fuck is *that shit* doin' on the screen? Get *that shit* off my television channel *now*!' The producer held up his

hands, palms upwards, and said, 'Well, sorry, Janet . . . er
. . . that's all there is.'

The lack of strong OB material and of a good supply of
filler material was a big problem for the daytime show, on
which presenter Simon London, with a single producer, a
researcher (often straight out of college and lacking
contacts and experience) and the intermittent services of
the Lone Runner, was expected to fill seven hours of
airtime, five days a week. The effort nearly killed him –
especially the primary instruction in the L!ve TV Editorial
Blueprint: 'Simon is Never Bored'.

A key element of London's show was a 'talent showcase', with viewers sending in homemade videos for
screening, thus, in theory, providing L!ve with hours of
free, viewer-friendly material. Before the launch an attempt
had been made to drum up some of this material and, for
once, H. L. Mencken's dictum that nobody ever went broke
underestimating the public's taste was proved wrong. A
great pile of vids arrived and it was some *poor sod*'s job
to sit through them all, and produce a report on what they
were and how long they lasted.

The purely pornographic or wildly defamatory efforts
were eliminated first. The rest were cleared for screening,
but were so awful that they were not even funny. A list
of the most promising material available for Simon
London's show included *Astrology: The True Answers
Revealed*, described by the *poor sod* as 'a very amateur documentary about astrology using some very strange drama-
tisation'. Then there was *Turkish Delight*, a demonstration
of amateur belly dancing ('technically OK, but women fat
and ugly. Duration: 3' 26"'); *Funky Diva* ('the trials and
tribulations of a Birmingham transvestite. Duration:
4' 02"'); *Ocean Images* ('some very fascinating footage of
fish. Needs to be edited to cleared music'); and *Carol and*

Brendan's Wedding ('the usual. Duration: *two hours*'). The real humdinger, however, was reckoned to be *Fred Smith's Favourite Journey* ('a trip on Docklands Light Railway with two girls miming to a Wham track; duration 4' 29". Tape no: 2161. *Cleared for use*'). More usable was a free promo tape from 'The RSVP School of Etiquette' with segments entitled 'How to eat sorbet from stemware' (3' 30"), 'How to tackle finger foods' (4' 47") and 'How to eat spaghetti' (4' 32").[5]

London's team was also handicapped by a lack of interesting studio guests. The *slebs* were unenthusiastic about traipsin' out to the wilds of Docklands to be interviewed for hours for the benefit of a couple of thousand viewers. The maximum booking fee was £50, which was not enough to interest somebody like Bamber Gascoigne, let alone Paul Gascoigne. At least once, an invited guest failed to show up and, although this was not on Simon London's show, the producer posed as an interviewee and the team bluffed their way through a few hours of output.

Sometimes clueless Americans, block-booked on to everything by their agents and not understanding the L!ve TV set-up, would turn up. The arrival of James Brown, the soul singer, booked on to Rhodri Williams's show, was one scoop. But the human Sex Machine was more interested in the strange office-cum-studio than in the interview. He ignored Rhodri and the cameras and wandered about playing with the computers and answering the phones.

All Rhodri's questions were answered with the interviewer's nightmare: either 'Yep' followed by silence or 'Nope' followed by silence. Janet's pre-launch announcement that L!ve would 'just cut to something else if it gets too borin' in the studio' now rang hollow. In the end Rhodri got Brown's attention by turning around Brown's own catchphrase: 'James, how do you feel?' Brown replied, still peering distractedly at a computer screen, 'Well, I *feeel awwwwllright*. 'Rhodri pressed on in his faint Welsh accent: 'All right?' Brown said, 'Yup! I'm *feeelin' . . . h'woooo . . . awwwwright*.' After a slight pause Rhodri asked, 'Are you sure?' and the conversation carried on like this for a while, because Brown couldn't be bothered to do an interview and L!ve had nothing else with which to replace the item.

There was a high point of sorts one day when, as Rhodri was wittering away trying to be amusing, reading out items from the papers and treading water, a man with suckers on his knees and hands came into view in the background climbing up the plate-glass windows on the outside of the building. The news crackled into Rhodri's earpiece and he rushed over to the window. There he was, unannounced and unscheduled: 'Spiderman', the French Nutter Who Climbs Up All The World's Tallest Buildings. Rhodri started banging on the window and gesticulating, but Spiderman ignored him. The Lone Runner was despatched to catch up with Spiderman when he had finished his crawl up to the viewing platform next to the Evil Pyramid on top of the tower and bring him into The Entity for a chat. Which he did. *Great telly!* But apart from this the lack of 'walk-in' stories at L!ve TV was notable.

Simon London, in general, had even less luck than Rhodri. There were rare hits like the time when Kelvin's old pal Max Clifford, the tabloid kiss 'n' tell expert, came on to talk about Hugh Grant's encounter with a prostitute in Los Angeles. But at other times he had to fill in by interviewing other members of staff, asking them what they were planning to do at the weekend, or getting them to impersonate *slebs* like Michael Caine. Once, in absolute desperation, he interviewed a visiting photocopy repairman about how photocopiers worked. People said it was the most interesting thing they'd seen on L!ve all week.

With the fatal combination of inexperienced staff and hours of airtime to fill, on-air gaffes were a certainty. Within a week memos from Neil Pepin were flying about, warning that the ITC might take a dim view of some of London's more desperate ad-libbing, especially a reference to 'sticking your finger up your bum' and an ad-libbed link involving a toy kitten which was put into a bag with London announcing he was going to drown it in the Thames. The lawyer thought this sort of thing ought to be avoided, really, on a programme designed, in part, to be watched by schoolchildren.

A more serious gaffe followed when a good-lookin' female presenter, recruited from the *sleb* circuit to brighten up Nick Ferrari's dowdy 'deconstructed newsdesk' (an oasis of beige disfiguring The Look), was ad-libbing about a crime story involving a man who had been accused in court of spending several thousand pounds a week on cocaine. The presenter pondered this and, after a bit of instant mental arithmetic, worked out exactly how much cocaine this would buy. She was impressed! Well-informed comment about his nostril capacity followed. *What a give-away!* It was later thought that broadcasting what amounted to an update on prevailing market prices for Class-A drugs was a mistake. The good-lookin' woman was transferred back to the *sleb* beat, where she worked with great success.

Most of the pressure was felt by the technical and production people, whom Janet and Rachel gathered together every week at a 'critical path' meeting, at which all the OB-unit, editing-system and other horrors were discussed. These meetings had started in the calmer times before the launch. They had been chaotic even then. Now they were often held in a mood of pure panic. Production staff would prepare carefully for these meetings, in the hope that the daily catastrophes engulfing their departments would at last be sorted out. The agenda was compiled in advance by Darryl Burton and consisted of a long list of problems and demands for extra money. Then everyone was shepherded into the room.

The meetings were dominated by the double act of Janet and Rachel. Rachel spoke very quickly and at great length, mainly explaining to people why something Janet wanted could not be done. Rachel was always on the ball and the logic of her argument was generally faultless – even crushing. Nevertheless, as often as not Janet would simply say, 'I don't care, Rachel. You can argue all day. I want it and that's that.' There were groans all round as Rachel recapped at great length, with Janet listening in a bored fashion and eventually replying, after a long pause, 'I told you: it doesn't matter what you say, I want it.' After three or four rounds of this, Burton would come to the rescue and propose that they move on and talk about the problem at the next meeting.

One especially long-running debate was about the small matter of why Rachel had failed to install some very heavy on-screen granite desks that Janet wanted. No matter what emergency was facing the production team, Janet would pull the conversation around to the Desk Question, week after week. Rachel would explain at length that they weighed many tonnes, that she was not sure they could be brought up in the lifts, and so on, trying to talk her round. Eventually Burton exploded: 'You can't have these desks, Janet, because they are three thousand pounds each!' But even that failed to remove 'The Fucking Desks' from the agenda.

From time to time there was progress of sorts, normally achieved by throwing money at smallish problems. When it was reported that nobody on the 24th floor could read their computer screen because of the glare from the television lights, Janet saw an opportunity to enhance The Look. It was decided to buy 'special edition' Anglepoise lamps, costing a total of £3,000. The management process was dominated by trivia. The committee never got through more than one or two agenda items. All the rest was left for the next meeting. So the agenda got longer and longer and ended up at three or four pages of densely typed points.

Rachel would emerge from these meetings with long lists of emergency 'things to do' organised with further lists of what these lists dealt with, summarised by one or two key lists of lists-of-lists controlled by a master list. 'I am the list lady,' she complained, tearing her hair out. The problems with the output, the inadequate staffing levels, the technical problems with the OBs and editing system, the relationship with the Mirror Group management, Janet's increasingly bleak moods in a place that lacked the BBC's resources and support services and, above all, the heartstopping series of crises she had to deal with every day and the sheer, exhausting effort needed to keep the show on the road – all this was getting to Rachel.

She was still dispensing determined, but increasingly implausible, jolly-hockey-sticks encouragement and chirpy morale-boosting bonhomie. But people knew she was fed up. When it all got a bit too much she would hide round the back of Janet's office, disobeying the strict non-smoking rule, furtively dragging on fags and muttering oaths under her breath before stubbing out the filthy dimp on an improvised ashtray. She would then take a deep breath, pull herself together, fix an encouraging smile on her face and bound out across The Entity to gee up the troops: 'Hey, come on! Cheer up! There's something happening over at HMV.' Her enthusiasm, proving less than infectious, was often met by groans. 'Yeah, Raych,' producers would say mournfully, 'but what do you want us to do about it?' Rachel, still under full steam, would gesticulate wildly: 'Well, y'know . . . use your initiative. Get over there and make it go *vmmmmfffppphhh* . . . y'know . . . easy *peasy*. Give it a bit of *pzzzzzmmmpffff*!'

It was OK to work in complete chaos for a while, especially if you thought things would get better. It was a bit like going on a course, Rachel thought, a sort of extreme Outward Bound obstacle course for TV programme-makers. After a slow start, the two-person features team working under her was putting together fifty pre-recorded eight-minute films a *week*. That was almost as much as some people in News and Current Affairs at the BBC made in a *year*. True, a lot of the stuff was diabolical, but some of it was really good. A lot of the new talent they had brought into television was *really fantastic* and they were already starting to move on. Adrenalin got you through it.

After a while, though, it became a grind. You could only get so far making a TV channel with no money, no staff and nothing to put on it. It was difficult keeping up the morale-boosting act. And Nick Ferrari kept going around telling people, 'I don't know why you are all working so hard. It's all gonna be changed round soon.' Anyway Rachel, for one, was holding good job offers from the BBC, MTV and others. She decided to leave L!ve TV. The long-running Janet-and-Rachel show was about to come to an end. And Janet was not going to like it.[6]

That was the problem with Janet. The personal was political. There was no dividing line between professional life and social life: they were the same thing. Any disagreement about telly-making was taken as a personal insult.

L¿ve TV

Any failure to do what she wanted was seen as treachery. So, naturally enough, when Janet heard of Rachel's decision to leave and take up an offer to work at MTV Europe, she threw the mother of all tantrums. Rachel tried to explain. They worked together well, that was true. They were friends; fair enough. They had helped each other out and watched each other's back over the years. Janet had given Rachel a break when she promoted her at *Def-II*, for which Rachel was still grateful. But, as Rachel put it at the time, they were not 'joined at the hip'. Many sympathised with Rachel when they heard that she had told Janet, 'If you were in my position, you would do the same.'

The separation caused a remarkable scene in the Groucho Club, witnessed by many. Rachel was having a drink with her prospective boss, Brent Hansen, president of MTV Europe, when she was set upon by an emotional Janet, who was out with her friend Mick Pilsworth from Chrysalis TV. To the amazement of the crowd of drinkers, Janet grabbed Rachel in a passionate embrace and started pleading, 'Don't leave me, Raych. Just tell me what you want. I'll double yer wages – anything.' But it was no good. Rachel was leaving.

The day after Rachel's official departure from L!ve TV, Janet received more bad news: the celebrated and bohemian Serbian–Canadian film-maker Frank Cvitanovich, the third of her official husbands, whom she had married in 1978, had died after a long series of illnesses.

Janet and Frank had split up in the mid-'80s and had been divorced in 1988, but they were still friendly and his death, although not entirely unexpected, was extremely depressing. On hearing the news MacKenzie quipped, 'That's bad news. Now L!ve TV is down to two viewers.'

Chapter Twenty-two

In which Janet goes to Edinburgh, fingers the M-People and complains about Dicks and Willies but is denounced by some and ignored by many others as she finally decides that It Isn't Going To Work Out With Kelvin And Me and leaves L!ve TV, precipitating the Death of the Infobar and the arrival of Grey Carpet Tiles, and is left facing an uncertain future

The MacTaggart lecture at the annual Edinburgh International Television Festival is an important event in the lives of many people in tellyland, highlighted in many a computerised personal organiser.

In 1995, the honour of giving the lecture was given to Janet Street-Porter, marking her arrival at the very top of the industry and giving her, at last, the respect and credibility she had craved when she was still at the BBC.

In recent years it had become something of a tradition to use the lecture to knock the new aristocracy of accountants and management consultants which had taken control of the TV industry, especially at the BBC and, after the disastrous, Thatcher-inspired ITV franchise auction, in the ITV companies. A few years earlier, Michael Grade, erstwhile head of BBC 1, who was then running Channel Four, had attacked his former friend John Birt for instituting 'pseudo-Leninist' management methods as BBC director-general, carried out 'with brutal zeal' by 'an army of accountants'. The following year Dennis Potter, by then dying of a cancer tumour he had named 'Rupert Murdoch', attacked Birt as 'a croak-voiced Dalek' dressed in an Armani suit. Janet chose to explore similar themes in a rambling and chaotic speech worked up with, among others, her old *Network-7* mucker John Cummins (Cummins had since left television and was running a media consultancy in the City).[1]

Janet turned up on time for the great event, which took place as usual in the hall of the Kirk of St Cuthbert, Edinburgh, in front of all the powerful and important people in British television. She took to the stage looking decidedly spaced-out and rumpled. Amazingly, for a person who lavished so much time and money on clothes, she was dressed in sweaty-looking tennis togs and hadn't even had her hair done. *Cool, or what!* ('She just said, "Sod that. I can't be bothered to change",' an aide later told a newspaper).

She began her speech with a general survey of the British TV scene which, she thought, was unremittingly bleak. In line with her usual solipsism, virtually everything she said referred to her own habits, preferences and state of mind. Janet did not find telly 'fun' any more, *ergo* telly was not fun any more. As ever, in this respect, her boredom was in tune with the very latest trends. A 'recent survey', she said, showed that most under-12s would – horror of horrors – rather play with their computers than watch the telly. *That's how borin' you are, you lot: more borin' than a load of techie nerds.*

The over-50s were opting out as well. 'Nowadays, if I want ideas, I don't watch TV. I go to a Brian Eno orra Laurie Anderson installation [*Y'see, I'm cool, me*] or I spend an hour inna greetin'-card shop, watchin' what wimmin are buyin' [*and street-wise too*] or I talk to my sister 'oo works in Sainsbury's [*Beat that, you Oxbridge wankers!*].'

Then Janet intoned her first major soundbite: 'A terminal blight 'as hit the Briddish TV industry. This blight' – dramatic pause – 'is management.'

This bombshell was followed by a rapid-fire round of interestin' and Completely Ironic infobar-worthy facts. 'The Briddish TV bizzniz is the worst-performin' of all our creative bizniz'iz. The British record industree exports nine times as much as we do.' More infobar wisdom followed: 'Briddish tellervision exports are now overtak'n by those of furtiliza [*'cos it's all shit*].' In the next century, she gravely warned, British television would be worth 'sod all' if things did not change.

The reason for this disaster was that the industry 'did not value talent' or promote talented and in-touch, street-wise people [*like me*] into senior management positions. In contrast, the pop-music racket did so well because the people who ran it were less middle-class and not so many of them had been to university [*unlike you lot of* sad *buttock-clenching tossers*].

Slowly, she built up to sound-bite Number Two, her voice quivering with the Sheer Bloody Momentousness of what she was about to say: 'Wivva a few notable exsepshuns, Briddish TV managers 'ave always been "M-people". That means midderl-class, midderl-brow, midderl-aged and male, Masonic in their tendencies and – *notta put too finer point onnit* – fairly mediocre.' ('I hope she didn't mean me,' twittered Alan Yentob, who had brought her into the BBC, indulged her pet projects such as *Der Vampyr*, promoted her and put up with her many foibles for five years.) The lack of Vision was such that 'the BBC is in danger of becoming the Clarks Shoes of the multi-media world, something that your mum would buy for you but which you'd never choose for yourself'. (L!ve TV, of course, was more like a pair of orange Patrick Cox brothel-creepers, and that was *official*.)

These M-people lived in a bubble world, Janet said, and had no idea [*unlike me*] what was goin' down on the street.

Live TV

"Ow can they respond to the pulsaytin' mass, that 'othouse of ideas in a multykultchural Briddish society [*me an' Normski*], if they all tawk in the same [*clenched-buttock*] accent polished at the same universities an' all end up shoppin' at the same delicatessens [*like the poxy Cheese Shop in Barnes*]. No wunder the prowgrammes they commission are all startin' to look the same . . . vets, hospitals, detectiffs . . .

'TV needs to innervate [*like what me and Raych used to do*] now more than ever, and that is exactly what it is not doin'. Vision is often ridiculed by mundane Briddish management [*Yentob used to wind me up no end*]. You carnt only folla' taste, y've gotta lead it [*like me and Zandra*]. Y've gotta be bold. You cannot dissolve risk out of the job [*'cos that's what they said, wasn't it? "Janet's an innervator, but she's a helluva risk"*]. Once, tellervision companies 'ad identities,' Janet remembered, 'but now they only 'ave cashflows as their owners care less 'n' less abaht creativity. But creativity is where the long-term profits will come from [*I mean, look at all the cash that's been made copyin'* Network-7 – *just ask anyone. What a mug I've bin*].'

And another thing. Willies! Dicks on Tables! Wimmin were often the most creative and most popular with the TV audience, Janet said, 'but 'oo commissions the comedy on Briddish tellervision? . . . Do you need a willie to 'andle creative talent like Michael Barrymore, Lenny 'Enry or Jennifer Saunders [*like I did in me BBC commissioning job*]? No you did not. That was the inescapable answer to this question. Wimmin are so woeferlee under-represented in TV management it makes me want to weep.'

Here she was on strong ground. The lack of equal opportunities for women in senior management was a source of profound guilt for many of the liberal, '60s-radical, university-educated men she was addressing. Not that the rock biz or fertiliser industries that she praised as more creative and efficient were less male-dominated: quite the contrary. Still, it was a strong card and she played it for all it was worth.

The speech was greeted with lukewarm applause and then everyone rushed off to bag a decent place at the George Hotel bar and get on with the main business of slaggin' off rivals to the hordes of waiting media hacks, suckin' up to potential employers and cuttin' deals with independent producers. Janet herself, who seemed to expect the earth to open with a volcanic roar and swallow the entire audience at any moment, marched up to Michael Southgate, the hapless 41-year-old commercial director of the ITV network; he had been one of her bosses way back in her old LWT days. 'You're the fucker I was referrin' to,' she rasped, 'and what annoys me is not only that you are a *suit*, but that y've made a lotta money out of it!'

The next day the papers played the story fairly big, zeroing in on the catchy 'M-people' phrase which, at least, made a decent headline. Leading the way was the *Independent*, which printed the speech more or less in full, partly because Monty had sacked many of its journalists and it had nothing else to fill its yawning designer pages. Comment was universally hostile. The *Financial Times* thought the lecture was a prime example of a greenhouse-dweller throwing stones. 'Have you watched L!ve TV?' the paper asked its readers, before revealing that 'it is a mixture of mindless music, vox pops, clubbing and chat among the ignorant. It looks cost-effective but devoid of talent. Precisely the qualities Janet Street-Porter so vigorously attacks.'

The *Daily Telegraph* wanted to know what all the fuss was about. Who is this Janet Street-Porter anyway? She runs a cable television channel which nobody watches, doesn't she? People who run cable television stations are ten a penny in any Soho wine bar. Who cares?

Janet had mentioned that her own 'inspiration' came in part from the Sex Pistols and the Pet Shop Boys. This allowed her critics to counter-attack, saying she was over the hill. Nick Elliot, a leading M-person from Janet's past at LWT, was reported as saying, 'The idea that Janet in her designer house is close to the grass roots is a joke . . . even if her sister does work at Sainsbury's.'

Other critics noted that Janet, when she had put herself forward as a potential head of Arts at the BBC just a couple of years earlier, had said very different things, emphasising, in a series of carefully planned press interviews, not her checkout-girl sister but the fact that her mum supposedly used to take her to sub-titled foreign movies, that a close relative had been a ballet dancer and that, in her own words, 'when it comes to the arts, I quite like elitist coverage'. Although she had not been to university, she had the opportunity to do so, but had instead chosen to go to the Architectural Association college, which was, if anything, even more swanky. In fact, the only thing that was working-class about Janet Street-Porter was her accent – and nobody was sure quite how affected that was.

After the exertions of Edinburgh Janet briefly returned to Canary Wharf in what was described as a 'power haze'. She rounded on Kelvin telling him that she should really have added a fifth 'M' to the 'M-people' list, so it would read 'male, middle-class, middle-brow, mediocre and – *MacKenzie*! *Ack, ack, ack*. But instead of crumpling as she intended, Kelvin shot back, 'Yeah, and a sixth – menopausal! *Hee, hee, hee*.'

Janet now seemed more bored than ever with havin' to put up with MacKenzie and the other Dicks and Willies and deal with all the tedious management responsibilities, especially now Rachel had departed (how *could* she do that to me?). At the same time, Kelvin had made it clear to senior people in the Mirror Group that he wanted her to leave. The teasing and mutual banter had been replaced by genuine aggro and neither Janet nor Kelvin could see things working out.

He had stopped taking her calls, switching his extension on to its Ansaphone so that he need not speak to her. If visitors asked how he was getting along with Janet, he would smile, say, ''Ere, just listen to this,' and turn on the Ansaphone. '*Kelllllvinnn!*' the machine would squawk, 'I *know* you're in there, Kelvin!' Click. Bleep. 'Yoooooo *bastard!* You can't just walk away from this, MacKenzie.' Click. Bleep. '*KELLLLVIN!!!* Grow up, come out. Look, you *won't* get away with this.' Click. Bleep. 'This is *JANET!* You fat *bastard*, stop hidin' – I know you're in there . . . ' Kelvin would let the messages run for a while, then turn the machine off and conclude matter-of-factly, 'She's nuts.'

Janet announced that she had been invited to take a short holiday on Sting's yacht on the Côte d'Azur, according to one version of the story, or, in another version, a motoring tour or something with Bryan Ferry, or, in yet another version, to play tennis in Spain with Ruby Wax and Lynne Franks. 'Great, innit,' she complained to her minions. 'I just get back from givin' the bleedin' MacTaggart an' I'm s'post to go off to the Sahf of France at the drop of an 'at an' hang abaht with a load of bleedin' pop stars on a boat for a fortnight. I dunno. Great, innit?' She said she could not wriggle out of the invitation, and told her staff, 'You lot are just gonna 'ave to look after the station for a bit.' And off she went.

As soon as she had left (on what was now being described as 'a walking holiday' in the South of France) Kelvin became more in evidence about the place, and Nick

Ferrari's attitude towards the staff cooled notably. A few days later Kelvin issued a press release announcing that he had completed negotiations to buy second rights to the early stages of the rugby union World Cup. The production people were baffled. There was no slot in the rolling schedule for live sport. It had never been discussed. It was not part of The Vision and there was no mention of it in the Blueprint. At the very least they would now have to redesign the schedule. Janet would have to approve all that. But where was she? The news filtered back that Janet was 'furious' about the rugby deal and would ditch the whole thing when she got back. In the meantime, heads were kept well below the parapet. Then, a few days later, corporate conformist grey – *grey!* – carpet tiles were laid over the funky metallic floor in Janet's office. The rumour machine went into overdrive. There was No Way Janet was coming back to set foot on *grey carpet tiles*.

There had been rumours and straws in the wind for a while. Rachel Purnell's departure to join MTV had, for many people, been the beginning of the end. The writing was on the wall. Just a matter of time. While Janet was away, Rachel had dropped back into pick up her things. She had bumped into one of the night-time producers, with whom she was friendly, and asked him what he was doing about getting out. When he said he had no plans, she became grave and warned him that 'big changes' were afoot and he probably wouldn't like them.

For Monty, this was crunch-time. He had courted Janet for a long time and, despite the obvious problems with L!ve TV, he still thought her the right person to run the national syndicated spine for his British 'Fox' idea. He seemed torn, and unwilling to have Kelvin in absolute control of the Mirror Group's TV interests without somebody like Janet to trammel him a bit. Monty and Kelvin had now sunk their differences, but the relationship was tense and Kelvin was already throwing his weight around, what with his special links to the cable companies on which the whole of Monty's television ambitions rested. Now Monty had to make a choice. He backed Kelvin. Janet was out.

The first inkling anyone at L!ve TV got of this was a strange atmosphere in the building on the morning of 12 September 1995. It was quieter than usual. *Too quiet*. No *screamin' an' shahtin'*, of course: Janet had been away on her holiday for nearly a fortnight. Nick Ferrari, who had taken over the day-to-day running of the place after Rachel went, was nowhere to be seen. There was activity in Janet's office. *Funny*. Blokes seemed to be moving carpet tiles and bits of wood and plasterboard in and out. *Very funny*. Maybe she was just having a bit of redecorating done; you never knew with Janet. Then, halfway through the morning show, the phone in the director's box rang. The producer recognised the voice: Kelvin MacKenzie. *What's he doing phoning The Box?*

'Take that fuckin' info-strap off the screen,' MacKenzie barked. 'It's full of spelling mistakes . . . Just get rid of it, got that? . . . OK . . . Straight away, if you don't mind . . .' Click. The producer blinked. It was Janet's Rule Number One that no matter what, no matter how out of date, misleading or stupid the 'data' on the infobar, it *had* to stay on the screen. It was the *cornerstone* of The Look. It was a tricky one, this. MacKenzie was Janet's boss, and therefore the producer's boss *in theory*, but day-to-day . . . No, the infobar had better stay, unless the order came from Janet herself. If she and MacKenzie were having one of their tiffs, they could sort it out between them. He was not getting involved.

The phone rang again. It was MacKenzie, louder than

ever: 'Look. *Didn't you hear me?* Are you fucking deaf as well as *BLIND?!* I told you, Get! that! fuck! ing! In! Fo! strap! *Off* the fuckin' *screen*. *NOW!* . . . Eh? What? . . . Janet? *Never mind Janet!* . . . No, no, you listen to me . . . I won't tell you again. I want you to *kill it*! *NOW!* Have you got that, eh? . . . Good! . . . Off. Now. *Straight away*. Got it? Right?' Click.

Blimey, he means it! The producer took a deep breath. The infobar was a pain in the arse, true, but it was like turning off the life-support machine in a hopeless case. Quite a step. But what could he do? . . . 'I won't tell you again' . . . He reached for the knobs on the mixing desk. He looked at the output monitor. The infobar faded and disappeared.

Not many people noticed at first. Everyone in The Entity had their head down, too busy to look at the output. The producer cut to a pre-recorded package and the cameramen in The Entity took a short rest. MacKenzie appeared, shirtsleeves rolled up, bowling along the puce carpet towards what was still thought of as Janet's office. He glanced once at a monitor suspended from a lime-green pillar to check and then, without missing a stroke, clapped his hands, shouted, 'The fucking infobar's gone!' and gave a little swooping clenched-fist gesture, like a footballer who had just scored a goal. A spontaneous cheer went up. MacKenzie, still swaggering under full steam, disappeared into 'Janet's' office, pushing past the Decorating Blokes, a broad grin on his face.

Most people at L!ve TV heard officially about Janet Street-Porter's resignation from the channel only when they read it in the papers next day on their way into work. In fact, when Janet went on holiday, she had had no intention of returning. She was worn out complaining about all the problems at L!ve TV and had made up her mind that nothing could persuade her to stay. She and MacKenzie had already agreed on a parting of the ways, to be finalised by the lawyers. Her departure, which was negotiated in 48 hours, involved her getting a substantial pay-off in return for folding the year that remained on her two-year contract.

The usual anodyne and mutually self-serving statements were agreed and appeared in the press, announcing her resignation. 'For almost a year I have lived and breathed L!ve TV,' Janet said. 'Now that it is successfully up and running I wish to move on to fresh challenges.' Monty replied for the Mirror side: 'Janet has done a terrific job for us at L!ve TV. I look upon her as a friend and wish her every success for the future.'

The Mirror camp added that Janet's Vision for the channel was different from that required by the Mirror board, who had reports from market research 'focus groups' and adverse comments from the cable operators to back them up. The channel Janet had created, said one 'senior Mirror manager' quoted anonymously in the trade bulletin *New Media Markets*, 'was too unstructured and difficult for people to understand, appealing only to a narrow market. The programming was too youth-oriented and not commercial enough. L!ve TV needs to accept that "commercial" is not a dirty word.' Also, 'there were too many pieces which were bite-size, thin, passive. The channel would just put a person in front of a camera or event in an insipid way.' It was also claimed that Janet had ignored the importance of local programming and had done little to help set up the local 'opt-out' affiliates which were such an important part of the business plan. Kelvin said that he intended to create 'an intelligent and accessible' channel in future.

That night the press pack descended on Janet's post-modernist pirate castle, perhaps hoping she would appear on the special 'papal balcony' which overlooked the street and which Piers Gough had designed specifically for occasions when she needed to address the masses. Instead she bounced out of the side door, told them all to fuck off and jumped into a waiting taxi, which whisked her off to God Knows Where. She was never again seen at L!ve TV.

A few weeks later Janet started giving interviews, but she didn't say much. She appeared on Clive Anderson's show and gave a carefully scripted teasy-weasy hint to the effect that she hated MacKenzie's guts, but could not talk because those horrid Mirror people had gagged her with a confidentiality clause (the reality was that she had been paid in return for agreeing not to talk to the press about L!ve TV in perpetuity).[2]

She was free, however, to talk about her main area of expertise, which was herself, and did so in a couple of lengthy recuperative interviews. 'Competition has been the driving force in my life,' she told one newspaper. 'But that'll change now. I've made money out of being opinionated, I've been self-centred but I was probably horrible to be with. Work dominated my life, and I came home brain dead. It can't go on, this life of money and achievement.' A new more mature, more mellow Janet was revealed: 'Do you know what? Yesterday I lost at Scrabble, and I didn't throw a temper tantrum. I hate losing at Scrabble, but for the first time in my life I managed to handle it.'

Soon after this she started writing a weekly column in the *Observer* (MacKenzie had once said he'd rather be 'rogered by a rhinoceros' than write for the *Observer*). In the first instalment, she said she was 'a happily unemployed ex-television executive'. Readers were then told that the column was Janet's 'space' and they were warned that it would be reflecting 'the bizarrely schizophrenic existence of this recently freed television executive, who no longer has to rise at dawn to sit at boardroom tables and indulge in time-wasting exercises like the conference call. These must have been invented by men to justify their existence . . . '

After this sideways reference to L!ve, Janet reverted to her standard repertoire: the sort of 'what I did on my holidays' material she had first written in the *Daily Mail* in the 1970s. 'I'm proud to say I've made a career out of being trivial. I think it's an art form . . . I'm a shameless groupie . . . I eat Sunday lunch with Neil Tennant from the Pet Shop Boys and go to Will Self's book launch . . . Damien Hirst is a pop star and that's what annoys the dreary art establishment . . . What does Britain's public do after 2 p.m. on Saturdays? We shop. We get our credit cards cooking.' And so on.

Some of her friends read the column and sighed. Poor old Janet. This stuff was *dire*. In the '70s the papers had taken her on as 'the voice of youth'. But now she was the voice of . . . well, the voice of what?[3]

Chapter Twenty-three

In which Kelvin Takes Control, promotes Nick Ferrari and tells the quaking Tellybrats to prepare for a future of Tits, Tarot Cards and Sport, leaving them to Reflect Bitterly that Janet has Left Them in the Shit, as the Gay Contingent flees, the Techies Readjust to the New Regime and Orange Shoes are banned forever

'Are you the pervert who makes all this fucking rubbish that goes out on Saturday night?' MacKenzie is now ensconced in Janet's hastily refurbished office in the corner of The Entity. He has been in full control of the station for about eighteen hours. He is making it his business to find out what everyone does – mainly so he can work out who to sack.

'No,' replies the night-time producer MacKenzie has summoned to his office. 'No, I'm the pervert who makes the rubbish that goes out during the week.'

MacKenzie, who tends to admire people who stand up to him, softens a bit. 'So you must be the one who did that . . . *thing* . . . with the baked beans.' He has obviously heard about the 'sploshers' incident on 'sex night' (which came to the attention of the station's lawyer), and is intrigued.

The producer decides to grab this opportunity and make a pitch to stay on board. Word is that others are being sacked without the chance to say anything at all. 'Look, I know you don't like what the late-night show is about,' he says, 'but I really think you should take a look at some of the stuff we've done. You've got nothing to lose.'

MacKenzie grunts: a good sign.

The producer explains that he was inventing 'a new type

of television', and that it really didn't have that much to do with Janet.

MacKenzie gives another encouraging snort.

They are doing sex features which nobody has done before, except on the pay-per-view channels. It is all late at night. The ITC is happy with that. It's cheap to do. I mean, a catering-size tin of baked beans from the *Mirror* canteen, what was that? A fiver? They have been attracting part of the pay-per-view audience and getting away with it: 'If you get rid of it you'll be missing a trick.'

MacKenzie grunts again. 'Awright, you're wasting my time, but, go on, make me a tape.'

The producer rushes off to make a compilation of what he considers his greatest hits and rushes back.

The Managing Director of Mirror Television clunks it into his video machine, muttering under his breath, 'Fucking perverts . . . I dunno what I'm watching this shite for . . . Fucking baked beans . . . ' The screen comes to life and displays a group of young women modelling padlocked chastity belts, prancing round The Entity in a spoof beauty-cum-fashion contest. The producer eyes MacKenzie, nervously awaiting his reaction. The muttering has stopped. MacKenzie's jaw hits the newly installed grey carpet tiles.

The girls on screen start to take their tops off. Kelvin begins to emit a low groan-like sound which seems to signify a mixture of horror and pleasure. *Oooowwwooorrrgggg . . . ooohhhhhhhhmmmm . . . ahhhh . . . eerrrrgggg.'*

After a while the producer interrupts. 'Well, whadda y'think?'

But Kelvin is miles away (*ooommmrrrggg hhmmmmmmmm*).

'Tell you what,' the producer enthuses, 'fast-forward it. You've just *gotta* see the baked beans. It's *fantastic!*'

At this point Kelvin wakes up. 'Fuck off,' he says. 'I am

not watching the fucking baked beans. This stuff . . . this *stuff* is *not right.*' Still, the producer has done enough to get Kelvin's attention. This man is no run-of-the-mill Planet Janet airhead luvvie. He has promise. He can *deliver.*

'Awright,' Kelvin says at last, keeping one eye on the topless chastity-belt women. 'I'll give it a go. But this stuff is *too* weird – it'll put people off. A *bit* of weird stuff is OK, but it has got to be *mainstream* weird.' The producer is told to go away and think about material to fill up a relaunched late-night sex show MacKenzie is already planning for the post-Janet schedule. It is to have the title 'Exotic Erotic' or 'Erotic Exotic' or 'Exorotic' or something. MacKenzie's own thinking, at this point, has not progressed much beyond conventional stripping. The producer is dismissed – MacKenzie is a busy man – 'But you'd better—*Gawd, look at that!* Oh my gawd, don't tell me *that* went out! Yeah, look . . . You'd better leave this tape with me, though.'[1]

Earlier in the day MacKenzie had marked the arrival of the new regime at L!ve TV by addressing the massed ranks of producers, on-screen Talent and assorted Tellybrats. He stood next to a desk just outside his new office – *Janet's office!* – flanked by Nick Ferrari. MacKenzie kicked off by giving a potted version of the official line about Janet's departure, adding that there had been 'an element of a personality clash there – *as you may have gathered* – but we've sorted it out. Somebody had to leave and it's all over and done with.' He gave Ferrari a withering look. 'Nick here will still be running things day-to-day *for the time being.*' Ferrari visibly gulped.

'Now, down to business.' Kelvin thumped a market-research report as thick as a phone directory down on the table beside him and started poking it with what many thought was needless force. 'This says the viewers are only interested in three things: sport, tarot cards and tits.' Sport, tarot cards and tits were therefore what the viewers were going to get. Did they understand that? There was silence and a few glum nods. Were they *sure* they understood that? More nods. Good. OK. All right. Excellent. 'Right then,' Kelvin said, building up to a crescendo, 'I'm *glad* you understand that because if you can't grasp this *fact* you might as well fuck off now! Got it? OK? All right? Excellent.' Would some people have to go? Probably. But only so that the channel as a whole could keep going 'financially speaking' and thus save the jobs of all the rest. 'Right, well, that's it for now. Nick and me will be seeing some of you one by one to have a word and see where we are, OK? Good. Excellent. Right.'

The meeting dissolved into nervy muttering. Some, presumably those who had been marked down as capable of adjusting to the new regime, looked smug or embarrassed. Other were close to tears. A lot of the gay and feminist contingent decided to resign immediately – why wait to be shot? Others worked out that if they waited to be sacked they would get better pay-offs. Resigning was a mug's game, financially speaking. Despite this a lot of the gays, especially, hissed through gritted teeth that as a matter of principle they were not going to work for Kelvin MacKenzie, probably the nation's Number One gay-baiter. They were going at once, even if it did cost them money. No gagging clauses, either. Others, uneasily hoping to stay on because they had no other jobs to go to, were impressed by these heroics.

At the same time there was bitterness that Janet had just cleared off and left them to their fate. She was all right. She had got her pay-off, rumoured to be £300,000 (the real figure was £100,000) but, whatever it was, vast by the standards of those left behind. She had tried to arrange things so that she came out of this . . . this *mess* . . . smelling of roses. M-people and all that. Blaming it all on rugby and Machovision and all that. The captain was supposed to go down with the ship, wasn't she? Where was 'women and children first'? If they had known she was going to leave after just twelve weeks on air, at least some of those who had folded other jobs, rather than just walking in off the streets, would not have joined up. These more experienced people, recruited from the extended family of Janetvision, were the ones most likely to face the chop: *she begged us all to come here and then jumped ship at the first excuse and left us in the shit!* The younger Tellybrats, generally speaking, were more malleable and therefore had a better chance of keeping their jobs.

The worst fears were soon confirmed. As people began to troop one by one into Ferrari's or MacKenzie's office, it became clear that mass sackings were under way. Ferrari dealt with people briskly. It was clear that he and MacKenzie had agreed in advance who they wanted to stay and who they wanted to go. Those fingered in advance, including some who had been hired by Ferrari in the first place, were sacked without mercy. In some cases, they were simply told their faces did not fit and they should go and see the Mirror group's lawyers about their pay-off. There was an important proviso. If, like Janet, they signed a 'gagging' confidentiality clause, which was described to them as 'a no-pissing agreement', the Mirror Group would pay the tax on their pay-off cheques. If not, they would have to pay the tax themselves.

Others found the whole process hilarious. Some had wanted to go for a while, but had been so wrapped up in day-to-day crisis management that they had never had the chance to lift their heads, ask 'What am I doing?' and walk out. For this minority, being sacked was a blessed relief.

One feisty and senior Janet-recruited features executive was sacked by MacKenzie, rather than Ferrari, on the grounds that she might not go quietly and, anyway, would be relatively expensive to pay off. She listened to MacKenzie's clipped hard-man tabloid-monster spiel, replete as usual with crude one-liners, and, when he stopped, burst into gales of laughter: yet *another* surrealistic episode of *Spinal Tap – the TV version*. Ferrari, taking a break between sackings, wandered along the corridor to see what all the noise was about. MacKenzie told him to get lost. Ferrari looked mortified: *What's she got to laugh about? Oh fuck, maybe Kelvin's given her my job!* The features executive corpsed again, before making her way to the lift to pick up her cheque from the lawyers.

After a couple of days of sackings, the number of victims was reckoned to be about forty, almost a quarter of the staff. The scale of the onslaught provoked some grim humour. Before the coup, somebody had scrawled on one of the many no-smoking signs in The Entity, 'I'm dying for a fag'. Within a few days of the coup, someone added, 'Too bad – Kelvin has sacked them all'.

There were still a lot of people on the hit list, especially in the technical department, but no action could be taken against them until MacKenzie and Ferrari had worked out what they did and whether they were needed in order to keep the Output hitting the screen. Kelvin treated the techies with great suspicion. To him they were the electronic equivalent of the old print unions, the 'inkies', who had stood between him and the finished product at the *Sun* and whom he had hated with a vengeance. The techies were just the same: always telling him that he couldn't do this, and he couldn't do that – or he could do it, 'but it'll cost you'. Yep. Just the same. Look at them. Sitting around all day looking at computer screens or wandering about trying to look busy. What did they all *do*? The more senior production people tried to explain, saying it was a bit like the NASA control centre. There was a satellite up in the sky and you had to have people in the control room looking at the screen to make sure it was still there. It didn't mean they weren't doing anything.

Kelvin's view was that the technical staff were disposable. They were lucky to have jobs. Technical managers told him that good Avid operators were hard to get. 'Bollocks!' MacKenzie replied. 'We put an ad in the paper and thousands applied.' That was true, the production people said. There were indeed thousands who wanted to have a go. But it was rare to find anyone who was any good at it. MacKenzie was unimpressed . . . *yaaaaahh . . . bollocks!*

MacKenzie indulged in what appeared to some managers 'experimental' or 'creative' sackings. If he could not work out what a person did, because the official job description was too complicated or technical, he might sack them just to find out what happened. He would charge into the gallery and demand: 'Who *are* you? What do you do? Tell me now . . . If you can't tell me in *twenty seconds* what you do, you're out.' The stunned production staff, including some freelance Avid operators, were often at a loss for words. *Who was this guy?* Didn't he realise they were in the middle of *live transmission*? They would attempt a faltering or cheeky reply and Kelvin would butt in, violently – 'Awright, I've heard enough. Out! *Now!*' – and point to the door. *But . . . err. . .* 'Never mind that. I said *Out!* Collect your stuff or I'm calling security. Got that? . . . Fine . . . Go *onnnn*! *OUT!*' And people were sacked – *just like that*.

If the programmes continued to go out, they remained sacked. If the person was *really* needed, MacKenzie reckoned, the production manager would come to see him on the verge of a nervous breakdown and then he would deal with the tricky problem of apologising and bring *really* vital people back on board again. His logic was impeccable – if in doubt, kick 'em out. After a while, some techies began to worry that they *hadn't* been sacked, at least temporarily, and that there must therefore be something wrong with them.

The first wave of sackings got rid of most of the 'Janet people' and Kelvin followed through by trying to remove all physical traces of the old regime. His team set about the place. The lavish supplies of booze in the greenroom 'padded cell' were replaced by his favourite tipple of Diet Coke, with only the odd can of lager on hand in case the *Loaded* team turned up again. Leasing agreements on company cars were cancelled, expense accounts and travel allowances were slashed. The vast sums spent on taxi fares during the Janet era became the moral equivalent of Imelda Marcos's shoe collection: evidence of the old regime's supposedly decadent ways. In the inner sanctum of Janet's office the huge multi-coloured designer table sculpted from molten plastic waste was discovered (there was a rumour that it had cost £8000). MacKenzie's Revolutionary Guards dragged it out of the room and dumped it unceremoniously round the back of The Entity. It was later used to park cameras.[2]

The great clear-out was assisted by the Janet people who had been sacked. They returned in cars and even hired transit vans to collect their gear and, in some cases, nick bits of designer furniture and other souvenirs. Once MacKenzie emerged from his office and spotted a couple of key members of the Janet team dragging an acid-coloured sofa across The Entity and into the lift. They had already taken a pair of giant silver-coloured wastepaper baskets. 'What the fuck do you think you're doing?'

MacKenzie thundered at them. But the sofa people held their ground. One, a remarkably strong-willed Amazon, growled at him, 'This was promised to me by Janet.' MacKenzie, nonplussed for once, backed down. He wasn't too bothered, anyway. The sofa was not grey. He wanted everything grey.

Next to go was the central Avid editing machine: the revolutionary new technology which was to have created The Look by allowing constant and rapid editing together of OB and other material to create seamless rolling output. The system had been asked to do something it was not designed for, and it had therefore never worked as Janet intended, notwithstanding the company's heroic attempts to rewrite its programming. Now MacKenzie had his people trade in the all-important central server, sending it back to the company in return for two or three more 'conventional' editing suites, better suited to making the individual scheduled programmes he wanted for his new and 'revamped' schedule. (Mike Spinks, the technical manager, later saw the server on a shelf at a trade exhibition in Amsterdam and gave the former bane of his life an affectionate pat.)

With the Avid server (and the infobar and weird graphics it was supposed to service) gone, and the whole idea of non-stop live broadcasting junked, all that remained of The Vision was the Amazing Multicoloured Entity itself. It was demolished at once. A small, cramped, cheap-looking studio was built at one end of the 24th floor, the rest of which was turned over to normal office use. The 'padded cell' was padlocked and then, eventually, designated a production area for 'top secret' special editorial projects (of which there were to be several).

The clear-out didn't stop there. Virtually everything ever transmitted by L!ve in the Janet era was wiped. An exception was a quantity of 'bloopers': various editing cock-ups (examples of presenters stuttering, on-screen swearing and other minor disasters) were copied on to tape, to be used partly for MacKenzie's own amusement and partly as potential ammunition to use against departed Tellybrats if they started slaggin' off L!ve TV. When presenter Imogen Edwards-Jones left L!ve and wrote a mildly critical article in the London *Evening Standard*, MacKenzie retaliated by broadcasting her 'bloopers' back to back. Likewise, he arranged for a (new-style) L!ve TV promo film to be made featuring footage of Janet stumbling over her words during the 'M-people' address in Edinburgh. The voice-over said, 'Don't you be like this. Get your message over clearly with L!ve TV.' Not for nothing had Kelvin always been reluctant to appear on the screen himself. 'It's a hostage to fortune,' he would intone sagely.

One day Rhodri Williams, the morning show presenter who had uttered the very first words on L!ve TV, came into work wearing his orange Patrick Cox shoes. According to legend, Janet had tried to make the wearing of orange shoes compulsory. Kelvin now banned them. Rhodri, who had quickly made the adjustment to become a key member of the new regime, was deeply grateful. Later, when the *Mirror* was puffing L!ve, the paper ran a questionnaire-based profile of him. One of the standard questions concerned the biggest fashion mistake he had ever made. Rhodri's answer was 'Buying a pair of orange shoes'. The in-joke was not explained to the *Mirror*'s readers.

PART IV

KELVIN'S L!VE TV

Chapter Twenty-four

In which Kelvin decides he does not wish to become a Television Personality even if he had the time and inclination to do so, which he does not, but nevertheless reckons he could do it if he wanted to, and in which the BBC puts out a Documentary showing him and Janet at work and Kelvin is Quite Pleased with it because it makes Janet look as though she has Gone Bonkers and also it has a Good Title and is the perfect launchpad for a Kelvin PR campaign featuring a great many Cunning Stunts

'Hello, good evening and – *bollocks*!'

Kelvin MacKenzie always maintained that the *Viz* character 'Roger Mellie, the man on the telly' was based on him. There was indeed a striking physical resemblance.[1]

Over the years various of MacKenzie's associates had tried to persuade him to become a TV presenter. Not a newsreader, like Roger Mellie, but a chat-show host, the ultimate presenter for the age of zoo television. After all, his fans reckoned he was one of the few people in the country who could make politics entertaining. He had all the right attributes, plus a thick contacts book full of people – ranging from top politicians to sportsworld big-wigs and showbiz stars like his great pals Barry Hearn and Jim Davidson – who could be leaned on to appear. He was quick-witted and a master of the instant cutting put-down. His voice was sonorous with the required estuarial twang. He was a natural. Everyone said so.

A lot of MacKenzie's cronies from his *Sun* years had made the move on to the screen, either as a career in itself or as a profitable sideline. Richard Littlejohn had become a fixture on ITV after limbering up on the Sky show Kelvin had fixed him up with on vast wages. Look at Andrew Neil. *Nice work if you could get it*. Other journalists like Roy Greenslade, MacKenzie's former number two at the *Sun*, had made the transition. Then there was the gangling, hi-pitched and speccy figure of Ray Snoddy, the *FT* media correspondent, who was briefly a MacKenzie hate-figure after fronting a TV series knocking the tabloid press.

Even Garry Bushell – *Can you believe it!* – Kelvin's side-kick from the *Sun*,[2] was fronting his own late-late show on Carlton. This was despite the fact that 'Gal' was ugly and bearded and found it difficult to speak off the cuff. 'I haven't got the right face' was how Bushell put it. 'I've got cirrhosis of the kisser. I've got a face like a map of Tenerife.'

Bushell's show was presented from the former skin-head's living-room in his ex-council house in *sahf* London, complete with its internal stone-cladding, home cocktail bar and proudly displayed print of the charge of the Scots Greys at Waterloo. One typical episode, a naked attempt to cash in on the *Loaded* wave, featured Bushell giggling about 'giving head', followed by some leering over sugges-tive chipolatas, and then some groaning while a skimpily dressed blonde stroked his beard. The blonde was asked to describe how she'd 'lost her cherry', Bushell ungallantly assuming this to be the case. He then did a spot of impromptu TV criticism over a few cheap clips. Poirot? 'I want to stick a spring up his arse!' Ulrika Jonsson's weather report about an overnight snowfall was greeted with 'I bet she had a good eight inches last night, ha, ha, ha.' Talk about 'dumbing down'. This sort of stuff appeared to be designed for people who'd have to take out a career-development loan to get a lobotomy. One critic described Bushell as making 'Forrest Gump sound like Professor Stephen Hawking'. Well, if Bushell could do it . . . ! And just look at the on-screen Talent at L!ve and all those other luvvies and bimbos at the BBC and Sky. Even Samantha Fox, Kelvin's favourite Page Three stunna, had done it for a while on Janet's old LWT *Six O'Clock Show*. Yep. *You could train a monkey to do it*. Street-Porter herself could do it. And they got paid a fortune, some of them. Being on TV? It was money for old rope.

After MacKenzie left Sky and before he washed up at the Mirror Group, he had hosted a one-off political chat show called *People, Power and Politics* on the Meridian ITV franchise. It wasn't a great success. Kelvin found it difficult to tone down his usual behaviour to match the requirements of mid-evening viewing. He spent a day or two on the venture, but then packed it in. At about the same time he had been approached by Hugh Dehn. Dehn trooped out to MacKenzie's fortress-like residence in Kent, which was surrounded by several acres of woodland to help protect his privacy, and tried to talk him into presenting a series for the BBC under the working title of *Kelvin on Britain*.

The idea was for Kelvin to make withering attacks on British social institutions – doing that sort of thing, he could afford to be much more 'himself' than was possible on a chat show. He might go to Ascot, for example, and rip the piss out of it. Then he might turn up at a Royal Garden Party and, in the nicest possible way, piss all over that as well. But Kelvin wasn't keen. The thing would take a whole year to make, and, anyway, he was busy at the time plotting his move into cable television.

There was another problem. If he moved on to the screen it would make him, for the first time, a celebrity who might be recognised by the tabloid newspaper audience. Kelvin took a pessimistic view of human nature and knew that everybody had at least a few skeletons in their closet. He was no exception. The *Mirror* had taken a few pops at him over the years – 'Is this Britain's most horrible boss?' and all that bollocks; 'Is MacKenzie "evil and demented?"' and all that stuff – but they were firing blanks so long as the readers had never heard of him and his market value to the paparazzi and intrusion specialists was zero.

There'd been the embarrassment of the *Mail on Sunday's* 1993 'GOTCHA KELVIN!' snatch picture of him with his mistress at the time of his 'temporary' resignation from the *Sun*, but that had been a comparatively harmless journalists' in-joke. If, though, he was a *bone fide* television *personality* – even a fairly minor one (never mind a *Frank Bough* or a *Michael Barrymore*) – it would be different. Once you were 'on the telly', *well* . . . Kelvin had seen it happen first hand, a thousand times. All sorts of people started crawling out of the woodwork. 'TEN TIMES A NIGHT LOVE-RAT MACKENZIE WHIPPED BY FAT HOOKERS DRESSED IN MILLWALL SHIRTS' or 'TELLYTOSSER KELVIN GLUES UP OWN BUM WITH EVOSTICK' – they might dream up *anything*! Before you knew it you were in Max Clifford's office sobbing on his shoulder, lining up with David Mellor to sign petitions in favour of privacy laws and working out the best way to make money out of limiting the damage to your smouldering career. No way! *Kelvin on Britain* was a non-starter.

However, Dehn's trip out to Fort MacKenzie had not been entirely a waste of time. It resulted in the eventual making of *Nightmare at Canary Wharf*, Hugh Dehn's 'fly on the wall' documentary about the launch of L!ve TV, shown as part of the BBC 2 business series *Trouble at the Top*.

The film was heavily promoted by the BBC. In the days before the screening, the *Mirror* camp also went into overdrive, phoning up all manner of journalists, telling them to watch it and, at the same time, putting the knife into

Janet. One journalist complained of receiving 'poisonous' phone calls from *Mirror* sources telling her that if Janet Street-Porter represented the top broadcasting talent in the country, the industry was finished: 'No wonder Murdoch is cleaning up.' Janet was attacked as 'long on office politics, short on ability and universally loathed'. She was 'a barking mad fag-hag' and it was Janet, not Kelvin, who was 'the *real* nightmare at Canary Wharf'.

The documentary showed lots of footage of Janet charging about the place, *screamin' an' shahtin'*. At one point she was seen raving at a group of techies who were trying to explain why the Avid system was not working: 'Don't fucking tell me 'ow it works – I'm *not interested*. Just *doooo* it!' In another scene, she was shown squabbling about the problems being caused by the lighting in The Entity: unable to win the argument with logic she abruptly broke off the conversation, put her head on her desk and mumbled, 'It's like a battle o'wills. The only way t'get me way is to be-yave liker child.' After this she was seen slumped against a wall waiting for the lift, apparently close to tears, and muttering, 'I'm depressed . . . I'm so fuckin' depressed.'

Rachel Purnell featured strongly, valiantly trying to make progress against the odds, cheerfully complaining about her lists of lists, trying be both assertive and efficient in her attempts to persuade the Mirror Group managers to supply equipment that worked and a few more hands on deck. Darryl Burton was seen trying to hold Janet in check and make her stick to the budget. Ruth Wrigley, who was in charge of the malfunctioning OB van operation, was seen reduced to tears. Nick Ferrari hardly appeared at all, for the simple reason that he had told the crew to 'Fuck off' and had refused to co-operate in any way.

In marked contrast to Janet, MacKenzie came over as

aloof, calm and in control. The final sequence showed him moving into Janet's office and speaking on the phone. The film ended with a freeze-frame on him squawking, 'Cut it to the bone,' to unknown persons on the other end of the line. That was fine by him – cost-cutting was precisely what he was supposed to be doing.

After the broadcast MacKenzie at first said nothing officially and the Mirror Group gave no corporate reaction. But members of Kelvin's top team arrived at work the next day with big beams on their faces, and indulged in their favourite game of imitating Janet – '*I'm deepwest, sah fahkin' deepresst*' – and saying that it was brilliant PR worth millions of pounds advertising.

Asked a few months later by a newspaper if he thought the documentary was fair and accurate, MacKenzie said he thought it was 'spot on'. He was sufficiently happy with it to allow Thirkell to continue filming, with the aim of making an updated version of the show, which included footage taken after MacKenzie had taken over. When the updated *Nightmare at Canary Wharf* was broadcast in due course, Rachel Purnell organised a special 'viewing dinner' at her house, with Janet as guest of honour. Janet, who by this time had formed the view that she had been badly stitched up by Thirkell and Dehn, was too scared to watch and hid in the kitchen. Rachel had to drag her to the TV set, saying, 'Come on Janet. Just sit down and watch it. It's not going to be *that* bad.' (Later still – in August 1997 – Kelvin also got Thirkell to edit an (official) promotional film for L!ve TV which was screened at the Edinburgh Television Festival – much to the annoyance of Janet Street-Porter.)

L!ve TV limped along after Janet's departure in September 1995 until the end of the year, when *Nightmare at Canary*

Wharf was broadcast. The channel was still reeling under the mass sacking of 'Janet people' and was working on a patched-up and largely improvised schedule. Now, on the back of the wave of publicity and interest created by Dehn's film, the channel was launched into the new year with a 'new schedule' consisting, in the main, of Cunning Stunts designed to get column inches.

This was meat and drink to Kelvin-the-showman. It was true that he did not understand the finer points of television-making, but he certainly did know how to start a fight and get everyone talking. And that was the important thing for cable television. People had to know it was there and want to take a peek at it. At this point, according to estimates published in the trade press, L!ve TV had a peak viewing figure of about 2500 people, meaning that the channel was 'buying' its viewers at a cost of about £30,000 each. At this rate it would cost £300 billion to get a decent ITV-size peak audience.[3]

MacKenzie got to work straight away, using his favourite trick of Winding Up the Royals: the ideal target, since they could not hit back. He dreamed up a stunt at the expense of Princess Diana which took the form of an advert for the channel's *Terry Tarot* show. The ad appeared in the *Mirror* and used the famous fifteen-year-old picture of Diana and Charles kissing on the Buck House balcony on their wedding day. This had been altered to replace Charles's head with Paul 'Gazza' Gascoigne's. The modified picture was run above the headline 'Who knows what the future holds?' and the ad copy told people to watch Terry Tarot exclusively on L!ve TV to find out. Buckingham Palace complained to the Advertising Standards Authority, pointing out that all requests to use pictures of the Royal Family had to be cleared by the Lord Chamberlain's office and that this had not been done in this case. The ASA upheld the complaint.

Kelvin was exultant. They had fallen for it! Not, as he was fully aware, that they had any choice. If the Palace allowed pictures to be used in advertising, a precedent would be created. They were not worried about L!ve TV, but if they had allowed the ad to go ahead there would have been nothing to stop, say, a toilet-roll manufacturer running an ad saying that its own brand was the best one to use 'on the throne' and illustrating this claim with a picture of Her Majesty sitting on the bog. With Buck House fighting a losing battle to hang on to the Monarchy's remaining shreds of dignity, this prospect had to be avoided at all costs.

Nevertheless, in the resulting massive press coverage, the Royals were derided as hopeless, out-of-touch fuddy-duddies and spoilsports over-reacting to a bit of harmless and inoffensive fun. MacKenzie issued an unabashed statement saying that L!ve TV would fly-post the advert all over London if it was banned from the papers and official poster sites. 'These days we need a Lord Chamberlain to protect us from the bloody royal family's bloody utterances,' MacKenzie thundered. 'People are writing books about who they are shagging. They're going on TV and confessing to adultery. So I can't see anything wrong with our advert and we intend to show it again.' The papers played this big as well, falling into the trap carefully laid for them. After this MacKenzie was seen motoring across the floor at L!ve, full of beans preparing stage two of the stunt. 'Right! We're in business!' he yelped with a clap of his hands. 'They don't like Gazza, so we'll be Good Boys and Girls and take his head off and put Will Carling's on – that'll be closer to the truth. Let's see what they do then!' The Carling-snogs-Diana poster duly appeared but by then the campaign had run out of steam. Kelvin dejectedly complained that the papers were not running with it. 'What the fuck's the matter with them? Carling kissing her is a much better story than Gascoigne – they should be running this one *much* bigger. What *are* they *thinking* about?'

MacKenzie followed up by granting interviews to media hacks from the posh papers, desperate for an angle on Diana in the wake of her famous interview on *Panorama*. In one interview he announced, 'The more Charles says, the less people like him. Diana's been waiting seven years to give him one in the guts. She'd obviously been working on that *Panorama* script. It was one of the great *tours de force* of modern acting, along with Robert Lindsay in *Cyrano de Bergerac*.'[4]

Kelvin moved on to his next Diana stunt, which involved getting a Diana lookalike to have a boxing match with a Queen lookalike and broadcasting it on L!ve as 'the boxing grudge match of the century'. The Di lookalike was then employed to make a 'major drama-documentary' about the princess's love affair with James Hewitt. After this the press were reliably told by Ferrari that L!ve possessed some 'dynamite exclusive footage' of Charles and Camilla and that this was going to form the core of yet another 'drama-doc'. In reality, he had about eighty seconds of entirely unexceptional camcorder material shot by a hack from the *Mirror*. (The search for Diana and Charles stunts remained a L!ve preoccupation until her death, at which point there was panic, with MacKenzie hiding in a bunker and praying that nobody would work out that Earl Spencer's 'blood on their hands' jibe was aimed mainly at him and Murdoch.)

Taking a pot shot at Diana was simple enough, because she had no way of hitting back. MacKenzie would have dearly liked to do the same to Janet, but this was fraught with all sorts of legal difficulties. Nevertheless he put a group of producers to work making a L!ve TV special called *Janet Street-Porter: The Tribute*. It was fronted by MacKenzie's avuncular old pal David 'Banksy' Banks (former editor of the *Daily Mirror* and, at the time, hosting a L!ve TV chat show staged in a Hammersmith pub). Banksy kept his face straight and delivered a moist-eyed eulogy along the lines of 'and then this *towering* talent of British television *got her teeth* into *Network-7*, probably the single most important and influential programme in recent television history'. This was intercut with crassly awful bits of *Network-7* and *Def-II*. A passage about how she 'then teamed up with Normski, perhaps the greatest young intellect of the age' was intercut with footage of Janet rambling on about 'M-people' at Edinburgh. That sort of thing.

Clips from Janet-era L!ve output were intercut with professional TV critics like Garry Bushell and Charlie Catchpole (another old mate of Kelvin's from the *Sun*) passing painstakingly 'objective' and agonised (but devastatingly negative) comment with furrowed brows: 'I can see what she is *trying* to do . . . mmmmmmm . . . but as a viewer . . . it tends to comes over as – how can I put this? – somewhat, er, *trite*? Perhaps a *little* self-indulgent . . . ' And then, more emphatically about L!ve TV: 'Well, the *infobar* was good – by far the best bit. But much of the rest was a little, er, shallow . . . boring . . . pointless . . . clichéd . . . unwatchable.' The *Tribute* was packaged with a graphic based on Janet's teeth, which snapped shut between sequences. Bushell's opinion was that 'yoof TV' was the biggest con-trick ever perpetrated in the history of the media.

Kelvin loved the show. He immediately sent a copy to the ITC in the hope that they would ban it or something, so as to get the old 'watch the film they don't want you to see' scam going. But the Mirror Group lawyers went spare, saying that Janet was bound to sue. At the very least she would have to appear on the film or be given the right of reply. There was no chance of that – the confidentiality clause in Janet's settlement with L!ve TV meant that she could not have replied even if she had wanted to. But MacKenzie had an answer even to this problem. They could send sample output from Janet's L!ve to the Royal National Institute for the Blind ('Let's face it, if all TV looked like that you'd be glad you were blind, wouldn't you? Eh?'). A blind person could review it and say it was great. L!ve would achieve the required balance and fairness. The suggestion was turned down, and in the end the film was shelved and (officially) all copies were destroyed.

Banned from screening *The Tribute*, MacKenzie still tried to humiliate Janet for the purposes of publicity, by basing her on a fictional character in *Canary Wharf*, a five-days-a-week, three-times-a-day 'soap opera' on her. In the light of the huge PR success of the *Nightmare* documentary, it was decided that L!ve was going to run a 'soap opera' about itself or, as it was explained, about a TV station in a parallel universe that *just happened* to be based on the 24th floor of Canary Wharf (not the *real* Canary Wharf, but the parallel-universe one) and so *any resemblance to real characters would be entirely coincidental*. Huge billboard adverts for *Canary Wharf* were designed showing a cameraman turning the camera on himself with the slogan 'You are never more than five minutes away from a snog'.

Having established the idea, there only remained the small detail of making the series, which was to be done as cheaply as possible. A few actors and actresses were hired to play such characters as Valentine Glass, the bisexual chief executive (thought by some to be an amalgam of various Mirror Group executives); and the Janet Street-Porteresque Andrea Cavendish, who was having an affair with Glass and with, well, virtually all the other male characters too. 'Benny', a former *Crossroads* star who had been down on his luck for a while, was brought in for a few episodes.[5]

MacKenzie told a journalist that *Canary Wharf: The Soap* cost £1000 an episode to make 'which basically undercuts what everybody else does by a multiple of ten, and sometimes a multiple of 30. Now, you might say, "Well, having seen it, I'm not surprised." But you look at it again and say to yourself, "Is this really 30 times worse than Coronation Street?" Right? Now you might say to yourself, "No, it's a hundred times worse," but you would be wrong. I promise you it isn't. It's bloody well done.'

The snogging was filmed in the most basic fashion in the L!ve TV offices, where people were trying to do real-life work, and so it looked completely unprofessional – a problem which was not helped by the fact that the actors were not wearing make-up (which the channel could not afford). If they filmed in other parts of the tower there was a danger that *Mirror* hacks would wander into shot, see what might look like attempted rape and ask what they were doing, in which case they would have to shoot it all again.

To get maximum publicity out of the show, media hacks on all the papers were sent an envelope containing a pair of knickers and invited to preview the first episode at L!ve TV HQ. There they were greeted by the producer, Bill Ridley, whirling about and shouting, 'Hello, did you get the knickers?' A story was then leaked to the papers to the effect that the BBC was 'negotiating' to buy the rights to screen *Canary Wharf* to 'fill the gap left by the collapse of *Eldorado*', a similarly ill-starred snogathon which had imploded a few years before. The 'story' was partly swallowed by the *Financial Times* before it wisely took the precaution of checking with the BBC. The BBC press office denied the rumour and asked, 'What sort of soap is it, then?'

Later in the year Kelvin and Nick set off for the Cannes Film Festival, where they tried to sell the programme to the world's TV networks and, amazingly, succeeded in doing just that. It was bought by a tiny local cable station in South Africa for a fee reckoned to be well below the average price of a bottle of designer beer at the festival bar. They bumped into Steve Timmins, the ex-Wire TV man, who took the opportunity to bend their ear about lack of progress on developing L!ve's local affiliates and other technical matters. But they were more interested in roundly denouncing him as a 'fucking poof' because he was wearing a pastel-coloured linen suit. Timmins later observed them involved in various noisy altercations with the locals. There was a queue at the airport, and Kelvin started shouting, 'The trouble with this fucking place is that there's too many fucking Frogs. I can't see what the fucking attraction is. It's too hot! Bloody foreigners! We're going back to our country. It's much better . . . I live there.'

Before long, it was decided that there was no more publicity mileage to be had from the soap, and the decision was taken to can it on grounds of cost. Soon after this Ridley, to whom Kelvin was taking a shine, came up with the idea of repeating episodes in the same slot in the same schedule but under the title *Canary Wharf 'Gold'*. Kelvin toyed with the title, saying with typical self-deprecation that it was a cheek to call anything as bad as *Canary Wharf* 'Gold'. At one point he considered *Canary Wharf 'Bronze'* in tribute to its unabashed third-rate status.

The last episode finished abruptly by cutting to an exter-

Live TV

nal shot of the Canary Wharf tower with the screen going all wobbly and then turning itself inside-out to the sound of Dr Who's Tardis. It was explained that both Canary Wharf (the place) and *Canary Wharf* (the soap opera) had been sucked into a time-warp, returning to the start of the first episode so that it could, in theory, be run as an endless loop for all eternity.

Chapter Twenty-five

*In which Kelvin tells of his Adventures in the Land of
Media Monsters, demands yet more Cunning Stunts and
Gets Them, tries to Save the Channel with the help of some
Goldfish and* The Clangers *and unleashes the full force
of Uncle Bill Ridley on an Unsuspecting Public, making
him Head of Weird*

'For fuck's sake, Nick, that's fucking shit. Don't even fucking bother speaking, mate.'

Feet now well and truly under the table, Kelvin is hosting his regular 8 a.m. editorial conference at L!ve TV. Half
a dozen of the top people in the new regime are brain-
storming, trying to think of material to fill the yawning
hours of airtime.

Nick Ferrari soldiers on. 'OK. All right. I get the feeling that you don't like that one – am I right? OK, well what
about this, then? What if we get some old footage, right?
and do a sort of—'

'Look, Nick, mate,' interrupts Kelvin, 'that's *so* shit I can't
believe it. Just go to sleep, will you? Go on, just *nod off.*'

There are titters and sniggers round the table. Kelvin's
givin' Nick a *hard time.* But he's being funny with it.

Taking the daily editorial conference had been a central
ritual in MacKenzie's life for some fifteen years, ever since
he became the editor of the *Sun* in 1981. He was an early
riser, and a creature of habit. He listened to *Today* on Radio
Four as he heaved his increasingly corpulent form out of
bed. Then he would flick through the day's papers to make
sure he was fully briefed and to see if there was anything

worth nickin' to put in the *Sun*.

Then came the early-morning walk with his dog, Chubbs. 'Stop that right now!' Kelvin would bark down the mobile to the newsdesk. 'Eh? What do you mean Kelvin,' they would reply. 'No, not you, silly fucker, the *dog*. Come 'ere, Chubbs!' The people at the *Sun* had come to curse the invention of the mobile phone. It meant that the only time in a 24-hour cycle when Kelvin was out of contact was when he was going through the Blackwall Tunnel on his chauffeur-driven journey up from Kent.

Once he reached the office, he used to bowl into his office, summon all his senior people and demand, 'Right, whadda you lot got for me today, then?' The tone in which this catchphrase was delivered had been important. If the paper was in the middle of a good, opposition-crunching run the question was upbeat, energetic, optimistic and rounded off with a sharp clap of the hands. Sometimes, though, it dripped with sarcasm. Then woe betide any journalist who had not been up as early as him or was not a fund of useful ideas, preferably ones that tickled Kelvin's funny bone.

If things were going well the conferences had often been hilarious.[1] If it was suggested that the *Sun* should do something about John Major, for example, Kelvin would expertly mimic the Major's voice and expect all the other hacks to carry on the conversation in character. If things weren't *too* busy, the mention of a celebrity name had sometimes led to Kelvin telling a rambling and usually filthy anecdote which had everyone in stitches. Or he might turn on one of the assembled hacks and enumerate their shortcoming in a humiliating but entertaining way. Any mention of Murdoch led to extended mimicry, with Kelvin even getting out of his chair to imitate the Boss's gait and gestures as well as his voice. When he did that, things had sometimes got really silly.

MacKenzie was determined to run L!ve TV in the same sort of way. Morning conference at 8 a.m. *sharp*. Crisp white shirts and ties. Of course it was nowhere near as good as at the *Sun*. L!ve was not in a position to react quickly to fast-breaking news (though MacKenzie was able to satisfy his craving for this activity by endlessly interfering in the editing of the *Mirror*). But the slower pace meant that there was more time for thinking up outrageous stunts and, generally, taking the mickey and having a laugh.

If he was in the mood he would regale the L!ve team with long yarns concerning the Amazing Adventures of Kelvin MacKenzie in the land of the Media Monsters during his heyday at the *Sun*. Especially his dealings with Rupert Murdoch. 'Bollockings? *I'll* tell you about bollockings. Murdoch was the *Grand Fuckin' Master* of bollockings,' he once informed his captive audience. 'I remember Rupert once gave me *The – Most – Fantastic – Bollocking – Ever.*' Tears of appreciation welled up in his narrowed eyes – like a connoisseur remembering the taste of a particularly fine brandy. '*Ahhhhh*, it was a bollocking on every conceivable level. *Ooooooohh*, it was foul-mouthed, it was abusive, it was *witty*, it was intelligent, it was *demeaning*. Yep' – shakes head in awe-struck admiration – 'it was the bollocking of a lifetime.'

He often brought Ferrari into these reminiscences ('Ain't that right, Nick, eh?'). 'L!ve TV's very own Mr Blobby', as Kelvin called him, always accepted the invitation with enthusiasm, usually taking the opportunity to brag about the lavish lifestyle he had enjoyed as a *Sun* showbiz reporter, and telling War Stories about his globe-trotting at the expense of News International, in pursuit of the likes of the Norwegian supergroup A-Ha. 'Ain't that right,

Kelvin? Great days, eh?' MacKenzie sighed. 'Yeah, Nick. Great days indeed.'

Others listened to this old pals' act with a mixture of wonder and alarm. It was interesting stuff, and very entertaining. But they had 24 hours of television to make with half a dozen cameras, a wonky studio and a bunch of semi-trained kids. *For fuck's sake put a sock in it and let's get on with making a bit of telly!* But – oh *no*! – they're off again: ''Ere, Nick, were you there that time Norman Tebbit came round to Wapping and old Monty said to 'im . . .'

Kelvin was a hard man to please. He was always very definite about what he did not want, but was vaguer about what he did want. A starting-point for brainstorming was other TV shows or even catchphrases which could be adapted with the help of the tabloid headline standby of sick or cringe-inducing puns. Kelvin himself was a master of the pun, creator of the headline 'TAMILA MOWDOWN', run over a story about a massacre carried out by the Tamil Tigers during the Sri Lankan civil war.

Compared to that, puns on TV programme titles were easy. Kelvin would set the others off and then they all joined in, with increasing hilarity. *One Man and His Dog*? What about a sort of profile thing where we do interviews wiv 'em sittin' on the toilet: *One Man and his Bog*! *That's Life*, hmmmm, let's see now . . . *That's Wife*? . . . er . . . *That's My Wife*? . . . er, no. How about *Twat's Wife*?' 'No.' 'You mean *This is Your Life*, do you, but done as *This is Your Wife* . . . naaaahhh,' 'I know, I know: *Call My Muff*! We get people to phone up their girlfriends or something – *fantastic*.' 'No, no, no, we get Page Three girls, right, in the studio and people can phone 'em up. *Call My Muff*! It's a runner, it's got *legs*. I'll get the press release out today – that should wind up the IT-fucking-C. Maybe they'll *ban* it – *fantastic*!' (Many were impressed by Kelvin's ability to outfox various media regulatory and self-regulatory bodies and, from time to time, turn them into virtual extensions of his publicity machine. At the same time when there was no publicity value in breaching ITC regulations he and Ferrari insisted they were strictly implemented, thus giving themselves yet another opportunity to bollock people.) In the end a version of *Call My Muff* was toned down to *Babe in a Basque* and went out during the late-night 'Erotic Exotic' slot.

Sometimes Kelvin took people to wine bars so that they could all get tipsy and the creative juices would really start flowing. There was one session in a West End wine bar when he came up with the idea of doing an 'adult' X-rated remake of one of his all-time favourite TV programmes, *The Clangers*. 'Whaddiwannaknow,' he kept repeating through the increasingly boozey evening, 'whaddiwannaknow [BURP!] 'scuse me – an' nobody's told me yet, right? – whaddiwannaknow *izzzzz thizzzz*, right? What [pause] noise [pause] would the fuckin' Clangers make if they wuz shaggin' each uvvver?' Collapse of all stout parties. 'Eeeehhh heeeeee arrrrfffff haaawww heeee. '*Ere*, Nick, aarrrrfff heeee heeee, Nick! Hey, *Nick*! *Go on*, make the noise the Clangers would make if they were *doin' it*! Aaaarrrrrhhh haaaarrrr, heeeee.' Ferrari composed himself and started making quiet, long *whoooowwwppp whooooowwwppp* noises, which went up in pitch and got shorter and louder until they reached a climax. '*Arrrrrhhhhh arrrrfffff haaaawwww haaaaarrrrrrr! Fuckin' brilliant! Arrrhh hhhhaaaaa. It's a runner . . . haaawwww!*'

And so it went on late into the evening, with all present having to make Clangers-on-heat noises and propose assorted filthy scenarios. The most amazing aspect of this episode, it was later thought, was not the fact that it had happened but the fact that it was a serious proposition.

Live TV

The next day one of the station's lawyers was instructed to phone Oliver Postgate, the creator of *The Clangers* (U-rated version) to find out *in all seriousness* if he would sell the rights to the show to L!ve TV. When it was gingerly explained what Kelvin was up to, Postgate gave them an 'until hell freezes over' answer and another great editorial idea bit the dust: *You wait. Somebody'll do it some day and make a million bucks – you'll see.* Thereafter, whenever sex came up on the agenda, especially if there was mention of a woman member of staff who was thought to be having an affair with a L!ve TV executive (now all male, of course), a round of excited Clanger *whhhoooowwwps* would break out.

When Kelvin was in the mood, any idea, no matter how daft, was given consideration. Once a newsdesk hand suggested turning the cameras on to the fish tank in reception, on the grounds that this was considerably more interesting than a lot of the stuff they were doing. Kelvin was intrigued. The idea was exactly what he was after. It would undoubtably be cheap and, better still, it was a potentially good Cunning Stunt. The media hacks on the posh papers were bound to give it a line or two. It would keep L!ve TV in the public eye, and bolster the channel's all-important 'recognition rating'.

The team was instructed to kick the fish tank idea around for a while. 'I know, we could have speech bubbles coming out of the fishes' mouths . . . Yeah, with headlines in the bubbles . . . *Yeah!* . . . What would you call it, though? . . . I know, what about "Fishy Business?" . . . *Naaah* . . . Hmmmmm, 'ow about "Fins Ain't Wot They Used to Be?" . . . Hmmmm, that's a *bit* better . . . I know, I know, what about "Hollywood Bowl"? . . . *Eh?* What? . . . You know, "Hollywood Bowl" and we could just use celebrity news . . . *Yeah*, yeah, and at the end you could have "Fin" like they have on them nude art films they have on Channel Four.' Kelvin's eyebrows went up – always a good sign! He assumed a demonic grin and tipped back in his chair, hands linked round the back of his head. There was a short pause as his eyes flicked back and forth. He lunged forward, smashing his fist on the table top: 'You're a fucking *genius*! You've *saved the station*!' – the table gets another energetic thump – 'It's brilliant, quite *brilliant*! "Hollywood Bowl!" *It's a runner*! Have you got any more like that?'

The fish feature made it to the screen, but, as was often the way at L!ve TV, the more ambitious aspect, which in this case was the animated bubbles, did not work out. Instead, the fish were shown without comment until one died live on air and it was realised that the stunt was not so cheap after all. You needed somebody to feed the slippery fuckers and generally look after them. Kelvin appointed a senior journalist, whom he considered a bit too pleased with himself, the official fish-tank cleaner: 'Right, your job is now to clean the fish tank. Got it? I want it nice and clean every day, OK?' Anything to cut people down to size. But Kelvin quickly grew bored with the idea. The media hacks had not risen to the bait this time. He'd spent all that money on fishfood and there wasn't a line of free advertising to show for it. The feature was axed as an economy measure: "*Ere! Which stupid fucker thought up that fishtank bollocks?*'

Other stunt-programme ideas included 'Blow Job of the Day', a cunning plan to throw a 'BLOW JOB OF THE DAY' caption up on the screen, fade to black and then show a man sweating and breathing heavily, before pulling back to reveal that he had been blowing a trumpet. That one didn't make it to the screen.

In spring 1996, when L!ve was getting into the stride of its 'all-new schedule', Bill Ridley, the maker of the

Live TV

Canary Wharf soap opera, was very much 'flavour of the month'. Ridley, who was British, was now getting on a bit but had started off in Fleet Street and was a tabloid man down to his boots. Kelvin and others described him as 'an inspired ideas man' specialising in 'wacky' features, 'zany' stunts and 'off-beat' competitions as well as very, very violent and bloodthirsty programming. Janet's former office was divided in two with a shoddy piece of wood. Ridley squatted in one half, and Kelvin in the other.

Ferrari called Ridley 'the Human Pipecleaner' because he was incredibly spindly and thin and tall and was always dressed in ill-fitting and crumpled but matching shades of grey. He was always incredibly nervous and jumpy and was never known to sit down. He used to stand up at the back of editorial conferences and ideas meetings, leaning against the wall and fidgeting. He had irritating nervous tics and habits, including 'imaginary smoking' which involved taking long, noisy drags on a non-existent ciga-rette and then making ash-flicking movements with his fingers. He also liked to roll pieces of paper into tight balls, throw them in the air and volley them across the room as an aid to concentration. Ridley also ate standing up, briskly shovelling food into his mouth in such quantities that his beanpole appearance was inexplicable. There was also a rumour that he had not slept for more than a decade and that, at night, he merely dozed standing up, like an upside-down bat.

'Uncle Bill', as the oddball Ridley was commonly called by more junior L!ve TV people, had his own nickname for Ferrari: 'the Fat Boy'. Like Ferrari, Ridley had done a stint at Fox working on *A Current Affair*, the grimly fascinating and profoundly unwholesome 'reality television' show with its diet of reconstructed murders, lovingly filmed slo-mo carnage and in-depth interviews with the terminally berserk. Ridley had been a great success on the show for a good while but had, according to news-room legend, eventually 'fucked up' by missing an aspect of the Oklahoma City bombing and so had joined Nick, Kelvin and many others, including Monty himself, in the ranks of 'Murdoch rejects' now congregating at the *Mirror*. Ridley's official job was 'head of development' but MacKenzie called him 'Head of Weird'. He was required to work alongside Ferrari, who stayed on as head of programmes.

The Head of Weird got down to work overhauling the schedule which, when he arrived, was a mixture of wreckage left over from the Janet era supplemented by desperate programme ideas, mainly dreamt up by Nick, such as *Stand Up L!ve*. This was described as a 'comedy showcase' and featured people with stage names such as 'The Mindless Drug Hoover'. Viewers were encouraged to join in by the presenter, who said things like 'If you want to be a stand-up comic, call us. If you think you're better than us, call us, and we'll kick the shit out of you.' The assistant producer on the show was a good-lookin' but inexperienced young woman, the first of many such people hired by Nick now he had a free hand, who had a habit of rewriting the scripts, many thought, so as to take all the humour out of the jokes.[2]

The main Janet remnant in the pre-Ridley schedule was the teenage pop show called *Buzzin'*, still presented by Bouncin' Bhavesh Hindocha: *'Buzzin'* ... *buzzin'* ... *maximum chaos in the house!'* *Buzzin'* had been left alone because Ferrari and, especially, MacKenzie did not understand the 'alternative' pop and youth scene and were not that interested in it. They nevertheless hated the show, first because it was broadcast in an experimental way involving strangely flickering freeze-frames and massively boosted-up colour which looked really cool in the studio but, once the signal had been compressed, sent down the cable and otherwise degraded, looked a right mess. '*Buzzin'!*' Kelvin would sneer. 'It's invisible television for the blind – the only TV programme in the whole world which you can't see when you look at the screen.' But mostly the programme was disliked because it did not show enough mainstream white 'boy bands' of the Take That ilk.[3] Bhavesh was required to have a quota of white faces on his show on the grounds of reflecting the teenage craze for (white) 'boy bands'.[4]

In the end Bhavesh was summarily sacked for an offence related to not wearing a poppy on screen in the run-up to Remembrance Sunday. *Buzzin'* was axed, thus ending the very last on-screen link with the Janet era.

With the immediate clear-out of the schedule completed, Ridley moved on to masterminding larger projects such as documentaries and series which, Kelvin fondly imagined, L!ve would sell on the open market, making him a player in the glamorous world of programme sales and exports. Ridley really got things moving with a project which was firmly in the Fox 'reality vision' mould: a 'major documentary' about the life and times of one Fred West, deceased, of Cromwell Road, Gloucester. The documentary, which was to be called *Natural Born Killers*, dealt with the trial of Fred and Rosemary West. Nick Ferrari as director of programmes and Ridley as Head of Weird had invested a lot of money (by L!ve's standards) in the project and were eager to see the results.

For once money was no problem. £10,000 had been allocated to make the programme, and permission was given to use experienced film crews, proper locations and professional actors. And £800 had been put into making an accurate and realistic-looking scale model of the West residence. This was the centrepiece of the ninety-minute show. A miniature camera floated round the rooms in slow-motion, dream-sequence style. The soundtrack featured a creepily distorted and wonky child's music box playing 'Twinkle, twinkle, little star', while a breathless voice-over described the horrors that had taken place in each part of the house: the room used as a knocking-shop by Rose West . . . the kids' playroom . . . Fred's home cocktail bar in the living-room . . . and, then – with 'Twinkle, twinkle' boosted up to maximum echo-chamber effect – down to the cellar where the rotting corpses were buried.

Every cliché of the semi-professional DIY horror video was used. The hatch on the scale model was unlocked, to the sound of horror-film creaking dubbed on to the soundtrack, and fell open with an over-loud thud. The mini-camera continued its guided tour, showing the position of all the corpses, each marked with the letter 'X'.

That was the mild part of the show. The soothing slo-mo tour was punctuated with sequences in which lookalikes acted out the crimes, with only grunts and yelps on the soundtrack. A voice-over hyped up the story to suggest that there had probably been sixty murders in total, with many victims still missing, lying in undiscovered graves. A bit of bogus psychobabble was dreamed up to run the thesis that the Wests had been involved in 'a love affair with death'. They were fated to find true love and each other only by inflicting pain and death on others, and there might be other such couples, well . . . picking up *your* daughter *right now*. This angle, which was basically bollocks, enabled L!ve to use the title *Natural Born Killers* for the film, which was important for the American market.

When the first rough version was made Ridley and Nick sat in a viewing-room and watched with rapt attention, while the production team awaited their reaction. At first the two bosses were silent, and Ridley even managed to sit still for a moment or two. Then they started making encouraging and delighted little comments: *'Fan-Tastic!* . . . This is it! . . . Here we go!' A reconstruction scene showing Fred and Rose lookalikes cruising around in a car, stopping to pick up a young woman, incarcerating her in the back seat and slapping her round the face, came on the screen. Nick and Ridley chuckled: 'Grrrreat! You don't get that on fucking *Crime Watch,* do you? Hee, hee, hee.'

There was another reconstruction showing a lot of gaffer tape being brutally applied to the mouth of a struggling young woman. (*'It's strong, isn't it?* . . . *Very strong.'*) She looked terrified, and her panic mounted as she listened to the sound of Fred West viciously beating somebody, complete with screams of pain and fear, off screen. *'Ooooohh, the Yanks will love this* . . . *Nobody else has got the balls to do this sort of stuff, have they?'*

The final credits ran and the production team was warmly congratulated. Nick and Ridley had specified a *Current Affair*-style reconstruction of the West case, dramatising all the evidence with actors, murder by murder and rape by rape, via prostitution, torture, kidnap and abduction. They had got what they wanted. The show was sordid beyond belief, of course, but once they had it in the can it would be valuable property which could be sold as average-to-good (only sixty or so murders, including possible undiscovered graves) to the flickering butcher's shop window that is American 'tabloid TV'. If the Yanks bought it, perhaps hundreds of networks around the world would follow suit. There was much talk of all the money they were all going to make. The producers were told to make a few minor and mainly technical changes before they showed it to Kelvin ('the Almighty One', as Ridley called him) for final approval.

But when Kelvin saw this first cut of *Natural Born Killers* he went bananas: 'What the *fuck* are you *playing* at? We can't run *this* – it's *hardcore porn*!' The team tried to talk him round, saying that they had included some over-the-top material to see how far he wanted to go. They could cut out the worst (*best!*) bits if he wanted. That was no problem. Maybe different versions could be produced. One to show on L!ve TV in the UK and the full-strength (*proper!*) version for the States. Kelvin was mollified. 'OK. But *use your fucking brains*! We'll end up in fucking *prison* if we show this sort of stuff.'

Natural Born Killers was duly toned down. One or two short scenes, including the most sickening (*tastiest!*) sequences suggesting sexual violence against under-age girls were cut and others re-edited. Kelvin looked at the amended version and pronounced himself satisfied.

But, after backing the project, a few days later Kelvin suffered a loss of nerve. At first the PR Outrage Machine had been cranked up to publicise the show, which was to be billed as 'L!ve TV's first major documentary'. As part of the PR strategy, *Natural Born Killers* was scheduled to be shown at 10 p.m. (which was certain to create a publicity-rich bust-up with the ITC: 10 p.m. was the earliest possible time available, if they were to stay even remotely on the same planet as the ITC regulations). There were to have been frequent repeats to milk the 'see the film they tried to ban' angle all week as the manufactured scandal hit the front pages, gettin' everyone talkin' about L!ve TV. Instead Kelvin ordered that the film be 'buried'. There would be no publicity and it would be shown after midnight with no repeats. The papers failed to pick up on it all and the £10,000 investment in producing the show was more or less written off.

After this, one of the producers bumped into Kelvin near the lifts and asked him what he thought of the finished, broadcast version. Kelvin feigned indifference: 'Ooohh, y'know . . . it was all right, I suppose . . . so, so . . . average stuff.' The producer, risking a major bollocking and, possibly, an on the spot sacking decided . . . *fuck it* . . . this was such a stupid thing to say that he would contradict the boss: '"*Average*"? Whaddayamean? You can't call a documentary showing Fred West shagging under-age girls "*average*"! You can call it *shit*, you can say it's a bad piece of journalism, but there's no way a thing like *that* is "*so, so*".'

Kelvin was unfazed. He gave a smug and patronising smile: 'I'll tell you what you do, right? What you do is that the next time you make one of these things use your head and come and see me first, OK.' The lift arrived and Kelvin got in. 'See me first, OK, then I'll show you how to do it properly.' He winked. 'OK?' The lift doors closed and he was gone.

Chapter Twenty-six

*In which Kelvin makes an Important Speech about the
future of Television News, denouncing prevailing News
Values as Perverse and A Million Miles Away from the
Concerns of Ordinary Folks, and regrets the Constraints
placed upon him by the regulators and arbiters of Taste,
Decency and Balance, but ploughs ahead anyway with a
Plan to hire the country's first Stuttering Newsreaders as
Nick sorts out the newsdesk*

MacKenzie had always hated speaking to large numbers
of people in public. Some said this was because it could
bring on a funny turn, related to his health worries. Others
said it was because gatherings like business conferences
bored him to tears. Whatever the reason, he much
preferred the intimate surrounding of the editorial conference room or dinner table when holding forth.

But in February 1996, riding on the wave of national
publicity generated by *Nightmare at Canary Wharf*, he
agreed to address a *Financial Times* conference, which was
entitled 'New Media and Broadcasting', on the subject of
news. The conference took place in a posh hotel in Park
Lane, and was attended by 150 movers and shakers in the
world of multi-channel television. Kelvin had promised
the organisers that he would play it absolutely straight.

He turned up at the conference looking serene and exud-
ing his version of gravitas, which normally involved standing around, sticking one hand in his trouser pocket and
playing with his keys while gently kicking imaginary tin
cans and dum-di-dum-dah-di-do'ing a disjointed monot-
one medley of Frank Sinatra's greatest hits. In due course,

he took to the podium, eyed nervously by the organisers. 'Good morning, ladies and gentlemen. Today I want to speak about . . . ' *No opening put-down. Excellent. What a relief!*

Kelvin droned on in a calm, reasonable and mildly self-serving way about how the multi-channel future would lead to dozens of news or news-related channels to which the existing ITC regulatory framework was not suited. He attacked the 'regimentation' of existing news shows saying that, at the moment, the viewers were being offered 'a long and boring show on Channel Four at seven o'clock; then a pretty dull half-hour on BBC 1 at nine o'clock; there's yet more on ITV at 10 o'clock. Why are they so afraid of letting the public have something different to choose?' *No swearing so far. It's going to be OK!*

He then criticised the ITC for demanding, when it advertised the Channel 5 tender, that the new channel should provide 'high-quality news'. This, he thought, meant 'more of the same' establishment news, 'light years away from the interests of the Great Swathes' of the general public. But the mention of Channel 5, lately the cause of much grief to Kelvin, seemed to make something snap in his mind. He looked up from his prepared speech, leant forward and started talking about David Elstein, the erudite head of the new channel, who until recently had worked at Sky TV.

'David Elstein, eh? Lemmmee tell you a little story about David Elstein.' *Oh-oh! He's starting going off the rails!* 'David Elstein, Daaaaavid Elstein, right? is soooo *big-headed*, OK, that one day he was in the lift at Sky TV alone with this Rather Attractive Young Lady, and this very attractive young lady says to him, "Can I give you a blow job, Mr Elstein?"' There is a ripple of embarrassed sniggering from the assembled suits. 'So, right, OK, so Elstein says, OK,

"Fine . . . *but what's in it for me*?"' Red-faced guffaws all round. The organiser glared at him full-blast, desperate to make sure that the speech did not degenerate into a full-blown shaggy-dog session. MacKenzie seemed to get the message. He waited for the laughter to subside, gave a little cough and returned to best behaviour.

'Anyway . . . as I was saying, ah yes . . . ' and he resumed reading his downbeat speech, attacking the ITC requirements for political balance in news output: 'Your neutrality is my bias . . . in the long term, impartial news is no more real than impartial drama.' An edited version of the speech was printed in the broadsheet papers the next day, shorn of the Elstein joke.

MacKenzie's first love was news. Although he reckoned the Great Swathes were not very interested in the formal news agenda and completely bored by all foreign stories, he read all manner of newspapers and magazines himself and listened to heavyweight stuff on the radio and was personally very well briefed on all these matters. The skill he prided himself on, and valued in all other journalists, was the ability to turn dull material like politics into rude, preferably sexy, personality-based entertainment.

He had always made sure that the formal news was there *somewhere* in the *Sun*, even if it had to be buried on page two, the 'graveyard page' which, according to newspaper lore, nobody ever looked at. Still it *all had to be there*. 'The readers aren't stupid,' he had warned. If the news was thrown out entirely, they would regard the paper as a comic: you entered *Sunday Sport* territory. 'Joke' newspapers might sell well for a while, but in the long term readers wanted to think they were buying a 'proper' newspaper. 'There's gotta be some beef in the sandwich' was one of his favourite slogans.

The same was true in television news, he thought. But

there were all sorts of problems, starting with the requirement to avoid political bias. It was all very different from
the newspaper scene, where the entertainment factor was
achieved in political reporting mainly by indulging hilar-
iously extreme and even spiteful partisanship which
allowed you to handle the party political game in a way
similar to supporting one football team against another.
You had the *Mirror*, which was for Labour supporters and
socialists (*God help them!*), and the *Sun*, which was for
Maggie's supporters and normal people. The Great
Swathes could choose between the two. But with the telly
they couldn't. All telly news had to be 'balanced', which
meant in practice it had to be bleedin'-heart foreigner-
loving unpatriotic elitist left-wing liberal piffle which cost
a fortune to make and nobody wanted to watch.

What that left you with was rubbish like the BBC *Nine
O'Clock News*. 'Every night you're listening to gobblede-
gook about fascists killing each other in Bosnia,' he told
a journalist. 'But you can be sure the most interesting thing
in Britain that day will not be on! Will Carling's divorce
will be the last item! It's *perverse*!' Kelvin reckoned if he
was in charge of the BBC he could get the *Nine O'Clock
News*'s rating up from 6 million to 10 million 'easy – and
without needing a Streaker of the Night'.

In the meantime he was stuck with the news effort at
L!ve TV, which was not going well. The balance requirement effectively ruled out Kelvin's normal style of political reporting, and thus a huge chunk of the daily news
agenda. If you couldn't show a graphic of John Major's
head as a vegetable and call him a plonker, what was the
point of talking about him at all? Foreign coverage was
obviously out on financial grounds. Even the posh papers
had slashed their once-mighty foreign desks as an economy measure and were often reduced to chopping and

repackaging wire copy, supplemented by the odd on-the-spot report from a superstar reporter. Foreign material was virtually banned from L!ve's news bulletins: 'Bosnia it ain't.'

Sport was out as well, because L!ve could not usually afford to buy pictures of anything other than ice-skating and off-cuts of rugby league. There was no football, cricket or boxing (the only things that mattered in tabloid sports reporting) because Chisholm owned it all. Sky had even bought up *fishing*! The problem was addressed partly by stealing as much footage from Sky Sport as possible and pushing the rules on 'fair dealing' (whereby channels are able to show tiny snatches of each other's exclusive material for purposes of comment) to the absolute limits. Apart from that, L!ve sport consisted of more Cunning Stunts such as running trailers for a 'game show' called *A Game of Two Halves* consisting of a snatch of Premier League footage which, at a quick glance, made it look as if there was some football on the channel (*coming up later . . .*) and various 'spoiler' stunts designed to latch on to publicity for whatever genuine sports sensation Sky was showing.

When Sky launched pay-per-view by charging £14.95 to watch the Frank Bruno vs. Mike Tyson boxing-match, Ridley cashed in by holding a press conference in the Sports Café in the West End and announcing that L!ve had hired two boxers who would re-enact the fight blow by blow. The channel would broadcast an 'exact simulation' with full commentary from a ring in its studio 'and it won't cost the viewing fight-fans a single penny'. The press release claimed that 'with the addition of sound effects and additional expert commentary . . . you could almost be in Las Vegas'.

The stunt went ahead. Erecting the ring was a problem. At one point one of the posts fell over and cracked one of the floor-to-ceiling plate-glass windows. Other difficulties such as obtaining permission from the Boxing Board of Control were bypassed in the normal piratical fashion. The L!ve version of the bout was, of course, a farce. But no matter. It had worked as a PR stunt and that was all that counted.

For good measure MacKenzie ordered that highlights of the real fight should be nicked from Sky and broadcast the next day. Even Ridley, hardly the most cautious of programme-makers, thought that this was outrageously risky. Sky was certain to sue. But he was overruled. 'If Chisholm wants a fight, he can have one,' MacKenzie said, trembling with jealous rage. In the event nothing happened and it was assumed that Sky simply couldn't be bothered to deal with such a minor irritation. As with a lot of MacKenzie's 'triumphs' at L!ve TV, everything depended on the basic fact that virtually nobody was watching the channel.

With no political reporting, no sport and no showbiz reporting, the last resort was the Royals. You could do stunts like the Diana—Gazza poster. But proper Royals intrusion was difficult, what with the rigmarole of sending a camera crew and OB van. The paparazzi who, when required, could hide in the bushes and get to work with the old 'grief-detector' telephoto lens would beat you to the story every time. Even then, if you were doing the Royals you needed reporters with specialist contacts, and such people were at a premium. The L!ve TV newsdesk had tried to get the *Mirror*'s Royals reporter, James Whitaker, to help out, but he turned them down flat, explaining that they couldn't afford his services: 'Richard and Judy pay me £500 and send a helicopter . . . You rotters don't pay!'

In desperation, L!ve resorted to reading out the *Daily*

Mirror on screen, but that meant getting whacked by the ITC under the cross-promotion rules. If you read out the *Sun* they might do you for copyright (if they could be bothered), and you wouldn't want to read out any of the others. The *Star* had no words in it. Reading that out would fill precisely six minutes and forty-one seconds (it was timed on the L!ve newsdesk) if you left out the stuff that was obviously and blatantly untrue. Reading out the *Guardian*, granted, would take all day, but it also would put all the viewers to sleep.

No, all you had, really, was raw wire copy which could be rewritten by someone with a smidgen of experience in a real newsroom and then be read out by tarty women (if you could find ones who could read a script and wear a push-up bra at the same time – *multi-skilling!* – which was not always the case at L!ve TV). The girly show would be supplemented by stunts, making the most of the useless OB equipment left over from the Janet era, supported by the old *Sun* stand-by of 'themed weeks' turning the news into an extended joke. These were to include 'custard pie week', when newsreaders got slapped in the face, splosher-style, at the end of each bulletin, and 'animal week', when they had to cuddle cute kittens, puppies and, memorably, a lion cub which, inevitably, pissed all over the newsreader while she was intoning the headlines.

During the Euro '96 football tournament the newsreaders had to paint their faces with the England flag like 9-year-olds. After Princess Diana's famous visit to a hospital operating-theatre, a woman presenter appeared in a white surgeon's gown, cap and face mask and sporting long false eyelashes matted with mascara. An off-screen assistant wiped sweat from her brow as she read the news. She punctuated each item by fluttering her eyelashes and saying, 'Tweezers . . . scalpel . . . swab . . . ' There were endless variations on 'glamour week' with the newsreaders wearing ball gowns, opera gloves and suchlike.

MacKenzie's own favourite newsreader stunt was a sadistic plan to hire people with a serious stammer to read the news. Most people at the channel got to know about the idea when, one fine day, they found him sprawled helpless over a desk in the newsroom in floods of tears, creased double with mirth. Representatives of the official British Stammering Association were sitting in his office. He had managed to keep a straight face for about ten minutes, solemnly giving them the dreamed-up pitch that L!ve TV wanted to combat prejudice by showing the world that, just because a person had a major speech impediment, it did not mean they were stupid or incapable of professional work. If stammerers could read the news on *national television*, well . . .

The association's representatives had, of course, enthusiastically agreed. MacKenzie was ready for that. He could handle it, he reckoned, with a few firm bites on the tongue. What sent him over the edge was discussion of the possible appointment of the country's first stammering air . . . air . . . air . . . (*hairdresser*?) . . . air . . . *air-traffic controller*. As the implications of this sank in, MacKenzie started to lose it. He excused himself. The minute he was out of the door he was silently convulsed. It took him a good few minutes to pull himself back together, dry his eyes and earnestly re-enter the room to complete negotiations.

A po-faced press statement was drawn up jointly by L!ve TV and the Stammering Association, in which MacKenzie was quoted as saying that the innovation would move L!ve TV's bulletins away from the 'dull and regimented' format used by all the other channels. He was enthusiastic but the final go-ahead, *of course*, could not be given until screen tests had taken place. Frances Sparkes, manager of the

Michael Palin Centre for Stammering (the father of the former *Monty Python* man had a severe stammer), said he was 'excited' by the plan, adding: 'I hope it's not a stunt. If it was, it would be a retrograde step, bringing back all the old stereotypes.' The stunt, after gaining the required column inches, was quietly dropped.

But whoever was reading out the news, there was the constant problem of gathering the information in the first place. MacKenzie ordered Nick Ferrari to hire 'proper journalists', which proved difficult, though he did turn up one or two talented and capable people from the lower rungs of the profession, tempting them with over-the-odds salaries for their equivalent status elsewhere and the promise of working with The Great Kelvin MacKenzie (an invitation which attracted a mixed response). In addition, some experienced people were brought in on freelance shifts from places like Sky or commercial radio newsrooms.

Mostly these people worked overnight preparing scripts for the morning breakfast show (which had been relaunched as a 'normal' make-over and health tips plus light news-based morning magazine show). It all struck them as fairly normal, a bit like working on news bulletins for Capital Radio or something, except that they might suddenly be confronted by a gang of topless models busy recording something for Bill Ridley.

The work-rate was ferocious, with news producers typically up all night using the L!ve editing suites to produce dozens of short news packages to be inserted into the bimbo-fronted news bulletins throughout the following day. After the chaos of Janet-era 'people news', they found they were able to improve things quickly by packaging easy-to-do tabloid gobbets (a true-ish piece about a man who had allegedly taken up a Pizza restaurant's 'eat as much as you like for £5' offer by stuffing himself with seventeen Deep Pan jobs and ending up in hospital, was fondly remembered). This sort of stuff would have taken the average Planet Janet airhead a week to do. A trained journalist could slap the footage together in ten minutes.

Kelvin turned up at the newsdesk from time to time, mostly showing round mysterious City types and unimpressed bigwigs with American accents who most people assumed were corporate assassins from the cable industry. It was always the same routine and script: 'And here's our newsdesk. It's not the BBC, as you can see. Bosnia, it *ain't*, ha, ha herm, ha.' Everyone winced, especially on hearing it for the ninety-ninth time. There was more excitement when Kelvin, immensely puffed up, ushered John Major – the *Prime Minister himself* – into the studio and headed for the newsdesk ('Bosnia, it *ain't*, ha, ha, herm, ha'). Major smiled gormlessly, as though this was the funniest joke in the world. Kelvin then drew his attention to the fabulous view, which Major politely admired, allowing Kelvin to wisecrack, 'Yep, on a clear day you can see a Tory voter.' Major chuckled audibly.[1]

The newsdesk was caused further difficulties by MacKenzie, Ferrari and Ridley intermittently sticking their respective oars into day-to-day operations. Ridley would spin up to the desk and make helpful suggestions about how to do graphics or something. These would be carried out. Then Ferrari would bowl over later in the day and denounce it all as terrible. After the Dunblane tragedy Ferrari organised blanket (by L!ve's standards) coverage of the funeral service but this was cancelled by MacKenzie who could not stomach it. He had not told Ferrari, who exploded when a newsdesk oppo told him L!ve was pulling out: '*You whaaaat!* You. Are. Sacked!' – points, à la MacKenzie, to lift door – 'Get your cards – *now*! No, wait a minute. You get this fucking story *on the fucking screen*, and *then* you're sacked.' The newsdesk oppo told him that he was following a direct order from Kelvin. Ferrari made an instant U-turn: 'Are you sure? Hmmmmm, right, good idea! It's not really a story for L!ve anyway – too depressing. Yeah, right, very good, excellent decision.'

At 3 o'clock every afternoon, Ferrari held conferences with the newsdesk team which were a trickle-down version of MacKenzie's 'Whaddayagot for me?' morning conferences for top executives. Ferrari would ask, 'Now, what have you got for me' – short, exasperated pause – 'that is *new* and that is *interesting*.' People made suggestions. 'No, no, no, wait a minute – you *are not* listening to what I am saying. What I asked was' – pauses, lowers voice to a near-whisper – 'is it *new* and is it *interesting*?' 'Well, Nick . . . ' 'Ah! No, no-no-no-no-no-no, there you go *again*.' – sigh and longer pause – 'Is it *new* and is it *interesting*? Do not tell it to me unless what you have got to say is' – pause – '*new* and *interesting*, all right?' 'OK, Nick. I've got an idea that is new and interesting.' 'Good! That's better. *New* and *interesting*. Simple, see? Good. Go *on* then, tell it to us!'

The ideas would then flow. Mostly they were *old* and *boring*, but Ferrari approved them anyway, unless he had direct orders from MacKenzie, in which case he would rage, 'What have you done about the Princess Di story today?' or 'Why aren't we doing more about Europe interfering with our bananas' or whatever was in the other tabloids or MacKenzie had heard on *Today*.

The hacks would patiently explain that there was not a lot they could do, because all the cameras were booked out for use by Ridley's Weird Features Department. All the staff reporters had been allocated to stunts by MacKenzie and himself and the budget to hire freelancers had been abolished. At this point Ferrari would explode and do a passable imitation of a MacFrenzie bollocking: 'That's not *my* problem, that's *your* fucking problem. If there aren't any cameras, *find* a camera. I want – *I want* – a half-hour Diana programme on the air in *two hours'* time!'

The news team now consisted of a mixture of journalists (who were more likely to tell Ferrari straight when something couldn't be done and could handle the bollockings) and airheads: a collection of prima-donnaish glamourpuss presenters (including disgruntled Tellybrat hangovers from the Janet era), and a growing band of unpaid media studies students and sundry junior relatives of MacKenzie and his friends.

Ferrari treated the airheads a bit more delicately. 'Now. I expect you have all heard of Naomi Campbell,' he would say as though talking to a group of 12-year-olds with learning difficulties. 'Now Naomi often has her picture in the newspaper doesn't she?' Nods all round. 'Right, well we just thought that we might want to talk about her as well, and perhaps have some pictures of her too. But she's a very busy lady so she probably won't speak to us, will she?' More nods. 'Right, well, so perhaps we could get her *mum* to come on the show. What do you think about that as an idea?' The airheads would agree that this was a splendid idea. 'Fine. So what I want you to do is phone Naomi's mum and get her to come on the show. OK, can you make that happen for me?' Nods. 'Good, because I don't want to see that *not* happening. You won't come back and tell that it *hasn't* happened, will you?' Heads swivel from side to side: no. 'Good, well off you pop then. Go on, shoo, *shoo*. Off you go. Bye bye.'

The airheads were a nightmare anyway. They made mistakes so basic that the more experienced people had forgotten such errors were possible. They copied out stories from newspapers without realising they had to attribute them or rewrite them slightly to avoid copyright problems. That was not hard to do; it simply did not occur to them it was necessary. The slightest difficulty defeated them. Their knowledge of legal matters was zero and they often added little asides along the lines of 'Well, I hope they lock him up and throw away the key' when reporting on a court case still in progress. They wasted time with daft ideas like interviewing witnesses in court cases, or trying to get defence lawyers to admit that their clients were guilty. The older hands were relieved whenever Ferrari managed to lure one of his tabloid cronies, no matter how horrible, to L!ve, because at least they would not land you in the shit every day.

Every time another new Autocutie presenter turned up, there were groans from the news hacks. 'What this place needs,' they would say to each other, 'is a safe pair of hands. Not another nice pair of tits.'

Chapter Twenty-seven

In which the L!ve TV newsdesk hacks are forced to go about their business wearing Bunny-Rabbit costumes, greatly enhancing the range and type of Stunt that can be performed and Boosting L!ve TV's Recognition Rating very satisfactorily, even though nobody is watching and it is, anyway, a Tremendous Wind-Up and talking-point for the Media

'Aww, Nick, come on. You can't make me wear *that*. It won't fit me. It's OK for these kids you've got round here, but Kelvin brought me here to do proper news. I'm a journalist, not a circus clown. Sorry, mate, there's no way I'm doing it.'

Ferrari sneers and tossed the grey and pink bunny-rabbit costume on to the desk next to David Nicholson, L!ve TV's twenty-stone, six-foot man mountain of a news editor, who has lately arrived at the channel after a lengthy career at, or near, the top in Fleet Street, including stints at the *Sun* and the *Sunday Times*.

But Ferrari is adamant: 'Take your jacket off and *put it on*. Everyone's got to do it. There's nobody else in today who can do it, anyway: we've sacked them all. Kelvin's orders. He's made *me* wear the fucking thing, so I don't see why you shouldn't.'

After more protests Nicholson struggles into the sweaty, airless, sticky nylon suit, which (as usual) reeks of the impregnated BO of the previous day's victim. He almost busts the zip, and mutters, 'I dunno. It's like *Monty Python's Flying Circus*, this place.'

The idea of making L!ve TV's reporters dress in bunny-rabbit costumes had come to Kelvin during one of his many 'ideas sessions' aimed at finding Cunning Stunts to fill the gap created by the impossibility of doing proper (tabloid) news. So when the idea of having a 'Human Bunny Rabbit' reading the news, or otherwise involved in the bulletins, was announced, some assumed that it was another PR stunt which would disappear into thin air along with the other duds.[1]

'News Bunny' had started life as a glove puppet. The idea was then developed to include a human-sized 'channel mascot', who would go out on the road doing stunts and getting the channel noticed and talked about. The afterthought of putting 'News Bunny' on screen behind the newsreader was suggested by a newsdesk hack at an editorial conference. Kelvin grabbéd the idea and elaborated: '*Yeah*, I like it! when the news is bad, it can look sad, and when the news is good it can sort of go like this', and he acted out a little skipping, hopping thumbs-up routine with a goofy, buck-toothed grin on his face. 'Nick, get it organised.'

Uncle Bill Ridley, standing on the other side of the room twitching away as usual, looked relieved that this particular brainwave did not come under the heading of Weird and was therefore to be Ferrari's headache, not his.

'And, Nick, I want it to have a carrot as well – a big one which it can wave about, sort of like *this*.'

This was bad news for Ferrari, who, at this point, was trying to carry out the previous Kelvin decision which was to do 'proper' (tabloid) news and hire some decent (tabloid) journalists to work alongside the 'fucking airheads' and the various blonde bimbos hired during the previous phase of trying to 'glamorise' the news. More than one tabloid hack got a call from Ferrari, who moaned that he was surrounded by morons who had no idea what a story was, armed with contacts books you could, in the standard phrase, safely fit up a gnat's arse. He could match the wages on offer elsewhere, just about, but most of the hacks wanted a substantial premium to compensate for the loss of career prospects, so not many came.[2]

Soon after the News Bunny discussion at editorial conference, Ferrari was gingerly interviewing a 'proper' journalist from one of the terrestrial channels, trying to lure him to L!ve, when the door flew open and MacKenzie charged in, yelling, 'Where's my fucking bunny, Ferrari?'

The Proper Journalist was stunned, but MacKenzie ignored him: 'Now, we *are* going to *have* the bunny, aren't we? You haven't *forgotten* about it, have yooooo? Because we *agreeeeeed* about the bunny, didn't we – y'know, *happy* when it's good news, eh, *sad* when it's not, big carrot as well.'

Ferrari cast a nervous glance at the Proper Journalist and replied, 'Erm yes, Kelvin. What colour would you like?'

MacKenzie turned to the Proper Journalist and said triumphantly, 'There you are! You can always tell when they're from News Corp. They don't argue or ask you why, they just *do it*. And another thing—'

Ferrari interrupted before MacKenzie could do any more damage: 'What *colour*, Kelvin?'

'Grey. It's *got* to be grey, and, er, *pink* – but only on the ears. I don't want a fucking pouffy *pink* rabbit. Er, grey, mainly, like actual rabbits, but a bit of pink, yeah. And *don't forget the carrot*! Right, got it?' and he rushed off. The Proper Journalist did not take the job.

An urgent search for man-sized grey-with-a-touch-of-pink rabbit suits was mounted, starting in Hamleys and working down until they found a place in Islington which would make them for £1200 each.

Then, of course, it was time to hit the publicity trail. An

interviewer from one of the posh papers was ushered into MacKenzie's office with the promise of an important story about L!ve TV. *Maybe they are finally going to face the facts and pull the plug . . . ?* But no. He was met by MacKenzie, who was bouncing the puppet version of 'Newsy' on his knee, clumsily pushing its paws into a thumbs-up gesture. 'This,' he said in momentous tones, 'is The News Bunny, the Future of Television.' He explained that Newsy would appear on screen during bulletins and would function as 'L!ve TV's very own opinion-former'.

The rabbit suits duly arrived. MacKenzie got Ferrari and others to model them and pronounced himself fairly satisfied. The costumes were stored just behind the presenter's desk in the studio. MacKenzie decreed that all L!ve TV staff (except himself) must take their turn at wearing them. But as the studio clock ticked towards news time people made sure they were very busy or, best of all, were sent out of the building on some mission or other, so they would not have to take their turn. The main objection was the smell, and a lot of people felt they needed a good shower after wearing it even for a few minutes. Then there was the problem of acting out the required signs of joy or grief on the spot as the headlines were read out. There was no time to rehearse or discuss in advance L!ve's editorial position on whether any particular news item was 'good' or 'bad'.

MacKenzie had given examples of bad (the death of the Queen Mother: *thumbs down*) and good (Frank Bruno winning the world heavyweight championship: *thumbs up*). But not everything was as clear-cut as that, so journalists, normally, tried to remain as neutral as possible. Trying to fall in with Kelvin's personal news prejudices stirred another wild card into the mix. What if there was a massacre in Bosnia or Rwanda or the Congo? How might Kelvin react? He might think it was sad, obviously, that thousands of people were dead (thumbs down) but good that there were fewer foreigners and blacks in the world (thumbs up); their children were now starving orphans (thumbs down) but their parents almost certainly deserved to die anyway (thumbs up). It might mean that British troops would be sent there for a bit of Falklands-style heroics (double thumbs up) but then they might get shot as well (thumbs down), but then again some of the endangered squaddies probably came from Liverpool (thumbs up) and they definitely deserved to be shot (double thumbs up plus exultant little jig).

Politics was very difficult. If Labour was doing well, that was thumbs up as far as official Mirror Group policy was concerned but thumbs down far as Kelvin was concerned (not to mention the strict ITC regulations preventing bias in favour of any particular political party). And there was the problem of genuinely tragic news requiring dignity of presentation. What then?

Kelvin, as usual, only told people when he thought they'd got it wrong. In an early outing next to the newsreader, the Bunny of the day had reacted, on the spot, to the news of the death of teenage boy in a car accident by pretending to wipe away imaginary tears with his little paws. Kelvin thought this looked insincere and bollocked everybody about it. He then banned any bunny activity in connection with the death of Leah Betts, the teenage girl who died after taking Ecstasy, but went berserk when it was left off a similar story which the newsdesk people thought was at least as tragic, if not so high-profile. The problem kept coming up. If they had the Bunny commenting on a major motorway pile-up, MacKenzie would bollock them for being insensitive. If they left him off he would come roaring out of his office shouting, 'Where's my fucking bunny? Don't you realise that this station *is*

Newsy Bunny?' The newsdesk team could not win, though after the Dunblane tragedy the bunny suit was put in mothballs – for two weeks; then it was back again.

It was safer to send the bunny out to do harmless stunts. A L!ve TV reporter changed his name by deed-poll to News Bunny so he could stand in a parliamentary by-election in Tamworth, near Birmingham. But as usual the stunt had not been thought through in advance. It was OK for News Bunny to appear as a candidate on ITN or BBC news (as intended) under the equal-airtime rule. But if he appeared on L!ve doing his 'normal' job all the other candidates would have to be mentioned as well and that was a nuisance because there were a lot of them, many also being desperate publicity-seekers. The problem was solved by renaming the bunny in the L!ve TV newsroom Dr Newsy von Bunny from Germany, and sticking a tacky 'moustache' cut out of black crêpe paper on his face to prove it. This seemed to satisfy the ITC regulators for the moment, but they let it be known that they were mortified by News Bunny in general. Late-night sex shows were one thing, but turning what was still (just about) the 'real' news for the day into a travesty was quite another, with all kinds of very bad potential consequences. The ITC made it clear that they would be watching very closely.

The News Bunny Party issued a manifesto during the by-election. The document was remarkably po-faced, relatively free of jokes and gave a fascinating insight into MacKenzie's political philosophy. 'All political parties have failed the little people of Britain', the document said, adding that the country was set to become 'a weak third-rate flop under the current no-hopers'. Detailed policies were resolutely populist, revealing an obsession with organising government on the basis of constant opinion polls and referendums, so that the bloke in the pub got his way at last. On education, Kelvin promised to abolish all new universities which, he said, were 'a front for students to spend three or four years drinking lager and taking soft drugs. Such training breeds only layabouts and "poor me" counselling victims.' He wanted a republic, and presidential elections to be held immediately. There had to be 'harsher sentencing for criminals' and European integration was to be resisted: 'The ECU is funny money and there is no need for it here.' During the campaign itself, Bunny generated minimal publicity until he was arrested for obstruction while giving out carrots.

Most of the news-presenting in Tamworth was done by Wendy Turner (sister of the more famous Anthea), who had been headhunted from Stoke-on-Trent where she was appearing in panto. Wendy had little training or experience as a journalist and, as she cheerfully realised, was brought in as a further publicity stunt. She screwed up in a mild way when covering the count on election night itself. She had been on stage with Bunny, finding it all very interesting, but when it got late she felt tired and went off for a kip. When she woke up it was all over. L!ve TV had missed the result and had to take a feed from the BBC. Kelvin, directing the output late at night from the phone in his bedroom (as was his wont) was not best pleased. The reporter who had worn the filthy, sweaty rabbit suit all week was meanwhile left to face life with 'News Bunny' stamped on his credit card, chequebook and driver's licence.

In March 1996, Turner was involved in another bunny PR incident. She and the bunny of the day had gone in an OB van to Princess Diana's health club in Chelsea to engage in a spot of mild stake-out persecution in the wake of her 'queen of hearts' performance on *Panorama*. The OB truck was parked on a bit of waste ground. Turner, bunny and the team were half a mile away, *en route* to the health-club entrance, when half a dozen police cars went scream-ing past, chasing a car full of gangsters into the wasteland where the L!ve OB truck was parked. There was a shoot-out and three bullets hit the truck. The team reported back to base, where there was great excitement. The next thing they knew the 'story' was splashed all over the front page of the *Evening Standard*, saying that 'Anthea Turner's sister' had 'almost been killed' and that News Bunny had been inside the OB truck when a 'hail of bullets' hit it. All lies, of course. But good publicity. Kelvin shook Turner's hand (the nodding-off incident at Tamworth was now forgot-ten) as 'L!ve TV's very own Kate Adie' and gave her the day off in tribute. (After a few more months of this sort of madness, Turner moved on to present cutesy animal programmes on normal television, which was much more her cup of tea).

One bunny stunt involved getting an 'exclusive' inter-view with Tony Blair, then leader of the opposition. L!ve had tracked him down to a themed pub-restaurant where he was having lunch on his way to a meeting. One of Blair's spin-doctors saw the OB van and bunny team hang-ing about in the carpark and wandered out to see what was happening. The interview request was turned down – 'You must be fucking joking!' – but minutes later, sens-ing that the ambush could not be avoided without an undignified run-for-it, Blair himself appeared and gave them an eight-second sound-bite to the effect that this was 'one of Kelvin MacKenzie's scams, wasn't it?' The picture of Blair talking to a man-sized rabbit was splashed all over the papers the next day. Another direct hit!

This triumph was followed up with a scam story to the effect that Newsy was feeling sex-starved so L!ve was going to supply him with a Newsy Bunny girlfriend (an old stunt that one, which had been used with success in the *Sun*'s war with the *Daily Star* over the welfare of Blackie, the persecuted Spanish donkey 'rescued' by the paper). The female Newsy Bunny, L!ve said in a statement, would look like 'Barbara Windsor with fur'. She would not commentate on the news but instead would 'give Newsy the eye and try to distract him'. There was more publicity when an 'alternative' comedian tried to kidnap Newsy Bunny as part of his own stunt-based show on Channel Four.

Any row with authority triggered by bunny activity was welcome. News Bunny had been sent, for example, to the 1996 state opening of parliament after permission to film inside the police security cordon was granted to two L!ve TV newsdesk bods. The police complained that one of them had turned up wearing a latex mask of Prince Charles and a blond wig, and the other in a bunny suit 'in contravention of the Palace of Westminster photographic regulations'. The police report quoted L!ve's representatives as saying, 'We are going to report the state opening of parliament with a man wearing a rabbit suit in the foreground and the soldiers and carriages in the background.' Black Rod made an official complaint and asked for an assurance that there would be no repetition of this. Everyone was delighted. The more aggro with the likes of Black Rod the better.

The bunny might be a problem, in terms of editorial judgement and ITC regulations, but *fuck that*! The scam was working beautifully as PR. The daily 3 p.m. news meeting, a replica of the morning conference but involving more junior people on the news side of the operation, came to be dominated by the search for bunny stunts. Ferrari conducted these meetings, copying Kelvin's (highly contagious) management methods: 'Right, whaddaya got

for me today? Whaddawe going to do with the bunny?'
And people would make suggestions. Maybe gatecrash
the Imran Khan libel trial at the High Court? No chance,
Nick. The clerk of the court will throw us out and make an
official complaint. Great! We can do with the publicity.
'Now then. Why aren't we bidding to buy Madonna's
dresses at the Christie's auction, eh?' 'We tried, Nick.
Christie's won't let a man dressed in a bunny suit into the
building.' *Heh, heh. I wonder why?*

'Bollocks! I want – *I want* the fucking bunny! I want the
fucking bunny – the fucking *bunny* – in the fucking *auction
room*, and I want it there *now*! . . . Just . . . all right? Bunny-
at-auction, eh? Right? Just get your act together, pal, or You
. . . Are . . . *Out*!' A minion would shuffle off to try and deal
with the request.

Soon everyone was writing about Newsy. He was even
referred to in the first paragraph of a heavyweight review
of a book about Bosnia in a broadsheet newspaper: 'L!ve
TV's News Bunny has been instructed to yawn whenever
the subject of Bosnia comes up; he will not like this book,
then, and neither will his pea-brained boss, Kelvin
MacKenzie.' Newsy was fast becoming a national institution – like Janet Street-Porter's teeth and accent – which
people would refer to out of the blue, or if they were stuck
for a metaphor or cheap joke. *Fantastic!* The recognition
rating was soaring. Apart from the Sky Channels, L!ve TV
was turning up in the market research as just about the
only cable or satellite channel anyone had ever heard of.
It was going like a dream.

Chapter Twenty-eight

*In which a Great Many Good-Lookin' Norwegian Girls
are carefully examined but L!ve TV misses out on Ginger
Spice, Posh Young Ladies are Teased over their Horsy
Looks and the female Tellybrats are told to Get Their Tits
Out for the Lads, a Dress Code is announced, and a
Worldwide search is launched to find some Topless Tarts
as Nick and Kelvin go to War against Hypocrisy in the
defence of the Common Man and his Bit of Saucy
Entertainment*

'Hei, hei, da skal vi se pa vaeret for i dag. Vi far det litt
kjoligere i England og Wales. Lett regn kommer til a
komme innom Northern og Eastern England pa
morgenkvisten, og strekker seg South West ettersom det
lir pa dagen . . . '

A good-lookin' blonde Norwegian woman called Anne-
Marie, dressed in an unseasonable bikini – which is *not*
the national costume of Norway – is reading the weather
forecast on L!ve TV. She gestures towards an ordinary-
looking electronic weather map. Ordinary, that is, except
for the fact that Overhalla in Norway is picked out with
a large red dot.

' . . . I Scotland blir det overskyet til a begynne med, men
her far vi mere regn som sprer seg fra sor utover til alle
kanter, men etterpa blir det solskinn her ogsa . . . ' And
with a toothy smile and a flutter of the eyelashes she breaks
into fractured Ingleesh. 'But in my home town, Overhalla,
it's tirribal tooday wid all dat snooo and eyes and warder
all mixed ooop into a big grey soooop – but nivver mind.
Hey, James frohm Brimminharm! You wrote to me a rilly-

graaate-ledda. Did you knoo yorr a fanny guy! [winsome giggle] I knoooo, vy don't vee get you onorrr commud-dyshow *Standuplive*, hahr, hahr! Ah bet yoo vish yoo had nivver written to me now!'

The idea of having the weather report in Norwegian came, as usual, from one of L!ve's drink-fuelled brain-storming sessions. MacKenzie had invited people to think about what they could do with the weather bulletin, prefer-ably to stretch it out as long as possible as a way of fill-ing up airtime and, at the same time, feed the publicity machine (the triumph of the stammering newsreaders was still fresh in everyone's mind). What sort of disability would be cruel and funny for weathermen? Well, they could go back to having old-fashioned magnetic rain-cloud and sunshine symbols and just be very clumsy and keep dropping them all the time. That would get a laugh. *Naaaah, too borin'.*

Bill Ridley came to the rescue: *dwarfs*! You could have weathermen who were too short and couldn't reach the fucking map to put the symbols on it. Pause; pin-drop silence as Kelvin tipped his chair well back and pictured this in his mind. Then, '*Fffwwaakin' 'ell, Bill, you mad old bastard! You're a fucking genius! You've saved the channel!*' Kelvin was pleased with the idea.

Everyone joined in: *yeah*, and they could have colds all the time, because of the weather . . . and hay fever in the spring. *Yeah! It's a runner!* I know, why don't we have Bill's *dwarfs*, right, jumping up and down to reach the map? *Great!* No, better than that – trampolines! *That's it!* Kelvin blocked out the slogan word by word with his hand, just as he had done many times at the *Sun* when painting imag-inary front-page headlines: 'Upper deck: "Only . . . On . . . L!ve TV". Lower deck: 'Trampolinin' . . . *dwarf* . . . weathermen". Yep. I like it!' A pair of trampolining dwarfs was therefore hired to present the weather on L!ve TV.

But MacKenzie soon got bored with the stunt, so the subject of weather bulletins was put back on the agenda. He glumly announced that L!ve was reverting to the standard idea of busty blondes as presenters, 'same as the news'. But Ridley again came to the rescue. Where did blondes come from? Norway, right? So why not get a Norwegian girl but . . . have her read it all out in Norwegian? 'No, no, hear me out.' All the stuff about isobars and depressions, it's like a foreign language. So why not go the whole way and do it in Norwegian, one of the world's most stupid-sounding languages?

MacKenzie was persuaded. Ridley set off to Stringfellow's nightclub in search of 'Norwegian Tit', as it was put, taking Nick with him as his guide. A number of hopefuls were lured for screen tests which Ridley organised in secret 'so as not to upset the dwarfs'. Ridley filmed dozens of girls on a Hi-8 camera. They had to wear bikinis and stand in front of a road map of England (procured from a petrol station) and, oh yes, read an old weather script, translating it into Norwegian as they went along.

Later MacKenzie, Ridley and Ferrari were seen in one of the tiny viewing-rooms, snickering and drooling over the girls like schoolboys looking at porn mags behind the bike shed. Some of their comments were recorded for posterity by a passing female presenter: 'Well, what about that one then? . . . Yeah, well, she's got OK tits, but she's got too much cellulite, hasn't she? . . . No, she's fine . . . six out of ten . . . '. Eventually two girls were chosen. They were told that they could present either in a bikini (which L!ve TV would generously buy and provide for them) or in a 'glamorous evening gown' (which they would have to buy themselves). The whole thing was judged a great success by Kelvin and was to become one of L!ve's main running gags, the ideal complement to News Bunny.[1] The following year Kelvin signed a sponsorship deal with his favourite football club, Millwall. The players ended up wearing the legend 'L!ve TV: The Weather in Norwegian' on their shirts.

It was reckoned that MacKenzie and Ferrari's obsession with getting good-lookin' women on the screen came partly from the success of Page Three in the *Sun*, but was mainly to do with the hard economic facts of pay television, given that, according to the research, the only things people would pay up-front TV subscriptions for were 'hot' sport, recent Hollywood movies and porn. Since L!ve had no access to the first two, it was bound to gravitate towards the third, though MacKenzie and Ferrari always maintained that what appeared on L!ve was 'saucy fun', not porn.

Ferrari had screen-tested numerous models, many of whom wrote in with publicity pictures asking for a presenting job on L!ve as a first step to 'being on the telly' (even if it was only cable). In this way Ferrari had turned up Geri Halliwell, later famous as 'Ginger Spice'. She had written to him in 1993 when Monty was bidding for a franchise to run London Live. After an interview with Ferrari she presented a pilot edition of something called *The Fashion Police*, in which she rushed around wearing a peaked cap, blowing a whistle and 'arresting' people who were badly dressed. 'She had tremendous enthusiasm,' Ferrari later told a newspaper. 'She looked great and wasn't fazed by anything and clearly loved performing.' She had been offered a job on L!ve TV but, Nick claimed, was rejected by Janet, who advised her to get some more experience by becoming a 'traffic announcer on Radio Plymouth'. Soon after this the Spice Girls took off. Just as they were starting to make it really big, the group appeared on L!ve TV performing their song 'What I really, really want', which was an amazing coup for the channel.

Teasing of women members of staff at L!ve TV about their appearance was frequent and understandable, given the nature of the channel. Normally it took the form of telling them to dress more sexily in line with the editorial requirement to have the channel fronted by good-lookin' women. One young woman was hired after Kelvin had spotted her on Garry Bushell's smut-drenched late-night show on Carlton. Others came from soft-porn channels. Several of the female Tellybrats left over from the Janet era were teased remorselessly, especially if they were at all 'posh'. Making well-brought-up young women behave in a vaguely sluttish fashion seemed to tickle Uncle Bill Ridley's fancy. One was told that if she wanted to keep her job as a L!ve TV newsreader she would have to 'show a bit more tit' when presenting the 'normal' news and also make regular late-night appearances 'reporting' on strip shows in Brighton and doing 'product reviews' of vibrators and similar 'sex aids'. She went sick to avoid these assignments and then left the channel.

Another woman, a highly qualified financial journalist, made the mistake of asking to do a series of high-profile interviews with politicians. She was sneeringly told that she could do the interviews, but there was a condition: she would have to wear a low-cut dress with a micro-camera concealed in a push-up bra, so that they could screen the politicians ogling her 'for a laugh'. Still others, hired both before and after the Janet coup, were told that if they didn't 'show a bit more tit' when presenting the news they would lose their jobs. If they refused, they were usually given increasingly repugnant late-night 'sex story' assignments until they either gave in and tarted themselves up or left the channel (as usual, it was pointed out that there was a long queue of others willing to take their place). Gayle MacKenna, a former *Sun* Page Three girl, was hired to front L!ve Sport. On her first night she wore a little jacket, but Nick told her that was in breach of the L!ve TV 'dress code'. It was explained to her that the dress code for L!ve Sport was 'Cleavage, cleavage and more cleavage'.

Step one in the process of glamorising the channel was to get blondes to present just about everything from the news and 'sport' to the weather, all dressed as provocatively as possible. Next came programmes which were supposed to be 'about' sex, or had a titillating element to them. Leading the way was *The Sex Show* (later renamed *Exotic Erotic*) which was shown after 11 p.m. and was built on the rubble of the Planet Janet TV era *Late Night Show*, with the gay and 'perverted' element removed. The new staple was 'normal' (or 'mainstream weird') striptease. This was supplemented with a sex-based late-night chat show which, like many things on L!ve, was long on sizzle and short on sausage. (Its early highlights included 'erotic dancing' by strippers, and a lot of interviews with strippers, both male and female, conducted by cringing female presenters. There was once a sofa-bound interview with Randy Shagnasty, a star of the rival Fantasy TV porn channel, whose gimmick was to approach women in the street and ask them to have sex with him.)

The presenter then did a sort of 'what the papers say' slot flicking through porno mags: 'This one's called *Big and Fat* . . . with lots of pictures of big, er, fat women enjoying themselves . . . ' The camera remained a tidy distance away so that all that appeared on screen was smudgy blancmange shapes. 'These ladies are big, big ladies [repulsed flick of pages] . . . certainly, very large, yes . . . ' On one level this was harmless smut. It was hated by the women who had to present it, not least because of the constant

387

danger of sexual advances – or even attack – by viewers who might recognise them off duty. This problem was made worse by the 'interactive' element, with constant requests for the nation's dirty-mac brigade to phone in. There was at least one case of a female *Sex Show* presenter being stalked by a man who, at one point, got into the Canary Wharf car park and tried to attack her. After that she had to be escorted to and from her car by a security guard.

But the main 'saucy' interest on L!ve TV was to be a daily stunt featuring girls who were paid on average about £70 to appear topless on the channel for about four minutes at a time. It was natural enough that MacKenzie should want a topless equivalent to Page Three in the *Sun*. But a televisual version of the feature was fraught with problems.

The main problem was, of course, cost. The top Page Three girls charged a lot of money for a photo session and, at the height of the craze in the mid-1980s, could earn £150,000 a year. On the other hand a photo shoot might produce dozens of pictures, so the cost of each picture was reasonable and the *Sun* could afford it. There were other spin-offs as well, ranging from calendars to sales of the pictures to other papers at home and abroad. The girls (and their agents) were often prepared to let the *Sun* have the pictures fairly cheap as a sort of loss-leader in return for positive publicity aimed at getting them extremely lucrative advertising and personal appearance work. So the whole thing worked just fine.

L!ve, by contrast, would have to hire at least five different girls per week, paying each the equivalent of a lengthy photo shoot just to fill up a few minutes per day. There was only so much a girl could do once she was topless, other than walk up and down a bit, and that would get boring very quickly. The best girls, especially the ones with 'wholesome' images to maintain, would be reluctant to do even this.[2]

So Operation 'Topless Darts' went into action. Simon London, the presenter who had done marathon presenting stints in the Janet era, was called at home by Ferrari, who told him that he was in luck. He was being sent to Australia to film topless girls on the beach. The idea for the 'topless darts' electronic Page Three was explained. London was appalled but, after a moment or two's thought, decided that in this world it was not possible to have both morals and a mortgage. He agreed to do it, so long as he did not have to present it or otherwise be linked with it in public. MacKenzie and Ferrari agreed, and before London knew it he was on Bondi Beach, dartboard under his arm and Kelvin's instructions to find 'girl-next-door types, but with nice tits' ringing in his ears.

For a couple of days London tried to find volunteers, but without success. Instead he phoned back to base to get permission to hire girls from a model agency. The 'models' arrived for the shoot with a gaggle of friends eager to do the work for relatively little money. London, somewhat to his horror, later came to the conclusion that some of them were prostitutes, but said nothing about it. None of the girls, of course, could play darts. He simply filmed them in pairs bouncing across the beach, getting ready to play the game by tossing a coin. He then got them to jump up and down with their arms above their heads, making their tits jiggle up and down, while they mouthed, 'I won! I won!' London himself then threw darts at the board and filmed that so that he could cut it all together in various combinations and produce numerous editions of *Topless Darts*. With this material in the bag, he flew back to London where, to his surprise, he found billboards all over the place advertising the contents of his hold-all: 'Coming Soon: Topless Darts. Only on L!ve TV!'[3]

The results of London's work were shown to MacKenzie, who seemed pleased enough, and the show went out in the schedule accompanied by the usual publicity blitz. 'Topless Darts will make you smile,' MacKenzie was quoted as saying, 'it's not designed to win a BAFTA award. People only say L!ve TV is tacky because of the job I did before. If I'd been editor of *The Times*, they'd have called it inspired programming.'[4]

Simon London had brought in the first *Topless Darts* in Australia under budget by nearly £4,000. But even this was reckoned to be too expensive. In a further attempt to cut costs, another producer was sent to a topless beach in Spain, where he tried with very little success to talk girls into appearing for free. Unwilling to go home empty-handed and receive a bollocking from Ferrari or MacKenzie, he hit the local red-light district of his own accord. The hiring of prostitutes was considered. But there was a problem with this. The inmates of provincial Spanish brothels were tremendously ugly. In desperation, *big* money (£200 a go!) had to be paid to attract various Scandinavian nightclub hostesses, waitresses and willing nightclub clientele to strip off.

After this, *Topless Darts* began to be filmed indoors in London at locations such as ice-rinks (*Topless Darts on Ice*) with 'special editions' such as *Topless Darts in Outer Space*, echoing the *Sun*'s old Page Three trick of 'themed weeks' (e.g., 'Pussy Week', when all the girls would be shown stroking kittens). Eventually it was supplemented by *Lunch Box Volley Ball*, which was similar to the Page Seven Fella feature that the *Sun* had run for a while. Ferrari defended *Topless Darts* as good clean 'saucy' fun, and counter-attacked his critics with a monumental wind-up. By now a lot of Janet-era former L!ve people were on the circuit complaining that MacKenzie and Ferrari had 'killed their baby' by substituting moronic old-fashioned soft porn for their more 'edgy' art-porn approach.

Ferrari hit back by taking the moral high ground, thus sending a 'ferret up the bum' of the Planet Janet people. 'All we are trying to do,' he said in an interview with a trendy style magazine, 'is get ideas that are genuinely entertaining, that are a little bit saucy . . . ideas that are moving on from the *Carry On* movies, if you like.' He was horrified, shocked, scandalised, indignant – even *hurt* – to find that the sort of Snooty Groucho Club Art-Porn mob who were responsible for the sort of thing you got on Channel Four were sniping at L!ve TV: 'We're not trying to do something tasteless like Channel Four's snog-a-granny or eat-from-a-bucket-of-sick. There's nothing funny, skilful, amusing, titillating, entertaining or saucy about eating your own sick. It's pathetic. It's vile. It shows a total lack of intellect.'

Unfortunately his standard defence of the Common Man and his right to enjoy a bit of harmless smut without interference from the *hypocrites* of the Stuck-Up Clever-Dick Spoilsport Holier-Than-Thou Television Establishment was somewhat undermined by events closer to home. After material like *Topless Darts* started washing up on the channel, Ferrari's wife, Sally, also an experienced tabloid journalist, had decided that L!ve TV was no longer welcome in the Ferrari household. It was 'an embarrassment'.[5]

Chapter Twenty-nine

In which a Bomb goes off next to Canary Wharf present-ing L!ve TV with a Great Story which, much to Kelvin's fury, the Airheads he is forced to Put Up With fail to make the most of, revealing their many Deficiencies and forcing him to Bollock Everyone Harshly amid much Injustice, waving aside their Excuses about Lack of Resources, and in which Kelvin's Reign of Terror creates much Fear and Loathing until, at last, the Head of Weird disappears suddenly

'Stay where you are everyone! . . . Don't try to use the lifts – they're not working . . . There might be another bomb somewhere in the building . . . The police say don't use the stairs, they'll get us out later . . . So just sit tight, OK, and stay calm.'

The L!ve TV newsroom on the 24th floor of Canary Wharf is a scene of pure panic. Some people are running around, others are sitting at their desks trying to make phone calls, paralysed with fear. There is debris every-where and fire alarms are shrieking in the newsroom and throughout the building.

Ferrari is striding about like a World War II naval captain on the bridge of a torpedoed destroyer. He clutches a piece of paper ripped from the news-wire machine. 'It's the IRA . . . it was an IRA bomb . . . Right, I want a bulletin writing and going out in *two minutes* . . . Get that camera and point it out of the window . . . I want to see what is going on.' The camera is pointed out of the window. But it is night and there is smoke in the air. There is nothing to see except the flashing lights of a clutch of fire-engines and police cars at the foot of the Canary Wharf tower.

At 7.01 p.m. on Friday, 9 February 1996, the IRA detonated a huge bomb near South Quay railway station in Docklands. It killed Inam Bashir and John Jeffries, who ran the station's news kiosk, and injured many more. Canary Wharf, half a mile away, was hit full on by the blast wave, while a L!ve news bulletin was being broadcast. There was a huge thudding bang, the building swayed violently, and many of the plate-glass windows rattled and cracked. Insulation and other debris rained down from the ceiling. The lifts locked in place and dozens of fire alarms burst into life.

At first the newsreader carried on with the bulletin. But as people began running around and shouting in the background, she started looking over her shoulder and mumbled, 'Er, hold on . . . I think something fairly serious has happened here . . . er . . . ' The bulletin was suspended.

For a while there was utter confusion. What had happened? Was it a bomb further down the building? Had a plane crashed into the tower? Was the place on fire? Were they all trapped? The phones were still working. Somebody got on to the police, who confirmed that a bomb had gone off in the area. It was *not* in the Canary Wharf tower itself. The safest thing was to stay where they were. They must, at any rate, keep off the streets. There was a danger that there might be another bomb. They were better off inside the tower which was 'bomb-proof'.

The news did not lessen the panic. The chance of being hit by an IRA bomb was a frequent topic of conversation for everyone who worked in the tower. In April 1993, the IRA had exploded an enormous bomb near the NatWest tower in the City, a few miles away, causing widespread devastation. After that Canary Wharf was the next obvious target. Sadistic sub-editors on the *Mirror* had taunted the vertigo-suffering contingent during cheery chats in the canteen. It was explained that '*bomb*-proof' meant just that: the building would survive a *single* bomb. They had looked it all up, as subs are apt to do. But the building wasn't bombS-proof, because the first explosion would weaken the tower and use up some of its shock-absorbing capacity.

A second bomb, the Sadistic Sub would continue in an ill-informed way, if it went off in, say, the basement, would work like the charge in a mortar, hee, hee, hee. The blast wave would be funnelled up through the building, up the staircases, lift and ventilation shafts, blowing out the weakened windows. If the charge was big enough, it would blow the fucking pyramid off the fucking top of the building and shower the whole of London with debris and rubble and, oh yeah, bits and pieces of us lot, of course, hee, hee, hee over a sixty-mile radius . . . Huh! at least we'd all get home quickly for once, ha, ha, ha! . . . What's the matter, mate? You've gone all green at the gills, tee, hee, hee . . . Unless we were all just sucked out of the windows of course which' – chuckle, chuckle – 'I grant you, is more likely . . . I mean, that's why I sit by the window myself. If you've gotta go, I'd rather go that way, myself . . . What's the matter, mate? Why aren't you – tee, hee, hee – eating your dinner?'

The 'not-bombS-proof' theory was remembered and rumours spread, making everyone feel sick. Did they ignore the cops and make for the stairs and the street and run the risk of being shredded by flying glass, or did they stay put and wait to be burnt to death and shot into the sky like a series of dismembered human cannonballs? It was a tough decision.

Meanwhile Ferrari, now joined by MacKenzie, was still

marching about barking at people. The Press Association news wire was filling in the detail. The IRA had put out a warning, claiming responsibility for the attack in advance, at some time during the previous hour. The newsreader went back on air to read the raw copy. Somebody on the news desk yelled, 'No News Bunny for these bulletins, everyone!' Ferrari, meanwhile, was more interested in negotiating with CNN, who he eventually persuaded to pay for a live feed from the camera pointlessly aimed out of the window. He shouted out the good news to nobody in particular: huh! *Great!*

By 10 p.m. the situation had calmed down a bit. There was no second bomb. The L!ve TV staff were evacuated by the police, leaving the camera pointing out of the window, feeding CNN with pictures of the Docklands skyline and pitch-black night sky and nothing else. A strapline was put on the L!ve output reading, 'Normal transmission will be restored tomorrow.' And everyone went home.

The L!ve TV morning shift struggled in the next day to find security, which had always been tight, massively beefed up. Through the week staff were issued with an additional ID card to get them through the 'ring of steel' security checkpoints the police had installed round the City of London, and another one to get into the carpark, a third to get into Canary Wharf itself, and yet another one to get them past the heavies newly stationed outside L!ve TV's reception area. Monty, as one of the country's most celebrated Orange Unionists, was naturally paranoid about the possibility of attack. After the bombing he stationed four security guards on each floor inhabited by the Mirror Group. They had nowhere to sit and so just floated about giving everyone the willies until they suddenly disappeared a few weeks later.

MacKenzie was paranoid as well, partly for the same reason as Monty. Over the years he had firmly nailed the 'hang the IRA scum' flag to the mast of the *Sun*. His home in Kent was a fortress to guard against not only Sinn Fein but the many other potentially or possibly murderous opponents he had persecuted or vilified over the years. These ranged from the 5000 print workers whose jobs he had played a key role in abolishing, through sundry Arabs, Muslim fundamentalists, left-wing activists and people ranging from Clare Short, John Major, Neil Kinnock and Alan Bennett to the entire population of Liverpool.

With the new security arrangements in place, work resumed. True to the spirit of the Blitz, L!ve's staff got to work on the Saturday schedule, dominated by a children's programme, as if nothing had happened. MacKenzie, who arrived early, was not pleased by this display of fortitude. He came screaming into the directing gallery yelling, 'What the fuck are you playing at? We are sitting on the biggest fucking story in town. Your own office was nearly blown to bits – and you are doing a fucking kids' programme.' He pointed accusingly at the output monitor. 'Get that *off* now. Well, *go on!*'

There was the familiar moment of confusion and shuffling hesitation. Kelvin's eyes turned skywards. 'Fffffffk'in 'ell! Do I have to do *everything* in this *fucking place*?' He rushed off to see if he could get more sense out of the newsdesk. There was more pointing, like a referee at a football match giving somebody the red card: 'Get out and start reporting the story!' A rolling news programme was specified to start at 8 a.m. and run all day.

There were only a couple of problems with this. First, there was no story to report. Apart from people sweeping up the rubble, there was nothing going on. Second, the reporters available were, in the vast majority, simply not up to covering a story like this, lacking contacts at a senior level in the police, with the anti-terrorism people, or the IRA themselves.

L!ve TV nevertheless shambled into action. Wendy Turner was sent out to conduct 'vox pop' interviews with passers-by in the street. The passers-by, of course, knew even less about what was going on than the newsdesk, who could at least read what the Press Association put out over the wire. Vox pops were the absolute pits, the last resort in any sort of journalism, and Wendy, with her showbiz approach, did not distinguish herself as a hard-news reporter. She asked people who were clearly fit and well, without a hair out of place, 'Were you injured in the blast?' When they said 'no', she followed up with 'Does this sort of explosion happen often around here?' and, to heartfelt groans on the newsdesk, 'Do you think this bomb incident will be bad publicity for Docklands, or not?'

This thin material was supplemented with a phone-in which immediately ran into the L!ve TV problem of having no callers because there were precious few viewers. In any case, by this stage, every radio station in the country was doing a bomb phone-in, so the nation's purveyors of homespun wisdom were fully occupied elsewhere. The task was made even more difficult by MacKenzie's strict instruction that he wanted on air only people who 'think the IRA are scum and should all be shot', and nobody else *at all*. The coverage was so awful, and the newsdesk kids' inability to cope so profound, that Kelvin was soon in a rage: 'Look, it's simple! – *Do I have to do everything myself*? – You just phone up a couple of MPs and get them to say the IRA should be hung – it's *that fucking easy!*' But the kids didn't know any MPs. Their contacts books were full of C-list showbiz celebs, faltering pop stars and wannabe fashion designers, if anything.

Live TV

They didn't have a 'rentaquote' MP between them.

During an ad break MacKenzie stormed over to the presenter and started raving at her, eyeball to eyeball. 'Who the fuck *are* you?! Who fucking *hired* you?! I have never – *never!* – seen anything so *shit* in all my life! You are *a fucking disgrace* and the *minute* you are off the air . . . You!' – stab of finger towards presenter's nose – 'Are! Out! *Got that?!!*' The young woman was reduced to tears. He stormed back to the newsdesk and berated one of the more senior producers: 'What the *fuck* is the *matter* with these people?' The producer had been turning his own contacts book inside-out trying to line up tame (but rabidly anti-IRA) academics and pundits to keep the phone-in going for six hours. He managed to calm Kelvin down slightly: 'Kelvin, you have got to lay off a bit. If you carry on like this, even what we've got is going to collapse. This is as good as it's going to get. They're just kids. They're not really journalists.' Kelvin seemed to get the point, but even so he flew into another impotent rage, made various additional impossible demands, announced his intention to sack 'every last one of them' and then stormed off.

Minutes after this confrontation the producer's phone rang. It was Ferrari calling. 'How's it going, mate? Having fun?' The producer winced and said, 'Well, Kelvin's just reduced the presenter to tears in the middle of a live show and he wants us to stop doing what we are doing and do something else, we have no idea what . . . but, yeah, apart from that everything's great.' Ferrari chuckled: 'Good, so in other words it's normal, then. OK. 'Bye.' Typical Nick.

After the IRA bomb L!ve TV's plunging morale fell by another notch. MacKenzie wouldn't let them forget that they had, as he saw it, missed the big story ('Now I've seen everything. They put a bomb under the office and we miss the story. Fucking brilliant!'), especially if there was the faintest criticism or any suggestion that something he wanted could not be done ('Ah yes . . . more words of wisdom from the man who had a bomb explode under his bum and didn't notice!').

The tighter security arrangements made Docklands even more unattractive, inaccessible and grim. As part of the relentless drive for economies, all expenses and perks were cut to the bone, especially for more junior people. The search for budget cuts extended to every corner of the operation. As in the Janet era there were various demands for extra spending in the technical areas, accompanied by dire warnings that output would splutter to a halt unless the stock of videotape or computer chips or something was replaced. MacKenzie now dealt with these spending demands personally. Not a penny could be spent without his direct approval.

His method was to say 'No' the minute anyone started a sentence which sounded like it was going to end up asking for money. 'Er, Kelvin,' the techies would say, 'we've got a bit of a prob—' And he would cut them off – 'Nope' – in mid-sentence, often without looking up from what he was doing. The petitioner would try to rephrase the question: 'Er, Kelvin, do you remember how you asked us to—' and again get 'Nope'. On one occasion MacKenzie was keeping up this routine with a senior techie who eventually said, in exasperation, 'Kelvin! You are just going to say no to everything I say to you, aren't you?' Without looking up MacKenzie said, 'Yep,' and carried on reading. However, if there was a disaster because of failure to buy a *thingymajig* or *whatchermacallit* MacKenzie would bollock everyone, authorise the spending and ask, 'Why the fuck didn't you *tell* me you needed this?'

Equipment was sometimes unavailable to programme-makers because it had been commandeered by MacKenzie for a pet personal project, such as the film that was made to be shown at his fiftieth birthday party, which was held in a banqueting hall in the City. Everyone had a good laugh at the expense of the stuttering newsreaders he had conned into making audition tapes, and then MacKenzie played the host and danced the night away to a medley of '70s disco hits and 'Hi Ho Silver Lining'. A spoof edition of the *Mirror* was produced for the event, featuring a picture of Monty and Kelvin eyeing each other. The caption was to the effect of 'Now we are fat cat bastards in suits doing nothing for a living'.

The cuts also meant that simply getting to and from work was sometimes difficult. In the Janet era Darryl Burton had been generous with travel expenses involved in getting to and from Canary Wharf, especially very early in the morning and very late at night. But now all taxis were banned, which not only increased the mugger/stalker risk to women but posed a problem for all staff working on the late-night output who had to get home after the inadequate local public transport had stopped running. People without cars were allowed, from time to time, to sleep on the editing-room floor.

There were difficulties in the early morning, as well. One fairly junior member of the production staff, who lived fifteen miles away, asked how he was expected to get into work by 6 a.m., when his show, *Morning Live*, started. 'Try cycling,' he was told. Similarly, a cameraman on the show couldn't get in without a taxi, because there were no tubes or buses. He was told to come in as soon as the buses started. Taking them at their word, he rolled in at around 8 a.m., to find the camera being operated by a cleaner. He was threatened with the sack unless he bought a car, at his own expense – difficult on his minuscule wages.

People had been relatively well paid during the Janet era, but as the first wave of annual contracts were folded in the spring of 1996, or as people were sacked or terrorised into leaving, they were replaced by people on very low wages or, in many cases, no wages at all. Some researchers were paid as little as £7000 a year, but were loaded with huge responsibilities. Long hours and unpaid overtime were routine.

People sometimes plucked up the courage to ask Ferrari for a pay rise for themselves, or for a particularly exploited member of their team on the old-fashioned grounds of fairness: 'Look, Nick, you earn £100,000 a year . . . ' Nick would smile smugly and say, 'Yup. Quite a lot isn't it?' All requests for pay rises were refused, Kelvin-style, with Ferrari saying that if they didn't like it they could fuck off. They were lucky. There were plenty of people who would do their jobs for less. This was true. L!ve TV was now using large numbers of media-studies students on 'work experience'. Ferrari would wade through the mountain of applications: 'Crap. [plonk in bin]. *Total shit* [plonk].' Applicants were told to send in ideas with their applications, which on the Give Enough Monkeys Enough Media Studies Degrees principle would, once in a while, provide something that could be copied and put on the screen. In accordance with normal criteria, most of the media-studies persons hired were good-lookin' girls, none of whom stayed long or seemed to get much out of their association with 'Britain's newest national television channel'. Eventually, L!ve started sending colleges posters that asked, 'Do you want to be a TV star?' and gave a number to ring. Alongside the students, assorted young relatives of MacKenzie – including his son Haydon – and his pals turned up. (Speaking at the Edinburgh TV Festival in August 1997, MacKenzie said, 'There is no middle-class friend of mine whose children I do not employ, including my own. I see them joining us as an extension of going to university.')

At one point it was reckoned that fully a third of L!ve's staff consisted of unpaid students and other semi-professionals. Most of them wanted to be presenters, leaving serious gaps in the staffing of difficult and skilled areas such as technical production and on the newsdesk. Kelvin had pushed out many of the purely technical people who controlled output in the main control room. He had inherited a production manager from the Janet era, an experienced director who had been trained at the BBC and who had instituted all sorts of procedures to prevent cock-ups, but MacKenzie got rid of him. The control room came to be staffed mainly by freelances who did not know anyone and were unfamiliar with the place. As soon as they got used to it they left or they were sacked.

Those who, for whatever reason, could not be sacked or easily replaced were subjected to the MacKenzie 'bollocking' process to keep them on their toes. He did sometimes praise people but usually his highest compliment was a snarled 'You're a clever cunt, aren't you?' which was taken to mean 'Well, you have done OK today, but you are bound to screw up one day and then I will take even more pleasure than usual in doing you in.'

The net result of all this was that there was often nobody in the control room to keep an eye on what was going out on the channel, especially overnight. Producers were told to put their edited tapes straight into the machine which transmitted them, without anyone to check. They just clunked the videos into the machine, pressed the button and hoped for the best. Inevitably, things went wrong. On at least one occasion the whole channel crashed for two hours (without so much as a test-card), leaving L!ve in danger of being in breach of its contract with the cable carriers. Another time a hard-core porn video, which was being edited for extracts to be shown on the *Sex Show*, was mixed up with the 'real' output (which was supposed to be sport) and broadcast for twenty minutes before anybody noticed.

The ultimate transmission-error horror was reckoned to be the danger of broadcasting the pre-prepared obituary for the Queen Mother which Ferrari had self-importantly produced and put on ice. With the production staff cut to the bone, there was a danger of somebody leaning on the wrong button and killing off the nation's favourite great-grandmother. MacKenzie issued a memo setting out a detailed checking procedure resembling a Pentagon plan for authorising the use of nuclear weapons. It was loaded with dire warnings and had the words 'The Queen Mother Obit is in two boxes and is kept in the top drawer in the Presentation Area' picked out in huge black type.

The lack of professionalism on the newsdesk, exposed during the non-reporting of the Canary Wharf bomb, became more of a problem as the unpaid and non-professionals got more and more involved. Coverage became haphazard. For example, the 'airheads' (for some reason best known to themselves) put a lot of effort into covering a visit by John Major to Wales, grabbing all the scarce equipment and bunging up the editing suites as they took all day to do a ten-minute job so that they could teach themselves video-editing by means of trial and error. But L!ve had no affiliates or, therefore, viewers in Wales. Meanwhile, a visit by Tony Blair to Liverpool, which was one of L!ve's key distribution areas, was ignored. People would come back with films which were shaky, with the horizon at a tilt, and abysmal sound quality. Sometimes they missed the job altogether.

Live TV

That sort of thing was bad enough, but the airheads quickly became addicted to the powerful drug of 'being on the telly' and, to the dismay of the older hands, were eager to please MacKenzie and Ferrari by signing the newsdesk up to all sorts of mad and even dangerous projects. MacKenzie had, for example, for a while been keen on creating a slot called *Caught in the Act* based on going round the regional criminal courts, obtaining a list of offenders and broadcasting their crimes and sentences, together with identifying film taken when they walked out of court, and other graphics. The idea was that a lot of criminals were getting away with soft sentences and it was L!ve TV's job to pillory and stigmatise them on television and, well, more or less brand them across the forehead if possible: especially if they were child-abusers, rapists, drug-dealers and so on.

The newsdesk had resisted *Caught in the Act* for a long time, risking MacKenzie's wrath. It was a practical proposition in a way, and even quite cheap to put on screen. The police loved the idea and were falling over themselves to help. The problem was that the criminals and their families were unlikely to take kindly to the journalists involved. Since a lot of these people were violent and, well, criminal, you would be able to count the days until they kneecapped the producer and/or burned his house down. A version was broadcast on L!ve's Birmingham affiliate for a while until the team realised they were riding for a fall and the idea evaporated.

All the while, the pressure was cranked up by Kelvin's bullying and his moods. He would pace around the office, flanked by Ridley and Ferrari, zeroing in on people at random – 'What do you do? What are we paying your wages for? What are you doing *at this minute*?' – and sometimes sacking them on a whim. He was once overheard saying to Ferrari, 'I'm bored. Let's go and sack somebody.' Another time he was heard to tell a senior hand on the newsdesk, 'You'll never make it to the top of journalism. You're too soft. You should try sacking a few people.'

Sackings were so frequent that MacKenzie eventually started shaking hands twice with new recruits when he welcomed them to L!ve: once to say hello and the second time 'in case I'm not in the office when you are sacked'. For a while he also insisted that L!ve TV executives introduce themselves to visitors as 'the current' director of programmes or news editor or whatever, so as constantly to emphasise that they were liable to be sacked at any moment. He would butt into conversations and correct people, saying, 'He means *current* director of programmes' or 'news editor *for now*, ha, ha, ha!'

On one of his boredom-inspired marching-about sessions, MacKenzie wandered past a desk where a young Australian woman was working. 'How's the programme going,' he asked in a concerned and almost polite fashion. Like many people, she was having problems putting her material together. She made the mistake of taking the question at face value: 'Look, Kelvin, what you don't understand is—' As she uttered these words, MacKenzie swooped towards her and, eyeball to eyeball, raged, 'No! Tell you what, eh, what yooooo "don't understand" . . . what *yooooo* don't understand, right, is that when you leave this building – which will be in *exactly* two minutes' time – this will be a helluva lot better television station. Now *walk*!' And, just like that, she was out.

Sackings sometimes were done on a pretext. A producer once mentioned in passing that one of the girl presenters had mumbled 'oh fuck' live on air, when she dropped her script. 'Right! She's out.' The girl collected her cards without further discussion. The turnover of the presenters was rapid. When they were on screen their picture was displayed on the corridor wall near reception. When they were sacked the picture was taken down. Sometimes it was like Kremlinology. The first you knew that the latest bimbo discovery had been given the heave-ho was when her picture disappeared overnight.

MacKenzie also went through a phase of 'suspending' people or imposing 'fines' of so many weeks' wages, just like a football team manager. A producer was filming a cutesy filler item called 'Kids Talk'. He asked one 4-year-old, 'What's the rudest word you know?' in the hope of getting a charming response such as 'bum' or 'pooh'. Instead the child said, 'Fuck'. The tape was sent up for editing with strict instructions to cut out the f-word before it was broadcast. This did not happen and the swearing went out on air. Kelvin sacked the producer on the spot but, when the circumstances were explained, magnanimously commuted the sentence to a 'two-week suspension' for the producer *and* the tape editor *and* the presenter.

Although Janet's infobar was gone, L!ve still ran a lot of graphics and captions. The newsdesk airheads often made spelling mistakes and so Ferrari, with Kelvin's enthusiastic support, initiated a policy of 'three strikes and you're out': after three attributable spelling errors, the culprit would be sacked. People were likewise threatened by means of round-robin memos telling them they must be at their desks at 8 a.m., regardless of how late they had worked the previous night. They were also expected to have read all the day's papers before they came to work and Kelvin sometimes tested people to see if they had.

Life at L!ve TV was not made any easier by the splits and feuds right at the top of the organisation. MacKenzie tended to set Ridley and Ferrari at each other's throat and made them compete for his favour. After backing Ridley at first, he seemed to have fallen out with him over some of his projects; the bones of contention included allocation of the credit and royalties for 'quality' development projects such as an animation series called *Boy Band*.

In addition, a major needle-match had brewed up between Ferrari, as head of programmes, and Bill Nicholson, the corpulent news editor; the latter complained about the many problems afflicting the L!ve news-gathering operation and was not keen on News Bunny either. There was another cause of friction. Nicholson had 'seen the light' and become a born-again Christian. He objected on a personal level to Ferrari's constant sexual banter in editorial conferences. Ferrari, for his part, seemed to worry that Nicholson would get into MacKenzie's good books and undermine his all-important relationship with the boss. Ferrari did what he could to make Nicholson's life hell, and eventually Nicholson left. He took a job on the *Sunday Mirror*, but then fell out with the paper's editor, Bridget 'Death' Rowe, who had been appointed by Monty, and left Mirror Group employment altogether.

After Nicholson, the next senior person to leave was Bill Ridley. Uncle Bill had always struck people as distinctly odd and nervy. But the months of coping with MacKenzie, who was increasingly on his back, seemed to be driving him towards the edge. His behaviour became, if anything, even more strange as the weeks passed. He suggested, in spooky, gaunt-faced, hollow-eyed seriousness, that L!ve TV should train the satellite dishes on the OB trucks on Mars and track the planet, to see if they could pick up anything. One day soon after this, like Captain Oates in the Antarctic, he simply got up from his desk and walked out into the wastes of Docklands and did not come back.[1]

Chapter Thirty

In which the Mirror Group lines up with Carlton TV to make a bid for the Premier League which comes to naught but is Very Useful for the cable companies in their continuing War against Sky TV and so they are very grateful for Kelvin's efforts and think he is a Wonderful Person

The Coombe Abbey hotel near Coventry had seen high-powered business meetings before, but nothing quite like this. At 5 p.m. on the dot, on Thursday, 6 June 1996, a pair of black Mercedes with darkened windows crunched up the gravel drive through the Capability Brown gardens and came to a smooth halt. The doors flew open in unison and a group of besuited executives leaped out and jogged determinedly up the steps to the hotel entrance, led by a stocky little cannonball of a man wheezing slightly as a result of his chronic asthma.

Sam Chisholm and the boys from Sky TV bounded past the reception desk, through the lobby and headed straight for the Court House Conference Room, a converted real-tennis court, where the chairmen of England's Premier League football clubs, the joint owners of the hottest and most coveted TV sports rights in Europe, were waiting for them. The Sky team burst into the room in a flurry of hearty greetings, back-slapping and knuckle-crushing handshakes.

At stake was the renewal of the Premier League's screening rights deal with a Sky–BBC alliance which had been signed in 1992 and had brought several hundred million pounds of additional income to the clubs and saved Sky TV's (and Rupert Murdoch's) bacon.

Earlier in the day the football chiefs had heard from Lord Hollick's MAI group, which was bidding against Sky in partnership with the group which owned the *Daily Express*, with the aim of buying the rights for exploitation on Channel 5 or ITV, in which MAI also had financial interests. Hollick's people had been working on their bid for over a year, and gave what was reckoned to be a superb presentation. Their offer was based on selling screening rights to a number of outlets in the UK and abroad, giving the clubs a share of income and profits, rather than just a straight fee as was the case with Sky. Hollick offered a cool £1.25 *billion* for the rights. But he wanted a ten-year deal. The chairmen were not keen. With all kinds of technical developments, including digital television, coming up, they did not want to be locked in for such a long time.

After a sandwich lunch, Kelvin MacKenzie and David Montgomery were ushered into the room to present a joint Mirror Group and Carlton ITV bid. Kelvin was offering £650 million in cash over five years, the money coming from merchant banks and American backers, plus a 50:50 share in a new channel to be called Goal TV, which was to be broadcast on the Eutelsat satellite rather than on the Astra satellite used by Sky. The option of running Goal on the cable networks had been ruled out by the 1995 'sweetheart' deal between Sky and TCI, which prevented any competitor channel to Sky being put out on cable. Combinations of live games and highlights programmes would be shown on either ITV or Goal TV.[1]

The Mirror–Carlton presentation was hesitant and unconvincing. Really MacKenzie would have been more comfortable attacking Sky and the way Chisholm had stitched everybody up by creating a distribution monopoly. The supposed benefits of his own bid were mainly couched in terms of Sky's supposed disadvantages. The

Mirror Group and Carlton, for example, would share the profits from subscriptions – unlike Sky. They would have the promotional support of the *Mirror* – just as good as the *Sun*'s support for Sky. Goal TV would properly package the matches into a continuous football 'lifestyle' channel – unlike Sky. The *Mirror* had links into the cable world, presenting possibilities for local 'club channels' – which was not yet possible with Sky.[2]

Alan Sugar, owner of Tottenham Hotspur, savaged the presentation. He was batting for Sky, just as he had done during the 1992 negotiations,[3] and he attacked Michael Green, the multi-millionaire head of Carlton, on technical grounds. Sugar knew that Mirror-Carlton couldn't get on the Astra satellite because it was fully booked by Sky. Cable distribution was out because of the 'sweetheart' deal between Chisholm and TCI. That left them with Eutelsat. And Eutelsat was no good, Sugar reckoned. He was the expert, he claimed, having been Sky's main satellite-dish-maker for many years. This technical line of attack went straight over the top of the heads of most of those present, including MacKenzie. But Green was well and truly kebabbed and his advisers ended up squabbling with each other. Sugar looked pleased with himself. The message was loud and clear. The club chairmen had already got a ton of cash from Sky, and were about to get tons more. Why risk it all? Jam today . . . bird in the hand . . . better the devil you know . . . stay with Sky.

After a break for tea and fruitcake, the chairmen gathered to hear from Sam and his team. Sky's presentation was fronted by Chisholm himself. He was confident, and exchanged banter with Doug Ellis of Aston Villa. Ellis said he wanted a share of Sky's advertising revenue this time round, to which Chisholm replied, 'This is some partnership y'want, Doug, when you are taking everything from us and leavin' us with nothing. Don't be so greedy!' There was nervous laughter. Chisholm then introduced the head of Sky Sports to make the main pitch. Sky offered £670 million for the rights, on terms similar to the 1992 deal. David Dein of Arsenal questioned Chisholm: would they raise the subscription price to pay for it all? (They had done that after the 1992 deal.) Chisholm was noncommittal. Latter, Dein was the only one to abstain on the Sky offer.

When they had finished, the Sky team briskly snapped shut their briefcases and rushed off again in a professional and mildly intimidating way. 'That's the way we liked it – arriving at the last minute, and leaving straight after-ward. That's Sky – you don't know what they are up to, you don't know what they are thinking,' Chisholm told the journalist Mathew Horsman.[4]

MacKenzie, in contrast, had hung about in the lobby after his pitch, chatting to Michael Green and jawing on to journalists, complaining about Sky's 'monopolistic prac-tices'. The debate on the merits of the rival bids, taking place meanwhile back in the conference room, was brief: only a couple of hours, all told. The Premier League stayed with Sky, which had always been a good bet since the Sky–TCI deal had killed off serious bid attempts from the cable industry. Sky was safe for another four years, though football at these prices was not likely to yield the super-profits enjoyed after 1992. Sky was to end up paying almost four times as much. The clubs were promised as much as £10 million each a year, which they promptly blew, in many cases, by importing ancient Italian foot-ballers on massive wages.[5]

MacKenzie, never a good loser, walked away mourn-fully. He told journalists, 'It's tough trying to compete against a monopoly. In the end it was money that decided it.' He began to mutter about the Premier League, saying it was a cartel that would one day be broken up, allowing individual clubs to sell their rights to anyone they liked, at last allowing cable into the game with its superior ability to customise local programming.[6]

The Mirror Group's bid was the fruit of a year's work by MacKenzie, his attempt to resurrect the ghost of the *Mirror*-backed SportsWire/Cable Sports Network which had been killed off by the deal between Sky and the two leading cable companies, TCI and Nynex. Had the Mirror–Carlton bid been successful, the value of Sky Sports to TCI would have declined substantially and, aided by the customary armies of lawyers on both sides, TCI and Nynex might have been able to wriggle out of the undertaking not to carry rival sports channels to Sky. At any rate, it would be hard to see how a Mirror TV channel with exclusive rights to show Premier League football could have stayed banned from the nation's screens for very long. It had been worth a try. Michael Green had phoned Fred Vierra, the deputy head of TCI in the US, before putting in his bid. Would TCI carry the Mirror–Carlton Goal channel if they beat Sky to the screening rights? Vierra's reply was categorical: 'Of course I would.' But TCI were not prepared to risk their contracts to distribute Sky in the UK by supporting the Mirror–Carlton bid, nor were they willing to put in money up front or join in a bidding war.[7]

Although the Mirror–Carlton bid failed, it had been extremely useful to TCI. The Mirror Group was not party to their deal with Sky over carriage of Sky Sports and so this was a way in which the cable industry could mount a 'backdoor' attack on Sky without getting involved in a bidding war. The effect of the Mirror–Carlton bid was to push up the price Sky had to pay, reducing their margins and, therefore, scaling down the vast profits Sky was making on the Premier League. David Dein's point in the negotiations was an important one: Sky could not pass on all the extra costs to subscribers, including subscribers via cable (since the price of getting Sky Sports via cable or via dish was fixed by the deal). In future, Sky would need every penny it could get, and that would make it, for the first time, really dependent on the income it got from cable subscriptions.

It was little wonder that the cable companies liked MacKenzie so much.[8] Overall, his activities both at Sky and then with Carlton–Mirror football bid greatly strengthened their hand against Sky, and the return has been worth hundreds of millions.

After all the fuss, without a dedicated football-led sports channel on cable, it did not much matter what the Mirror Group put out over the cable system under the heading of L!ve TV. As a business proposition it was not so much a TV channel, more a method of paying the *Mirror* to hype cable subscriptions and steadily turn itself into a cable-TV programme guide. But without cable-exclusive sports and movie channels, there was nothing much to hype. After the collapse of the Mirror–Carlton bid for the Premier League all that remained was Monty's original plan for a chain of city TV stations. And so, without any great enthusiasm, MacKenzie turned his attention back to L!ve's local affiliates.

Chapter Thirty-one

In which a U-Turn is performed and Monty's plan for City TV is revived, local L!ve stations become Top Priority, Kelvin admits that Nobody with the choice would pay to watch L!ve TV and Monty berates the Cable Operators and tells them they are Doomed . . .

On 12 June 1996, L!ve TV celebrated one year on air with a series of predictable Newsy Bunny stunts. By then it was available in 1.4 million 'cable homes'. The deal (£3 per year per subscriber) with the cable companies gave the channel an income of about £4 million, but the cost of producing the channel was running at around £14 million, even after dramatic cost-cutting. L!ve TV was losing £10 million a year. Cable subscriptions would have to reach about 5 million before it started to break even.

Subscriptions were creeping up slowly, but this was almost entirely due to the fact that the country was not yet entirely cabled up, and each month more homes came onstream. Every time another street was dug up, a few new subscribers were added to the list. But the proportion of people who bought cable when it was offered to them was stuck at around 20 per cent, which was catastrophically low.[1] And of this heroic 20 per cent, market analysts such as Zenith discovered, the vast majority were hooking up because they wanted a cheaper telephone connection. Others were being 'sold' on subscriptions to Sky's sports and movie channels. The only other reason to buy cable was to receive porn, which was not easily or conveniently available elsewhere.

Since demand was driven mainly by people's wish for

cheap phone lines and porn, it would be a long slog before cable subscriptions reached the 5 million L!ve needed to stem its losses – let alone start making profits. Even if the figure was reached, it would take years of operating profit before the losses made in the early years could be paid off.[2]

The only bright spot was the fact that L!ve TV was managing an audience share of 1 per cent in cable homes, which meant that by cable standards its 'reach' and 'recognition' figures were good – doubtless the result of MacKenzie's many Cunning Stunts. But recognition did not earn the Mirror Group a single extra penny. All it did was create a fuss around cable TV in general, which was great for the cable operators, in a way: their marketing was so dire that a lot of the punters did not even know cable existed. But L!ve TV on its own could do nothing to move the penetration take-up rate up from about 20 per cent towards the 40 per cent originally foreseen in the L!ve TV business plan.

But from the cable companies' point of view L!ve TV's image was a double-edged sword. For every person who became aware of, or interested in, cable TV as a result of hearing about *Topless Darts* and the like, there might be ten (or ten thousand) turned off by it. There was another problem. Cable was starting to get a very down-market image around the edges.[3] Porn subscriptions were booming. There was a distinct danger that, by word of mouth, the idea would spread that cable was a way of getting porn videos delivered without having to locate the seedier sort of video hire shop. L!ve TV did nothing to alter this impression.

There was another obvious problem with Kelvin's Cunning Stunts strategy. In many cases the Stunts were in practice *only* advertising gimmicks. The programmes behind the Stunts were made almost as an afterthought or were unwatchable or became boring after a few minutes. News Bunny or a Norwegian weather girl might be hugely amusing the first time you saw it but, once you had enjoyed the joke, that was it. Most of the funny or mildly erotic material that went out on the channel in any given 24-hour period could easily be compressed into a half-hour comedy show with modest ITV-type audience appeal. Put the other way round, L!ve was like a single episode of a cross between the *Benny Hill Show* and *Monty Python* with the jokes extruded out over a whole week. The central irony was that L!ve TV only worked – on any level – so long as nobody watched it.

Apart from the uneven spread of cable subscriptions, the problem of 'churn' worried the operators. Of the small numbers of people who were taking out subscriptions, as many as half in some franchise areas were failing to renew their subscriptions for the second year: exactly what happens with marketing campaigns which, like L!ve TV's, are based on the 'sell the sizzle' principle.

Some of the cable operators started looking for a way out. They did not see why they should pay a sort of £3 poll tax to the Mirror Group every time they happened to sell a telephone line or a subscription to Sky Sport. One operator in particular, CableTel, wanted to renegotiate the Mirror Group's 'carriage contract' so that it would only pay the £3 fee if a customer asked for cable TV, as opposed to a phone. They wanted the right to sell phone connections only, with a free 'promotional package' of cable TV channels. If the customer liked the promotional material and bought any of the channels, all the basic 'tier' of channels would be supplied (including L!ve TV) and the Mirror Group would get its money. But if the customer bought only the phone line and promotional package, the Mirror Group would get nothing. CableTel tried to put all this positively to L!ve, saying that the phone-only deal would 'punch' the cable into people's homes, after which they were much more likely to buy television channels, at which point the Mirror Group would be paid. In this way, the cable people said, the Mirror stood to make much more money, more quickly in the 'medium term'.[4]

MacKenzie was mortified by the proposal, and told the Mirror board that 'we declined their kind offer for us to cut our own throats'. If L!ve was sold *à la carte*, it would hit the station 'enormously badly', he said, because L!ve 'did not look attractive to viewers'. In public Monty was saying that he was proud of the way L!ve TV had extended 'consumer choice'.[5] In private the board of Mirror TV was told the truth. If the public really did have the 'choice', precisely nobody would buy L!ve TV.

The Mirror Group had its own priority: how to stem L!ve TV's mounting losses. One side of the equation had already been addressed: Kelvin had cut costs to the bone, staffing the place with media-studies students and slashing the budget. Only one item remained sacrosanct: his own salary, which already accounted for a grotesque and growing proportion of the channel's total expenditure.[6]

The only possible way forward after the failure to get hold of Premier League football was to concentrate fresh energies on Monty's original idea of a city TV network. This rested on the creation of local affiliates (sometimes called 'opt-outs') in the hope of luring some cheap advertising away from the local newspapers and free-sheets. But here too the extremely slow rate of cable growth and low levels of penetration were a real problem. In a city the size Glasgow (where L!ve planned a local affiliate), there were about 15,000 cable subscribers in 1995. A viewing figure of 1 per cent (which was reckoned to be very good going indeed) gave you an audience of 150 people. How much could you charge an advertiser to reach 150 people tuning in between very cheaply produced local 'news items' about cats stuck up trees and national 'features' such as News Bunny?

For MacKenzie, the renewal of interest in local versions of L!ve involved an abrupt U-turn. When Channel One was launched in London in November 1994, both in public and in private he had vigorously denounced it and the whole idea of news-based City TV as a waste of time, in a way that both astonished people and made them wonder why on earth, then, Monty had hired him. These attacks on Channel One were not just the usual wind-up against a competitor, but part of a carefully thought-out and considered position.

MacKenzie showed no interest at all in the local opt-outs, or in doing news in competition with Channel One: 'that's not our game,' he had told Julian Aston, head of Channel One. He derided the idea that a city TV station could work, saying that 'a house fire in Peckham is of no interest to people in Ealing', and that 'in fact they would be secretly pleased'. His considered view made a lot of sense, as Channel One had found to its cost. Local news could only work on a scale so small (replicating a local newspaper which circulated in a single borough) that it would never be economic, and would never happen. MacKenzie had emphasised to Aston that he wanted L!ve to be a national sports and entertainment service 'like Sky' and ridiculed Richard Horwood's and Monty's city TV idea.

The way in which MacKenzie had been able to ignore Monty's strategic plans and, in effect, rip up five years of careful preparatory work for city TV struck many as odd. Likewise his general demeanour towards Monty struck many as a reversal of the formal power relationship. He behaved much more like a fellow chief executive (with a salary to match), or even like Monty's boss, than like a subordinate, and always appeared able to overrule Monty at will. Why Monty had backed MacKenzie's 'topless darts' vision of L!ve TV against Janet's 'nightclubbing' approach, when the later had created (in a somewhat different way) just as much 'recognition' for the channel, was a 'mystery' to all the senior people in the Janet camp . Their explanations were in the main psychological. MacKenzie had charisma and was tougher than Monty, who was a bit of a wimp, was the general impression. But still others, who had met Monty on the social circuit, had seen him roll his eyes and look to the heavens in deep embarrassment when asked about what MacKenzie was up to. The fact was that MacKenzie was able to get his way with Monty on any important matter of policy and, basically, do whatever he wanted and thought best. The same was true of the *Mirror* itself where, according to several people we spoke to, Kelvin was 'consulted' over any important decision made by Piers Morgan, the paper's titular editor. Did Kelvin achieve all this by sheer force of personality? It was all very odd.

Now, suddenly, the local opt-outs were Top Priority. Monty and MacKenzie ploughed on, filling the vacuum left by the collapse of the Premier League bid by announcing, two weeks after the Coombe Abbey débâcle, a plan to launch up to twenty affiliates by 1998. Each station was to have around thirty staff to cover all functions including ad sales and administration. They would run a 24-hours-a-day operation, filling up part of each hour with local material to supplement the programming being pumped out from MacKenzie's 'mother ship' at Canary Wharf.

The first ones on air were Birmingham, Liverpool and Westminster in November and December 1995, followed by Glasgow, Edinburgh, Manchester, Newcastle,

Nottingham, Leeds and Thames Valley. In contrast to Kelvin's grandiose statements when he joined the Mirror Group, he was now claiming more modestly, 'All we are is an electronic form of local media. It is not rocket science.'[7]

Birmingham L!ve was launched on schedule in November 1995, jointly operated with Midland Independent Newspapers, which the Mirror Group had bought into mainly with the launch of a local TV station in mind. At this point there were about 80,000 cable subscribers in Birmingham, so the opt-out's nominal share of L!ve's national income was about £240,000 a year plus whatever it could earn in terms of advertising revenue, which, it was recognised, would be virtually nothing to begin with. Operating costs were very low, about £1 million a year, but the station was still likely to make losses for many years to come.

Whereas national L!ve TV worked on a budget of around £2000 a hour, the local opt-outs had to be made even more cheaply. The production budget for Birmingham L!ve worked out at about £300 an hour, for that part of each hour the channel was on air. This was maybe *one-hundredth* of the cost of making 'old-fashioned' local television news and, as the Birmingham L!ve chief Dan Barton boasted (like MacKenzie and Nick Ferrari, Barton was a graduate of the Dan Ferrari news agency and had the customary School of Hard Knocks approach to life) was far less than even the cost of local radio.

Birmingham L!ve, Barton said, would be going in for 'people news' in the sense of 'putting mum, dad and the kids on television.' He added, 'We will be looking for who makes the best cup of tea in Birmingham,' but, given the production budget, those chosen for this accolade would probably have to provide their own teabags. 'Birmingham

L!ve will be "people television",' Barton emphasised. 'It is easy viewing TV. Our slogan will be "Birmingham L!ve: Good News for Birmingham".' The results were predictably dire.[8]

The Birmingham studio was plagued with the same sort of technical production problems which had dogged the launch of national L!ve TV, and they stemmed from the same source: the efforts to use untried electronic equipment operated, in the main, by inexperienced and low-paid people, in an attempt to avoid hiring anybody who could command a decent salary. Birmingham (and the other opt-outs) soon suffered from an 'out of sight, out of mind' problem which was the downside of MacKenzie's famously hands-on approach to editing. There was no talk-back loop from the affiliates and so MacKenzie was unaware what was happening (apart from what he learnt in a general way when Nick Ferrari or others were sent on 'bollocking' raids). The terrorised staff in Canary Wharf concentrated on keeping MacKenzie happy, and if that meant missing an advertising break by a minute or two, so be it. As long as MacKenzie did not notice, that was OK. The result at the end of the line was that Birmingham L!ve adverts, the source of revenue in due course for the whole network according to plan, would be wrecked, or would crash into the middle of a programme or overrun a Canary Wharf news bulletin, making the whole thing look like Amateur Night.

Liverpool L!ve launched a month after Birmingham, but little had apparently been learned. The station launch was based around a rights deal to show Liverpool FC playing against FC Sion in a European match which coincided with the launch day. This would have been a good idea had it not been for the fact that the match was larded up, on Canary Wharf's orders, with promotional material for

Topless Darts and other sex material, drawing a barrage of complaints and bad publicity from angry dads watching the match with their kids.

In Liverpool there was the additional problem that MacKenzie was a major liability. As architect of the *Sun*'s coverage of the 1989 Hillsborough disaster (he had virtually blamed the victims for their own deaths and injuries and had carried false reports that Liverpool fans had attempted to rob the corpses), he was a major hate-figure in the city and was in some danger of being attacked if he turned up there. Any association in the public mind between Liverpool L!ve and MacKenzie (or indeed the *Sun*) would be fatal.

When MacKenzie eventually visited the Liverpool station, he had to be secretly whisked into the studio, which was only 200 yards from the *Liverpool Echo*, where he was deeply hated. (When, for a while after Hillsborough, it became impossible for *Sun* reporters to work in Liverpool, Kelvin had told them to pretend to be working for the *Echo*. This ruse had been rumbled, making life difficult for the local hacks, who, even a decade later, could still face unpleasantness as they went out on a mundane job, only to find everyone uncooperative and accusing them of being *Sun* journalists.) To everyone's horror, MacKenzie suggested that they all pop down to the local pub for a pint. This they did, with great trepidation. MacKenzie was recognised, but the anticipated lynching did not take place and he left the pub and the city unmolested.

MacKenzie's main interest in Liverpool seemed to be the fact that Channel One, his main rival, also had an affiliate there, so he could organise a passable imitation of a newspaper circulation war. Latching on to some good reach and recognition figures, he hired one of the rejected Norwegian weathergirl glamourpusses to stand outside Channel One's Liverpool offices wearing a placard saying, 'L!ve TV – three times more viewers than Channel One', and shouting slogans in her native tongue. The fact that this meant L!ve had about 300 viewers against Channel One's total of 100 only went to show that there are lies, damn lies and statistics.

Liverpool L!ve was contracted to provide thirty minutes of local news in the hour, which was achieved by means of doing a fifteen-minute bulletin and showing it twice, thus achieving the promised 'half-hour' before crashing in and out of the national output in the established cack-handed, home-video L!ve TV house style. The quality of the news-gathering was very poor and editorial judgement appeared to be lacking. This resulted in, for example, a decision to run an item about a pet dog being put to death at 8.15 in the morning, in the middle of the pre-school kiddievision slot: *Mummy, what are they doing to that doggy?*

Besides this, the normal chaos reigned. The station had four or five chiefs in the first few months, the result of unannounced commando-style 'sacking raids' from London. Some of the L!verpool people thought Bill Ridley was barking mad, but quite nice. Nick Ferrari was regarded as a straightforward hatchetman, and was intensely disliked by many. The whole style of the station was changed several times over. One week it was all meant to be serious-ish, hard-ish, local-ish news, the next all entertainment-ish, listings-ish, comedy-ish and then back again it swung to hard news. The name was changed from Liverpool L!ve to L!verpool News 18 and back again. There was a big turnover of technical staff, who were hired and fired more or less willy-nilly.

There were many other minor catastrophes leading up to the failure to get a report on the postponement of the

Live TV

1997 Grand National because of an IRA bomb threat, one of the biggest stories to come out of Liverpool for years. The staff blamed it on the fact that all the locks in the office had been changed the day before the race and they could not get in. There was a 'bollocking and sacking raid' from London anyway.

Westminster L!ve, launched slightly later than Birmingham and Liverpool, was a different story. To begin with it was something of a success, editorially at least. Whereas Birmingham and Liverpool were joint ventures with local newspaper groups, Westminster was a wholly owned subsidiary of Mirror Television. Richard Horwood had done the deal with the local cable franchise, held by BT, himself and continued to run it as a semi-autonomous operation.[9]

Westminster L!ve was run by a two fairly experienced producers who had been keen to get away from the madness of Canary Wharf and run their own show. They used a single OB unit and hired two or three directors. After the station's initial success, the news bulletins were extended to provide a half-hour central London entertainments listings service called *West End L!ve*, which was also much admired. At first MacKenzie and Ferrari seemed content to stay at arm's length and let Horwood get on with it, apart from occasional visits by MacKenzie during which he would interfere by sub-editing the local news scripts, changing them from scripts suitable for reading against pictures into perfect tabloidese, which would have been great if they had been producing a newspaper. They were not.

Disagreements between the Westminster team and Canary Wharf started when Ferrari promoted a good-lookin' but very inexperienced young woman to read the national news. The idea was to bring Westminster L!ve into

424

line with the house-style of glamourised presenters. But she was regarded as hopeless and seemed incapable of reading a script without stumbling at least one or twice in every item. (It was hilarious in a way, and some wondered if MacKenzie had secretly revived his plan to hire stuttering news readers.) The Westminster L!ve people started running a sweepstake on the number of errors she would make in a bulletin.

People who worked on the national newsdesk at Canary Wharf tell the same story from the other side of the camera. The woman simply could not read from a script, and she knew it. In addition to stumbling over words she would flush bright red and, at least once, was so embarrassed that she ended up close to tears.[10] After a while the Westminster team got permission from Horwood to read the national news themselves, having arranged with the Canary Wharf newsdesk to fax over the scripts. The results were much better but Ferrari exploded when he found out.

He counter-attacked not only by insisting that Westminster ran the national news read by his choice of presenter, but by denouncing the woman who read the local Westminster news as fat and ugly. She was told to go on a diet, even though she was not fat. Eventually, in what she saw as a form of punishment, the slimmish but 'non-bimbo' Westminster newsreader was transferred to work on an 'interactive slimming' programme called *Weigh to Go*, produced at Canary Wharf. Her place was taken by yet another low-paid but good-lookin' female L!ve TV recruit. Shortly afterwards the other experienced news producer was also transferred back to Canary Wharf, to experience various humiliations and bollockings before leaving. The original Westminster L!ve team took the view that their station had been crushed because it was reasonably good (for what it was), and therefore reflected well on Horwood and showed up Nick and Kelvin to some extent. The new version of Westminster L!ve was soon engulfed in the normal chaos.

The other local affiliates were set up in due course. Glasgow suffered from the problem of having only 15,000 cable subscribers (or a maximum of 180 viewers at full tilt). But MacKenzie was particularly taken with Jockvision, trying to negotiate deals with the Rangers and Celtic football clubs for a football 'lifestyle' channel. The Mirror Group had taken a highly profitable 20 per cent holding in the local ITV franchise and had all sorts of plans in Scotland, where, importantly, the *Mirror*'s sister paper, the *Daily Record* outsold the *Sun* and was therefore much courted as a promotional partner in TV ventures. 'Funnily enough,' Kelvin told the papers, 'of all of local L!ve stations, I think that Glasgow will be the most successful because people in Glasgow are interested in Glasgow and, quite frankly, not much else. And what they're not interested in is a load of bloody Herberts wearing expensive suits in the South.' Glasgow was joined by Edinburgh L!ve, scheduled to go on air in January 1997, and a studio was built in the Hibernian football stadium. Edinburgh was one of the better prospects.

Negotiations aimed at setting up Manchester L!ve were stalled by the fact that the local cable operator, Nynex, would not join in the venture unless the *Manchester Evening News* was roped in and this was to prove difficult.[11]

In these somewhat desperate circumstances Monty came up with a madcap plan to place the Mirror Group at the centre of yet another national cable programming group to take the place of the now defunct CPP-1 consortium and start a renewed attack on Sky. In October 1996 he addressed a cable operators' conference on the subject. 'I don't want to keep you long *becoize*,' he said, '*fronklee* [frankly], I don't think you, the British cable operators, have that much time left.' He castigated them for bowing down before Murdoch and allowing Chisholm to get away with his divide-and-rule strategy, especially over the Premier League deal.

'*Thos yor* [this year] cable had the chance to prove it had real muscle, by rolling in behind Carlton and the *Mirror* to secure control of Premiership football. But again the big gorilla in the Sky grabbed the prize.' He added, 'Sky and its master have built an empire in part through bullying, bluff and bluster, the extent of which has terrorised and subordinated cable.' Murdoch had turned the British cable industry into a colonised distribution system for his programming, Monty said. When he didn't need them any more – when he had the 'Death Star' digital satellite – he would kill them off.

Monty's solution was a new 'umbrella' company for cable. It would borrow $1 billion, to create and brand cable-exclusive channels, including sports and movie channels. The new umbrella company would invest in the cable companies in order to get its money back. The choice was simple, Monty said: 'Sign up to this new force and make the most of the billions already sunk into British cable, or remain in the doldrums to eventually see your investment swept away by the sudden and savage Osterley [Sky's headquarters] winds. For a measly billion dollars or so of some new investors' money, you can finally be *Moisters orv yoirownunivoirse* [Masters of Your Own Universe].'

The mention of Sky digital satellite was important. The prospect of hundreds of new potential satellite channels was bound to open up new opportunities for Mirror Television, since its problem had always been distribution more than anything else. The approach of digital had caused a flurry of activity as media organisations of all sorts, not least the BBC, looked for new partners with which to develop channel ideas. But the Mirror Group, which had been courted avidly by the cable companies before MacKenzie arrived in 1994, was to remain on the sidelines.

Monty was cold-shouldered, and his plan for an 'umbrella' company was ignored. Instead, three major cable companies, Videotron, Bell CableMedia and Nynex, merged with the Mercury phone company to form Cable & Wireless, leaving the Mirror Group out in the cold. The group did its own marketing campaign, spending huge sums on television and newspaper advertising. The promotional support of the *Mirror* was already in the bag because of L!ve TV.

When the new wave of digital franchises was announced, Richard Horwood wrote a report on how the Mirror Group might get involved, but MacKenzie, managing director of Mirror Television, showed little interest. A couple of weeks later the various media groups put in their bids for the new franchises, but it quickly became obvious that the other media groups had teamed up and deliberately ignored the *Mirror*. The group was now treated rather like a leper by the rest of the industry.

Postscript

In which Kelvin leaves L!ve TV, patches things up with Rupert and, having failed to become first King of Sky and then King of Cable, settles for being Arch-Duke of Radio, while Monty's Grand Strategy comes to nothing and Janet sets off on a very long walk.

The first edition of this book was finished in November 1997, by which time the saga of L!ve TV as a business story was well and truly over. It had, in effect, ended in May 1995 when the cable companies had done their 'sweetheart' deal with Sky. The minute the big cable companies had obtained Sky's Sports and Movie channels at wholesale prices they were happy with, L!ve (conceived as the 'shop window' for a series of 'cable exclusive 'channels) became an irrelevance and, frankly, a bit of an embarrassment.

L!ve's income was tied to the number of cable subscribers in the country. In the heady days of 1994, when Janet and Kelvin had been attracted to work for Mirror Television, it seemed that the Americans were serious about attacking Sky head on. If all had gone to plan, the Mirror and L!ve would have been swept along on a highly profitable surge of cable subscriptions as the punters dumped their dishes and switched to cable to watch the all-important exclusive live Premier League football. But Sky kept the football and the number of cable subscribers crept up very slowly. This was not too bad for the cable companies, who now concentrated on getting more money out of each subscriber, rather than basing their plans (as the Mirror had done) on a big increase in the total number of customers. At the same time they were biding their time and waiting for the next battle with Murdoch – over the internet. Round one of the war to 'punch' a pay-TV or satellite link into peoples' homes had been fought with TV channels as the 'drivers'. Round two, with even more billions at stake, would be fought with internet connections, home shopping, 'e-commerce', video and video-games on demand . . . This time the cable companies would have the whip hand.

The sweetheart deal had thus killed off the original L!ve TV project. The first casualty had been Janet Street-Porter. She had been a great signing for the sort of shop window channel that Monty had planned. But once L!ve had been locked into a much more modest future, she was surplus to requirements and quickly left to resume a career as a TV presenter and personality. She was still complaining that the media (and now the authors of this book) were wrongly trying to make her out to be a bit of a weirdo. Despite this, one of her first acts after leaving L!ve TV was to voluntarily appear in a spoof 'Swedish porn movie' as part of a guest appearance on the Lilly Savage Show. The viewing millions were treated to the sight of a 'teenage' Janet Street-Porter pretending to have sex with a donkey. She did the rounds of chat-shows and panel games and even tried her hand alternately presenting a late night heavyweight-ish political discussion show on the (previously loathsome) BBC. Eventually she settled into the groove of making programmes about her hobby of long-distance walking, limbering up with a meander around England, stopping off to visit various intrestin' people and places, before departing for more walking adventures in fascinating New Zealand. Janet's admirers in the business were pleased that things were working out relatively well for her. She was again playing to her strengths, as a quirky but undeniably attention-grabbin' on-screen presence, who also tossed programme ideas into the system. She went on the radio to say that she had no intention of running a TV channel ever again. Several of the tellybrats, meanwhile, went on to have meteoric careers as presenters. One of L!ve TV's proudest and most reasonable boasts was that, while some of it was pretty awful in itself, it did function as a springboard for young talent.

After Janet's departure L!ve TV had continued more or less as a zombie channel, lacking purpose and veering about according to whim and ever tighter budgetary constraints. MacKenzie cut the costs to try and fit the channel's new and more modest future. There was a reversion to Monty's original plan for City TV, but everything was confounded by the crushingly slow rate of growth of cable subscriptions. MacKenzie amused himself with the channel for a while and then he was off as well. In the spring of 1998 he handed over the running of L!veTV to Mark Cullen and moved up in the Mirror Group hierarchy becoming chief executive and, in effect, editorial director of the *Mirror* newspaper. There was only one major piece of unfinished business as far as L!ve TV was concerned: the constant attempts by some of the cable companies to wriggle out of paying the 25p per month per subscriber fee to the Mirror Group for the supply of L!ve TV.

After getting their fingers burned in the run-in with Sky over exclusive programming, several of the smaller UK cable operators wanted to concentrate on selling the cable system as a phone line. The fact was that many of the operators were able to offer phone services more cheaply than BT and so had a massive advantage. The problem was that the combined cost of subscribing to the phone together with the basic package of cable TV channels was much more expensive than simply having a BT phone line. The obvious answer, for some, was to dump the cable TV channels and just sell the phone lines. Or, just sell the phone lines and then offer channel subscriptions (e.g. Sky Sport) one by one, to people who wanted them.

By the time of MacKenzie's elevation to deputy chief executive, one of the cable operators, CableTel, had been trying to offer customers a cheap phone connection and an *à la carte* choice of cable channels for more than a year. As MacKenzie had himself told the board of Mirror Television, if consumers were given the choice in this way, very few would decide to take L!ve TV. If CableTel got away with 'unbundling' (as it was known in industry jargon) L!ve would loose its drip-feed from the cable system and its income would drop, basically, to zero over night. MacKenzie dragged CableTel through the courts and won an injunction, forcing them to provide all its customers with L!ve TV (whether they liked it or not) and, more importantly, continue to pay the Mirror 25p per month every time they signed up a new customer.

But then in May 1998 the Independent Television Commission announced that it was investigating 'bundling' with a view to banning the practice on the grounds that it was not in the consumer's interests. MacKenzie called on MPs to prevent the move, saying that unless L!ve was included on the 'basic tier' of channels supplied with every cable connection, the Mirror Group would have 'no choice but to close the station' losing 200 jobs. In the event, the ITC did ban bundling but made a specific exception for L!ve TV. The channel's charmed and strangely un-dead existence was thus guaranteed – for the time being.

After the narrow escape of the ITC bundling decision, there was even a moment of optimism at L!ve, when the ITC said it was about to relax its regulations on cable TV 'advertorial', the practice of advertisers paying for the

production of programmes which, with varying degrees
of subtlety, were passed off as ordinary content.
Advertorial was already widespread in the world of
consumer magazines and local newspapers, where
anything from the opening of a new shopping mall, to
fashion, food, cars, computers and even the human rights
and economic records of places like Malaysia, were advertised in the form of 'editorial' spreads. Now the green light
was given for cable TV to run the same sort of thing. The
station itself talked of lengthy co-productions with DIY
stores and supermarkets. Lengthy 'advertorial' productions for L!ve TV would enable the Mirror Group to get
paid, in effect, three times over. The advertorial hours
would cost nothing to make: the bottom line was the video
loops already run by DIY stores for the delectation of bored
punters queueing at the checkout. L!ve would be paid for
running this stuff and the cable operators would pay the
Mirror Group to supply it, via the 25p mandatory subscriptions. Of course very few people were likely to watch it.
But, financially speaking, from the Mirror Group's point
of view, that hardly mattered.

Re-thinking L!ve as a non-stop 'advertorial' channel, the
electronic equivalent of junk mail, might be one way for
the channel to go into the future and the Mirror embraced
the idea with gusto – just as L!ve TV had, frankly, enthusiastically embraced every retrograde step in television
since its inception. The fact that, less than two years earlier,
L!ve had been threatened by the ITC for fairly mild
episodes of 'product placement' and 'undue prominence',
and had been warned over the fact that a week's
programmes had been sponsored by a chocolate bar,
merely showed how quickly things were moving in the
world of television. It was the same with L!ve sex content.
The ITC had always been more relaxed about this. By the

time of Monty's departure L!ve was running soft-porn in the evening more or less non-stop. But by 1999 this attracted little comment since Channel Five (having discovered, like L!ve, that if you don't have many decent Hollywood movies or much live football, soft porn was the only way to go) was running a lot of sex as well, with the others basically following suit in order to compete.

MacKenzie's defence of 'bundling' in the cable business was his final piece of work for L!ve TV and the Mirror Group. In the summer of 1998 he left the group to take over at Talk Radio, the national FM speech-only station, which was bought out with the financial backing of Rupert Murdoch. After his original move from the *Sun* to Sky, and then from Sky to the *Mirror*, this was MacKenzie's third 'bombshell' move in just a few years. But really there was no mystery. MacKenzie had worked out that possession of rights to broadcast 'premium' or 'hot' sport combined with electronic, broadcast media was a licence to print money. He had seen it happen first hand at Sky. When it became clear that he could not become top dog at Sky he moved over to become King of Cable. That had not worked out and so he had settled for radio. The fact was that the commercial radio business was on the up in the late '90s, drawing some advertising away from the fragmenting worlds of mass-market television, newspapers and magazines. But the most successful channel was not commercial. It was the BBC's Radio Five, which had grown a mass audience from nothing on the back of its exclusive radio rights to the Premier League. The BBC had signed up the Premier League until 2002, paying over £10 million for the deal. MacKenzie would have to wait for a while, but a serious bid for the rights, backed by Murdoch's millions, would transform Talk Radio overnight from a small, minority channel to a major player.

In the meantime MacKenzie amused himself with the radio station, bringing in old pals from L!ve, including both Ferrari and Uncle Bill Ridley. The Cunning Stunts machine was duly cranked up. Adverts for Talk were produced showing a thick-rimmed pair of glasses perched on a naked female breast, further decorated with a greasy hair-piece and made up to look remarkably like MacKenzie's old foe, David Mellor. The former Minister of Fun was now presenting a phone-in on Radio Five, Talk's direct rival, and the general idea was that Talk's rival phone-in was much better because Mellor was 'a tit'. The ad had a run-out in a few small circulation magazines, generating the required outrage and column inches. As with L!ve, Talk Radio's 'recognition rating' was soon massively out-stripping its audience figures, to the extent that the channel landed an exclusive interview with Tony Blair and Gordon Brown after the 1999 budget. The MacKenzie marketing 'magic' was working like a charm.

MacKenzie's departure from the Mirror Group had coincided with boardroom changes which were, ultimately, to lead to David Montgomery's departure from Canary Wharf. Montgomery had been put in charge of the Mirror Group by the terrified bankers who formed the board after the massive debts of the Maxwell era were converted into shares. The board, led by Sir Robert Clark, had backed Monty's strategy of cutting costs to boost operating profits and, just as importantly, to bolster the Group's share price by moving into television. At first, from the board's point of view, he had done well enough, cutting all the group's operation to the bone. The papers were now very lightly staffed compared to rivals such as the *Daily Mail* which was on course to overtake the *Mirror* in the circulation stakes, making it the second best read paper in the country after the *Sun*.

Live TV

After the first deep cut-backs in the mid-90s Monty had come back looking for more. In 1997 he announced a plan to re-train all the group's journalists in a newly formed 'Academy of Excellence' (instantly nicknamed 'The Academy of Excrement'). The idea was to reduce staff levels by abolishing traditional distinctions between sub-editors (the technical specialists who write the headlines and actually put the pages together), reporters and other writers. In other words, in future Mirror Group reporters and feature writers would have to sub-edit and layout their own pages, possibly taking the pictures as well, in the manner of a school magazine. In the end, the plan did not have much impact, other than to emphasise Monty's increasing desperation. Drastic cost-cutting had been an effective financial strategy. But it was a trick which could only be performed once.

The other prong of Monty's strategy, to expand out of trouble, had come to nothing. L!ve TV was stillborn, his Grand Alliance with the cable giants had ended in acrimony and the Mirror had been frozen out of the next leap forward into digital television. Likewise the purchase of the *Independent*, which was intended to give the Mirror Group a foothold in the broadsheet market, had not worked out well (although, for various reasons, most city analysts thought it would have a brighter future than that facing the tabloids). Cost-cutting at the *Independent* had been so savage that the paper was forced to more or less give up the fight to cover the news as effectively as the other broadsheets and, for a while, experimented with the idea of being a sort of upmarket daily magazine. The circulation started to slide badly; no more cuts were possible and so Monty decided to sell it off, thus releasing money to re-launch the old Mirror-owned daily horse-racing tip-sheet the *Sporting Life* as the country's first daily sports newspaper. In the end the *Sporting Life* re-launch became another fiasco. The re-launch was cancelled at the last moment in typical Monty 'Mr Sneaky' style. The editor and sixty journalists, lured by Monty to Canary Wharf with talk of a bright future, suddenly found themselves out on the street before a single edition had been printed and distributed. Monty unfairly explained the turnabout by saying that the editor had been 'a crap journalist and a crap employee' and that the paper wasn't worth printing.

Still desperate for a way to expand, Monty had turned to local newspapers. He had made investments in regional papers in the Midlands and Northern Ireland then, in the spring of 1998 opened talks with two large local newspaper groups, Newsquest and Trinity International. The talks dragged on until the German media company, Axel Springer, made a potentially much more profitable takeover bid. The board, delighted by the prospect of at last getting their money back, encouraged the bid and were reportedly 'disappointed' when the Germans did not go ahead. Boardroom discontent with Monty's performance was growing.

In July 1998 Group chairman Sir Robert Clark retired. Monty had attempted to assume total control by succeeding Clark, but the board and larger shareholders had turned instead to Sir Victor Blank, a multi-millionaire banker and lawyer. A board member was quoted anonymously in *The Times* as saying: 'We didn't trust Montgomery to have absolute power. Victor is intelligent, wealthy and independent. He won't be bamboozled by David.'

After Blank's arrival the attempt to find a merger partner was replaced by the realisation that the Mirror Group was more likely to become a takeover target. The rest of the year was occupied with approaches and rumours of approaches

437

from larger media companies eager to swallow up the Mirror. Potential purchasers, including Regional Independent Newspapers, backed by the venture capital company Candover, and Trinity, who came back on the scene after the collapse of talks with Springer and the Germans, made it clear that they were only interested in the Mirror's national titles. Monty's stunted television empire, with what remained of L!ve TV and a stake in Scottish ITV, were seen as disposable; as was Monty himself.

In January 1999, after months of boardroom discontent, Monty was called to see Tony Dye, head of the Philips and Drew pension fund, one of the Mirror's biggest shareholders. Dye gave him an ultimatum: either he resigned at once or face a boardroom vote of confidence which he was more or less certain to lose. Monty left the Mirror to be relaced by the Group's finance director, John Allwood. There was much gloating and rejoicing among Monty's enemies, and many rounds of drinks bought by the army of ex-Mirror bods he had shown the door – until they were hit by a sobering thought. Many had made a career out of fleeing from papers where Monty had been the editor or an executive. He had gone to ground for the time being. But where was he going to turn up next?

Allwood made the most of the good PR, in the media press at least, following Monty's departure. This was the first good news about the Mirror for years, as far as many were concerned. 'David had his style,' Allwood told the press, 'and I have my style. We are friends, but we have different personalities.' He said he wanted a more 'consensual' style of management at the Mirror in future.

Allwood's first moves were to encourage a renewed takeover bid for the Mirror and put L!ve TV up for sale. The Mirror was looking for an offer of around £10 million for the channel, with Allwood admitting that the whole value of the operation was the ITC-protected contract with the cable suppliers which would give whoever bought the station the 25p per month subscription fee for every cable subscriber. This was now worth about £8 million a year; and was creeping up every year as the number of cable punters slowly grew. If the Mirror got £10 million for the channel, its overall loss on the venture would be around £50 million.

In the meantime L!ve had closed its local affiliates in Newcastle and Liverpool. The Edinburgh, Birmingham, Westminster and Manchester stations were still running – just. Mark Cullen, L!ve's new managing director, had declared at the time of the Newcastle and Liverpool closures that the future of Edinburgh L!ve was 'extremely bright'. Cullen added: 'Edinburgh is one of the most successful stations, we are absolutely committed to Edinburgh.' In the event it was closed a few months later. 'We are wasting our time trying to break into the television market in any meaningful way,' Allwood said.

Notes

PART I

1 Tim Street-Porter was the first of Janet's four official
  husbands (there have been additional 'common law'
  arrangements, making about six 'husbands' in total, at
  the last count). It has been noted by Janet's friends that
  her husbands have become steadily less posh over the
  years and tend to match whatever she is doing in her
  career at the time. So in 1965 she married Tim Street-
  Porter when she thought she might become an architect.
  Next she married Tony Elliot, owner of the 'alternative
  lifestyle' magazine *Time Out*, when she was an 'alternative lifestyle' journalist. When she was making her way
  in television she married the celebrated Canadian-
  Serbian television film-maker Frank Cvitanovich. Her
  association with Normski (a dancer and rap artiste) came
  when she was producing dance and rap music
  programmes for the BBC; and so on. More recently, when
  she waded into the tabloid world of Mirror Television,
  she married a working-class *Mirror*-reader-type bloke.
  Along the way she had a long-term relationship with
  Tony James, a minor 'post-punk' pop star, when she was
  making *Network-7*, a 'post-punk' television programme.

Friends also note that Janet gets married so frequently because 'well, basically, she just loves the drama of organising a wedding'.

2 Williams later became famous for writing an epic poem called *Whale Nation*, set to music made from whale noises. Janet appeared in a production of his play *The Immortalist* at the ICA in 1976.

3 According to a 1993 survey by academics at Kent University, the country's leading estuarial-speaker is Lord (Norman) Tebbit; others include Michael Caine, Danny Baker, Jonathan Ross, Ben Elton, Ken Livingstone, Nigel Kennedy and Paul Merton. The report's author noted that it was now 'almost impossible to host a TV chat show or make yourself understood on the right wing of the Tory Party without complete mastery of Estuarial'. The glottal stop was found to be widespread among university students, and the survey forecast that middle-class professions would be forced to accept large numbers of estuarial-speakers within ten years. Most surprisingly, the researchers found that aspects of estuarial speech had spread north, producing 'hybrid' speech as in 'Eeh bah gum, am goin' *dahn* yon *vidjo* shop to hire a *vidjo f'free pahnds*, reeet, inn-eye, ecky thump, *leeeve it ahrt,*' which was apparently the sort of thing that confused 'yoof television'-watchers in Barnsley were apt to say.

4 One close working associate told us, 'With Janet what you see is what you get,' and 'She is an easy target for lazy journalists, and she can be criticised in all sorts of ways. But the fact is that more than almost anyone else she is responsible for breaking the old middle-class Oxbridge monopoly in television. She brought in people who would never have stood a chance before.'

5 Since her youth she had been an avid collector of odd

artefacts, and by the mid-'80s she had so many that they had to be stored in packing cases in a warehouse. Her collections included Japanese masks, copper fish-shaped jelly moulds and, importantly, a collection of lovingly restored art deco and other *objects d'art*, absolutely *the Thing* in the post-Biba 1970s. As ever the boundary between Janet's personal and professional life was non-existent and in her early television manifestations at LWT she always insisted on an art deco look for programme graphics and the studio set.

6 Birt has remained an admirer of Janet, though over the years the relationship has had its ups and downs. They have similar backgrounds. Both were working-class, and at first regarded themselves as outsiders in the television world. Unlike Janet, Birt went to university. He didn't drop out, as Janet did, but like her he seemed in some ways too bright for the disciplines of academic life – he spent most of his time dabbling in the alternative arts scene and obtained only a third-class degree (in engineering). Janet later came to resent the fact that people like Birt, whom she regarded as her equal and whose background was like her own, were able to rise to the top of the industry. She was apt to put this down to sexism and the 'incorrect' image foisted on her by the press.

7 As usual, Janet was remembered both as a technical perfectionist and as someone who was moody and would throw tantrums to get her own way, especially in her dealings with senior management.

CHAPTER TWO

1 McLaren gloated over his Sex Pistols scam in a film called *The Great Rock and Roll Swindle*, in which he outlined his 'tips for success' in the modern media age. A McLaren

figure appears in the film pasting pictures of Myra Hindley over the tombstone of Karl Marx in Highgate cemetery as a publicity stunt, and then wearing a rubber bondage suit and croaking the following instructions (here slightly paraphrased) to a midget henchman:

• Never use professional media performers. Make sure [members of the group] hate each other.
• Concentrate on creating generation gaps. Terrorise, threaten and insult your own useless generation. Suddenly you become a novel idea and everyone wants to join in. You can become a story you can sell.
• Con the production companies into thinking they are missing out. Panic them into thinking they might miss out on the next fashion craze.
• Be as difficult and obstructive as possible with production companies, in order to fulfil their fantasy that they are getting the bargain of the century.
• Bullshit the production company as much as possible. Make them believe you are an anarchist. Push scandalous stories about yourself to the papers. Move on quickly to a new production company and repeat the trick.
• Cultivate hatred. This is your greatest asset. Force the public to hate you.

Throughout her television career, Janet Street-Porter appeared to be following this advice to some extent and with great success.

2 Until 1979 the ITV network broadcast output from Thames TV until 7 p.m. on Friday, when it handed over to LWT for the weekend. Thames had no interest in handing over a big audience to LWT, which was its direct competitor for advertising, so the station tended to surrender the crucial early-evening primetime slot to the

BBC. LWT successfully campaigned to take over the airwaves at 6 p.m. and the extra hour was filled by *The Six O'Clock Show* which had to be aggressively populist. The launch of the show had unleashed an internal battle between LWT's Light Entertainment and Current Affairs departments. Current Affairs won and took over the programme, putting Greg Dyke in charge. Dyke was keen to have Janet on board, teaming her up with yet another suave counterfoil, this time Michael Aspel. Essentially this was the same formula as the old LBC Callan vs. Janet mutual teasing act.

3 Baker's stint on *20th Century Box* was shortlived and he ended up on *The Six O'Clock Show*, where he was teamed up with ex-Page Three girl Samantha Fox. After that he was out of work for eighteen months before resurrecting his TV career with a proposed chat show for satellite co-hosted by two monkeys (ruled out by objections from animal-rights campaigners). He revived his flagging fortunes in the '90s by hosting a 'controversial' football phone-in on BBC radio and with a couple of fairly disastrous stints as a game-show and chat-show host on the BBC, as well as starring in a number of adverts for Daz washing powder. This was exactly the sort of fate a street-cred person like Janet feared and wanted to avoid.

4 In 1978 ITV had had a go at 'punk television' for teenagers with a show called *Check it Out*, made in Newcastle. The local Tyne-Tees ITV company handed over cameras and editing suites to selected groups of young people, who made their own mini-features which were slotted into a more conventional magazine show. The result had been a lot of feeble, out-of-focus camera work, messy editing and stuttering voice-overs: all genuine enough, but extremely earnest and boring. The verdict was that a programme held together by the theme

of 'youth' did not work, since young people were just as diverse as any other segment of the population. *Check it Out* was judged fairly unwatchable and pulled after a couple of short series.

5 Some members of minorities protested loudly protested if Minorities Unit programmes were not wholly sympathetic to their problems. During a series on gays, which advertised itself as being about all homosexuals, male and female, a large gang of furious lesbians picketed the LWT Tower with placards proclaiming, 'LESBIANS ARE PEOPLE TOO'. They resented being lumped together with gays, who were in many ways even more revolting than heterosexual men. Hewland invited them into the LWT canteen, where she was roundly denounced as a fag-hag and a hypocrite. They wanted their *own* programme, nothing to do with gay men. Then there was another argument. Lesbians who were into sadomasochism announced that they were a 'minority' in their own right, separate not only from gay men but also from other lesbians: they wanted their own show. Some were black. They violently objected to the obvious prejudice and absurdity of lumping them together with gay men (either black or white), or white lesbians (either sadistic or masochistic). And what was this 'lesbian' crap, anyway? Some wanted to be called 'dykes': anything else was an outrageous insult. What about disabled dykes? What was being done specifically for them? *Nothing*, that's what! At the same time as working with Jane Hewland on programmes for Channel Four, Janet devised and produced a series of short films for Channel Four under the series title *Paintbox* (1982) produced a series called *Bliss*, also for Channel Four (1983) and produced *Get Fresh*, the ITV Saturday-morning children's show (1984–5). All were generally well

thought of in the industry.

6 LWT had already experimented with a long 'channel-within-a-channel' programme, broadcast overnight and called *Night Network*. For a time in the mid-'80s when LWT closed down at about 11.30 p.m., the channel was 'taken over' by *Night Network*. It was aimed at people in their late teens and early twenties coming back from pubs and nightclubs, and included such things as recorded-as-live disco dancing at 4 a.m., live 'game shows' filmed on the roof of the LWT centre, generally featuring versions of hopscotch or skittles, a motley collection of camp technicolour American 1960s sitcoms and other trivia. Officially, the phrase 'deconstructed television' was borrowed from the world of structuralist literary criticism in order to explain *Night Network*. Put more simply, this was meant to be television that made a virtue out of its extremely cheap production values: it was so bad that it worked as a joke 'about' television. The advertisers were less keen and *Night Network* was closed after a couple of years, due to lack of advertising revenue. But the magic word 'network' had also been used by Sidney Lumet as the title of his 1970s film about American televison. The film's central character was a power-mad American TV executive who swept all before her. *Network* also featured 'Howard Beal, the Mad Prophet of the Airwaves', a demented newsreader who started his bulletins by chanting, 'We're as mad as hell and we aren't going to take it any more!' and many other televisual innovations which were to come to pass, or were perhaps copied, in the 1980s and '90s.

Notes

1 In its heyday the *Mirror* had been selling the best part of 5 million copies every day. Murdoch's much-derided *Sun* was launched in 1969 and presented an immediate competitive threat. It was still way behind the *Mirror* but reached sales of over a million in its first hundred days of publication. The *Sun*'s circulation rose to 4 million in 1978, overtaking the *Mirror*'s, and peaked at 4.25 million on the back of newspaper bingo.

2 Larry Lamb, the paper's pioneering editor through the 1970s, had written off the *Star*, which he believed was so tacky that it posed no threat. Murdoch begged to differ, worried that the *Star* would do to the *Sun* what the *Sun* had once done to the *Mirror*. He also thought that Lamb, now knighted and Sir Larry Lamb, was getting too big for his boots: 'a prickly pommy bastard' who had lost his touch. The final straw was Lamb's demand that he should be promoted to edit *The Times* as well as the *Sun*. Lamb and Murdoch parted company, leaving the editor's chair at the *Sun* vacant.

3 *The Gown*, 20 January 1970. The article also said that Montgomery had a 'high-handed manner' with other student journalists, because he had 'once been a tea boy for the summer in the offices of a provincial daily of ill-repute. Consequently he bears a supercilious but kindly contempt for all the amateurs which student journalism forces him into contact with.' The paper referred to was thought to be the *Ulster Newsletter*, the pro-Unionist Belfast paper which Monty, many years later, was to buy and make part of the Mirror Group.

4 The Mirror Group had bought a chain of local newspapers based in Plymouth mainly for the purposes of training, for which tax exemptions were available at the time.

Live TV

The course ran for only a few years. Its graduates include the ferocious Alastair Campbell, later the *Mirror*'s influential political editor (he resigned in protest when Monty took over the paper) and then Tony Blair's press secretary.

5 Unsurprisingly, in a letter to the authors, Monty said the totality of newspaper articles written about him amounted to a 'mixture of fantasy and legend spiced with malice', though he declined the opportunity to reply to his critics and did not say which articles were inaccurate or in what way.

6 Murdoch got the point. During a 'regal' visit to this latest far-flung addition to the Empire, a *Today* hack was introduced to the Boss as the paper's 'consumer editor'. Murdoch smiled. You mean, our "greed editor",' he smirked.

7 These women produced a lot of health and lifestyle material with a slightly right-on feel, much of it in the style of the women's magazines, with a lot of personal horror stories, triumphs over tragedy and ghosted first-person confessionals. Power dressing was the order of the day and female hacks who turned up in the office more casually dressed were required to borrow a impressive suit from the fashion department before going out on a job.

8 Janet's column reflected a fascination with 'people-watching' – the '80s newspaper and magazine game of defining new sociological groups like Sloane Rangers, yuppies, buppies and dinkies – which was, in turn, related to the development of niche marketing in advertising and the media. She believed that TV audiences were fragmenting or, as she put, it 'going crumbly' as the audience split up into ever more subtle consumer groups and sub-groups, defined by what they bought. In one article she divided the upper and lower middle classes between

those who 'live in Esher or Wimbledon, have a wine cellar, a couple of cars and give dinner parties' and those who 'Like The Price Is Right, shop at Tesco and eat oven-ready chips'. She described her own idea of consumer heaven as 'putting your feet up with a drink and a tangerine for a really blissful hour of Dynasty', and was delighted to discover that only a credit card and a tele-phone transaction stood between herself and Joan Collins-style chic. 'Britain has become a place where Yuppiedom can be purchased without even leaving the house,' she reported early in 1988. 'You just pick up the phone and use your Next catalogue'. The solipsistic style of her previous writings was maintained. 'I've just stuffed down a Marks & Spencer Indian dinner and was tuck-ing into my M & S luxury chocolate mousse' was her way, for example, of beginning a review of a science programme about human metabolism.

CHAPTER FOUR

1 The kitchen took the form of an aluminium tube like the inside of an aeroplane. The bathroom was built round a sunken bath with gold and jewelled tiles radiating out and up the walls. The bedroom resembled something like the inside of a gigantic vulva: the walls were covered in pink tulle and decorated with masses of puffy pink nylon netting surrounding an egg-shaped bed. There was a television set dangling from a blackamoor statue. Zandra's wardrobe, of course, had a room to itself, wall-papered in pink and green; there was a filing system for her huge quantities of clothes. The rest of the place was done out with fake Greek pillars, Sumerian ziggurats, mosaics and murals, mostly featuring Zandra. There was a gigantic chandelier designed by Andrew Logan, 'the

Alternative Miss World', and a Logan bust of Zandra done in tiny pink tiles. Both Zandra and Janet thought that Logan, who also specialised in over-sized chunky jewellery, was Completely Brilliant.

2 James himself played bass guitar in the group, dressed in a peculiar collection of fishnet body-stockings and wearing heavy make-up. Although they were white, Sigue Sigue Sputnik sported long Rastafarian dreadlocks which they dyed with streaks of green and pink and pulled up on top of their heads in great fuzzy plumes, making them look like over-fertilised pineapples. They did their best to get their record, a risible effort called 'Love Rocket No 1', banned, and said they represented a new 'cult of ultra-violence'. But, unlike the Sex Pistols, this latest manufactured threat to the moral health of the nation's youth was widely ignored.

3 'Infocrawl' was jargon for text moving across the screen; *Network-7*'s was reckoned to be at least three times faster than anything that had been seen before. The words appeared in a red box which flashed on and off the screen very quickly. This was designed to deter people over 30 from watching. It was reckoned that younger people had grown up in a 'multimedia' environment, and so, in the archetypal case, had mastered the art of 'looking at' a tabloid newspaper while simultaneously glancing at the telly, fiddling about with a computer game, listening to disco music on a Walkman and, quite possibly, doing all these things while rolling around the living room in a circle balancing on a skateboard. *Network-7* had T-shirts made boasting, 'I can read the captions'.

4 On his arrival at the BBC, Birt linked up with another ex-LWT luminary, Michael Grade, who was managing direc-tor of BBC Television and had played a role in bringing Birt to the corporation. But the two men soon fell out.

5 In 1997, after leaving L!ve TV, Janet claimed that she was not a 'channel surfer' and preferred to watch 'substantial' TV shows (despite recently producing the exact opposite). But then again, many people noted that Janet was always changing her mind about things, including her own past. She also had a knack, according to some, of holding two directly opposed opinions at the same time and regarding this as a good and sensible, rather than bad and barmy, thing to do.

CHAPTER FIVE

1 The move anticipated a 1983 Act of Parliament which authorised the first local multi-channel cable monopoly franchises. Cable operations started in Croydon and then, slightly later, Swindon. These two towns, very much strongholds of social group C2, popular capitalism and tabloid newspaper circulation wars, thus got the chance to make a permanent contribution to the development of world culture. The original Sky channel was broadcast by satellite to cable 'hubs' which distributed the signal to cable homes. The signal could also be received by DTH ('direct to home') satellite dishes. One of the many problems afflicting Sky's early years was that, while the cable network crept steadily and slowly across the country in the 1980s and 1990s, few punters were prepared to subscribe until there were some decent programmes available. But until they subscribed there would be no money to buy or make programmes: Catch-22. In the end, when Murdoch relaunched Sky as a much bigger operation, he decided to bypass the cable networks by promoting the purchase of individual DTH dishes. This decision unleashed a war between Sky and the cable operators (and between the many individual,

local cable operators) which delayed the arrival of American-style multi-channel television in the UK by at least a decade.

2 In May 1989 he was guest of honour at the Chequers dinner held to mark Mrs Thatcher's tenth anniversary in office. By then he was well aware of changes she wanted to make to ITV, which would also have the effect of making it easier for Sky to compete and get a foothold in Britain. Murdoch needed all the political help he could get. The cost of launching Sky almost sank his entire Empire.

3 For a detailed account of the failure of BSB see *Dished! The Rise and Fall of British Satellite Broadcasting*, by Peter Chippindale and Susanne Franks (Simon & Schuster, 1991).

4 In Britain, city TV was more or less the preserve of cable television, because satellite could only broadcast signals to the whole country. But at this point there were a number of vacant channels on the Astra satellite used by Sky. It might mean that 'the London station' was on channel 23, Birmingham on 24, Manchester on 25, or whatever. These channels would be available all over the country in the same way that a few copies of a newspaper like the *Evening Standard*, aimed at London, were available at railway stations in other cities. They would only be watched by people in, or with an interest in, the appropriate city.

5 Monty believed there was annual advertising revenue of up to £20 million available for city TV, if Sky became available in enough homes. It was a simple commercial equation. If city TV stations could be set up along the lines of local commercial radio stations or local advertising 'freesheets', they could syphon off the purely local advertising. Businesses such as large garden centres, the

emerging hypermarkets and big used-car dealers might buy a lot of advertising on a purely local TV station, just as they did in local newspapers. A car dealer in, say, Liverpool could only advertise on Granada, which covered the whole of the North West, which he could not afford and which anyway involved a lot of waste showing his wares to people in Manchester. Local TV would be cheaper and would reach people in the dealer's catchment area only. An added sales pitch was that TV was a better bet than local newspaper advertising because items like cars could be shown in action and generally drooled over by the camera.

CHAPTER SIX

1 Apart from the globe-trotting Magenta, the rest of the *Network-7* crew were left behind in Limehouse in their beat-up caravans under the control of Charlie Parsons, who replaced Janet as editor for the second and final series of the show. (Janet said that she did not watch *Network-7* after she went to the BBC because it was screened on Sunday lunchtime when she was 'at the seaside learning to jet-ski').

2 On-screen 'Talent', Janet thought, was entirely disposable, which was why she had got out of the presenting game herself. There was an endless supply of wannabees who could be 'styled' (by Janet) to look good on the screen. The Show (i.e., Janet) was the star. She seemed genuinely to despise some of the Tellybrats.

3 Other shows inspired or produced by Janet at this time included *Move Over Darling* (BBC 1, 1990) which was a series, fronted by Pamela Stephenson, about the progress of women; the alternative comedy series *Paramount City* (BBC 1, 1990); *283 Useful Ideas from Japan* (BBC 2, 1990);

Rapido (BBC 2, 1990); *Extra* (a European co-production for BBC 2, 1990); and the football programme *Standing Room Only* (BBC 2, 1991). *The Full Wax* won a silver medal at the New York television festival.

4 An influential rap ensemble called the Disposable Heroes of Hiphoprisy had made a record with the refrain: 'Television! The drug of the nation. Breeding ignorance and spreading radiation', which seemed to sum up the general attitude. The contradiction could only be ignored, or answered by asserting that *Def-II* was not a 'normal' television station at all. Of course, this idea would only really work if it was an independent station like some of the black-orientated channels in the US which traded on the image, if not the reality, of being 'anti-television'.

5 Janet had set up the Groucho Club with her ex-husband Frank Cvitanovich and a couple of other friends in 1984. The PR campaign itself was orchestrated by Charlotte Ashton, who, later, also organised Janet's press relations while she was at L!ve TV.

6 Janet, most displeased with Heller's article, later told the authors she had 'terminated the interview after 15 seconds' because Heller had started asking questions about her early life. 'I have a policy of never discussing that,' Janet told us, despite the fact that there are numerous articles under Janet's own by-line doing just that. Janet also claimed that Heller had 'made up' most of the interview. Heller remembers the interview vividly. She told the authors that Janet was 'tetchy and semi-cooperative throughout'. Janet had criticised her during the interview, asking her to frame questions about 'serious' concerns, rather than about her personal life. Far from lasting 'fifteen seconds', the interview lasted three-quarters of an hour and Heller retained the tape. After the article was published Janet confronted Heller in the

Groucho Club and roundly abused her, claiming that the article had made her cry. Janet said it was 'horrible', and accused Heller of deliberately selecting the ugliest photo she could find to go with the article, even though this had nothing to do with the journalist. Heller, feeling mildly intimidated, patiently explained that she had no axe to grind and had just expressed her own views in good faith. Janet could not expect that everyone would always see her the way she saw herself. But Janet was not consoled. Another journalist was accused by Janet of being 'blind drunk' when writing a profile containing what struck the authors as reasonable criticism of her. Another was accused of making up an interview after Janet had terminated an interview after '15 seconds', and yet others were accused of sexism in wanting to write about her personal background, and so on. 'Everything that has been written about me is wrong,' she assured the authors. 'There are two Janet Street-Porters, the one y'see in the papers and the real one.'

7 An account of Janet at work in Manchester is given in Ginny Dougherty's book *The Executive Tart and Other Myths: Media Women Talk Back* (Virago, 1995), according to which Janet spent all day in meetings and shouted so much that, at the end of the day, she had to remain silent for an hour to get her voice back. Working relationships were tense. Janet is quoted as saying, 'People don't like working with me because I interfere too much,' and telling another executive, 'Look, it's no good being nice to them [the presenters]. They hate you.' Over lunch (Malaysian noodles) Janet name-dropped the Pet Shop Boys and produced 'a big notebook, like a doodle-pad, from her plastic bag and writes MOST IMPORTANT THINGS TO DO in scrawly capitals.' The Most Important Thing on this particular day was to get more black people

on the screen as presenters. A meeting with Alan Yentob
was observed for posterity: 'Yentob sits up only when
JSP informs him with the most dazzling grin that she
would like a substantial sum of money, please, for her
pet project, *Der Vampyr*.' Janet denounced Dougherty's
book to the authors, saying it was all based on hearsay
because she, in her standard phrase, had 'terminated the
interview after about fifteen seconds'.

CHAPTER SEVEN

1 Alan McKeown is the son of a bricklayer from Hainault
who left school aged 15 and became a hairdresser, working for Vidal Sassoon. He got into producing TV commer-
cials when he was hired as a hairdresser for a shoot. After
a time making ads he moved to the USA, where he
organised the production of a comedy series written by
Dick Clement and Ian La Frenais, creators of *Porridge* and
The Likely Lads. Friends remember him as something of
a raver (women, champagne and hairstyles) and 'a
hustler in the best possible sense of the word'. He
returned to England to form an independent production
company with Clement and La Frenais called Witzend
Productions. The company's numerous series included
Girls on Top, which was how McKeown met and married
Tracey Ullman. In 1988 McKeown merged Witzend with
another company, SelecTV, which was run by Michael
Buckley, a City wheeler who had started life in humble
circumstances: he had been found, aged six months, in a
telephone box in Sloane Square. At the time of the merger
with Witzend, SelecTV was owned by Robert Maxwell.
The merged company, trading as SelecTV, was a huge
success. Following the introduction of the independent-
production 'quota' at the BBC, the million-pound

commissions came rolling in for hit series like *Lovejoy*
and, above all, *Birds of a Feather*. But McKeown thought
there was no money in production, compared to owning
rights and back catalogues and to becoming a broadcaster. Thus in 1992 he joined up with Lord (Clive)
Hollick's MAI/Meridian group to make a successful
franchise bid for control of the southern ITV area, ending
up with a 30 per cent stake in Meridian/ITV. McKeown
had been careful to hang on to the copyright of
programmes like *Birds of a Feather*, sensing that they
would be worth a fortune in the multi-channel future.
They could be run back to back on a 'Gold' repeats channel, generating a second wave of income for each show
by way of cable subscriptions: hence his interest around
1993 in joining up with Associated Newspapers and/or
the *Mirror* (or anyone else) to be a partner in operating a
cable channel. After a disagreement with Associated he
tried to launch his own SelecTV cable channel over the
national cable networks, but ran into the familiar 'they
are a nightmare to deal with' scenario. McKeown was
also to join up with Montgomery, MacKenzie and others
to mount a bid for the Channel 5 franchise which was up
for auction in February 1995.

2 The formula was a great success. By 1992 when Monty
was working on his British version, Fox's total revenues
had grown from next to nothing to almost $200 million
a year, with previously becalmed local affiliates reporting ratings increases of between 50 per cent and 100 per
cent. Fox was being 'rolled out' to other affiliates, now
eager to sign up, right across the continent. A senior Fox
executive told the television trade press that this success
was based on 'narrowcasting' and 'targeting specific
demographics'. The network was weaning the 18–25
'demographic group' away from the existing channels

with 'aggressive and innovative' shows which created 'distinctive brand-name identity'. There had been an increase of 31 per cent in a single year among the 18–25s, who regarded the network as 'cool' and 'like a club, reflecting their values and aspirations' typified by the cartoon series *The Simpsons*. Because it had started small, Fox could 'get away with things that the majors could not risk'. For example, it had several programmes with specific appeal to gays, enabling the company to tap into the booming 'pink economy' of fashion-conscious, high-spending 'dinkie' (double income, no kids) couples, who had vast appeal to advertisers but were hard to reach through advertising on the existing networks: in other words all the rhetoric used by Janet at *Network-7* and *Def-II*.

3 Janet stayed at the BBC for another two years. People who knew her then were aware that she was helping Monty with his plans to break into television, was advising him on programming and was even considering becoming his new channel's programme head, but they were sworn to secrecy. She didn't want to leave unless she was absolutely sure the new channel was going ahead.

4 As late as 1996 Monty was still complaining bitterly about Murdoch's 'vertical monopoly' on satellite distribution, encryption and subscriber management, and hinting that it was underwritten by News Corporation's web of political influence.

5 Channel One's editorial plans were, to a large extent, based on the New York cable news station NY-1, and it was staffed by a new generation of 'video journalists': mostly newspaper reporters (or recently qualified trainees) who went out on the road with their own camera and with no support staff at all. The hope was

that it would achieve a 10 per cent 'reach' (meaning people dipping in and out from time to time) in the 300,000 or so cable homes in London. Associated Newspapers expected to lose up to £50 million in the first few years of operation, but believed they would make profits when more people hooked up to cable. In other words, like everyone else involved with the cable industry, they were basing their plans on 'subscription growth'. This was slower than many experts predicted, for reasons including a continuing lack of attractive cable-exclusive programmes, ferocious competition from Sky and the cable industry's own ineptitudes, especially when it came to marketing. By 1997 Channel One was in serious financial difficulties and had to cut back its already inexpensive production base.

6 Cox had left Sky when it started 'raining Australians' and moved to NBC, setting up NBC Europe (later NBC Superchannel), a cable channel very similar to 'European Sky', except that instead of showing old movies and British TV repeats it repackaged NBC's American output such as golf marathons and American stock-market reports.

7 TCI had come from nowhere to become one of America's biggest and fastest-growing companies in the space of a couple of decades. By 1997 TCI had annual revenues of over $8 billion, derived from 14 million subscribers (and numbers were still rising), assets worth $30 billion and an annual profit of nearly $300 million. Its chief executive, John Malone, had risen to become one of the richest businessmen in the world with a personal stake in the company worth around $2 billion, despite spending a huge part of TCI's money mountain on setting up home-shopping and Internet services. Through the 1990s TCI branched out from

simply distributing programmes to boost profits by making (or, rather, buying and re-selling) its own programming. TCI's American programming arm, Liberty, specialised in repackaging old TV programmes from around the world into special-interest niche channels. The company would, for example, buy in old soaps from all the American channels and throughout the world, and re-edit them to produce a non-stop soap channel. But it could do this for any particular type of programming: science fiction, fishing, cookery, jazz music, black interest. TCI's UK arm followed suit, developing a former oil company called Flextech into a mini-version of Liberty. Flextech made whole channels for sale to the UK cable distributors and to Sky.

8 The members of CPP-1 were TCI's UK subsidiary TeleWest and the other major players: Nynex, CableTel, ComCast, Bell Cablemedia and TCI itself. Together they controlled approximately 95 per cent of the total cable network in the UK. Wire was managed by Joyce Taylor and Nigel Haunch at the TCI-owned company United Artists.

9 The daytime element of Wire TV was produced by a man called Steve Timmins, an unlikely media mogul, who ran a small independent production company based in Bristol. The live element on Wire was pretty much like talk radio – lots of phone-ins and chat shows – except, of course, that it was radio with pictures: 'radio-vision'. Flower-arranging was big on Wire TV. You couldn't do that on the radio.

After getting the station off the ground and running it for less than £2000 an hour, Timmins had found it hard going, especially in 1993, the second year of his two-year contract to supply the channel. Wire's output steadily degenerated towards the broadcaster's last resort: a national radio phone-in programme, with the added but entirely pointless attraction of pictures of the man on the end of the phone line appearing on the screen. 'We are cheap tarts,' Timmins cheerfully told a newspaper.

CHAPTER EIGHT

1 Finch, one of BBC Arts' star film-makers, was famous for having made *My Way*, a 1979 *Arena* special about the semiotics of the old Frank Sinatra standard – heavy with significance as the song had recently been re-recorded in a punk version by good old Sid Vicious. The show got a 9 million rating when it was shown on BBC 1. Finch had followed this triumph with a documentary about the Ford Cortina, another smash hit.

2 The winners of the three main awards at the September 1993 Prix Italia were the Dutch drama *I am Going to Tahiti*, the documentary *Silverlake Life*, and *Der Vampyr*, which won the music and arts prize.

3 Will Wyatt told the authors that he had not asked Janet to make the application or, at least, that he had no recollection of doing so. He remembered that she was keen to apply under her own steam. 'Janet does not take very well to rejection,' he observed.

4 On 25 August 1993 Pilsworth had left SelecTV to become chief executive of Chrysalis TV and on 1 October he announced plans for a massive expansion of the company's activities. He dissolved Chrysalis TV and launched Chrysalis Visual Entertainment. He told the trade press that the company 'now had a very clear strategy' of focusing on the production of peak-time programmes in which the company would retain copyright, and noted that the value of such rights was set to increase massively as more and more cable and satel-

lite channels came on stream: in other words a version of the SelecTV strategy. Pilsworth launched or bought a number of individual production companies, taking a 50 per cent stake in each one. The idea was to create a cluster of companies pulled together under the Chrysalis banner, again much in style of SelecTV. Pilsworth signed a deal with Jonathan Powell's Carlton TV giving the latter first refusal on sit-com ideas from a clutch of Chrysalis production independents including Assembly Film and TV, Bentley Productions, Red Rooster Film and Television, Stand and Deliver Television and Clive James's production company, Watchmaker. In addition, Chrysalis already ran a substantial sports department which produced Italian football for Channel Four and organised sports programming for the cable-exclusive SportsWire channel, which was being developed by the cable companies as a competitor to Sky Sport.

5 Janet's job was described by the BBC as 'developing and commissioning comedy and entertainment ideas from independent companies'. The *Guardian* noted, 'The task of working with independent companies like Hat Trick, which makes *Have I Got News For You?*, and SelecTV, makers of *Birds of a Feather* and *Goodnight Sweetheart*, will become increasingly important within the BBC. The corporation has a government quota of 25 per cent production by the independent sector.' In her own 'official' CV, produced in 1996, Janet said that she was responsible for buying *Clive Anderson, Our Man In . . .* and *Paul Merton's Life of Comedy*, and for overseeing the continuation of around twenty series, including *Fantasy Football League, The Detectives, Jasper Carrott, Men Behaving Badly* and *This is Your Life*.

CHAPTER NINE

1 Clark denied the further allegations as 'tosh' but was otherwise contrite. He apologised for boasting about his sexual adventures. 'I ought to be horsewhipped,' he said. 'But I have changed my ways and I am a reformed character now.'

2 This account is given in *Full Disclosure* by Andrew Neil (Pan, 1997, pp. 216–17). Neil goes on to speculate that MacKenzie's revolt 'led directly' to his move to Sky, the implication being that he had demanded an eventual move to Sky as a condition of returning to work for Murdoch. This was confirmed to us by another source. MacKenzie *did* demand a move to Sky after taking the decision to 'get into television' in the spring of 1993. At one point he told people that Murdoch would allow him to spend three years 'learning the ropes', with a view to taking over from Sam Chisholm, with Chisholm's blessing.

3 For a detailed account of Kelvin MacKenzie's career, see *Stick It Up Your Punter! The rise and fall of the* Sun, by Peter Chippindale and Chris Horrie (2nd edition, Simon & Schuster, 1999).

4 A senior Wapping executive involved in the resignation drama told the authors that Kelvin could 'dish it out to Murdoch, as well as take it', and described their relationship as being like that of 'an old married couple who would shout at each other a lot across the kitchen table and feel safe with that until one day something just snaps'.

5 One senior editorial executive who had daily dealings with Kelvin at this time told us that he found Kelvin's behaviour 'eerie' in the period from approximately June 1993 until he left the paper to go to Sky. 'Suddenly Kelvin

wasn't hands on, he wasn't all over the paper like a rash, he wasn't lapping the office and going talking to the sports editor, talking to the features editor, geeing up the writers, banging on to the news desk, shouting at the picture people, all that aspect of the daily ritual and performance that he used to put on had gone because he was clearly distracted. Nobody had any idea what was going on but there was something happening in his head.'

6 Bruce Smith, a senior TCI executive who was involved in financing sports acquisitions for Wire and SportsWire, told the authors that TCI headquarters had given its UK subsidiaries the green light for all-out competition with Sky. 'It was full-steam ahead,' he said, adding that even the hundreds of millions spent on sports rights could be seen as 'peanuts' compared to the billions spent on cabling up the country. TCI headquarters would have financed a bid for the Premier League, 'if push came to shove'. At the same time as the 'full-steam ahead' attack on Sky in the sports area, the cable companies were also developing a proposed cable-only movie channel to be called Home Box Office. TCI and the cable consortium were also in discussions to sell the daytime LiveWire operation to David Montgomery and the Mirror Group with the aim of hooking in the *Mirror* to promote cable subscriptions. All these developments were part of the same strategy: to get UK cable 'out from under the yoke of Sky'.

7 The plan was to keep the main matches live on BBC, with more minor matches and various highlights available on cable for hard-core tennis nuts. The deal between SportsWire and the BBC was loaded with significance for Sky because it meant the two organisations would gain experience of working side by side on a major sports

event, and mirrored the way Sky and the BBC worked together to screen the all-important Premier League. If the cable companies could woo the BBC and break up the *de facto* Sky–BBC alliance over football, they would greatly increase their chances of getting the football when negotiations opened in 1995. Nigel Haunch, the executive in charge of running SportsWire, told the authors that the Wimbledon deal was a 'dry run' for a BBC–cable Premier League bid. Will Wyatt, managing director of BBC Television, confirmed this but said that 'dry run' was 'a bit too grand'. Wyatt, understandably, was keen to emphasise the BBC's independence from both Sky and the cable companies, pointing out that the corporation was happy to work with either as the opportunity arose.

CHAPTER TEN

1 The deal with Lewis had been signed in 1992 by MacKenzie's predecessor, Gary Davey. Sky paid £3.4 million for the rights to three guaranteed fights together with first refusal on the rights for Lewis fights against Riddick Bowe and Mike Tyson if these could be arranged, as seemed likely at the time. This was the biggest single sports-rights contract in UK television history, and Sky hyped it as 'the deal of the century', boasting that Lewis was 'in line to become the nation's first world heavyweight champion of the 20th century'. On the main point, Sky also boasted that Lewis's first fight against 'Razor' Ruddock had sold an extra 100,000 dishes.
2 MacKenzie's intervention in boxing was estimated by some commentators to have cost Sky up to £20 million in terms of inflated rights money paid for the unattractive Eubank fights and lost revenues from the Lewis fights. Eubank was signed up for eight fights in twelve

months. He was to be paid £10 million but was allowed only one defeat. At the time Steve Bunce, the respected boxing correspondent of the *Daily Telegraph*, said that the deal 'defied logic'. Eight fights in twelve months was 'ludicrous'. If defeated, Eubank had one chance to fight again to win back the title, or the deal would be terminated. Many people noted that this was an incentive to fight the weakest opponents he could find. Eubank's manager, Barry Hearn, coincidently an old pal of MacKenzie's, said there would be no 'patsies', meaning soft fights. But Eubank's first fight for Sky was against the unfancied Brazilian Mauricio Amaral, who was not even in the WBO rankings. The Eubank deal was not good box office for Sky. After his defeat in a fight in Dublin against an undistinguished opponent in September 1995, even Sky's own analyst, Barry McGuigan, was moved to say that Eubank should retire: 'He's had 46 hard fights and they've taken their toll and there's nothing left in the tank. There is nothing he can do. . . . he has nothing to give at any weight.' By this time Lewis was ranked Number 2 in the world, after Mike 'bite yer ears off' Tyson, by the WBC. Lewis's agent, Maloney, formed the view that MacKenzie's dealings with him over the Lewis contract were one of the reasons why MacKenzie left Sky. The minute MacKenzie was gone from the channel, Chisholm got on the phone to Lewis's training-camp, trying to persuade them to come back on board, using 'industrial language' to abuse MacKenzie roundly.

CHAPTER ELEVEN

1 About 1 million people had signed up, which would have produced an income of only £3 million a year. But

the figures used by the *Mirror* predicted that by 1998 the number of subscribers would have grown to over 5 million, generating £15 million a year. This would have been enough to produce an 'operating profit' for L!ve TV and enable it to starting paying back some of the money invested in the launch and early loss-making years. In addition, by 1998 L!ve would have finished 'rolling out' the channel to local affiliates, thus tapping local advertising revenue. Ad revenue would therefore grow and, together with further cable subscription growth predicted by 2000 and beyond, L!ve would start to make substantial profits.

2 As part of the purchase agreement, the CPP-1 companies, led by TCI, were given a 10 per cent shareholding in L!ve TV and two seats on the board so they could keep an eye on things. It also gave them an incentive to renew the ten-year contract to supply L!ve when the time came.

3 In a business plan presented to the Mirror Group board in December 1994, cable-subscription growth predictions prepared by the independent analysts Zenith were used. These figures were more than double the subscriptions predicted by other analysts such as Goldman Sachs. Predicting future cable subscriptions is a tricky business. The predicted number of 'homes passed' (i.e., homes where the cable could be connected if people wanted to buy it) was the easier figure to work with, since it was based on the known plans of the cable companies busy digging up the streets. More risky was 'penetration', the proportion of people who actually bought a subscription when it was made available to them. Zenith predicted penetration of 40 per cent compared with figures much nearer 20 per cent from other analysts, which was the historical figure. This meant that Zenith, whose figures are normally extremely reliable, had some reason to

believe that cable would suddenly become much more attractive to subscribers during 1996. The obvious candidate for this reason was Premier League football, which was up for auction in 1995–6: if cable won the bid the matches would start to appear on cable in September 1996. A Zenith analyst told the authors that in 1994 his company 'knew a great deal about what was going on in the market' but that they could not comment on 'any specific assurances' that had been given to them. When asked directly if the optimism was based on certain knowledge that cable was going to get the Premier League, the answer was a very firm 'No comment'.

4 If MGN's papers did a good job and promoted sales, as a reward they would get more money in the form of the 25p per month per cable subscriber laid down in the national subscription agreement the group had inherited from Wire TV. However, until the Premier League football came on stream (according to plan) in September 1996, there was nothing for the *Mirror* to promote and therefore no additional subscription revenues available from which the cable companies could pay the group its 25p per subscriber. MGN evidently believed that the subscription revenues after September would more than compensate for the fifteen-month 'subscription holiday' it had given the cable companies.

5 The announcement of MacKenzie's appointment was made on 4 October 1994 and became effective on 25 October.

CHAPTER TWELVE

1 Frank Presland told the authors that the *Business Age* team had behaved in an 'annoying' way, reminding him of people on a student rag mag. But he could not remem-

ber if they had offered to cut his client's grass.

2 Nick Ferrari, then head of the programme-making side of Mirror TV, refused to discuss the circumstances of MacKenzie's arrival but, according to his wife, Sally, he had been as much in the dark as everyone else. Sally Ferrari, also a national tabloid journalist, remembered hearing the news of the appointment on the car radio when she was driving her kids to school and said she had been astonished. The MacKenzie and Ferrari families had been close for years – Kelvin and Nick used to play ball in the Ferraris' back garden when they were children, and Dan Ferrari, Nick's father, had employed the young Kelvin as a reporter for his news agency; and Nick and Sally Ferrari and Kelvin and Jacqui MacKenzie had the same wedding-anniversary date and lived in the same relatively up-market area of Kent – but Sally, at least, had no recollection of any discussion that MacKenzie might move to the Mirror Group in any capacity, let alone as managing director of Mirror Television.

3 Kelvin, for his part, was tickled by the way in which numerous former Wapping associates were turning up at the *Mirror* and trimming their political stance, and by the fact that they were pulling down huge salaries while, at the same time, professing allegiance to Labour. Shortly after his former Wapping pal David Banks was appointed editor of the *Mirror*, Kelvin yelled at him across a crowded social gathering, 'Oi, Banksy! Are they giving you socialism lessons yet, eh?' The ideological about-turns were made easier by the arrival of 'Blairism' in the Labour Party. This enabled Piers Morgan, Banksy's successor as *Mirror* editor to say, 'I used to be a true-blue Tory. Now I'm a true-blue Blairite.' (This attitude was summed up, after Labour's landslide win in the 1997

general election, by a brilliant *Private Eye* cover. It showed John Major beaming at Tony Blair and saying, 'There. I told you the Tories would win.') During the 1997 election campaign Kelvin, by then installed on the Mirror Group board, voted Tory and instructed his minions at Mirror TV to do the same. He told one associate that 'you could drop a nuclear bomb on the *Mirror* newsroom and not kill a single socialist'.

4 Flextech had started out as an oil services company. In 1990 its owner, Roger Luard, bought a 25 per cent stake in the Children's Channel, a pay-TV channel then available to the minuscule number of cable subscribers, but later sucked into Sky's multi-channel package. In 1992 he went into partnership with TCI, which had lately spent billions laying cable systems around the country but had nothing much to show on those systems except output from the existing BBC channels, ITV, Channel Four and Sky. TCI was therefore interested in cable-exclusive channels which it could both run on its own cable systems and also use to strengthen its hand in negotiations with Sky (and also sell or swap with Sky as a sideline). In 1993 Flextech was 'reversed into' the TCI-owned programme-making company United Artists. Rapid development followed, with Flextech buying up or developing numerous channels such as Bravo, Discovery, QVC and The Box for sale to the cable operators and to Sky. By 1996 Flextech was valued by the City at £1.5 billion (and Luard had become exceedingly rich as a result). Its latest activities involve partnership with the BBC, and the strategy is to get hold of the BBC's priceless catalogue of programmes and package them for sale world-wide (e.g., all old editions of *Horizon* to go on to a new Horizon science channel; all arts material to go on the Arena channel, etc). At the same time as TCI was

developing programming through Flextech (TCI took the chairmanship by means of Adam Singer after buying a 60 per cent stake in Luard's company in 1994), it joined the CPP-1 consortium to develop cable-exclusive channels, beginning with Wire TV in 1992. All this left TCI nicely placed. Its own programmes were sold to Sky, thus giving it a foothold inside the golden circle of monopoly pay–TV. It bought and distributed Sky's premium channels, and it was developing cable-exclusive channels in really expensive areas like sport and movies and sharing the cost with (rival) cable companies under the aegis of the CPP-1 consortium.

5 Adam Singer told us that MacKenzie had been 'in the wilderness [after leaving Sky] and that's when we [TCI] met him – though we'd met him a few times at Sky – and we liked him, and wanted him in our group somewhere because he was a talent.' Singer also said, 'David Montgomery had his own relationship with Kelvin. We didn't suggest Kelvin to David. There was never any hint of that. We would have loved to have found a way of hiring him ourselves but at that precise second we didn't quite know where to put him . . . But we were quite keen to try and find a place for Kelvin. At which point, we were talking to David Montgomery, and David says to us, "Oh, I'm thinking of hiring Kelvin," and that made a lot more sense to all concerned.'

6 In an interview given to the *Sunday Telegraph*, MacKenzie went to great lengths to emphasise his gratitude to Monty for taking him on at the Mirror Group at a time when he had been 'in the wilderness'. MacKenzie had raved at the journalist that she could write anything she liked about him, so long as it was made clear that Monty had hired him out of the blue, as it were.

7 After joining Mirror TV, Kelvin made further visits to

TCI's Denver headquarters – there were approximately fifteen visits in a six-month period – and had talks there about the finances of sports rights with Jonathan Spinks, whom he had met in London through Bruce Smith, a friend of both men. Spinks had then been at Sky, but in 1989 had left and was now working in TCI's sports-rights department, Prime Time.

8 In his history of Sky TV, *Sky High* (Orion, 1997), media analyst Mathew Horsman reports that Sam Chisholm and other senior Sky executives took the threat extremely seriously and that their attempts to counter-attack were 'feverish'.

9 One reason for the bitterness against Singer and TCI on the part of CPP-1 consortium members was the fact that he had gone out and bought sport like World Cup cricket and Lennox Lewis boxing at vast cost, and then demanded that they all pay their share. Now that SportsWire was a dead duck, these rights were sold on to Sky on the usual over-a-barrel Chisholm terms. The overall effect was that the cable companies had paid a total of £10 million for the cricket, boxing and other bits and pieces. These rights were now handed over to Sky for next to nothing.

PART II

CHAPTER THIRTEEN

1 More than one of her BBC colleagues had noted that with Janet the personal, the political and business were often mixed together. She was apt to take any criticism of her programmes as a personal attack or insult. Technical cock-ups, a bad reaction from the critics – frequent enough in any sort of TV production operation – or even simple failure to get her own way tended to be viewed as betrayal.

CHAPTER FOURTEEN

1 Canary Wharf had been built by the Reichmann Brothers at the height of the '80s property boom. Mirror Group managers had long contemplated a move to low-cost Docklands, but Maxwell had hocked the old *Mirror* building in Holborn, central London, and as part of the mortgage agreement had promised that the paper would stay on in the building at an enormous rent (just another of the ways in which Maxwell had channelled the *Mirror*'s income to cover the debts on his failing personal business ventures). With Maxwell out of the way, Monty was free to move. The half-empty Canary Wharf building, offering knock-down rents, was perfect. The two *Telegraph* papers moved in, taking floors 11 to 16, and the Mirror Group (now including the *Independent* and *Independent on Sunday*) took floors 18 to 24, creating a so-called 'vertical Fleet Street' in one building. (What went on on the floor separating the two newspaper groups, the 17th, remained mysterious; some people were

convinced that it was used by MI5.) There was a great fear, widely discussed from day one, that it would make a brilliant and obvious target for the IRA. Though there was proximity between the journalists, there was none of the old Fleet Street intimacy. The hacks were only vaguely aware of each other's existence. Lifts did not stop at the floors occupied by rival papers or other businesses. Another difference from Fleet Street was that the accommodation was generally very cramped. The Poor Sods on the *Independent* were reckoned to have the worst of it, because they were shoehorned into a single floor and at first some hacks didn't even have their own desks (the problem was soon solved, when Monty sacked half of them). *Mirror* hacks were likewise crammed in, and some were told to work from home. It was all a far cry from the pre-Maxwell glory days when hundreds of feature-writers hung about in the spacious *Mirror* office block, where whole floors in the basement were commandeered by printers who turned them into drinking dens or improvised non-stop blue-movie cinemas (at one point they converted the basement into a veritable shopping-mall of stolen goods). Now the printers – the inkies – had gone. Gone, too, were the printing-presses: you no longer, as you had in the *Sun's* filthy old pre-Wapping headquarters in Bouverie Street, heard or felt them revving up in the basement, something that was remembered fondly by older hacks like Kelvin. But nostalgia was to be avoided. Going on about the good old days made you stand out as an old fart, ripe for sacking.

2 The main technical consultant at L!ve TV in the run-up to the launch was a man called Terry Lee, who had previously set up the technical side of L!ve's rival, Channel One, and who had also worked for Channel Four and others.

3 Orsten started his media career in commercial radio before moving to TV-AM to work with putative media giants like Greg Dyke. Orsten then followed Dyke to LWT, where he worked as a director on *The Six O'Clock Show*, going on to work on current-affairs output with Jane Hewland. Janet and Jane brought him into direct *Network-7* and he picked up a BAFTA along with them. In 1990, after cutbacks at LWT, he moved into the independent sector and joined Chrysalis Television. He stayed there until summer 1994, when he joined L!ve TV on a one-year contract as a 'start-up' expert.

CHAPTER FIFTEEN

1 Cox, backed by NBC's head office in New York, had decided to mount a breakfast TV bid when it was discovered that Gyngell and TV-AM were prepared to offer only around £15 million to renew the existing franchise. It would be easy to offer more than this, Cox and the others reckoned, and still have plenty of money left over to run a profitable business. The plan was to design an 'up-market' breakfast service using the mid-market/broadsheet approach of ITN and the *Daily Telegraph*, shaped by NBC's huge scheduling experience in the competitive world of American early-morning sofa-vision. This would replace TV-AM's formula of cartoons, Roland Rat and cheerful nonsense for housewives since, it was predicted, the housewives and teeny tots market was shortly going to be swallowed up by a new wave of non-stop cartoon and lifestyle channels on Sky and on cable.

2 Patrick Cox remembers that MacKenzie 'left Sky and surfaced pretty quickly at the *Mirror*'. He also remembers that the two of them held their first meetings in

September, which was a month after Kelvin left Sky and month before the official announcement of his appointment at the Mirror Group. This timescale was confirmed to the authors by Robert Clarke, chairman of the Mirror Group board, who remembered that board members had been telephoned about a month before the October board meeting with the news that MacKenzie planned to join the company. Clarke said that the appointment had been entirely uncontroversial.

3 McKeown's long-standing ambition to become a broadcaster had been partly realised in 1991, in SelecTV's link-up with Lord Hollick's Meridian TV, but that had not been a happy experience. McKeown found Meridian insufficiently keen to commission new productions, and, with a relatively small (15 per cent) minority shareholding, he had less influence than he would have liked; and there were rows over the value of McKeown's shareholding. He therefore sold his stake. In 1993 he had lined up SelecTV as a partner in the *Evening Standard* bid for Channel One, but had pulled out when he found it was to be a news-only channel. After that, he had set up an entertainment-only cable-exclusive channel, which he managed to get most the country's cable operators to take.

4 McKeown joined the Mirror–NBC bid in September 1994, by which time MacKenzie had been running the Mirror Group side of the bid for a while. Before this, and after parting company with Associated, which was at first going to be the outlet for his re-runs on the cable system, MacKeown had been busy trying to persuade the cable companies to run an exclusive SelecTV channel on the same subscription basis (25p per subscriber per month) as they had agreed with Channel One and Wire (now L!ve) TV. He told the trade press that his plans had been

'pipped to the post to a certain extent' by L!ve TV. After joining forces with the *Mirror* and NBC he abandoned his plans to be a cable broadcaster in his own right. The background to McKeown's involvement was somewhat fraught, and demonstrated the soaring value of holding rights to repeats of any half-decent programming as the 'multi-channel universe' began to emerge. Only a few years before, there had in effect been only two channels, BBC 1 and ITV, bidding for his material. Now he was being courted by dozens of outfits which wanted either to screen the repeats on new channels or else to own the rights in anticipation of even more demand in the future. In the year prior to McKeown's involvement in the Channel 5 bid, SelecTV's turnover had soared to £24 million, bringing a 19 per cent increase in profits. In many ways MacKeown's position was similar to that of football clubs, which saw the value of their television rights increase by a factor of 100 in just a few years. This potential for vast profit had led McKeown into all sorts of squabbles with former partners. There had been a monumental battle over control of SelecTV between him and Michael Buckley – co-founder with McKeown of the company – which blew up when two men were on holiday in Barbados over Christmas 1992. This had been followed by legal action over the conduct of SelecTV's affairs (in which McKeown was vindicated).

5 McKeown knew Janet vaguely, mainly through his friendship with her ex-husband Frank Cvitanovich. SelecTV sold a lot of material to the BBC, and had done so when Janet had her Light Entertainment commissioning role during her last year at the Corporation. But they had had no direct business dealings. All SelecTV's deals were done with the channel controllers or with Janet's boss, David Liddiment, or programme depart-

ment chiefs, such as the head of Drama.

6 McKeown was playing a larger and larger role in the Channel 5 bid, partly because of the media regulations controlling shares in the bid. The Mirror Group was limited to a 25 per cent stake and NBC, as a non-EC-owned company, to 20 per cent, leaving SelecTV with a 55 per cent stake, which was too big. Cox and Monty talked to McKeown about buying into SelecTV so that they could, in effect, increase the size of their stake in the bid, via their stakes in SelecTV. Under this arrangement McKeown would also be made chairman of the Channel 5 bid and of the station when it went on air. But this did not work out. Instead the *Daily Telegraph* agreed to join the consortium, although this was to remain a secret. This left the four partners with roughly equal shares. Cox, especially, would have liked a bigger stake, and the element of control which came with it. But he was content with the arrangement, so long as the others did not sign up to any really major risks.

CHAPTER SIXTEEN

1 Janet told the authors during a telephone conversation that 'hot desking' is now the standard arrangement throughout television: 'So don't go bangin' on about that 'cos you'll look really stupid.' The point she was making was that, once again, she was ahead of her time and at the cutting edge of innovation. This is perfectly true. Many other Janet-inspired ideas have also been copied throughout the industry. In fact, numerous interviewees pointed out that much of Channel 5's style was a straight-forward rip-off of the work that Janet did at L!ve TV.

2 A system like this had been installed by Avid at a TV station in Honolulu and worked after a fashion, and there

was a less ambitious version up and running in Belgium. But in both of those stations it was used on live news shows for an hour or so a day. The idea of running it for 24 hours a day was new. The minute the system was installed it was realised that the idea of linking the five editing suites via the server would not work. Each editing suite on its own was basically fine, though there were a number of normal installation bugs which took a while to sort out. The Avid server was set up deal with the five individual editing suites as 'clients', serving them raw material from its memory and taking the edited material back and broadcasting it. The main problem concerned Janet's infobars. For one reason or another, the message had not got through that the infobars were not merely normal graphics but a whole portion of the screen which would be edited separately, like a second channel appearing on the same screen. The infobar requirement meant that each editing suite was really *two* clients. So instead of five editing suites the maximum the server could cope with was two. This would not have been enough to put Janet's Vision into action. There was a further problem. Even for this to work the server would have to be persuaded to deal with couples of editing suites, one for the vision and one for the graphics, and treat them as a single unit. That would be tricky. Avid put in a team of engineers to try and sort the problems out. It was said by some that the server would have had to be as big as the Canary Wharf tower itself to have enough power to realise The Vision.

Live TV

1 Mucking about with malfunctioning equipment in people's homes was bad news. General Electric, owners of NBC, knew all about this sort of problem. Once, one of their refrigerators – *just a single machine* – had gone wrong and caused its owner's house to burn down. General Electric had had to recall every fridge of that model to check and repair each one. That had cost £500 million. Some had been sold on, second-hand. The (untrue) rumour circulated that all GE goods were dangerous, hitting sales. A decade later they were still finding the bloody things. *Nightmare.*

2 McKeown jumped ship and joined a rival team, led by the Canadian company Canwest, which bid enough money but was ruled out on the grounds of being foreign-owned. The Channel 5 franchise was won by a Pearson-led group, which did the retuning and launched the channel the following year with the help of the Spice Girls, but was soon in trouble for the reasons Cox had identified. After this setback McKeown decided to sell SelecTV to Carlton, pocketing £6 million, and moved to Los Angeles, where he started building a new business based around his wife Tracey Ullman's show for NBC.

3 In the end L!ve TV in its first year of operation, when Janet was in control, was produced for £1 million less than the figure budgeted for before the June crisis. But the cuts, despite ruining much of Janet's vision, were nowhere near big enough to cover the reduced level of income due to slow take-up of cable subscriptions. The Mirror Group had budgeted for a 40 per cent national take-up of cable. The real figure was to be 20 per cent, cutting L!ve income by half. The figures for cable subscriptions in this period, on which L!ve TV's income

is based, are given below:

Mirror TV Projections[a]

	1995	1994
All cable homes passed	5,080,000	3,623,000
All cable homes connected	1,618,000	929,000
Average penetration	31.9 %	25.6 %

Actual Numbers[b]	1995	1994
All cable homes passed	5,562,513	4,178,910
All cable homes connected	1,185,553	871,409
Average penetration	21.3 %	20.9 %

Shortfall

In homes connected	432,447	57,591
In nominal annual income (£)	1,297,341	172,773

Sources:
a: Zenith/L!ve TV business plan, December 1994;
b: Independent Television Commission (as of 1 July 1996)

In fact this income would not have been paid to the Mirror Group because the first subscription income was not due to be paid until the start of the Premier League season in September 1996. But from 1996 onwards the gap between L!ve projections and the reality of subscription growth was to grow wider, meaning that the income shortfall got worse each year. It is worth noting that Zenith had, with due and proper caution, *underestimated* the speed at which the country would be cabled up ('homes passed'), which was one source of subscription and therefore of income growth. But they seriously over-estimated the penetration rate, the number of people offered a cable connection who decided to take it up. Commenting on this Bruce Smith, the TCI representative on the L!ve TV board, attributed the miscalculation purely to optimism and wishful thinking. Zenith, for whom wishful thinking is the ultimate sin, told the authors that they had significant information about 'developments in the market' which would 'drive' subscription sales to the much higher level of penetration predicted, but, as a matter of company policy, would not discuss this information. It seems very likely that this was the fact that Premier League football (and possibly a new premium movie channel called Home Box Office) would come on stream. Zenith has a deserved reputation for great accuracy in these sorts of forecast and they must have been assured that something spectacular was going to happen in order to predict a rate of penetration (around 40 per cent) by 1996 that was almost double the real rate (around 20 per cent). Zenith was also keen to point out that in 1995, after the deal between TCI and Sky that killed off SportsWire/CSN, they had revised their figures downwards to something more realistic. It would also be fair to say that all independent predictions for cable growth offered in the early '90s were over-optimistic. But the figures offered by Zenith were the most optimistic of all, and these were the ones used by the Mirror Group to predict the income derived from L!ve TV.

4 There was another downside to Ferrari. As a *Sun* show-biz reporter he had upset a lot of the *slebs* who Janet hoped would get involved with the station. Elton John, for example. Elton was a Personal Friend of Janet's. But

Ferrari had famously got into a punch-up with Elton's minder, and then there was the little matter of Kelvin, the *Sun*'s ELTON'S KINKY KINKS story and the £1 million libel settlement which followed. Many of the best *slebs* hated the tabloids with a passion, and preferred to deal with *Hello!*, where they got purely positive coverage. Soon after Janet's arrival MacKenzie had teased her about her endless celebrity name-dropping, the contacts and the favours she could call into help with programming. 'How come you know all these people, then?' he had demanded, rudely. 'Because,' she shot back, 'I haven't been in tabloid jernerlism f'fifteen years slaggin' 'em all off . . . '

CHAPTER EIGHTEEN

1 Apart from anything else the infobar needed a couple of skilled people to operate it full-time, one to think of what to say, the other to type it all out with no errors, twenty-four hours a day, working eight-hour shifts of non-stop typing. So you probably needed about ten people to run it. That was half the total production staff at any one time.

2 According to L!ve's 'editorial blueprint', the official target audience for this well-informed-slightly-guilty-laddish-puppy was to be 'mothers, young kids, students, older people and the unemployed' between 1 p.m. and 3 p.m., reduced to just 'students, older people and the unemployed' from 3 p.m. to 4 p.m., then joined by 'schoolkids, teens, office workers and parents' when he started his second slot at 5.30.

3 It was true that there were a million cable punters, but the vast majority had signed up mainly, or mostly, to get a cheap telephone line. Moreover, people who had cable only watched it (as opposed to ITV, etc.) for less than 20

per cent of the time they had the TV switched on, and when they did watch cable they watched premium channels like Sky Sport or Sky Movies most of the time.

4 There was a much bigger production number on the release of *The Bridges of Madison County*, directed by Clint Eastwood (which needed all the PR it could get). For this L!ve had pushed the boat out with a filmed report from the film's premiere in Leicester Square (*'We'll be, like, taking people to all the parties and premieres they're not invited to'*). Unfortunately, the OB reporter failed to get anywhere near the event or the director. Instead she collared Twiggy, who passed the opinion that Eastwood was 'a brilliant director'. The Avid eco-system went into action and this gem was recycled at regular intervals for the rest of the day.

PART III

CHAPTER NINETEEN

1 Senior production staff who were at L!ve TV in the run up to launch emphasised to the authors that the idea of live OBs, going out and about and mixing with celebrities all the time, was very much Monty's idea. They called it 'Montyvision' and, left to their own devices, would never have done L!ve TV in this way 'in a million years'.

2 Steve Timmins of Wire had used his Big Yellow Bus, functioning as a single large OB 'satellite truck' (and now rotting in Bristol), for his daytime 'roadshow' tour round the nation's shopping precincts. That had worked just fine, in technical terms. The cable consortium CPP-1 had a cheapish contract with Intelsat to send the live signals via the satellite from Timmins's bus to Wire's headquarters in Bristol, from where it was mixed into the Wire output and pumped out of the cable system. L!ve inherited the contract with Intelsat when it bought the Wire operation from CPP-1. It had been modified slightly, and at no extra cost, to allow three trucks to use the link and bounce the signal back to Canary Wharf instead of Bristol, which was fine with Intelsat.

3 The camera-to-truck cable was a problem anyway. In 'old-fashioned' telly there were rules stating that you had to have a certain number of technicians per metre of cable to make sure that people did not trip over it or, perhaps, in Soho, take a meat-cleaver to it just for fun. Cable care was especially important if you were going to snake

wires up and down stairs in dark, crowded places full of drunks, such as nightclubs. The greatest danger was of somebody tripping over and breaking their neck, which would land L!ve with a massive uninsured public-liability claim. Then, even if you could lay a cable, it would not (on L!ve's budget) be capable of establishing 'talkback', the jargon for two-way communication between the cameraman/presenter and the producer in the van. Without talkback orders from Canary Wharf could not be transmitted to the presenter's earpiece, so directing him or her was impossible.

4 All the time the presenters had to pretend to be filming live while cassettes were periodically taken out of the camera to be jogged back to the OB truck by the producer for transmission. At first the people in charge of output back at The Entity tried to direct *Desperate and Dateless*, looking at the material as it came through, asking for changes and making helpful suggestions. But this merely led to more creative 'Do it again, please' vs. 'You must be fucking joking' exchanges. Eventually, any attempt at directing or quality control was abandoned, and the producer just sent the stuff through and quickly checked that it had been received before sprinting back to join the cameraman and presenter – who'd been left stranded in hostile territory – in the hope they had not been lynched in the meantime. At least when the presenter was there, he or she could talk to the bouncers and generally look after the team, releasing them from the constant and sickening worry that somebody would sneak up behind them while they were filming and whack them over the head with a bottle. This particular concern grew as the night wore on and the punters became more and more drunk. Since the filming was being done in pick-up joints, many of the customers could be assumed to be

engaged in two-timing or adultery and they did not take kindly to the presence of cameras.

5 Still, Janet glumly conceded that the nation's youth were obsessed with computers, to the extent that her friend Jane Hewland was running a series called *Games Master* (which Rachel had worked on immediately before coming to L!ve TV). Later, after leaving the Mirror Group Janet, ever the iconoclast, made a television programme bitterly denouncing the whole scene: 'Every decade needs some kind of blotting paper to soak up the socially challenged. In the past it has been things like designer drugs, religious cults and colonic irrigation. The seventies gave us the Moonies, the eighties aura-cleansing and rebirthing. Now the nineties have spawned the mega-cult of all time, the ultimate tool to keep nerds off the street – the Internet.'

CHAPTER TWENTY

1 The 'Dinner Party' took place every night though, naturally, the 'best' ideas tended to be saved for Saturday.

2 At first the title *Saturnalia* had been considered, but it was rejected as too obviously gay and, also, as suggesting that it would feature Roman-type orgies. It sporadically carried the strap line 'Come to the parties you are not invited to' and was by far the most important part of the output as far as Janet and Rachel were concerned, and the closest to The Vision of clubbin' TV. In theory, Rachel and Nick Ferrari shared responsibility for the output as co-directors of programming in alternate weeks. In reality, the split meant that Rachel was in practice in charge of the night-time stuff, especially on Saturdays, and Ferrari was in charge of the more lightweight daytime output dominated, as it was, by his protégé Simon

London's seven-hour daytime show.

3 In following weeks the production team resorted to bringing in their flatmates and girlfriends, if they were good-lookin' enough. The next step was to send out invites at random to minor DJs, or trawl the pubs and clubs to find Party People, preferably gay or cross-dressed. But these nonentities had nothing much to talk about and soon got borin' and bored. They would squabble with each other and wander around The Entity pressing buttons and muckin' about. Hence the emergency call to Mike Spinks. Several people the authors spoke to emphasised that a version of the Dinner Party idea was immediately copied by Janet's pal Ruby Wax for terrestrial television.

CHAPTER TWENTY-ONE

1 One of the proudest boasts of those involved with L!ve in its first year of operation was that overall it came in a million pounds *under budget*. But that was the overall figure. At the operational level budgets were too tight and there was no money for anything. The radio mikes that were used to broadcast from the studio picked up interference from the computers. The staff was minuscule and largely untrained. The lack of support staff was making senior programming people pull their hair out. In a normal operation on the scale of L!ve at, say, the BBC there would have normally been a pool of lowly but extremely useful minions known as 'runners' who could be called upon to do anything: meet studio guests when they arrived; go and buy sandwiches at lunchtime. At L!ve there was only one such post and, since some holders of it were instantly promoted to fill the gaps in the staffing structure, the person kept changing. On one occa-

sion a senior producer asked the receptionist to carry out a menial task but was told to get lost as she had just been promoted to become an assistant producer and was now looking for her own runner. Darryl Burton, who at the BBC had become used to sorting out Janet's sometimes chaotic operating methods, had taken the precaution of salting away sums of money in various official and unofficial contingency funds. He had written large sums into the budgets under headings such as 'taxis' and other miscellaneous expense accounts. This cash was now raided to pay for vital items like videotape for the cameras which, according to the plan, L!ve was not supposed to use because the whole system was meant to be digital and therefore tapeless and this was one of the channel's proudest boasts. Burton often paid for these items on his own credit card and claimed the money back as expenses. The production staff were deeply grateful for his foresight. Without it the whole operation might have ground to a rapid halt. He had also established his own lines of communication with the *Mirror's* senior management and was reckoned to meet MacKenzie early each morning to discuss the previous day's spending and authorise demands for extra cash needed to keep the show on the road.

2 At one point, Thirkell approached various L!ve TV people and said it seemed obvious to him that Janet was going to 'come a cropper': she would largely be blamed for the failure of L!ve TV in its original form. MacKenzie and Monty obviously felt that way but were refusing to criticise her directly. The trouble was that Janet was not really co-operating either, so Thirkell needed a bit more material to point up how and why Janet was going wrong. Eventually it fell to Tony Orsten to deliver the only direct criticism of Janet featured in the programme.

He was filmed saying, in a very mild way, that 'Janet isn't quite the creative force she once was.'

3 Phelps then complained that day two of L!ve was full of even more product placement. 'There is a great deal of brandname mentioning on L!ve,' he noted, adding that the constant mention of *Hello!* during the 'people news' slot 'appears to be a straight promotion for the magazine and, unless I have missed something which justifies this, it should not be repeated.' He was also worried about a much-recycled clip featuring a Tellybrat eating in a restaurant called Cranks and 'saying how good the food was, and so on'. This, Phelps wrote, was 'dangerously like a plug for the restaurant'. He warned L!ve over the 'undue prominence' of competition prizes and told the channel to avoid 'puffery' relating to any giveaway prize: 'it should not be described as "fantastic" or anything like that' (though he wrote again later, after taking specialist advice, with the 'good news' that the word 'fantastic' was OK after all, helpfully adding that 'some vaguely hyperbolic addition should be acceptable if kept within reason').

4 The Disney Corporation, Phelps noted, was still getting a lot of free advertising on L!ve TV: 'the release of a new video possibly justifies some coverage but the ever-present Disney publicity in most shots was not really necessary and the presenter seemed to go out of her way to help the MD of Disney Home Video to plug the product. Not surprisingly he accepted the invitation eagerly, finishing with a "buy the video" message.' Phelps noted that companies would no doubt be keen to give L!ve TV access on these terms, but he warned: 'If there is no real story, don't do the item!'

5 Free, sent-in music videos were also to form part of the material for *Buzzin'*, the daily music show handicapped

by the lack of sound-proofing and the resultant complaints from the Swiss banker neighbours. The music videos were a cut above the 'talent' material, since the whole music-telly business was awash with at least semi-professional videos made by bands hoping to make it. Here the material ranged from *Scream Jesus*, *Babe Rainbow* and *Beekeepers* ('three very good unsigned bands. Duration: 8' 54"') through *Technogasm* ('around twenty minutes of technobollocks') to *Cliff Ashmore* ('man in bathroom with guitar and singing') and *King Stan and Peebles* ('father and son duo – terrible. Duration: 4' 16"').

6 The day before launch Steve Timmins had visited the 24th floor (he had been retained as a consultant by the *Mirror* and had been watching the development of the channel closely). Rachel asked him if it was all going to be all right: 'I've been in some messed-up situations with Janet over the last eight years, but I've never seen anything like this. I'm not sure I can to do it any more.' Timmins told her, 'Janet doesn't know what she's doing. She has no idea.' Rachel's brow furrowed. She emitted a long, deep, thoughtful 'Hmmmm', and sloped away.

CHAPTER TWENTY-TWO

1 Janet had also been in contact with Lynne Franks around this time, helping to promote the launch of a wimmin's radio station called Viva! which involved Eve Pollard and most of the usual ex-*Petticoat* suspects. Franks was to become a presenter and boldly announced that she would not be basing anything on press releases: 'as a former PR, I'm the last person who's ever going to take notice of one of those'. On launch day Janet had appeared on Lynne's show to hold forth on the familiar topic of the 'hard time' women suffered at the hands of the *meedja*.

She assured the world that Liz Hurley was a good actress, and it was *so unfair* that she was best known for 'wearing that dopey dress'. Besides this, Janet helped out by joining 'networking breakfasts' to promote the station. 'It all gets pretty yacky as I'm sure you can imagine,' the station manager said of these events. (Viva!, or 'Vulva' as it was known to many in the advertising trade, was denounced by critics as 'Lite, Lo-Cal middle-aged power-dressed radio for the cerebrally anorexic' and was soon ploughing it).

2 Janet told the authors that MacKenzie and Monty had also signed an agreement that they would not talk about her activities at L!ve TV.

3 Much later, in November 1997, Janet said on Radio Four that she was no longer interested in working on the management side of television. 'I had a time at L!ve TV and I parted company with them. I've done my stint as a television executive' (*Sentimental Journey*, Radio Four, 25 November 1997).

CHAPTER TWENTY-THREE

1 Not all members of the late-night sex team fared as well as the baked-beans man. One producer had been working for weeks to set up an OB from a suburban semi which, *for the very first time live on national television*, would feature a number of middle-aged businessmen having talcum power and baby oil rubbed into their bottoms and being dressed up in nappies by a Cynthia Payne-type person. He had got permission from the brothel-keeper and, amazingly, from six or seven of her clients. MacKenzie got wind of this, sauntered over to the producer's desk and gave him a strange look: 'You must be mad if you think we are doing that. We don't

want that sort of rubbish, we only want normal weird. Get rid of it.' The producer, who was very proud of the careful access he had negotiated for his impending scoop, resigned immediately.

2 The purchase of this object was likewise presented as evidence of Janet's extravagance. In fact, her spending had been nothing out of the ordinary for television. She remained within budget and the programming she produced or inspired, such as it was, represented great value for the Mirror Group. The fact that L!ve TV could no longer afford it was more to do with the failure of cable subscriptions to grow as quickly as expected – a disappointment which had nothing to do with her.

PART IV

1 The editorial team at *Viz* told the authors they were aware MacKenzie likened himself to Roger Mellie, but the character was actually based on a former local Tyne Tees presenter. *Viz* had considered running a new cartoon strip based on MacKenzie to be called 'Fat Cunt', but it never happened. MacKenzie once got the chance to play Roger Mellie for real when he and his drinking buddy Roger 'the Dodger' Luard of Flextech locked themselves into the newsroom of European Business News (EBN), a channel partly owned by Flextech, and started reading a bulletin to camera along the lines of 'And here are the headlines. EBN is a load of crap. The Dow Jones index? Bollocks to that' and so on.

2 Bushell's relationship with MacKenzie had been through its ups and downs. The high point came when MacKenzie gave him the honour of writing the Page One Comment on the front of the sixteen-page Maggie Thatcher tribute printed to mark the Tory 'stab in the back' which got rid of her. After this Bushell had moved to the *Daily Star*, from where he regaled Kelvin with stories of life on his down-market rival: 'I told him they were all pissed all the time, which they were. The whole paper was adrift on a sea of alcohol. It was terrifying. The guy who did the editorials once came into my office with a crossbow, shot at a chair, then fell over on to the floor. I had to go and write his editorials! Then another guy came in and we had the same conversation twice.

He'd totally forgotten the first, and it was only 10 in the morning!' Kelvin listened to this tale of woe, nodding sympathetically. Later, he printed every word in the *Sun*.

3 Unlike ITV, L!ve TV's income did not depend in the main on the number of people who were watching the channel at any given time. Income was guaranteed in the form of the 25p per month per subscriber agreed with the cable companies. There was a slight premium in terms of selling advertising if L!ve TV could claim a lot of viewers, but this was marginal to the business. What counted was 'recognition', meaning the fact that people knew that L!ve TV existed and, most importantly of all, *you could only look at it if you were hooked up to cable*. It was vital that the punters were aware that cable-exclusive channels existed. Also important was 'reach', meaning the number of people who looked at the channel in any given month, no matter how briefly. Good reach figures were needed to make sure the cable distributors did not dump the channel as a complete waste of time. In essence L!ve TV, tied into the *Mirror*, was more of an advertising campaign for cable in general.

4 MacKenzie further revealed that he had discussed world affairs with Charles and Diana at a special lunch a couple of years before. He claimed that they had begged him to leave them alone for a bit, and that 'Diana hardly said a word and Charles spoke endlessly about that South African guru Laurens van der Post. I wasn't quite sure whether Charles was taking the piss, so I decided to adopt a position where I basically narrowed my eyes and nodded sagely, on the basis that if he was taking the mickey he would think I understood, and if he wasn't he would think I was enormously intelligent and had got to the bottom of his philosophy about life.' Diana, he said, 'didn't bother to look the vaguest bit interested in him,

which made her go up in my estimation'. He concluded, 'If anyone honestly believes that people divorce and separate and have affairs 'cos of tabloids, I suggest they lie down in a darkened room.'

5 Patrick Cox, MacKenzie's former partner on the aborted Channel 5 bid, had been keen on a plan to revive *Crossroads*. He investigated buying the screening rights to the ancient soap so that he could make it under new ownership with a weird story line about distant relatives returning and rebuilding the motel, which had burnt down at the end of the last ever episode. But the owners smelt a rat and the plan came to nothing.

CHAPTER TWENTY-FIVE

1 MacKenzie told a member of the L!ve TV staff that he had once made the entire executive staff of the *Sun* sit in a line on the floor of his office, legs round the person in front, pretending to row a boat and chanting, 'We smashed the *Mirror*! Hurrah! Hurrah!'

2 *Stand Up L!ve* naturally attracted complaints to the ITC. One complaint, upheld by the ITC, concerned 'a scathing attack' on 'born-again' Christians delivered by a man dressed as a woman. L!ve argued that the attack had been carried out 'in an intelligent and satirical way'. But the ITC did not agree, saying that it was 'uninformed by either wit or telling observation'. Doubtless there would have been more complaints about 'taste and decency' issues if L!ve TV had had more viewers. The ITC can not act against a channel on 'decency' unless it receives a viewer complaint and there were so few viewers that the channel could get away with a lot. The ITC, which is not a censor, would act against other breaches of its code; and warnings were legion over things like 'cross-promo-

tion' of the *Mirror*; and 'product placement' advertising. The ITC took a particularly dim view when L!ve started operating a premium-rate phone line involving live tarot-card reading, as part of the *Terry Tarot* show. This breached Rule 18 (ii) of the ITC Code of Advertising Standards and Practice, which prohibits advertisements for products or services coming within the recognised character of, or specifically concerned with, the occult.

3 MacKenzie's racism at least matched his sexism and homophobia, though in the witches' brew of prejudice and nonsense he actually rated the presenter Simon London, who was black (but not, er, '*black*'), as the channel's finest talent. MacKenzie had once described the film *Gandhi* as 'a load of fucking bollocks about an emaciated coon'. His view of the end of apartheid in South Africa was equally trenchant: 'There'll be a bloodbath when the blacks come down from the trees.' Following his lead, the *Sun* had always tried to avoid having pictures of black bingo winners, whereas stories involving violent crime by blacks were given extra prominence.

4 The new interest in boy bands eventually led to a hush-hush project codenamed, er, 'Boy Band', which was to be a partly animated, partly enacted cartoon series about a pop group. The idea originated with Ridley and was never discussed at the ordinary ideas meetings and editorial conferences. But things started to happen when MacKenzie mentioned 'Boy Band' at a meeting with L!ve equipment suppliers Sony, whom he persuaded to part-finance the production. Sony asked to see a demo and Kelvin promised to get them something in a week. This was rash, since there was nothing at all in production and animation is notoriously slow. A group of animators was hired and put to work in the former 'padded cell', which was henceforth padlocked as the computer graph-

ics people slaved away day and night with Kelvin chewing their ears off about their work rate. 'Boy Band' was soon bogged down in an argument between MacKenzie and Ridley about who had invented it and could claim the credit and royalties.

CHAPTER TWENTY-SIX

1 The quip was mild by Kelvin's usual standards. His loathing for John Major was fierce. It had begun with Major's role in the downfall of Kelvin's beloved Maggie and intensified after Black Wednesday, when the UK crashed out of the ERM, causing interest rates to rocket. In summer 1997, Kelvin made a rare appearance on television to describe his conversation with Major during the evening of Black Wednesday. Major had called him at about 7.30 p.m. and Kelvin had wondered why the Prime Minister was bothering to call a 'tabloid tosspot' like himself in the middle of such a serious crisis. Major asked him how he was going to 'play the story', to which Kelvin replied, 'Prime Minister, I have in front of me on my desk a very large bucket of shit. And I am just about to pour it all over you.' Major responded by saying, 'Oh Kelvin, you *are* a wag!' The next day the *Sun* appeared carrying one of Kelvin's most inspired headlines, cleverly linking the heavy political story to the sexual antics of senior Tories: 'NOW WE'VE ALL BEEN SCREWED BY THE CABINET.'

CHAPTER TWENTY-SEVEN

1 The bunny concept was far from original. When TV-AM had difficulty attracting viewers in the early 1980s, Greg Dyke came up with Roland Rat, a glove puppet, to

replace Anna Ford, Peter Jay and the station's original 'mission to explain' posse. It was now tellyland folklore that Roland Rat had saved the station, making Dyke's name in the process. Dyke was now a multi-millionaire – all because he had persuaded somebody to stick their fist up a rat's bum. Thereafter, whenever a station was in trouble a variety of furry puppets would often arrive on screen, with mixed results. It was to be the same formula at L!ve TV.

2 David Nicholson's arrival had been part of this process. He had been out of work after resigning as editor of a newspaper in Yorkshire and had phoned Kelvin, an old pal from his *Sun* days, to see what the prospects were like at the *Mirror*. 'You'll never get a job anywhere else, you fat fucker,' he was told, 'so you may as well come and work for me.' Nicholson took the plunge, and was joined by one or two other 'proper' journalists hired from places like Sky. They often worked extra reporting shifts after their 'normal' jobs, partly to see how an ultra-cheap operation like L!ve TV worked (information which, they grimly realised, might be extremely useful in the multi-channel future).

CHAPTER TWENTY-EIGHT

1 The two women were Anne-Marie Foss and Eva Bjertnes; the latter was also allowed to present *Eva's Seventies Pop Show* ('that was my own idea', she later revealed in a newspaper article). The weather information itself was lifted off the news wires and the scripts didn't always match the graphics: the weather girl might be forecasting rain, sleet and snow while the graphics showed sunshine and cloudless skies. This didn't matter too much, though, because the tapes were often put out on

the wrong days. Eva found it difficult to cope with the 'chaos' she found at L!ve TV but said, 'Maybe it was my Viking blood which helped me survive'. She also claimed to be 'a psychic with healing hands'. When she left L!ve TV she made a somewhat desperate pitch for a job in the form of a *Guardian* article stressing that she was available to present children's programmes: 'I go goo-goo ga ga when I see soft toys,' she reported, adding, 'I have over 30 teddy bears.'

2 Women prepared to do anything other than static poses would also be very expensive to hire, since the channel would have to compete with the money available from straightforward porn movie-makers and the new wave of 'lap-dancing' strip clubs, where a night's tips might amount to over £300. L!ve was prepared to pay between £50 and £200 for women to appear on *Topless Darts* and *The Sex Show*, and there was the added incentive of being on television. Even so, one woman who spoke to the authors and who had appeared topless numerous times at Stringfellow's club, was embarrassed to admit she had appeared on L!ve TV.

3 Soon after this London left L!ve TV to join the BBC, where he worked on the National Lottery show with great success. He was soon being tipped to rise to the top in BBC Light Entertainment.

4 There were murmurs from time to time from the cable companies, some of which had worries about this sort of stuff going out over their networks as part of the 'basic tier' of channels the subscribers got whether or not they had asked for them (even if, for example, they were signing up mainly because they wanted a cheap phone line). There was a different situation with the 'official' soft-porn channels, which were available on cable but required the subscriber to 'opt in' by paying extra money. But for the

time being at least, they were stuck with L!ve TV. At the time the old Wire operation had been transferred to the Mirror Group, to be re-launched as L!ve, Montgomery had been keen to 'negotiate out', as he put it in his report to the board, any sort of 'quality control' clauses which might give the cable suppliers a veto over the content of the channel. Montgomery had bragged about this coup, noting that Channel One, the rival news channel owned by the Associated group, was burdened with such a clause. In the case of L!ve, Montgomery reported, the cable operators had not insisted on quality control because they were satisfied that 'we would not wish to broadcast poor quality material'. All that counted was the evenings, when people started surfing. The companies had signed up in the expectation of getting *Daily Mirror*-meets-*Def-II* and had ended up with *Sunday Sport*-meets-*Electric Blue*.

5 Sally Ferrari told the authors: 'Shall I tell you a secret? L!ve TV is pretty much banned in my house. In fact, most of cable television is. At first we used to have it all over the house. Now only it is in one room, well out of the way.' She also said that 'it is embarrassing for my kids to go to school and say they watch cable TV – let alone L!ve TV'.

CHAPTER TWENTY-NINE

1 After a period of illness Bill Ridley returned to work at L!ve TV in the autumn of 1997.

CHAPTER THIRTY

1 Janet Street-Porter told the authors that she had done a lot of the work in the previous year developing the

proposal for Goal TV, drawing on her experience at the BBC where she had been in charge of series like *Fantasy Football League* and *Standing Room Only*. 'MacKenzie had no idea how to do it,' she said.

2 Various cable companies had been in talks with several clubs, including Manchester United, during the year-long bidding period for the Premier League rights. United had been unimpressed by the mainly shambolic presentations, which included offering the club its own Red Devils lifestyle channel, additional money for rights to games that Sky did not have space to show and, maybe, for reserve and youth team games which United nuts would watch round the clock. (There was later much excitement about a divorce case in which a woman dumped her husband because he habitually watched videos of old United matches for up to twenty hours a day – thus proving that there was a market of addicts and obsessives out there who would, doubtless, pay vast sums to feed their habit.) But the club had picked up 'vibes' indicating a vicious and not entirely above-board war between satellite and cable, and had gained the (correct) impression that they were being used as pawns in a multi-billion-pound battle to control the future of British pay TV. The plans for pay-per-view seemed hastily prepared and the club was not sure that the market was ready yet. Anyway, the digital version of Sky would have the capacity for hundreds (perhaps thousands) of new channels within a few years. They saw no reason to switch to the untested waters of cable. Sky immediately counter-attacked, working with the local ITV company, Granada, to create an exclusive Manchester United channel accomodated on digital satellite with its hundreds of spare channels.

3 Sam Chisholm and Rupert Murdoch himself had put

enormous and careful effort into buying up football in spring 1992, stealing it from under the noses of ITV and freezing out potential competitors like cable. There had been two major problems which might have led to the clubs rejecting his offer, no matter how much money he put on the table. The first was Sky's minuscule subscription base. Sky might pay more than the ITV or BBC, but the big clubs in particular were worried that if they went into a subscription service they would lose sponsorship money and, more generally, disappear from the national consciousness. Chisholm dealt with this by cleverly by encouraging the BBC to make a parallel bid. Sky's bid was to screen whole games live, but the BBC would revive *Match of the Day*, its Saturday-night highlights show. The relationship with the BBC was sensitive, but remained absolutely crucial to Sky's success.

4 Horsman is author of *Sky High* (Orion, 1997).

5 Other bids had been contemplated by two American consortia, one of which was Nasdaq (New York Stock Exchange) and the other a subsidiary of United Artists. A third American-financed group, fronted by investment bankers Merrill Lynch, had shown an interest but, like a German consortium, dropped out a few days before the Coombe Abbey meeting.

6 The idea of anyone wanting to buy, for example, Wimbledon vs. Southampton *à la carte* to put into a pay TV system seemed slight. Cable's technical advantage in respect of local customisation was soon overtaken by Sky anyway. Murdoch's new digital satellite, known in the trade as 'the Death Star', was due to be up and running by the year 2000. The Death Star will have at least 500 channels so, although these will be broadcast to the whole country, there would be no problem in having 100 local channels (with or without football) if there was a

demand for them. Sky's negotiations with the Premier League over digital broadcasting and pay-per-view, which could bring all concerned yet more millions, were set for 1998. After that, according to cable pessimists, all that remains is for Darth Murdoch Vader to manoeuvre the Death Star over the headquarters of the cable companies and blast them to atomic dust, a bit like the White House in *Independence Day*.

7 As Adam Singer, head of TCI in the UK, put it to the authors, 'Why take the risk? What would happen is this. We put £100 on the table, Sky puts £101 pounds on the table. They know that if they keep bidding one of two things will happen. Either they put up the price to such a high level that if we win it we are dead. Or they win it and they pass the price-cost straight back to us because we can't afford not to carry it . . . How do we win that? Murdoch has us totally over a barrel and we cannot win.'

8 In 1995 and early 1996, MacKenzie spent time at TCI's TeleWest subsidiary, officially 'on secondment' from the Mirror Group. He was notably shy about discussing his work there, though he told the trade magazine *Cable and Satellite Europe* (October 1996), 'I am a friend of Adam Singer and Stephen Davis [head of TeleWest] in the same way as our companies are friendly . . . they simply asked me if I had any ideas they might find helpful. And I have ideas, and it is up to them if they decided whether to use them or not . . . to be honest it's in our interest that major companies like TeleWest are as successful as possible because as they get extra subscribers we get extra cents. It is a virtuous circle for us.'

CHAPTER THIRTY-ONE

1 The 20 per cent overall figure was bad enough, but it

masked a very patchy take-up. Cardiff had the highest penetration (over 30 per cent) and Coventry the lowest (under 10 per cent). Unsurprisingly, some of the cable operators took this as evidence that an evenly spread national marketing campaign based on the *Mirror* (which was read by just as many people in Coventry as in Cardiff) and L!ve TV was a waste of time and money which could better be spent on focused local subscription campaigns in places like . . . Coventry. MacKenzie told the trade press that L!ve TV's budgets and business plans had been based on the assumption of 40 per cent cable penetration and so things were 'very tough' now that half its income was missing, confirming the fact that L!ve had thought much higher penetration was a bankable fact for some reason (probably because he believed that Premier League football was in the bag for cable before the deal between TCI and Sky). 'You will be able to spot the man who works out a way of increasing the figure to 40 per cent,' he said, 'because that man will have the biggest smile in the whole country on his face.' Achieving the increase would now be difficult, he thought, because the sales reps would have to go back to millions of homes and sell to people who had already rejected cable the first time. Trying to sell to people who have already decided not to buy is the textbook case of a marketing impossibility.

2 A June 1996 study by Goldman Sachs predicted that the total number of cable subscriptions would overtake dishes by 2000, with about 5 million subscribers. That would bring L!ve TV into operating profit, but the losses were unlikely to be paid off by profits in the years immediately thereafter. The Mirror Group's contract with the cable companies was due to come to an end in 2004, and the study thought there was every likelihood that the

Mirror Group would register a loss, possibly a big one, over the ten-year operating period. In the meantime the total investment to be sustained in covering the loss-making years was unlikely to be less than £60 million, double the figure originally provided for.

3 A report by media analysts Zenith noted that the strong demand for soft porn on cable and satellite had led to the start-up of Television X – The Fantasy Channel (which was to be a source of recruits for L!ve TV under MacKenzie's management) and the Playboy Channel on Sky (slogan: 'Moregasms!') which was packaged by Flextech, run by MacKenzie's pal Roger Luard. However, there was a high rate of 'churn', Zenith added, on the porn channels (as with all cable TV) as people signed up to sample the material and found it to be merely another Cunning Stunt, more sizzle than sausage and so on. Julian Aston, head of Channel One, complained (as might be expected) to the authors that L!ve TV was 'schlock TV' which was getting the whole cable industry a bad name. Monty, he thought, was 'nuts' to allow L!ve TV to run material which could be described as soft porn, given the damage it could do to the *Mirror* brand. To a large extent, the *Mirror* based its business and market position on being the 'decent' tabloid, for example by resisting Page Three pin-ups and refusing to carry certain types of sex phone lines. The way things were going, and the way MacKenzie was able to ignore the needs of the Mirror Group as a whole, struck Aston as astounding and inexplicable.

4 Despite the Mirror Group's opposition to being taken off the 'basic tier' of TV channels supplied automatically to telephone subscribers, CableTel pushed ahead with the phone-plus-promotional-package offer, prompting immediate legal action from the Mirror Group. In March

1997 the group sought an injunction against CableTel, with the backing of Flextech, whose business was also affected. Flextech threatened to refuse to supply *any* of its channels to CableTel franchises if they went ahead with the changes. The legal wrangling went on all year and had still not reached a conclusion in November 1997 when this book was being written.

5 In a letter to the authors, Monty said that 'the Mirror Group is extremely proud of what its TV team has achieved in providing greater choice for the viewer and in helping expand our media activities'. He chose not to comment further, complaining that we had asked him too many questions, and declined to confirm or deny the accuracy of a number of points of fact that we put to him.

6 In October 1995 it was reported that Monty's salary had risen to £473,000, an increase of more than £100,000 since 1994 and a wage packet, the financial papers noted, far fatter than those of the National Lottery 'fat cats' at Camelot, who were being daily castigated in the pages of the *Mirror*. He had also been given an option to buy a large block of shares at 61p each which by October 1995, the earliest date at which he could exercise the option, was a substantial discount on the market price of about £1.70. When the option date arrived, 'MGN insiders' were quoted in the financial press as saying that 'David Montgomery has no intention of exercising his options because he is confident the shares have much further to go, and will be worth much more in the future.' He nevertheless started selling shares in the following months and in 1996 made a total profit of around £1.4 million. Including his salary Monty could expect to earn about £1 million a year on average, by dipping into his options whenever the Mirror Group share price stirred. Charlie Wilson, chairman of the Mirror Group board,

was also generously remunerated. His salary was over £200,000, topped up with pension contributions of £13,000, share options and bonuses, meaning that he was drawing almost £700,000. *Mirror* editor Piers Morgan earned about £200,000 a year.

7 Again the public and private statements did not match up. Julian Aston of Channel One told the authors that he met Kelvin socially several times around the time of the Mirror Group's push into local programming and that Kelvin had cheerfully confessed that the figures in L!ve TV's business plan did not add up and he 'just could not see it ever working'. Aston sympathised. Channel One was in trouble as well, despite having the best pitch in the country, London, and links to Associated Newspapers, owners of the local paper, the *Evening Standard*. Aston said that part of Associated's thinking in running the channel was to protect the *Standard*'s advertising revenues. The Channel One exclusive deal with the London cable companies meant that the Mirror Group (or any one else) was prevented from coming in and selling advertising time to people who might otherwise advertise in the *Standard*. Channel One was a loss-maker but, taking into account the vast importance of the *Standard*'s advertising revenue to the company as a whole, it made much more sense. In terms of the London advertising market, they were pouring money down the drain, but at least it was, in a manner of speaking, their own drain. If city TV could not be made to work in London, it was unlikely to work in Birmingham or Manchester, where the potential ad revenue was much smaller.

8 Barton left Birmingham L!ve shortly after its catastrophic launch, and went to work for Central Television in its busy Nottingham newsroom.

9 The Westminster cable franchise was operated by BT, which was not a member of the London Interconnect Group which ran Channel One, London. A deal was signed with BT in August 1995 which took Westminster L!ve instead of, and in competition with, Channel One. It went on air in December 1995. Channel One had attempted legal action to prevent L!ve TV being run on the London Interconnect System in London and even on the regional franchises of companies, such as TeleWest, which were members of the Interconnect consortium. Channel One's argument was that its ten-year agreement with the cable operators gave it the exclusive right to run a news (and entertainment) channel. L!ve TV was a competitor channel which was competing with it for advertising and 'reach'. TeleWest came to L!ve's rescue, offering to carry Channel One in its franchises outside London as a *quid pro quo* for the fact that L!ve TV ran in London. The legal action rumbled on and added to the extremely bitter competition between the two channels, overlaid with the normal MacKenzie wind-ups.

The young woman eventually left L!ve TV. She told the authors she was grateful to Nick, who had given her a chance she would not otherwise have got to become a TV presenter and had then helped find her a job in journalism in another part of the country. Several young journalists and would-be TV presenters, including those who otherwise had a fairly unhappy time at the station, said that the good thing about L!ve TV was that 'it gave people a chance'. Most were grateful for this and several went on to have on-screen careers after leaving Canary Wharf. A report to the L!ve TV board on progress in Manchester intriguingly mentioned 'our especially close relationship with Nynex'.

Chronology

1975
Janet Street-Porter arrives at LWT.

1981
Kelvin MacKenzie becomes editor of the *Sun*.
Janet Street-Porter becomes a TV executive.

1983
Act of Parliament creates local cable franchises.

1986
News International moves to Wapping.
US Cable companies begin to sink £10 billion (over ten
  years) into digging up the streets.

1987
David Montgomery becomes editor of *Today*.
Janet Street-Porter becomes editor of *Network-7*.

1988
Janet Street-Porter becomes head of youth at BBC; wins a
  BAFTA for *Network-7*.

1990
Sky TV takes over BSB. Sam Chisholm creates pay TV
  monopoly for Sky in the UK. Cable 'frozen out' of the
  pay-TV market.

1991
ITV franchise auction.
Robert Maxwell dies. David Montgomery pushed out of
  News International.

1992

Sky TV exclusive five year deal with the Premier League worth £304 million.

Cable Programming Partners One (CPP-1) formed to make cable exclusive programming in competition with Sky.

David Montgomery arrives as Mirror Group chief executive.

1993

Mirror Group bids for a London-based 'City TV' franchise, but loses out to Associated Newspapers.

Kelvin MacKenzie makes 'swan song' appearance before the Calcutt Committee. He decides to move into pay-TV as managing director of Sky.

Janet Street-Porter's *Der Vampyr* wins Prix Italia; she fails to become a channel controller and decides to leave the BBC, but becomes co-ordinator of independent production at BBC TV Entertainment Group on her way out.

1994

January: Kelvin MacKenzie leaves the *Sun* and joins Sky as managing director.

Wire TV (backed by TCI and CPP-1) begins a concerted attempt to buy up sports rights, starting with World Cup Cricket.

Mirror Group buys control of the *Independent*.

March: Mirror Group moves to Canary Wharf.

April: Wire TV buys second rights to Wimbledon for £600,000.

May: SportsWire evening service is launched. A serious attack on Sky's monopoly.

SportsWire lures Lennox Lewis away from Sky.

Kelvin MacKenzie signs Chris Eubank to Sky.

L*i*ve TV

Mirror Group buys (daytime) Wire TV, with plan to relaunch it as L!ve TV, funded by cable industry (negotiations continue through summer; deal announced in February 1995).

June: Kelvin MacKenzie has huge rows with Sky News over its lack of tabloid values.

August: Kelvin MacKenzie leaves Sky TV and soon afterwards starts talks with cable industry about setting up a cable-exclusive sports channel backed by the Mirror, to compete with Sky Sports.

September: Janet Street-Porter is announced as head of L!ve TV.

Mirror Group buys 15 per cent stake in Scottish TV.

October: Kelvin MacKenzie joins the Mirror Group.

December: Sky floatation values company at £4.4 billion. Kelvin MacKenzie misses out on share option income of approx £1 million.

1995

February: Mirror Group bid for Channel 5 in conjunction with NBC Superchannel is announced.

April: Mirror Group/NBC Channel 5 bid is aborted.

Mirror Group press launch for L!ve TV.

May: TCI/Nynex–Sky 'sweetheart' programming deal is announced, on eve of Premier League bidding period.

Mirror Group and Carlton Communications announce joint bid for Premier League football.

June: L!ve TV launches.

David Montgomery dips into his Mirror Group share options to the tune of £1.1 million.

August: Janet Street-Porter's 'M-people' speech at Edinburgh.

September: Janet Street-Porter leaves L!ve TV.

David Montgomery announces Mirror Group profits

surge, despite falling circulation on titles.

December: *Nightmare at Canary Wharf* is shown on BBC 2. L!ve TV's News Bunny unveiled.

1996

January: L!ve TV new schedule announced: *Topless Darts*, etc.

February: Canary Wharf bombed. L!ve TV shaken, but stays on air. News Bunny away, standing in Tamworth by-election.

March: Kelvin MacKenzie's libel action against *Business Age* is settled. Murdoch pays costs to avoid a trial.

April: Advertising Standards Authority denounces L!ve TV's montage adverts of Paul Gascoigne and Princess Diana.

June: Sky renews exclusive rights (with BBC to show highlights) for Premier League football.

David Montgomery announces that L!ve is going ahead with its plan to open approximately 20 local affiliated stations by the year 2000.

1997

May: Mirror Television in dispute with the cable distributor CableTel in the High Court. CableTel must carry L!ve TV or be in breach of its contract.

June: Second injunction by Mirror Group on CableTel fails. CableTel plans to carry on excluding L!ve TV from some of its packages. The Mirror Group appeals against the decision.

July: Mirror Group is granted leave to appeal. At stake is the future of L!ve TV.

Select Bibliography

Peter Chippindale and Susanne Franks, *Dished! The Rise and Fall of British Satellite Broadcasting*, Simon & Schuster, 1991.

Andrew Davidson, *Under the Hammer*, Heinemann, 1992.

David Docherty, *Running the Show: The Inside of Story a Television Station*, Boxtree Books, 1990.

Ginny Dougherty, *The Executive Tart and Other Myths: Media Women Talk Back*, Virago, 1995.

Roy Greenslade, *Maxwell's Fall*, Simon & Schuster, 1993.

Mathew Horsman, *Sky High*, Orion, 1997.

Jerry Mander, *Four Arguments for the Elimination of Television*, Quill, 1978.

'Roger Mellie The Man on the Telly', *Roger's Profanasaurus*, Fulchester University Press, 1997.

Andrew Neil, *Full Disclosure*, Pan, 1997.

Index

515

Index